INTEREST GROUP POLITICS
IN THE
NORTHEASTERN STATES

INTEREST GROUP POLITICS
IN THE
NORTHEASTERN STATES

Edited by

Ronald J. Hrebenar
and
Clive S. Thomas

The Pennsylvania State University Press
University Park, Pennsylvania

Library of Congress Cataloging-in-Publication Data

Interest group politics in the northeastern states / edited by Ronald
    J. Hrebenar and Clive S. Thomas.

        p.   cm.
    Includes bibliographical references and index.
    ISBN 0-271-00900-4 (alk. paper) : $45.00. — ISBN 0-271-00901-2
    (pbk. : alk. paper)
        1. Pressure groups—Northeastern States.   2. Northeastern States—
    Politics and government.   I. Hrebenar, Ronald J., 1945–   .
    II. Thomas, Clive S.
    JK1118.I5665   1993
    322.4'3'0974—dc20   92–19898
                                                                CIP

Published by The Pennsylvania State University Press,
Barbara Building, Suite C, University Park, PA 16802-1003

It is the policy of The Pennsylvania State University Press to use acid-free paper for the
first printing of all clothbound books. Publications on uncoated stock satisfy the minimum requirements of American National Standard for Information Sciences—Perma-
nence of Paper for Printed Library Materials, ANSI Z39.48–1984.

This book is dedicated
to the memory of

Charles G. Bell

Political Scientist and
Astute Observer of Practical Politics

Contents

Preface

While western, southern, and even midwestern politics are often seen as distinct, the concept of northeastern politics is not as solidly established. Unlike the other large regions, the Northeast has not been the subject of a regional focus of analysis. The scholarly and journalistic books on the region have focused on the Northeast's subregions, especially New England. Rather than thinking of the Northeast as the part of the United States left over after the more distinct South, West, and Midwest have been defined, we strongly believe that the Northeast is a distinct region, which includes the nation's historical centers of finance, communications, and political leadership. Perhaps the most famous of these subregional books is Duane Lockard's *New England State Politics* (1959). Lockard's examination of the six New England states (Maine, Vermont, New Hampshire, Massachusetts, Connecticut, and Rhode Island) was largely organized around political parties and the changes in the six states in terms of party competition after 1945. To his credit, Lockard paid much more attention to interest groups than John Fenton did in his 1966 book, *Midwest Politics*.

During the three decades since *New England State Politics* was published, parties have declined in importance as significant actors in our state and national public-policy-making process, and more and more attention has been focused on interest groups. Still, little is known about the number, types, significance, and roles of interest groups in the policy-making processes of many states, and for many states there have been no efforts to study the interest-group systems and their impact on state politics in a systematic manner.

Comparative research on state politics using a regional unit of analysis also has been rare. Studies by V.O. Key, Duane Lockard, and Frank Jonas looked at politics in the South, the Northeast, and the West using the region to establish geographical boundaries of analysis. But these regional studies have been the exception rather than the rule. Much more common are individual state studies, such as the volumes in the series on government in the fifty states published by the University of Nebraska Press. We believe there are significant advantages to using regions in a comparative examination of interest groups.

Interest groups have exerted enormous influence on the public-policy-making process of all northeastern states. In fact, in most cases they have been the dominant political forces. This is not to say that the literature on northeastern politics ignores interest groups and their importance. There are many treatments of group systems in the literature on individual states. Yet, in virtually all these studies, including the University of Nebraska series, interest groups are treated only incidentally. This book's focus on interest groups provides a different perspective and therefore adds to the general understanding of the politics of the Northeast and its individual states.

But augmenting the general understanding of northeastern politics was not one of the major purposes we had in mind when we first conceived of a book on interest groups in the Northeast. This book was actually planned as the fourth in a series of four books that we have co-edited on interest groups in all fifty states. Each book focuses on a region of the country. The first covered the thirteen western states and was published by the University of Utah Press, the second book (University of Alabama Press) covered the South, the third book (Iowa State University Press) focused on the Midwest, and this book, on the northeastern states, is the fourth and final regional volume. A fifth volume (to be published by Harper Collins) will compare all fifty states and all four regions.

Seventy-eight political scientists were involved in the entire project, which took eight years to complete. This is the most extensive treatment of interest groups in the states yet produced. As with the other three regional books, this one on the Northeast grew out of a sense of frustration. We, and several colleagues throughout the country who are primarily interested in researching and teaching about interest groups, were particularly concerned about the dearth of material, and especially hard data, on groups at the state level. These books will serve as foundation material on interest-group politics in the states.

In planning these regional books we identified four primary objectives and one secondary objective. One major objective was to provide the first overall analysis of interest groups in states where there was no existing research on the subject. About twenty states fell into this category. Second, we wanted to provide an update on group activity in states where there was some previous work. Taken together, these first two purposes would provide an up-to-date data base for the comparative analysis of state interest groups to an extent that had never before been possible. That was our third major objective. Our fourth primary objective was to be able to assess our findings against previous research on state groups by such scholars as Harmon Zeigler, Sarah McCally Morehouse, Wayne Francis, and Belle Zeller. Such an assessment would make it possible for us to suggest modifications to existing theories and develop some new theories and propositions of our own.

Because interest groups are so central a part of all political and governmental systems, we realized that, if our methodology and analysis were rigorous enough, our study would also shed light on state and regional politics in general. That was our secondary objective. As our research progressed, we found that studying interest groups provided a new perspective on politics in individual northeastern states and the region that had not been previously explored or at least not expressly treated. Hence, our belief that this book will make a contribution to an overall understanding of northeastern politics. Nevertheless, this book focuses on state interest groups in the Northeast. It is not a treatment of northeastern politics that focuses on interest groups. First and foremost, we are interest-group specialists and—despite immersing ourselves in the literature on the region for the last several years—we do not claim to be experts on northeastern politics. We leave to those experts the task of discovering the deeper implications of our study for understanding politics in the region.

A few words about the format of the book are in order. The introductory chapter uses a conceptual framework combined with a historical methodology to set the scene for understanding the place of interest groups in northeastern state politics. It also explains our methodology. This is followed by the twelve state chapters, alphabetically by state. To provide some background for understanding the specifics of interest-group activity in each state, each chapter begins with a brief overview of the state and its politics. The concluding chapter summarizes the story of northeastern interest groups by using the conceptual framework set out in Chapter 1 and by drawing on the information in the other chapters to provide a comparative analysis of the current role, operating techniques, and power of northeastern state interest groups. It also compares and contrasts recent developments in northeastern interest-group politics with those in other regions.

More so than in most political science books, this book is the result of the efforts of many people. In this case, however, the people are neither "too numerous to mention" nor large enough in number to warrant a separate acknowledgments page. At the top of the list are our sixteen contributors. In particular, we appreciate their willingness to bear the cost of their own research efforts. The University of Utah and the University of Alaska Southeast provided us with some basic resources for our project—not the least of which was regular employment. Our copyeditor, Peggy Hoover, and Penn State Press key personnel were of immense help to us. Marilyn Miller, Debbie Frye, and especially Laurie Johnson typed the manuscript and tables while teaching us a few lessons in presentation and style. Josephine F. Milburn and John G. Grumm read an early draft of the manuscript and gave us valuable insights on how to improve it. Robert S. Friedman read the manuscript carefully and gave us innumerable suggestions on how to improve it, and we were able to implement many of those. For his time, effort, and patience, we are very grateful. Finally, our families have been understanding and supportive, and we express our appreciation and apologies for the time we have taken from them over the years.

Finally, we must make a few comments about how we shared the work in putting together this book. A lengthy and comprehensive set of guidelines that channeled the efforts of the individual state contributors was the work of Clive Thomas. Other editing, proofreading, and press corresponding tasks were divided into roughly even proportions, even though in the final tally we each feel we did 51 percent of the work. That's not to say that we shared equally in each of the myriad tasks involved in producing an edited book, because, like all good partnerships, ours is based on the fact that we complement each other.

Ronald J. Hrebenar
Salt Lake City, Utah

Clive S. Thomas
Juneau, Alaska

April 1, 1992

1

The Role of Interest Groups in Northeastern Politics

Ronald J. Hrebenar

The Northeast is a special region of the United States. It was the birth-place of the American Revolution, the center of the nation's early intellec-tual and academic life, and the home of the industrial revolution in North America.[1] The Northeast is also where this country's first competitive party and interest-group politics originated. Included within the region are some of America's most industrialized states; some of the most agricultural states; states dominated by metropolitan giants; states characterized by population scattered in dozens of small cities and towns; states with political traditions of honest politics; and states with long histories of corruption. Even states with a common historical experience, such as the former slave states of Delaware, Maryland, and West Virginia, have quite different styles of poli-tics.

The Northeast is also the region with the most diverse population pat-terns. Archetypal of the so-called Snow or Rust Belt, the Northeast as a region has been in relative economic decline for decades. Recently, the Northeast has been the slowest growing in the nation in terms of income, and one of the worst in terms of unemployment. When the recession began in 1990, the five New England states, especially Massachusetts, were hard hit. As the 1990s began, no other region of the nation was in as much economic trouble as the Northeast.

The entire range of types of interest-group systems and behavior emerges from the twelve northeastern states. The corrupt politics of New Hamp-shire, where railroad and timber interests had great power, makes a clear contrast to the clean politics of adjacent Vermont. Lobbying styles range

---

1. See Josephine F. Milburn and Victoria Schuck, eds., *New England Politics* (Cam-bridge, Mass.: Schenkman, 1981), xi.

from "super-lobbyists" of New York to the amateur citizen lobbyists of New Hampshire. In various historical periods, some of the northeastern states had periods of political domination by one or two powerful interests. Harmon Zeigler wrote about the domination of Maine by a few powerful interests: timber, the shoe industry, and utilities. Duane Lockard noted that Maine was one of a handful of states in which a few interests almost completely controlled a state's politics.[2] and according to one scholar, Standard Oil did everything to the Pennsylvania legislature except refine it.[3] Population heterogeneity and economic diversity tended to support more pluralist interest-group systems in some of the remaining states.

The pattern of dominant interest groups controlling state politics was common in other regions, such as the South in the 1800s. One reason interest groups played a more dominant role in state politics in the South than in most other regions is that the one-party Democratic dominance in southern states failed to provide a check on interest-group power. In the Northeast, interest-group power historically was checked by competitive party systems operating in some of the states, and not checked in states that had dominant parties in one era or another, such as New Hampshire, Pennsylvania, Maryland, and West Virginia.

Change, often significant change, has affected almost every aspect of life, culture, and politics in the Northeast. As the following chapters indicate, interest groups, like all human systems, have both been affected by this change and helped bring it about. In each northeastern state there have been significant changes in the interest-group systems, compared with just a few decades ago. There has been growth both in the number of groups in the state capitals and in the strata of the population represented by interest groups, as well as growth in the professionalism of lobbyists and group leaders. Explaining exactly what the nature of this change, transition, and growth has been in recent developments in northeastern interest-group politics forms the primary objective of this book.

To achieve this, we combine an in-depth analysis of individual states with comparative analysis of the region as a whole. This involves four distinct but interrelated lines of inquiry. First, we provide an update on the types of groups operating in each state and the tactics they are now using

2. Duane Lockard, *New England State Politics* (Princeton: Princeton University Press, 1959), 77–79.

3. George Thayer, *Who Shakes the Money Tree? American Campaign Financing Practices from 1789 to the Present* (New York: Touchstone, 1973).

to achieve their goals. For several states this constitutes the first comprehensive treatment of interest groups past or present. Second, we assess changes in interest-group politics in the Northeast as a whole, especially the role that groups play in the public-policy-making process. Third, we place the Northeast in contrast by comparing past and present trends with those in other regions. Finally, by combining the findings from these three lines of inquiry, we hope to enhance general theories of interest-group activity in the states.

This chapter outlines the framework for accomplishing these objectives. Most significant is the analytical framework provided for understanding the changes, transition, and growth in northeastern interest-group politics. The chapter also reviews the relatively small body of literature on northeastern groups prior to this research project; briefly traces the development of groups in the Northeast up to the 1980s and the factors that have affected change; explains some key definitions and methodology; and identifies recent changes in other regions as a means of assessing the developments identified in the individual state chapters. However, neither this chapter nor this book claims to be a book on northeastern politics. That book has yet to be written. The present book simply seeks to highlight the topics and themes of the region's politics that are essential for an understanding of northeastern interest-group politics.

Chapter 14 summarizes the current state of northeastern interest groups up to the present. It does this in a comparative context by drawing on the information in the individual state chapters. In addition, drawing on research done in the other thirty-eight states, the chapter compares recent interest-group developments in the Northeast with such developments in other regions.

THE NORTHEAST REGION

The Northeast is a difficult region to define; the West and South are regions that are relatively distinct. We defined the West by drawing the boundary at the 100th meridian, where the farming culture of the prairie ends and the ranching culture of the West begins. The South was defined as the eleven states of the Old Confederacy plus Kentucky, which was added because it is predominantly more southern than midwestern in terms of its social, economic, and political variables. Our "Midwest" almost completely coincided with Neal R. Peirce's "Great Plains States" and "Great Lakes States," with the removal of Texas to the South.[4] This leaves the northeastern states as the artificial merging of the twelve remaining states of the often quite different subregions of the New England and the Mid-Atlantic states.

The Northeast is almost never examined as an overall region. Research has focused, as we will see shortly, on one subregion or the other. Actually, even the two subregions are not very homogeneous. New England, for example, must be divided into rural and industrial sectors. Half the New England states have had one-party histories, while the other half have had two-party competition patterns. Vermont has been one of the most one-party Republican states in the nation since the Civil War. Massachusetts, on the other hand, has become a Democratic party stronghold since World War II.

Of the two regions, New England is more of a logical and meaningful unit. It has a much more homogeneous culture, population, and history. The Mid-Atlantic, with no regional identity or regional history, is more an artificial construction—especially with our addition of West Virginia to the other more traditionally grouped states.

PREVIOUS RESEARCH ON NORTHEASTERN POLITICS AND INTEREST GROUPS

To our knowledge, no book or article on the subject of northeastern interest-group politics has been published. The Northeast is not unique in this dearth of material on interest groups. The West, the Midwest, and the South have had extensive bibliographies published on their politics, parties, and regional issues. Yet, even in the cases of the West and the South there is little on interest groups in those regions, primarily because research on U.S. interest groups has focused on group activity at the national level. Such national-level research focused on a single city, Washington, D.C., was comparatively easy to accomplish because all major actors were often

4. Neal R. Peirce, The Great Plains States of America: People, Politics, and Power in the Nine Great Plains States (New York: W. W. Norton, 1973); Neal R. Peirce and John Keefe, The Great Lakes States: People, Politics, and Power in the Five Great Lakes States (New York: W. W. Norton, 1980).

found within a few blocks of each other. Researching state-level interest groups or lobbying in capitals thousands of miles apart, often in small, out-of-the-way cities, and operating in many different political cultures and traditions, was a nearly insurmountable research problem.

Duane Lockard's *New England State Politics* remains the seminal work on the postwar politics of the New England subregion. Lockard was discussing political parties and therefore only secondarily mentioned interest groups. Lockard's book has been updated by two recent studies on New England parties and politics. Josephine Milburn and Victoria Schuck's *New England Politics* is a broad-based study of political change in the subregion during the 1960s and 1970s,[5] while Josephine Milburn and William Doyle's *New England Political Parties* is primarily an examination of political parties up to approximately 1980, with some discussion of interest groups and their impact on party organizations.[6] John Fenton's study of border-state politics includes several of the southernmost northeastern states included in this volume.[7]

Six types of studies have touched on some aspects of interest-group activity in the Northeast. First, there are the Lockard and Milburn books on New England politics, discussed above. Second, there is the treatment of interest groups in books on the government and politics of individual northeastern states.[8] While all twelve states have been the subject of

5. Josephine F. Milburn and Victoria Schuck, eds., *New England Politics* (Cambridge, Mass.: Schenkman, 1981).

6. Josephine F. Milburn and William Doyle, *New England Political Parties* (Cambridge, Mass.: Schenkman, 1983).

7. See John Fenton, *Politics of the Border States, a Study of the Pattern of Political Organization and Political Change Common to the Border States: Maryland, West Virginia, Kentucky, and Missouri* (New Orleans: Houser Press, 1957).

8. Wayne R. Swanson, *Lawmaking in Connecticut: The General Assembly* (New London, Conn.: Connecticut College, 1984); James Phelan and Robert Pozen, *The Company State* (New York: Grossman, 1973); Mary Lou Wendell, ed., *A Citizen's Guide to the Maine Legislature* (Augusta: Maine People's Resource Center and Maine Common Cause, 1985); James F. Horan et al., *Downeast Politics: The Government of the State of Maine* (Dubuque, Iowa: Kendall/Hunt, 1975); David Levitan and Elwyn E. Mariner, *Your Massachusetts Government* (Newton, Mass.: Government Research Publications, 1984); Gerald Pomper, *The Political State of New Jersey* (New Brunswick, N.J.: Rutgers University Press, 1986); Richard Lehne and Alan Rosenthal, eds., *Politics in New Jersey* (New Brunswick, N.J.: Eagleton Institute, 1979); Richard J. Conners and William Dunham, *The Government of New Jersey* (Lanham, Md.: University Press of America, 1984); Peter W. Colby, ed., *New York State Today: Politics, Government, Public Policy*

books, the treatment of interest groups varies widely. Some books devote a separate chapter to interest groups, others provide just a small section buried in a chapter on political parties. These treatments also display a wide variety of approaches, from the purely anecdotal to the more conceptual and quantitative treatments. They also vary in scope and depth of treatment, and most are now outdated. A third category includes books that use northeastern states as examples or case studies. These are usually well written, but length limitations prevent them from paying more than cursory attention to interest groups.[9] Fourth, there is a small body of literature that has a public-policy focus and has taken a case-study approach to investigating the impact of individual groups. William Browne's recent book on agricultural interest-group politics provides the reader with a wealth of information on the nature of these agricultural groups and their roles in both national and state political, economic, and social life.[10] A fifth category of literature on northeastern groups has taken what might be termed a "micro" approach to the study of group theory. These have looked either at a specific aspect of the internal organization and operation of groups or at how they affect a specific part of the political process, such as the legislature. Sometimes these studies have been concerned solely with specific states, such as Belle Zeller's study of lobbying in New York State.[11] Finally, a sixth category of books also contains information on northeastern interest groups. John Gunther's 1940s survey of politics in America, *Inside U.S.A.*, contained valuable insights on group activities in many

---

(Albany: State University of New York Press, 1985); Joseph F. Zimmerman, *The Government and Politics of New York State* (New York: New York University Press, 1981); Paul Beers, *Pennsylvania Politics Today and Yesterday* (University Park: Pennsylvania State University Press, 1980); Andrew Nuquist, *Vermont State Government and Administration* (Government Research Center, University of Vermont, 1966); Duane Lockard, "Vermont: Political Paradox," in Lockard, *New England State Politics*, 35–45; Frank M. Bryan, *Yankee Politics in Rural Vermont* (Hanover, N.H.: University Press of New England, 1974); John A. Williams, *West Virginia: A Bicentennial History* (New York: W. W. Norton, 1976).

9. See, e.g., Alan Rosenthal and Maureen Moakley, eds., *The Political Life of the American States* (New York: Praeger, 1984).

10. William P. Browne, *Private Interests, Public Policy, and American Agriculture* (Lawrence: University of Kansas Press, 1988).

11. Belle Zeller, *Pressure Politics in New York: A Study of Group Representation Before the Legislature* (New York: Prentice Hall, 1937). See also Judith C. Meredith, *Workbook: Lobbying on a Shoestring* (in Massachusetts) (Boston: Meredith & Associates, 1985).

states, including those in the Northeast.[12] The modern manifestations of Gunther's book are the nine volumes written by Neal Peirce on the people, politics, and power in the various subregions of America. Peirce profiles each state and mentions in an informative but impressionistic manner the major interests that have had an impact on the state's politics.[13] Another source of information on the various states (and occasionally on their major interests) is the individual state profiles that introduce each state's congressional delegation in such books as the *Almanac of American Politics*.[14]

These six categories are a useful starting point in a study of northeastern interest groups, particularly group activity in individual states, and numerous references will be made to the studies throughout this book. Yet, because of the great variation in methodology and scope and in depth of analysis, these studies are of limited value for purposes of comparative analysis, and often for individual state studies as well. There is, however, a seventh category of literature that has been comparative in focus and has included the northeastern states as part of nationwide studies of state interest-group activity. The books in this group have taken what we might term a "macro" approach by attempting to understand interest groups in the context of the state as a whole and particularly in relation to the state's political and governmental system. The most notable work here has been conducted by Belle Zeller, Harmon Zeigler and Hendrik van Dalen, and Sarah McCally Morehouse.[15]

---

12. John Gunther, *Inside U.S.A.* (New York: Harper & Row, 1947, 1951).

13. Neal Peirce's regional books, in addition to the two noted in previous footnotes, are *The Megastates of America, The Pacific States of America, The Mountain States of America, The Deep South States of America, The Border South States of America, The New England States of America*, and *The Mid-Atlantic States of America* (with Michael Barone), all published by W. W. Norton. See also Neal R. Peirce and Jerry Hagstrom, *The Book of America: Inside Fifty States Today* (New York: W. W. Norton, 1983).

14. *Almanac of American Politics* (Washington, D.C.: Congressional Quarterly Press, 1989).

15. Belle Zeller, *American State Legislatures*, 2nd ed. (New York: Thomas Y. Crowell, 1954), 190–91 and chap. 13, "Pressure Group Influence and Their Control"; L. Harmon Zeigler, "Interest Groups in the States," chap. 4 in Virginia Gray, Herbert Jacob, and Kenneth N. Vines, eds., *Politics in the American States: A Comparative Analysis*, 4th ed. (Boston: Little, Brown, 1983); L. Harmon Zeigler and Hendrik van Dalen, "Interest Groups in State Politics," chap. 4 in Herbert Jacob and Kenneth N. Vines, *Politics in the American States: A Comparative Analysis*, 3rd ed. (Boston: Little, Brown, 1976); and chap. 3, "Pressure Groups Versus Political Parties," in Sarah McCally Morehouse, *State Politics, Parties, and Policy* (New York: Holt, Rinehart & Winston, 1981).

Despite the valuable contributions of these studies, all of them suffered from the same weakness. Their attempts at comprehensive analysis of both the Northeast and other regions were based on original data from only a few states and drew on other information (such as that referred to above) that varied in its methodology from the impressionistic to the highly quantitative, a divergence that was not ideal for comparative analysis. Therefore, the theories and propositions developed from these studies were arrived at by extrapolation, or by reliance on secondary sources, and sometimes, in the absence of data, by speculation.

Whatever their methodological weaknesses, however, these studies made significant contributions. Each was a major source for the evaluation of interest groups at the subnational level—including the Northeast—at a time when little other data existed. Zeller was the first to categorize states into strong, moderate, or weak interest-group systems. Zeigler, and Zeigler and van Dalen, developed several theories and propositions about how the economic, social, and political system in a state influences the composition, operation, and power of the state's interest-group system. Most notably, they developed a four-category classification of group power within strong interest-group states and advanced knowledge on the relationship between party strength and group power. Morehouse has built on this work, in particular expanding on the relationship of parties and groups and refining the threefold classification system of interest-group power vis-à-vis a state's political system (strong, moderate, or weak). She also developed the first listing of the most "significant" groups in all fifty states. All this has acted as a benchmark to scholars conducting subsequent research, and it certainly provided us with an important point of departure for our study of northeastern interest groups.

COMMON TERMS AND DEFINITIONS

Because each of the above-mentioned researchers used different definitions, the usefulness of previous studies of state-level interest groups for purposes of comparative analysis, whether comparisons within a state over time or between states at any point of time, is reduced. Five of the most important of these terms are *interest group*, *interest*, *lobby*, *lobbyist*, and *group power*. That previous studies used various definitions of these terms is understandable, as disputes over their meaning have been common for years.

To achieve methodological and analytical consistency, we developed a common set of definitions of these terms for use by our contributors in all fifty states. Here we will define the first four and leave "group power" for later, when we explain our methodology in more detail.

From most specific to most general, the most specific term is *interest group*. Over the years, researchers have used a variety of operational definitions of this term. Most common has been the legal or regulatory definition, which therefore made the groups required to register under federal and state laws the focus of study, and excluded groups not required to register. In certain limited cases such a definition may be adequate, but for most research on state interest groups, particularly research with a comparative focus or component, it is inadequate.

The major problem with this legal or regulatory definition is that the fifty states vary considerably in what groups and organizations they require to register as lobbying entities. Some states, such as Oregon, have relatively broad rules, requiring even state agencies to register. Others, such as Georgia, have very narrow regulations.[16] Many of the interest groups that are not required to register in Georgia are quite active in the state capital. Exclusion of these nonregistered, or "hidden," groups and lobbies, and especially state government agencies, greatly distorts our understanding of the role and impact of interest groups in such a state's public-policy-making process. For these reasons, using group registration lists as the sole basis for comparative state interest-group research is unsatisfactory.

We attempt to overcome these problems by using the following definition of an interest group in our fifty-state study: *An interest group is any association of individuals or organizations, whether formally organized or not, that attempts to influence public policy.* The State University of New York is an example of a specific interest group, as is the Teamsters Union. This definition is a variation of what is probably the most widely used definition of "interest group," that of David Truman and, indirectly, that of the "father of modern interest group politics," Arthur Bentley.[17] Our definition is shorter and more concrete. It embraces the various concepts that Truman

16. For the provisions of the lobby laws in the fifty states, see COGEL, *Campaign Finance, Ethics, and Lobby Law Blue Book 1988–89: Special Report* (Lexington, Ky.: Council on Governmental Ethics Laws Through the Council of State Governments, 1988), 157–68.

17. David B. Truman, *The Governmental Process* (New York: Alfred A. Knopf, 1951); Arthur F. Bentley, *The Process of Government* (Bloomington, Ind.: Principia Press, 1949).

included and at the same time eliminates some of the shortcomings of his definition.[18] All definitions have some drawbacks, and ours is no exception. It is very broad, and it creates some problems in securing data, as some of our contributors discovered. However, the findings from this project demonstrate that our definition produces a much more comprehensive and balanced view of interest-group activity in the states, including many aspects previously unnoticed or treated only superficially in some previous studies.

The term *lobby* has a much broader connotation than "interest group." In our study we use it as a collective term as follows: A *lobby is two or more individuals, groups, or organizations concerned with the same general area of public policy but that may or may not be in agreement on specific issues.* The education lobby in most states, including those in the Northeast, is comprised of state boards of education, parent-teacher associations, education associations, boards of regents of higher education, student groups, vocational-education institutions, special-education groups, and representatives of major individual institutions, such as research universities. These groups all share a general interest in promoting legislation and funding to enhance the quality of education, yet on any given issue members of this lobby may be on opposite sides. Because funds for education make up half or more of many state budgets, education lobby members agree that this proportion should continue or be increased, but exactly how education monies should be distributed may cause intense conflicts among the lobby's members.

The term *interest* has a broader connotation than "interest group" but is more specific than "lobby." We can again use education groups as an example. Individual universities, such as the University of Rhode Island, Penn

18. Truman's definition is "an interest group is any group that is based on one or more shared attitudes and makes certain claims on other groups or organizations in the society for the establishment, maintenance or enhancement of forms of behavior that are implied by the shared attitudes" (Truman, *Governmental Process*, 33). Despite its insightfulness, the Truman definition has been criticized on the basis of its emphasis on "shared attitudes" and the modes of political behavior that result from this. Subsequent work, especially that by Clark and Wilson and by Olson, persuasively challenged the notion that group members share common reasons for joining or maintaining membership in a group or that all members are concerned or aware of the political goals of the group. See Peter B. Clark and James Q. Wilson, "Incentive Systems: A Theory of Organizations," *Administrative Science Quarterly* 6 (1961), 219–66; Mancur Olson, *The Logic of Collective Action: Public Goods and the Theory of Groups* (Cambridge, Mass.: Harvard University Press, 1965); see also Terry M. Moe, *The Organization of Interests* (Chicago: University of Chicago Press, 1980).

State, or the State University of New York at Albany often lobby directly and therefore can be considered specific interest groups. These are part of the education lobby in their states, but they can also be in the interest category of "higher education," which also includes community colleges, vocational education, and other institutions, depending on the state. Exactly where an interest ends and a lobby begins is not always clear. But it is often a useful distinction to make because public officials refer to similar types of interest groups that often act in concert as an "interest"—that is, "the higher education lobby."

We defined a *lobbyist* as a person an interest group designates to represent it to government for the purpose of influencing public policy in that group's favor. From our definition of "interest group" we know that the interest represented by the lobbyist need not be a formal organization, such as the International Ladies' Garment Workers Union or the New York State Cable Television Association. It includes informal and ad hoc groups, such as a group of neighborhood residents who are dissatisfied with their community leaders, or an informal association of business people who are concerned about a specific issue. As we define them, lobbyists are not limited just to people representing groups that are required to register under state law, but include all those who lobby, whether they are required to register or not.[19]

Not all lobbyists are the same, just as not all lawyers perform the same roles in our nation's judicial system. Lobbyists can be divided into five major categories or types:

1. *Contract lobbyists* are hired on a contract for a fee specifically to lobby. They may represent more than one client.
2. *In-house lobbyists* are employees of an organization, association, or business who act as lobbyists as all or part of their job. They represent only one client, their employer.
3. *Government lobbyists or legislative liaisons* are employees of state, local, and federal agencies who as part or all of their job represent their agency to the legislative and executive branches of state government. These also represent only one interest.
4. *Citizen or volunteer lobbyists* are people who, usually on an ad hoc and unpaid basis, represent citizen and community organizations or

19. See COGEL, *Campaign Finance, Ethics, and Lobby Law Blue Book 1988–1989,* 157–68.

informal groups. They rarely represent more than one interest at a time.

5. *Private individuals, "hobbyists," or self-styled lobbyists*, act on their own behalf and are not designated by any organization as an official representative.

These five categories of lobbyists are viewed differently by those they seek to influence. While those in each category have the identical goal of influencing public policy, their background, their experience, their resources, and the organizations they represent are different, and that means the different types of lobbyists will probably lobby in different ways.

A FRAMEWORK FOR UNDERSTANDING INTEREST-GROUP ACTIVITY

In order to understand interest-group activity in states, it is useful to consider the basic factors that influence that activity—that is, what determines (1) the types of groups that are active in the states, (2) the methods those groups use in pursuing their goals, and (3) the role those groups play in state political systems and, in particular, the power they exert within those systems. Scholars agree that a complex set of economic, social, cultural, legal, political, governmental, and even geographical variables affects interest-group activity and that these variables both by themselves and in combination will differ from state to state. Therefore, each state's interest-group system will be unique.

Nevertheless, we have identified seven sets of factors that appear to be important in all states and that we developed into a conceptual framework, set out in Table 1.1. This conceptual framework for understanding what influences interest-group activity is a synthesis of previous research and of findings from our fifty-state study. While all seven factors and their various elements are not new, what is original is the way many of these elements have been used here and the integration of the seven factors into a single conceptual framework. These seven factors and their components are very much interrelated in that they influence one another. A change in one factor may result in a change in one or more of the other factors. Any change at all is likely to affect the nature of group activity, and major changes will have a significant impact on the interest group and the lobbying scene in a particular state or in the states as a whole.

Table 1.1.   Major Factors Influencing the Makeup, Operating Techniques, and Impact on Public Policy of Interest-Group Systems in the States

1. *State Policy Domain.* The constitutional/legal authority of a state affects which groups will be politically active. The policies actually exercised by a state affect which groups will be most active. The policy priorities of a state will affect which groups are most influential.

2. *Political Attitudes.* Especially political culture and political ideology viewed in terms of conservative/liberal attitudes. Affects the type and extent of policies performed; the level of integration/fragmentation and professionalization of the policy-making process; acceptable lobbying techniques; and the comprehensiveness and stringency of enforcement of public disclosure laws, including lobby laws.

3. *Level of Integration/Fragmentation of the Policy Process.* Strength of political parties; power of the governor; number of directly elected cabinet members; number of independent boards and commissions; initiative, referendum, and recall. Influences the number of options available to groups: greater integration decreases the options, while more fragmentation increases them.

4. *Level of Professionalization of State Government.* State legislators, support services, bureaucracy, including the governor's staff. Has an impact on the extent to which public officials need group resources and information. Also affects the level of professionalization of the lobbying system.

5. *Level of Socioeconomic Development.* Increased socioeconomic diversity will tend to produce a more diverse and competitive group system; a decline in the dominance of one or an oligarchy of groups; new and more sophisticated techniques of lobbying, such as an increase in contract lobbyists, lawyer-lobbyists, multiclient/multiservice lobbying firms, grass-roots campaigns, and public-relations techniques; and a general rise in the professionalization of lobbyists and lobbying.

6. *Extensiveness and Enforcement of Public-Disclosure Laws.* Including lobby laws, campaign finance laws, PAC regulations, and conflict-of-interest provisions. Increases public information about lobbying activities that has an impact on the methods and techniques of lobbying; this in turn has affected the power of certain groups and lobbyists.

Table 1.1. *Continued*

7. *Level of Campaign Costs and Sources of Support.* As the proportion of group funding increases, especially that from PACs, group access and power increases.

Sources: The Hrebenar-Thomas study; and Mark S. Hyde and Richard W. Alsfeld, "Role Orientations of Lobbyists in a State Setting: A Comparative Analysis," paper delivered at the Annual Meeting of the American Political Science Association, New Orleans, 1985; Wayne L. Francis, *Legislative Issues in the Fifty States: A Comparative Analysis* (Chicago: Rand McNally, 1967); Sarah McCally Morehouse, *State Politics, Parties, and Policy* (New York: Holt, Rinehart & Winston, 1981); John C. Wahlke et al., *The Legislative System* (New York: John Wiley, 1962); L. Harmon Zeigler, "Interest Groups in the States," in *Politics in the American States: A Comparative Analysis*, ed. Virginia Gray, Herbert Jacob, and Kenneth N. Vines, 4th ed. (Boston: Little, Brown, 1983); Harmon Zeigler and Hendrik van Dalen, "Interest Groups in State Politics," in *Politics in the American States: A Comparative Analysis*, ed. Herbert Jacob and Kenneth N. Vines, 3d ed. (Boston: Little, Brown, 1976); and Harmon Zeigler and Michael Baer, *Lobbying: Interaction and Influence in American State Legislatures* (Belmont, Calif.: Wadsworth, 1969).

THE NORTHEASTERN INTEREST-GROUP SYSTEM

Politics in the Northeast is characterized both by homogeneity and by complexity. The region's political heritage ranges from the most rustic and conservative antigovernment bias of the upper New England states to the powerful urban political machines that dominated so many major northeastern cities just a few decades ago. Despite the great differences in political background, we can identify certain themes that were and continue to be characteristic of northeastern political life.

The population mix of the region is perhaps most significant to an understanding of Northeastern politics. The Northeast is the most heterogeneous of all the main regions of the United States. Wave after wave of immigrants swept across the Northeast after landing in the major entry ports of Boston and New York. Initially, the population was largely English, but in the mid-1800s the Irish arrived in large numbers and changed the nature of politics for a century. Soon after, successive waves of immigrants came to the Northeast from seemingly every nation and ethnic group on earth. And not only did the ethnic groups organize to make their demands on government, but the religions of these immigrants, especially the Roman Catholics, facilitated the entry of the later-comers into the political system. The continuing political and social conflict between Protestant and Catholic adherents continues to define much of the region's politics into the 1990s.

The Northeast, unlike the South and Midwest and large parts of the West, does not have a strong economic base in agriculture. In some northeastern states, such as Pennsylvania, New York, and Maryland, agriculture has been and continues to be an important but not dominant part of the economy.[20] But the real power of the region is based on its political, intellectual, financial, and corporate resources. New York City is the corporate and financial headquarters of the United States, and the Boston metropolitan area serves as the intellectual center of higher education in the nation, as it has for nearly two hundred years. Finally, on the southern edge of the region lies Washington, D.C., the home of interest-group politics in its most sophisticated and complex manifestation. More than any other region of the nation, the Northeast has been the leader of this nation in many significant characteristics and continues in this role in the 1990s.

The interest-group patterns of the northeastern states during the 1800s were, like those in most states, narrowly based both in terms of the types of interests represented and in terms of those who wielded power. Railroads were probably the first "super-interest" because they were important as employers and power brokers and because for several decades they held a transportation monopoly. In most states, early in their histories, agricultural interests were also significant economic interests. Agricultural interests continue to be significant only in Vermont. In such states as New York, Pennsylvania, and New Jersey, strong industrial bases that came to overshadow the agricultural sector were built.

The Northeast was a stronghold of a laissez-faire philosophy of state government. Up to the mid-1900s this meant that the role of the states was far less extensive than it is today. In no other part of the nation was higher education considered to be a natural part of the private sector, and consequently the development of the great state universities was significantly resisted in the Northeast. State bureaucracies were kept small, and the level of state civil service professionalism was low. Professionalism was a mixed pattern among state elected officials, especially legislators. Some

---

20. Bureau of the Census, *Statistical Abstract of the United States: 1991* (Washington, D.C.: Government Printing Office, 1991), 1135.

states, such as New York and Massachusetts, gradually developed traditions of professional legislators, and other states, such as Vermont and New Hampshire, revered the "citizen legislator" as its model.

Business has dominated politics in the Northeast, as it has in the South, the Midwest, and the West. Railroads and financial institutions have traditionally been important political forces in all the region's state capitals, and agricultural groups have been powerful in each of the northeastern states but have recently declined significantly in power as their numbers and economic role diminishes.

Since the 1930s, business and agriculture have been joined by labor unions, which have probably been more powerful political actors in the Northeast than in any of the other three regions. Most recently, local government groups, labor unions, and education interests, especially school-teachers, have become important actors in state government in the Northeast, as they have in all fifty states. Together these five interests—business, agriculture, labor, local government, and education—made up the major interests operating in state capitals in the Northeast and in state-houses across the nation.

Because of their less-regulated styles of politics, some states, such as New York and New Jersey, developed the most famous (or perhaps notorious) of stereotyped lobbying styles: the wheeler-dealer. This style is easier to recognize than to define, but in general it refers to a powerful lobbyist who operates in an aggressive and flamboyant manner and is willing to use a variety of methods, some of which may be suspect, to achieve his goals. As with many other aspects of the pre-1960s lobbying community, it is impossible to determine how widespread wheeler-dealers were in the states, but the nature of politics at the time, resulting in part from the lack of public disclosure and professionalism, leads to the conclusion that this was the dominant lobbying style.

METHODOLOGY

If we could have designed the perfect methodology for this study of interest groups on the state level, we would have used an identical research methodology, including identical survey instruments, in each of the fifty states. However, the real world, including a lack of research funds, does not permit such absolute methodological consistency on such a scale. In fact, the practical problems of conducting identical social science research in fifty state capitals has kept other state-level researchers from achieving absolute methodological consistency for all the states.

In each state we first attempted to find a contributor who was a qualified political scientist as well as an interest-group specialist, but for some states it was difficult to find any suitably qualified political scientist, let alone an interest-group specialist, who was willing to take on the project. Even when we had contributors for all fifty states, certain factors precluded imposition of an identical methodology. First, literature on interest groups already existed for some states, while in others—the majority—our contributors had to start from scratch. Second, because the registration and reporting requirements vary so much from state to state, some information (lobbyist fees or the percentage of campaign funds contributed by political action committees) is simply not available. Third, a demand for an identical and restrictive methodology would have precluded individual contributors from identifying certain unique and perhaps crucial aspects of their state's interest-group system that would be valuable both for an understanding of that system and for comparative purposes. Fourth, a demand to impose an identical methodology on dozens of volunteer, unpaid, unsupported contributors would have been impossible for the editors to enforce.

We strongly believe that, even if we could mandate it, a purely quantitative approach would be inadequate because, unlike other areas of political science, such as voting behavior, we are not yet able to understand the role, influence, and impact of interest groups simply by quantifying their activities. That would fail to convey the highly personalized and dynamic nature of several key aspects of interest-group activity. One of the most important aspects is the interaction between lobbyists and group leaders, on the one hand, and policymakers, both elected and appointed, on the other. Much of the dynamics of this relationship, and especially what ultimately determines influence, requires a qualitative as opposed to quantitative methodology. A purely quantitative approach has similar shortcomings when it comes to assessing the various aspects of group power. Quantitative approaches need to be combined with a qualitative approach—"soaking and poking," as Richard Fenno would say—interviews, observation, and associating with lobbyists, group leaders, legislators, and bureaucrats. Accordingly, we encouraged our contributors to use qualitative methods in conjunction with quantitative research, and to place both within a conceptual framework.

In view of the aforementioned practical problems, we devised a methodology that would provide as much quantitative and usable qualitative data as possible in order to maximize our ability to make comparisons between states. We also wanted to give each contributor enough flexibility to identify the unique aspects and nuances of interest-group activity in their respective states. To achieve this, we developed a set of guidelines that required each contributor to use a methodology that incorporated certain specified elements. These are presented in the Appendix.

Having already presented the common definitions for interest group, interest, lobby, lobbyist, and group power, we now turn to an explanation of our approach to group power. The concept of interest-group power can encompass two separate though interrelated ideas. It can mean the ability of an individual group, coalition, or lobby to achieve its policy goals, or it can refer to the strength of interest groups as a whole within a state's political and governmental systems, or to the strength of groups relative to other organizations or institutions, particularly political parties.

Those with only an acquaintance with interest-group theory will know that individual group and lobby power is a concept that poses problems based on methods of assessment rather than definition. There are so many variables affecting both long- and short-term group power that it is difficult to develop a methodology to assess and predict that power in more than a general way. Three methods have been used to assess individual group power: the use of purely objective criteria; the perceptual method, relying on the perception of politicians, bureaucrats, and political observers; and a combination of those two approaches.

We decided to adopt the combination approach. The perceptual method is used, but we also attempted to inject a high degree of objectivity and consistency into the research by using quantitative techniques to analyze the responses. This study's definition of individual group power, which also incorporates our method of assessment, is as follows:

> *The power of any particular interest group or lobby is its ability to achieve its goals as it defines them and as perceived by the various people directly involved in and who observe the public-policy-making process (e.g., present and former legislators, aides, bureaucrats, other lobbyists, journalists).*

The weaknesses both in our methodology and in the results are unavoidable. Yet, despite these weaknesses, our findings represent the first comprehensive assessment, based on a consistent research method in all fifty states, of the most effective interest groups and lobbies in each of those states.

The problem of assessing group power as a whole within a state's political system is even more problematic. In fact, this is probably the most difficult aspect of interest-group activity to assess, primarily because there are so many variables to consider, many of which have not yet been identified, let alone defined. Consequently, assessments of overall group power are crude at best. Many scholars, however, have taken a valiant stab at the question. As we mentioned earlier in describing our conceptual framework, Zeller, Zeigler and van Dalen, and Morehouse have classified states as strong, moderate, or weak with regard to the overall impact of their interest-group system. One key factor in these studies is the inverse relationship between party strength and group strength. This relationship does not always stand up to more detailed investigation.

No definitions or methodologies involving overall group power and its assessment were mandated by the editors. We saw this as an opportunity to develop some new approaches to assessing group power. With nearly eighty researchers involved in our fifty-state study, we decided to turn our contributors loose on the problem because no other acceptable alternative was available. As a starting point, we asked them to consider existing methods and the findings on overall group impact. They were to critique these and offer alternative methodologies and assessments. We suspect that this is the largest number of people who have ever focused on this problem at any one time. The individual state chapters and the concluding chapter explain these results.

Because this is the first study of state-level interest groups to include all fifty states (or even the twelve northeastern states), even a less stringent methodology would have added considerably to our knowledge of interest groups in state politics. However, we believed that our research method would enable us to go beyond this and produce data that would make extensive and original comparative analysis possible. Perhaps of equal importance is the ability of our data to verify or suggest modifications in general theories and propositions that have been based on extrapolation from information on a handful of states. Our project results have made all this possible.

STATE-LEVEL INTEREST-GROUP POLITICS
IN COMPARATIVE PERSPECTIVE

The central theme of this book is change and transition in northeastern interest-group politics. Therefore, as a basis for comparison, it is useful to identify the major changes and trends that are occurring in the other three regions: the Midwest, the West, and the South. Then, as the individual states are discussed, the changes and trends in the Northeast can be assessed against the other regions.

These overall changes and trends in state-level interest groups have been examined in detail in other writings.[21] For our present purposes, we need only discuss the highlights. Ten such changes and trends appear to be of major importance in the other regions.

1. A substantial increase in the number of groups active in state capitals.
2. A simultaneous expansion in the range or types of groups that attempt to affect public policy in the states.
3. The rise of public-service unions (especially teachers and public-employee associations), state and local government agencies as lobbying forces, and public interest and citizens groups.
4. An increased intensity of lobbying, because of the increased number and wider range of groups spending more time and money on lobbying state government than ever before.
5. More sophisticated interest-group tactics, which now include public-relations campaigns, networking (using a member contact system), and grass-roots lobbying, as well as coalition-building, newsletters, and more active participation in campaigns.
6. A phenomenal rise in the use of political action committees (PACs) by certain groups as a means of channeling money to favored candidates. Business, labor, and professional groups account for the bulk of PACs and their contributions.
7. Notable changes in the background and style of contract lobbyists (those hired for a fee specifically to lobby). The wheeler-dealer is

21. See Clive S. Thomas and Ronald J. Hrebenar, "Interest Groups in the States," chap. 4 in Virginia Gray, Herbert Jacob, and Robert Albritton, eds., *Politics in the American States: A Comparative Analysis*, 5th ed. (Glenview, Ill: Scott, Foresman / Little, Brown, 1990).

being replaced by the technical-expert lobbyist, and more and more contract lobbying is being done by multiservice lobbying firms, law firms, and public relations companies.

8. An increase in the public monitoring of interest-group activity, as evidenced by the passage and strengthening of lobby laws and campaign finance and conflict of interest regulations.

9. Major shifts in interest-group power in the states, whether individual groups or groups as a whole. Business is having to share power with an increasing range of groups, and group influence as a whole appears to have benefited, among other things, from the decline of political parties.

10. The role of interest groups within state political systems has expanded overall, and partly due to the decline in parties. In particular, interest groups have become more important as vehicles of political participation.

In summary, interest-group activity outside the Northeast is becoming much more professionalized and more and more like the interest-group system operating in the nation's capital.

UNDERSTANDING INTEREST-GROUP ACTIVITY IN THE NORTHEASTERN STATES

This first chapter sets the scene for understanding northeastern interest-group politics in three contexts: in individual states, in the region as a whole, and in the context of the fifty states. Our seven-point conceptual framework, a review of major characteristics of midwestern society and politics, and the identification of the ten most significant changes in interest-group activity in other regions are our primary means for understanding group activities. In addition to the central theme in our analysis—the extent of change and growth in northeastern interest-group politics—we also address two other broad political questions: Is the interest-group system in the Northeast significantly different from the systems in the other three regions? Are there common elements in northeastern interest-group politics?

2

Connecticut: Political Parties Court the Interest Groups

Sarah McCally Morehouse

Lobbyists in Connecticut must wear badges and stand behind red velvet ropes. Occasionally their cause is championed by the capital newspaper, which claims they are being "milked" by the parties. These indicators of their powerlessness overstate the case, for interest groups abound in the state, and their influence is significant. However, the traditional strength of the political parties in electing and governing, as well as the diversity of the state's economy, which generates opposing coalitions on most issues, limits their power. For instance, Connecticut is known both as a strong labor state and as a strong business state. This chapter will describe the economic, political, and governmental parameters within which the interest groups operate; the laws that regulate their activities; the interdependent operations of the political parties, the PACs and the lobbyists; and the balance of power that exists between them.

THE SETTING

Three and a half centuries ago, the first session of the general court marked the birth of the state of Connecticut. Perhaps the heavy weight of history provided her title "Land of Steady Habits," which describes a phenomenon that plagues those who seek change yet rewards those who accomplish it—for laws, once passed, are steadily observed. History is only one of the many reasons for the stability of Connecticut's political system.

The Economy

The economy in Connecticut reacts to the national trends, but at a slower rate and with buffers to moderate the peaks and troughs of economic cycles. The state is seventh in the nation in dependency on manufacturing. One sobering component of the manufacturing sector in Connecticut is defense-related business. The state ranks seventh in total defense dollars awarded and first in per capita dollars awarded. Major products include aircraft engines and parts, submarines, helicopters, fabricated metals, and electrical equipment. Manufacturing has been the foundation of Connecticut's economy for most of the twentieth century, but in the last thirty-five years the percentage of the labor force so employed has dropped from 50 percent to 25 percent. Most of the work force is now employed in the financial and service sectors. Connecticut is one of the few states whose service sector exports a product: insurance. According to the U.S. Department of Commerce, the consumer is more security-conscious today than at any time since the Great Depression. Thus, Connecticut can depend on national insecurity to help keep her economy stable, since over 95 percent of insurance sales are derived from out of state. The southwestern part of Connecticut—Fairfield County, known as the "Gold Coast"—is the home of many corporate headquarters providing affluent white-collar employment. Forty-one of the Fortune 500 U.S. corporations are based in that county.

Connecticut's steady economy hides many contrasts. The state claims to have the highest per capita income in the nation. Movie stars and millionaires live a short drive from cities of poverty and despair. Two of the nation's poorest cities—Hartford, the state capital, and New Haven, the site of Yale, the state's most prestigious university—see their children go to bed hungry. A survey of twenty large cities shows that Hartford has the second-highest child poverty rate in the nation; almost 40 percent of the city's children live in poverty. New Haven was sixth, with slightly more than 35 percent, and Bridgeport was eighth, with 34 percent.[1] Connecticut is ranked 50th in the nation in state and local government spending combined as a percentage of personal income. According to Matt E. Melmed, executive director of the Connecticut Association for Human Services, "In relation to what we and the state could be doing to address human needs, we are in some respects the cheapest state in the nation."[2]

More surprising than the contrasts between the wealthy and the poor in Connecticut is the way the state raises and spends its revenues. Until

---

1. Valerie Finholm, "State Has Fine Year, but Riches Unevenly Distributed," *Hartford Courant*, January 1, 1987, A-1, A-22.
2. Quoted in ibid., A-22.

1991, this wealthiest state did not have a personal income tax. Instead, revenues were collected by means of many different state taxes plus hundreds of fees.[3] Most of these taxes are regressive in that they take proportionately more from a poor person than from a wealthy one. The income-tax question has been a continuing one in the politics of the state. Traditionally opposed by leaders of both parties and a majority of the citizens, it passed by a narrow margin in the summer of 1991 after a brutal battle between the governor, Lowell Weicker, and the state legislature. The leaders of the Democratic party were split as well, with the Senate president and the majority leader opposed to the tax, and the House leaders in favor. Not content to abide by the legislative decision, opponents in both parties went to work to rescind it.

It is not surprising that Connecticut is not a leader in generosity to its poor and in educating its youth. While its welfare recipients live in one of the ten most generous states, the children's education is not funded as generously. Connecticut spends less on education in proportion to its population than twenty-eight other states. However, sturdy advocates for the poor and for education funding have been making the state face up to its responsibilities. To the dismay of its public colleges and the University of Connecticut, the state ranks 32nd in per capita spending on higher education, relying on the fact that its private colleges and universities will educate some of its students and that 30 percent will get their education elsewhere.[4]

The People

The Yankees who populated the state for the first two hundred years and who were the architects of the "Land of Steady Habits" were jolted by the arrival of waves of immigrants who came to build the roads, canals, railroads, and dams and work in the factories that made Connecticut famous. First came the Irish, fleeing the potato famine of 1846; then came Germans, Scandinavians, and Italians. The Poles followed and became an important ethnic group. Ugly times developed around the politics of immigration, but the early viciousness was drowned in the tide as immigrants

3. State of Connecticut, *Economic Report of the Governor, 1987–1988*, 110–12.
4. Statistics from Department of Commerce, Bureau of the Census, *Statistical Abstract of the United States 1990* (Washington, D.C.: Government Printing Office, 1990), 20, 159, 281, 368.

outnumbered the old Yankees.[5] By 1920 Connecticut had the third largest proportion of first- and second-generation immigrants in the nation.[6]

The last two groups, the blacks and the Puerto Ricans, who make up 12 percent of the present population, have not found conditions as supportive as earlier ethnic groups did.[7] The factory jobs that had originally been the source of livelihood for those who came during the industrial revolution are few and far between, and they, as well as the new service jobs, take more skill and sophistication. Thus, the last two of Connecticut's immigrant populations have not yet had the chance to grow free and pursue their dreams.

The Parties

Those who have analyzed parties in Connecticut agree that the party organizations are strong and cohesive.[8] Duane Lockard's analysis of the relationship between Connecticut parties and interest groups rests on the premise that the parties were strong enough to use the groups to accomplish their ends and could occasionally discipline an unruly group.[9] The strength of Connecticut's parties is a result of three factors: electoral competition, control over nominations, and internal ideological agreement.

Connecticut has generally been a closely competitive state since 1930, although in the last decade it has been placed in the "modified one-party Democratic" column. It took nearly a century for the ethnic groups to wrest control from the old Yankees in the Republican party, which dominated the politics of the State until the Great Depression, and for a quarter of a century after that, elections were close. After 1954, the Democrats began to build a registration advantage and have controlled the statehouse for all but the four years from 1971 to 1975, when Thomas Meskill was

5. See Clyde D. McKee Jr., "Connecticut: A Political System in Transition," in Josephine F. Milburn and William Doyle, eds., New England Political Parties (Cambridge, Mass.: Schenkman, 1983), 15–18.

6. Neal R. Peirce, The New England States (New York: W. W. Norton, 1972), 187–88.

7. League of Women Voters, The Connecticut Citizen's Handbook, 3rd ed. (Chester, Conn.: Globe Pequot Press, 1987), 3.

8. See Sarah McCally Morehouse, State Politics, Parties, and Policy (New York: Holt, Rinehart & Winston, 1981), 117; Duane Lockard, New England State Politics (Princeton: Princeton University Press, 1959), chap. 9; David R. Mayhew, Placing Parties in American Politics (Princeton: Princeton University Press, 1986), 27–32.

9. Lockard, New England State Politics, 289–90.

governor, and for the years following 1990, when Lowell Weicker, an independent, was elected. Close electoral competition is commonly believed to bring about cohesive parties because it takes internal organization to defeat the enemy.

In Connecticut, the two party machines that have received the most notice have been on the state level, perhaps because Connecticut does not have a "major city" from which a machine could gain control over the state party. Middle-size cities vying for control may have necessitated a state "boss." The Republican boss was J. Henry Roraback, who held sway from 1912 until 1937. Roraback combined rural organizational strength, businessmen's money, conservative government policy, and a disciplined organization. And his power was not only political—he was president of the Connecticut Light & Power Company, the leading utility in the state, and at the time of his death he was president of five lesser utilities, a director of four insurance companies, and a director of at least one bank. He maintained control over legislation by "passing the word" to the Republican legislators, and he also chose committee chairmen. By judicious use of patronage and other rewards and punishments, Roraback kept the support of the local leadership. His main control over the party lay in his ability to determine who would run for office. He controlled the state conventions of the party and hence the slate of statewide executive officers. No successor to Roraback has held the power he had, but subsequent party chairmen have been able to exert power over nominations and party strategy in campaigns.[10]

The Democratic counterpart, John Bailey, held power from 1946 until his death in 1975. Gone were the days when a state chairman could exert dictatorial power. Bailey had to consolidate and persuade. He had to work around a challenge primary law that took effect in 1955 and provided that convention nominees could be subject to primary challenges. The structure of the Democratic party forced him into alliances with various city bosses, the labor unions, and ethnic minorities. At the height of his power, Bailey was able to control nominations as well as legislative policy, but it was by patronage and consensus.[11] Since his time, party chairmen have tried to keep the party unified for nominations and legislative loyalty.

While the two parties today are not as unified as they were under

10. Ibid., 245–51.
11. See Joseph I. Lieberman, *The Power Broker* (Boston: Houghton Mifflin 1966); and idem, *The Legacy* (Hartford, Conn.: Spoonwood Press, 1981).

Roraback and Bailey, they are still among the most cohesive in the nation. Competition between the parties for control of the legislature has reoccurred, and the Republicans can smell a gubernatorial victory. Broad areas of ideological agreement exist within each party, although both have internal disagreements along conservative-liberal lines. The convention system remains strong, and it is rare for a candidate for statewide office to be unseated in a primary election after winning the endorsement of a majority of convention delegates. State law provides that the winner of the party endorsement may be challenged in a primary only by someone who receives 20 percent of the vote in the convention. The party norms against challenging in a primary are strong. Only four gubernatorial primaries have been held since 1955, and only in the Republican challenge of 1986 did the convention nominee lose.

Because party registrants do not participate in primaries regularly, there are more unaffiliated voters in Connecticut than in most states. In late 1990 the voters were registered as follows: Democratic, 39 percent; Republican, 27 percent; unaffiliated, 34 percent. It is interesting that the voters perceived themselves somewhat differently, according to a Connecticut poll. Some 31 percent said they were Democrats, 27 percent said they were Republicans, and 38 percent said they were Independents.[12] Faced with this electorate, the parties must organize to win, for disunity spells defeat.

The Government

The state has transformed its governing apparatus into a modern system capable of performing professionally in demanding times. While the political relationship between the governor and the legislature is more important to policy-making than the streamlining of the two institutions, both branches of government have been modernized to serve the policy-making process. Since 1970, after the Eagleton Institute Report entitled *Strengthening the Connecticut Legislature*,[13] Connecticut has been in the forefront of legislative reform. Members of both houses of the General Assembly are elected from single-member districts in even-numbered years for terms of two years. While membership may be larger, law establishes the size of the

12. Connecticut Poll 106 (October 16–23, 1990), University of Connecticut, Hartford Courant / Institute for Social Inquiry.

13. David B. Ogle, *Strengthening the Connecticut Legislature* (New Brunswick, N.J.: Rutgers University Press, 1970).

Senate at 36 members and that of the House at 151. Following the recommendation of the Eagleton report, the state constitution was amended in 1970 to provide for annual sessions, although even the longer session may not last more than five months. The committee structure has been modernized and professionalized. The Office of Fiscal Analysis enables legislators to improve their ability to make judgments concerning taxation and spending. The Office of Legislative Research improves the quality of information available and provides professional staff to all committees. The Program Review and Investigations Committee provides help in oversight.[14] Salaries, staff, and physical facilities have been significantly improved.

Not too long ago, Connecticut's legislature was one of the most malapportioned in the United States. At one point in the 1950s, slightly more than 11 percent of the population could elect a majority of the House of Representatives. The rural areas and the Republican party dominated the House, while the Senate was inequitably apportioned in favor of urban areas, which were Democratic. From the depression until 1967, the legislature operated under divided control and the urban areas were particularly disadvantaged. After the U.S. Supreme Court ruled that both houses of a state legislature must comply with the equal-population requirement, Connecticut went through the throes of reapportionment, with the result that the Democrats have retained control of both houses for twenty of the last twenty-four years. In 1984 the Republicans won a comfortable majority of both chambers, and the balance has been reasonably close since then.

The state also provides substantial formal powers for the governor. A four-year term with no restraint on reelection places the governor in a strong position to exercise leadership over the legislature. A moderate appointive power is subject to legislative approval. The 1977 Executive Reorganization Act consolidated the state bureaucracy and created an Office of Policy and Management to assist the governor in managing the bureaucracy. The head of this agency is the governor's chief fiscal adviser, who is appointed by the governor with the confirmation of both houses of the General Assembly. The governor, through the Office of Policy and Management, is in control of the budget in the executive branch and also chief lobbyist for the budget in the legislature. At the other end of the budgetary process, the governor has the power to veto items in appropriation bills, subject to a two-thirds override. (The general veto power is also subject to

14. Wayne R. Swanson, *Lawmaking in Connecticut: The General Assembly* (New London, Conn.: Connecticut College, 1984), 3.

a two-thirds override.) If bills are vetoed after the Assembly has adjourned, a "trailer" session reconvenes to consider them, preventing a pocket veto. All these formal powers do not guarantee that the governor will exert strong leadership, however. The governor's ability to influence legislation depends on party leadership and the expectation of the legislators that the governor will use power. Party leaders and the rank-and-file legislators are traditionally disposed to cooperate with a governor of their party to pass a party program.

A wealthy and economically diverse state with an independent-minded electorate, cohesive political parties, and a strong governor and professional legislature mandates that interest groups share in the policy-making process but not dominate it. Connecticut has enacted comprehensive campaign finance and lobby legislation to publicize as well as control the flow of money and influence.

PAC LAWS AND LOBBY LAWS

An interest group has two major avenues for influencing the policymakers: giving money to political campaigns and lobbying. Of increasing importance is the relationship between political action committees (PACs) and the lobbyists. The recent focus on the power of PACs has obscured this relationship in which the lobbyists may have become the dominant partner. In Connecticut it is common for lobbyists to establish PACs and become their treasurers. Most lobbyists steer PAC decisions on endorsement and allocation of campaign funds, which indicates a natural flow of influence because the lobbyist knows who the supporters are. Conversely, money raised by a PAC is used to send a lobbyist to a $500 party caucus breakfast. This "cozy triangle" (Figure 2.1) is of concern to some lobbyists and legislators, for reasons that will be discussed later.

Campaign Finance Laws

At the office of Connecticut's secretary of state, the public may inspect campaign finance reports for several years back. Party committees, candidate committees, and PACs are required to report receipts and expenditures. Because labor organizations and business "entities" are prohibited

Figure 2.1. The Cozy Triangle of Power

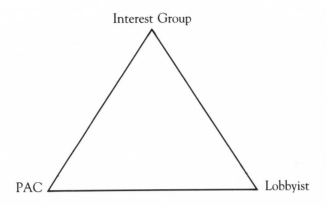

from giving directly to candidates, they establish PACs for that purpose. It is of interest that labor PACs may be funded either out of union treasuries or by voluntary donations, but not both. Business organizations may pay only for administration costs of their PACs. Permissible contributions to candidates by these two types of PACs differ dramatically because business PACs may give twice the amount that labor PACs may give. For instance, business PACs may give as much as $5,000 to a gubernatorial candidate but a labor PAC may give only $2,500. Individuals are held to the same contributions as labor PACs. Finance reports are not computerized. No state agency verifies, analyzes, or compiles the information, which is used chiefly by the press and by candidates' opponents. Violations of the law are handled by the Elections Enforcement Commission.

Codes of Ethics for Lobbyists and Public Officials

In Connecticut, lobbying is defined as communicating directly with officials in the legislative or executive branch for the purpose of influencing any legislative or administrative action. A lobbyist is defined broadly as a person who in furtherance of lobbying makes expenditures or receives compensation of $500 or more in any calendar year. Because this definition is so comprehensive, most organizations that want to influence policy-making are covered; notable exceptions are public officials and employees of state government. Lobbyists complain that department liaisons can go to the floor of the state House and Senate and speak to the legislators while lobbyists must stand in designated areas. For instance, the lobbyist for the Connecticut Food Stores Association must watch from the balcony while the Department of Consumer Protection liaison lobbies freely on the floor.

Lobbyists must register with the State Ethics Commission each year, as either a client lobbyist or a communicator lobbyist. Client lobbyists are the groups that pay for the services of communicator lobbyists. The clients must report expenditures for regular employees who lobby, for fees to retained lobbyists, and for advertising and solicitations in furtherance of lobbying and other related expenses. The communicator lobbyists too must register and report payments received. Quarterly financial reports are required of all lobbyists, and those who lobby the General Assembly must also file monthly reports.

The state Code of Ethics requires that no lobbyist may give to a state employee, a public official, or a candidate any gift costing more than fifty dollars in a calendar year. An exception is food or drink consumed on a single occasion, so a lobbyist can take a legislator or official out to lunch frequently, as long as the cost is modest. A major exception to the "proper gift" category may be a political contribution reported to the secretary of state by the political party, the PAC, or the candidate committee that receives it. However, neither a modest gift nor a political contribution should be given to any employee, public official, or candidate "based on the understanding that the vote, official action or judgment of the public official, state employee or candidate for public office would be or had been influenced thereby."[15] The pieces of a complicated puzzle are assembling. While a lobbyist may not do much more for a legislator than buy him or her lunch from time to time and a couple of bottles of champagne for New Year's, the lobbyist may personally contribute several hundred dollars to the legislator's campaign and influence the client PAC to give double that amount.

INTEREST GROUPS: AN OVERVIEW

In 1987 some 400 interest groups registered with the Ethics Commission to apply pressure on the government. The "communicators" who applied the

15. Connecticut State Ethics Commission, *Code of Ethics for Public Officials* (chap. 10, part 1, Connecticut General Statutes), sec. 1-84 (f) and (g).

pressure—or, more genteelly, lobbied—numbered over 500. In the same year, the Campaign Finance Division of the secretary of state registered 307 PACs of an economic, social, or ideological nature prepared to give money to political campaigns. The list of interest groups (or client lobbyists) and the list of PACs overlapped in 68 cases, which provide the model for the influence "triangle."

Many types of interests are represented in the governing circles (Table 2.1). As of 1985, sixty-three groups represented manufacturing, a sector that employed one-quarter of the labor force. In addition, the corporate tax provided 15 percent of the general fund revenue, a percentage the manufacturers do not want increased. Most of the groups represented interests in the nonmanufacturing sector, reflecting the service economy, the increasing concern with health, education and welfare, and the rise in advocacy groups. The groups representing business make up 59 percent of the total, which is remarkably close to the 58 percent Harmon Zeigler gives as characteristic of weak-interest-group states.[16] In strong lobby states, Zeigler claims, 75 percent of the powerful groups are in business, and business dominates the system. Connecticut's businesses, while influential, do

Table 2.1. Interest Representation in Connecticut: Groups with Registered Lobbyists, 1985

Interest	No. of Groups	Interest	No. of Groups
Manufacturing	63	State and local government	16
Health / social services	56	Communications	15
Finance / real estate	29	Education	14
Public interest / consumers	29	Transportation	11
Personal and business services	28	Religious and nonprofit	11
Trade	24	Construction	10
Insurance	21	Gaming	5
Labor	20	Law	3
Utilities	16	Agriculture	3

Source: Connecticut State Ethics Commission.

Note: 402 groups registered; some could not be assigned to a category.

16. L. Harmon Zeigler, "Interest Groups in the States," chap. 4 in Virginia Gray, Herbert Jacob, Kenneth N. Vines, *Politics in the American States*, 4th ed. (Boston: Little, Brown, 1983), 99–103.

not dominate, however, because labor and many other interests can influence policy too.

Money spent on lobbying is one indicator of the strength of the interest group and the salience of the issues before the legislature. Table 2.2 gives the top ten spenders of the legislative lobbying groups in 1986 and the money they spent to lobby. Four of the groups are consistently among the top ten year in and year out: the Insurance Association of Connecticut, the Connecticut Business & Industry Association (CBIA), the Connecticut Conference of Municipalities, and Northeast Utilities. Three additional groups, the two banks and the retail merchants, have appeared on the list more than once. Three groups are unique to 1986: the trial lawyers and the two medical societies, reflecting the controversy over tort reform in that year. Some of the nation's biggest insurers, located a stone's throw from the capitol building, sought action to limit the amount of damages awarded for "pain and suffering" and to control the fees of attorneys who file liability lawsuits. Two broad coalitions formed: one representing the insurance industry, business, the state medical society, the conference of municipalities, and those who did not want to see premiums increase; the other combining the trial lawyers, the state AFL-CIO and various public-interest groups. Unquestionably, business interests dominated the lineup.

Table 2.2.   Top Ten Spenders Among Legislative Lobbying Groups in Connecticut, 1986

Group	Amount Spent	Associated PAC
1. Insurance Assn of Connecticut	$294,154	Yes
2. Connecticut Business and Industry Assn	236,507	Yes
3. Connecticut Trial Lawyers Assn	150,041	No
4. Connecticut National Bank	130,018	No
5. Connecticut State Medical Society	99,686	Yes
6. Connecticut Conference of Municipalities	95,038	No
7. Northeast Utilities	84,952	Yes
8. Connecticut Retail Merchants Assn	84,563	Yes
9. Northeast Bancorp	83,326	Yes
10. Connecticut State Radiological Society	71,125	Yes

Source: Connecticut State Ethics Commission.

Why was the resulting compromise not exactly what they wanted? The power of organized labor and public-interest groups backed by numbers and votes is credited with influencing the outcome too.

Another method of exerting influence is to establish a PAC to distribute money to candidates for election. Committees formed for that purpose in Connecticut are required to register, and the list includes all Democratic and Republican town, district, ward, and state committees; women's clubs; and about eighty-five committees whose primary purpose is to elect their party's candidates. Included in the voluminous report are the 230 PACs or political committees established by business, labor, or other interests (see Table 2.3). Labor, professional, and public-interest PACs dominate in number. However, the manufacturing, finance, and insurance PACs represent interests that can outspend them many times over.

Most of the top ten spenders among the legislative lobbying groups have established PACs (see Table 2.1), thus forming a triangle of power that uses money to influence both elections and legislation. Not all interest groups have a PAC as well as a lobbyist, but sixty-eight of them do. It is the lobbyist-PAC combination that has been the subject of concern, and several bills have been introduced to control this concentration of influence. The groups that have both lobbyists and PACs can be divided into

Table 2.3.   PACs in Connecticut, 1986

Interest	No. of PACs
Labor	52
Professions	52
Public interest / consumer	32
Education	5
Manufacturing	17
Finance / real estate	17
Business	16
Construction	11
Insurance	9
Transport / utilities / trade	9
Law	6
Communications	4

Source: Connecticut Secretary of State, Campaign Finance Division.

four policy types based on the dominant interest of each (see Figure 2.2).[17] Each type is a different combination of who pays and who benefits. If the public pays through taxation, the costs are dispersed; if private enterprise pays, the costs are concentrated. Likewise, benefits may be public (dispersed) or private (concentrated). For each policy area there are major proponents. For instance, the CBIA, the Connecticut Retail Merchants, and the banks are placed in the "distributive" policy cell. This type generates publicly funded policies and programs promoting private activities by subsidies, price supports, contracts and the like and thus conveys tangible benefits to private individuals, groups, and corporations. Distributive policies are said to be desirable to society as a whole (what's good for business is good for Connecticut), so the costs are dispersed while the benefits are concentrated. Competitive regulatory policies and programs are aimed at limiting the provision of specific goods and services to only one or a few designated deliverers. Some decisions regulate the character of services de-

Figure 2.2. Lobbyist-PACs and Public Policy

POLICY COSTS

	Dispersed	Concentrated
Dispersed	Redistributive Education Public interest 4	Protective Regulatory Labor 10

Concentrated	Distributive
	
	Business 16
	Banks 9
	Construction 2
	Food <u>4</u>
	    31
		Competitive Regulatory
		
		Sports 1
		Professions 9
		Real estate 1
		Insurance 8
		Utilities <u>4</u>
		    23

POLICY
BENEFITS

Source: Computed by author.

17. Randall B. Ripley and Grace A. Franklin, *Congress, the Bureaucracy, and Public Policy*, rev. ed. (Homewood, Ill.: Dorsey Press, 1980), 20–26; the authors describe the four basic policy types.

livered; some grant and review licenses. Real estate, insurance, and the professional groups are major proponents in this category. In this case, both costs and benefits are concentrated, and there may be competitive or monopolistic regulation. Protective regulatory policies are designed to protect the public by setting the conditions under which private activities can be undertaken. Prohibition of unfair business practices is an example, and hence labor unions are major proponents of this policy. Here the costs are concentrated (business pays) and the benefits are dispersed. The last category, redistributive policy, reallocates wealth, property or some other value among social classes or racial groups in society. Integrated schools, open housing, and public welfare programs are examples. The Legislative Electoral Action Program (LEAP), a coalition of labor and citizen action groups founded in 1980 to propose progressive policies and candidates, is placed in the "redistributive" policy cell. Inspection of Figure 2.2 reveals that few of the interests with the heaviest clout are located in the public-interest (dispersed benefits) cells of the Table. In fact, protective regulatory and redistributive interests are barely 20 percent of the total. Because business, industry, and banks are overconcentrated in the policy-making process, legislators and lobbyists both questioned the wisdom of allowing lobbyist or PAC campaign contributions while the General Assembly was in session. Some legislators believed this practice was not in the public interest, while the lobbyists felt they were being coerced into giving in return for policy preference. As a result, in 1990 a law was passed that prohibits legislators, their campaign committees, or party caucus PACs from receiving funds from lobbyists or lobbyist PACs during the legislative session.

LOBBYISTS, PACs, AND ELECTIONS

The strength of the political parties in Connecticut's politics means that the PACs are courted but do not control. The parties are able to endorse nominate, elect, and govern, and the interest groups provide money, time, and information. In Connecticut the interests align themselves with one or the other party. Labor aligns itself with the Democratic party, and business generally aligns itself with the Republican party. However, because the Democrats have regularly controlled the governorship and both houses of the legislature in the last sixteen years, the business interests have adjusted to this situation by giving money to the governor, the party leadership, and the incumbents.

Elections for Governor

In 1982 each gubernatorial candidate spent slightly more than $1 million on their campaigns. In 1986 Governor William O'Neill raised nearly $3 million, while his Republican opponent, fresh from a bruising primary, raised less than half that amount. All the technology is used. Phone banking is employed and tied to direct mail. Weekly tracking polls are now the norm. Peter Gold, executive director of Connecticut Republicans estimated that in the 1986 campaign about 60 percent of Republican Julie Belaga's resources were devoted to television and radio ads, and the remainder to staff and consultants. In the Democratic gubernatorial campaign, television advertising was the greatest expense with more going to the national firms that designed the spots than to the channels that aired them. Next came staff and office operations, costing $35,000 a month on average. Computerization and direct mail was the third largest expense, followed by costs for radio, billboards, and bumper stickers.[18]

Surprisingly enough, most of the money comes from individual contributors, who are limited to giving $2,500 to gubernatorial candidates. In 1986 neither the governor nor his Republican challenger received more than 5 percent of their total from PACs. A scrutiny of PAC money for 1982 and 1986 confirms the well-known fact that the incumbent enjoys a tremendous advantage even when he or she is a Democrat. In 1982 Governor O'Neill, running for the first time, after succeeding to the office, received $22,250 from labor unions in gifts of $1,000 or more. He received $10,500 from business in similar-size donations. His opponent, Lewis Rome, rounded up $16,725 from business. By 1986 the size of most business contributions had doubled to the legal limit of $5,000. The *Hartford Courant Business Weekly* listed the corporate PACs that had given $500 or more to both campaigns by October 2. O'Neill had raised well over $50,000 from business, bank, and insurance PACs, while his rival had received less than $17,000. Several firms give half as much to the challenger as to the incumbent.[19]

Probably more significant and less easily traced are the individual do-

18. Janis R. Latham, "Campaign Finance: Connecticut and Other States" (Hartford: Connecticut General Assembly, Office of Legislative Research, December 8, 1986), 5.
19. "A Businesslike Approach to the Election," *Hartford Courant* October 27, 1986 (*Business Weekly*), 1–24.

nors. They may be lobbyists or business magnates, contractors or state commissioners. The lobbyists must identify themselves; their names appear in the campaign finance reports of the candidates and the parties. The 1982 trial of the commissioner of transportation revealed that the head of the Democratic party, as well as the governor's chief aide, had requested contracts for fiscal supporters of the party. The governor ordered this practice stopped. However, party fund-raising is being fed generously by the same consultants and their firms that have received lucrative contracts over the years. Three private developers who were among the largest contributors to the state Democratic party and the governor's campaign received $47 million in low-interest loans from the Connecticut Housing Authority in 1985. In addition, the authority's bond counsel is among the top contributors. While it is not illegal for those who do business with the state to contribute to campaigns, the Democratic challenger in 1986, Toby Moffett, called on the governor to disclose the names of all campaign contributors who had contracts.[20] A recent law, passed as a result, asks contractors to identify themselves if they give more than $1,000 to a statewide campaign.

Elections for the General Assembly

In the 1986 election the governor raised $2,824,745 for his statewide campaign. All 355 candidates for the state Senate and House, both winners and losers, raised only about $1 million more—$3,921,080. As mentioned, the governor received less than 5 percent of his total from PACs. The legislative candidates, on the other hand, received 20 percent of their total contributions from business, labor, and ideological PACs.

Costs of the average legislative campaign have risen from $16,716 for a Senate campaign in 1984 to $29,468 in 1988; for the House, it was $5,786 in 1984 and $10,660 in 1988.[21] Although these statistics may seem alarming, they appear modest when compared with costs in other states, although the value of making comparisons when the district populations are not compared too appears futile. Connecticut legislators serve only part-time and are not campaigning for their only source of income. The state contains fewer media markets than surrounding states to tempt expendi-

20. "Three of O'Neill's Top Donors Get Agency Loans," *Hartford Courant*, April 29, 1986, B-1, 5.
21. Common Cause / Connecticut and Election Enforcement Commission, "Facts About Connecticut Campaign Finance" (Hartford, Conn.: Common Cause, 1989).

ture. Public-access cable may keep advertising costs somewhat lower. Still, the voter is demanding more sophistication in terms of information, and the candidates send more mailings, which are issue-specific and colorful. Jonathan Pelto, former director of political development for Connecticut's Democratic State Central Committee, says candidates are making more use of radio and public access television, but estimates that one-half to three-quarters of a General Assembly candidate's budget goes for mailings.[22]

PACs feel the effects of increasing costs in the form of demands to give more, so it may be fortunate that there are more of them every year. Common Cause has documented the growing number of business, labor, and ideological PACs: In 1982 there were 104; in 1984, 207; in 1986, 246; and my records show 300 in 1987. Their pattern of giving resembles that of other states. PACs give twelve times more money to incumbents than to challengers. For the 1990 legislative campaign, PACs gave an average 34.5 percent of the money raised by House incumbents and 6.4 percent of that raised by challengers.[23] Apparently, PAC executives as well as lobbyists are aware of the nationwide tendency of incumbents to win. Malcolm Jewell and David Olson estimate that only 5 or 6 percent of all incumbents who seek an additional term are defeated in the general election.[24] In Connecticut this trend is not as pronounced; local parties are strong, and most races are contested. In 1986, a presidential midterm year, the success rate for House incumbents was 81.6 percent, a decent return for the PAC money but not the overwhelmingly favorable odds realized elsewhere. In the Senate race, however, only 67 percent of the incumbents won. PAC money spent on many Senate Republican incumbents was therefore wasted. Furthermore, the minority Democrats won back majorities in both chambers lost in 1984. By 1990, however, 95 percent of incumbents who ran were successful.

While the PACs were putting their money on incumbents, the legislative party caucus committees were engaged in a different allocation pattern. These partisan caucus PACs have an entirely different purpose from that of the business, labor, and ideological PACs. They put money into races to get party members elected and to forge a party esprit de corps for

22. Latham, "Campaign Finance," 4–5.
23. Common Cause, "Money in Politics: A Study of Campaign Financing in the 1990 Connecticut State Legislative Races" (Hartford, Conn.: Common Cause, August 1991), 16.
24. Malcolm E. Jewell and David M. Olson, *Political Parties and Elections in American States*, 3rd ed. (Chicago: Dorsey Press, 1988), 216.

the legislative session. A comparison of the pattern of campaign giving between the business, labor, and ideological PACs and the partisan caucus PACs in the 1986 Senate campaign illustrates this hypothesis. While party caucus PACs fund an average of 12 percent of the money given to the state senatorial campaigns, closer scrutiny reveals how the minority and majority party caucus PACs distributed their funds. The Republicans were trying to hold onto their majority for dear life. They gave, on average, the same percentage of funds to incumbents as to challengers (10 to 12 percent). The minority Democrats used a different strategy. Believing that their hard-core incumbents were secure, they contributed an average 7.4 percent of their money but doubled that percentage for the Democratic challengers who were to do battle against Republican incumbents.[25] This strategy paid well. These targeted races brought ten Democratic challengers into office. Thus, the political party can use the unusual competitiveness of the Connecticut legislative districts to help its legislators win elections and bind them to the organization.

One might ask to whom the average legislator is beholden. He or she receives about 24 percent of total contributions from business, labor, and ideological PACs. The first two types are limited in the amount they may give to any one candidate. Business may give $1,000 to a senatorial candidate and $500 to a House candidate, while labor can give half that. So candidates are beholden to the extent of the permissible giving on the part of business and labor PACs. Party committees are not limited. They do not give as much as the PACs, but the average legislator knows that 10 to 12 percent of his or her campaign money comes from one source—the party caucus committee—and the legislator who faces stiff competition owes much more of the funding to the party. We shall now consider this new type of party legislative caucus PAC, which has been observed in other states as well.

Legislative Caucus Committees

Legislative caucus committees—with such names as the Committee for a Democratic Majority, the Democratic Leadership Committee, the House

25. I compiled these statistics from Common Cause, "Campaign Contributions to Candidates for State Senate and House Seats in the November 4, 1986, General Election" (Hartford, Conn.: Common Cause, March 6, 1987), and table 3 from a study by the Office of Legislative Research, "PAC Contributions to Candidate Committees, 1986" (Hartford: Connecticut General Assembly, October 6, 1987), 25–28.

Democratic Campaign Committee, the Majority Project, the People for Republican Majority in the House, and the Republican Senate Victory Committee—raise money and disburse it with the intent of helping the party win seats or of strengthening the leadership's hand in dealing with its legislative caucus members. Table 2.4 shows how contributions to these committees grew between 1983 and 1986. While the Campaign Finance Law limits the amount individual PACs can give to these caucus committees to $2,000, PAC giving increased from an average of 17.5 percent of total contributions in 1983–84 to 26.8 percent two years later. For the Republicans, the majority party, that increase was even more spectacular, rising to 35 percent of the total. Individual lobbyists also give to these legislative PACs, although not to the same extent (11 to 15 percent of total giving), and they are limited to $1,000 a donation. A recent study of lobbyist and lobbyist PAC contributions to legislative caucus PACs indicates that they give on average about 45 percent of the money.[26] Most of these contributions are made in October during the legislative campaign. However, the substantial PAC giving to legislative caucus committees and leadership committees raises questions about the relationship between the PACs and the parties.

Protect the PACs from the Parties?

The usual scenario has the needy legislator at the mercy of the affluent lobbyist who can promise campaign support in return for a favorable vote, but in Connecticut the roles are reversed: The lobbyists are pleading for mercy. The assumption that the parties are milking the lobbyists underlies the surveys of the State Ethics Commission and the State Elections Enforcement Commission. The following statements from their report suffice to affirm this assertion: "The second major focus of these surveys was to elicit whether pressure was exerted upon lobbyists to make campaign contributions, and, if so, has such pressure remained constant or varied from term to term." The report added that one-quarter of the lobbyists felt pressured by legislative leaders to contribute. Some 47 percent of the legislators also agreed that such pressure was exerted. Half the lobbyists reported receiving unsolicited tickets to fund-raisers to purchase or sell to clients.[27]

26. Common Cause, "Money in Politics," 21.
27. State Elections Enforcement Commission and State Ethics Commission, *Report to the Connecticut General Assembly Pursuant to Section 10, Public Act No. 86-240* (Hartford: January 1987), 19.

Table 2.4. Lobbyist and PAC Contributions to Connecticut Legislative
Caucus Committees, 1983 and 1986

Committees	Contributions 1983 / 84	Percent of Total	Contributions 1985 / 86	Percent of Total
Democratic Majority	$58,218		$83,875	
LP	10,350	18%	20,575	25%
IL	7,675	13	15,237	18
Democratic Leadership	15,715		5,273	
LP	1,830	12	0	0
IL	3,120	20	650	12
House Democratic Campaign	46,700		99,210	
LP	9,450	20	13,505	14
IL	2,925	6	10,700	11
Majority Project (D)	92,793		57,346	
LP	10,075	11	9,600	17
IL	6,675	7	4,975	9
People for Republican Majority in House	70,083		122,870	
LP	10,446	15	38,080	31
IL	4,450	6	21,585	18
Republican Senate Victory	50,236		53,493	
LP	14,625	29	18,425	34
IL	7,542	15	6,275	12
Retain Our Republican Majority	—		13,246	
LP	—	—	5,250	40
IL	—	—	2,151	16

Source: Connecticut State Elections Enforcement Commission and State Ethics
Commission, *Report to the Connecticut General Assembly Pursuant to Section 10, Public
Act No. 86-240*, January 1987, Appendixes E and F.

LP = Lobbyist PAC.
IL = Individual lobbyist.

In a 1990 study of campaign financing, Common Cause questions whether
this assumption of control from party to PAC or lobbyist is accurate. It
claims that some of the top business lobbyists in Connecticut contribute
thousands of dollars to legislative candidates each election. Lobbyists would
not spend so much money on campaign contributions if they were not
convinced it would have an effect on the legislators. The fact that so much

lobbyist money was given to incumbents, who are heavily favored, suggests that the contributions are designed not so much to influence election outcomes as to buy access.[28]

Howard Reiter would agree that PACs are not pawns in the party game, for he states:

> One final indication of the clout of PACs is shown by comparing their total spending on candidates in 1982, which was about $2,252,000, to that of the two major political parties, about $1,026,000. This means that the influence of the parties on public officials is limited, as candidates become more and more dependent on PACs for their funds. This may make it more difficult for a governor to get his or her program through the General Assembly, as legislators are more beholden to interest groups than they are to their party.[29]

We therefore have two perspectives on the same political process, both driven by the theory that there is a relationship between parties and pressure groups and that the strength of one varies inversely with the strength of the other. I too subscribe to the "strong party–weak pressure group" theory, but I find the assumption that the parties are milking the pressure groups to be overdrawn. And I do not believe, as those who claim that pressure groups are dominant do, that there is a counterplot on the part of clever lobbyists who appear to be weak when in fact they are strong. There is probably a power-draw here. The parties are strong, and their leadership expects to wield power to see that legislation is passed or defeated. Control over raising and spending caucus PAC money can translate into the power to deliver votes on key issues. Legislators facing close elections, and challengers who win because of party caucus money, owe a debt to the party leaders. At the same time, the party leaders must raise the money to gain such influence. Because the PACs and lobbyists want to shape the outcome of legislation through the leaders, the arrangement is of mutual benefit.

What is remarkable is that PAC money is considered so monolithic. Unions, banks, corporations, insurance companies, and issue groups are lumped together as "PAC influence." Can a candidate receiving 10 percent

28. Common Cause, "Money in Politics," 14–15.
29. Howard L. Reiter, "Interest Groups and Political Parties" (Prepared for a book on Connecticut politics, Department of Political Science, University of Connecticut), 5.

of his or her campaign funds from business and 10 percent from labor be "bought" by either? Even receiving 20 percent from business alone can hardly ensure individual attention or the voters might retaliate. Since PACs and lobbyists may not give during the legislative session, the fear of undue influence over individual legislators is not realistic. The party leaders encourage donations to the party committees, but they must have overall party policy in mind.

LOBBYISTS AND THE LEGISLATURE

As many as 400 interest groups consider access to the General Assembly vital to their survival. For 330 of these, lobbying is their major technique because they have not established PACs. Depending on their resources and the skill with which they use them, groups gain access. Because parties are strong and the legislators are guided by the party position, the interest groups work through the party leaders and committee chairs. Further centralization is made possible by a system of joint committees with House and Senate co-chairs. Operating within these partisan and structural parameters, the lobbyists are considered an integral part of the legislative process. Their advice is considered vital to the passage of legislation, and they are counted on to obtain an accurate assessment of the views of their interest groups—or clients, as they are called.

Strong Parties

The political parties in Connecticut are ideologically distinct. Labor aligns itself with the Democrats, and business and industry line up with the Republicans. But these distinctions are not drawn as sharply as they used to be. The status of workers has improved to the point where a large percentage of the labor vote is conservative. In addition, because the Democrats have regularly won elections, business and industry accommodate to them, trying to convince them that what is good for Travelers Corporation and General Dynamics is good for Connecticut. Democratic governors Grasso and O'Neill were both considered friendly to business. Until 1991 neither a plant-closing bill nor an income tax was espoused by the administration or passed by the legislature. In that year, with a Democratic governor replaced by an independent governor, Lowell Weicker, both business and the Democratic party favored an income tax. However, Table 2.5 shows

Table 2.5. Legislative Support for Business, Labor, and Consumer Issues, Connecticut, 1987

| | House | | | | Senate | | | |
Group	No. of Issues	Rep. Support	Dem. Support	Avg. Support	No. of Issues	Rep. Support	Dem. Support	Avg. Support
Connecticut Business & Industry Assn	9	90.5%	62.1%	73.1%	9	78.0%	58.0%	64.5%
AFL-CIO	7	37.3	91.3	70.4	6	56.1	98.7	85.6
Connecticut Citizens Action Group	14	43.0	75.3	62.9	6	53.9	72.5	66.8

Sources: Computed from Connecticut Business & Industry Association, *General Assembly Report*, August 5, 1987; AFL-CIO, 1987 *Cope Scorecard*, Fall 1987; Connecticut Citizens Action Group, CCAG 1987 *Legislative Index*, Fall 1987.

that there is a different center of gravity for each party. Here the distributions of individual voting loyalty within each party for three policy areas are compared. The Connecticut Business & Industry Association, the AFL-CIO, and the Connecticut Citizens Action Group annually report on Assembly votes that are important to their memberships and publish individual legislator ratings. An analysis of voting favorable to business reveals that the average Republican legislator's support is high while the average Democratic legislator's vote is much lower. On labor and consumer issues the situation is reversed. The Democrats are much more likely to support labor and consumer legislation. Hence, the lobbies in Connecticut recognize that they have built-in support in *one* party and must work hard if they are to shake loose supporters in the other.

In addition to representing different public-policy concentrations, the parties exhibit high partisan voting loyalty. A recent study indicates that in 1981–82 more than 60 percent of the Democrats in both houses produced cohesion levels above 80 percent. The Senate Republicans were even more cohesive than that, while the House Republicans scored lowest, with 48 percent on that measure. Party votes, when majorities of each party oppose each other, occurred 61 percent of the time in the House and 70 percent in the Senate.[30] The legislators in the General Assembly expect solutions to the major problems to be partisan.

The center of party activity is located in the Democratic and Republican caucuses. The leaders are still influential in deciding what happens in caucus and on the floor. Party positions are hammered out in the caucuses. Most observers agree that the party leaders in Connecticut are more powerful than those in most state legislatures, because once a party position is determined in the caucus they are expected to see that it holds on the floor. The source of their power stems in part from the fact that the president pro tempore in the Senate and the Speaker in the House make committee assignments and decide on the chairpersons. Hence, the members and chairs know that both their present position and their future lies with the leadership. In this extremely partisan structure the interest groups maneuver.

Legislators' View of Lobbyists

In general, the legislators view the lobbyists positively. As many as 81 percent of a sample of 100 legislators approved with minor reservations the

30. Swanson, *Lawmaking in Connecticut*, 35–37.

activities of the lobbyists. Some 61 percent agreed that they got valuable help in drafting bills and amendments from interest groups. However, opinion was evenly divided on whether lobbyists and special interests had too much influence over the Assembly. Members asked to identify the interest groups that were most effective in lobbying named business, education, labor, insurance, banks, health agencies, transportation, and liquor and gave the reasons for their choices as size, economic power, and particular lobbying techniques. Lobbies with large memberships, such as education, health care, and labor, were obvious choices because of their potential impact on the vote back home. The business, insurance, and bank lobbies were cited because of the quality of their presentation of facts and evidence.[31]

The Lobbyists

It caused a stir when the governor's legal counsel of eleven years retired in 1990 and became a lobbyist with Aetna Life & Casualty Company six weeks later. Apparently this does not conflict with the "revolving door" statute, as long as Jay Jackson did not lobby the staff in the governor's office for a year. In fact, more than 25 percent of the professional lobbyists are former members of the General Assembly.[32] Two former House Speakers, Nelson Brown and James Kennelly (husband of U.S. Representative Barbara Kennelly), became lobbyists for the American Petroleum Institute and Connecticut Bank & Trust respectively. Joseph Coatsworth, a former deputy House Speaker, represents the Connecticut Hospital Association, a coalition of hospitals and medical facilities throughout the state. Lewis Rome, former Senate minority leader and candidate for governor, lobbies for fourteen clients, among them Connecticut Association of Realtors and the Motion Picture Association of America. A previous chairman of the Joint Insurance and Real Estate Committee, Felix Karsky, is now a lobbyist for the Insurance Association of Connecticut, which represents the numerous and powerful insurance firms based in the state.[33]

The lobbyists listed above represent several types. For instance, heads of associations that contact legislators are required to register as lobbyists even if they hire a lobbyist to do most of the contact work for them. The presi-

---

31. Ibid., 55, 59.
32. Ibid., 58.
33. Reginald Johnson, "Even with Controls, Lobbying Is Thriving Business," *Fairpress*, April 7, 1988, A-7.

dent of the Connecticut Retail Merchants is registered but hires an aspiring young lobbyist to do most of the retailer's legislative communicating. Many lobbyists are full-time employees of the companies they represent, and lobbying may be only a small part of their jobs. All the staff attorneys of Southern New England Telecommunications are registered with the Ethics Commission, although the bulk of the lobbying is done by two or three specialists. Some of the lobbyists are law firms that have drifted into lobbying, such as Updike, Kelly & Spellacy of Hartford, the second largest lobbying organization (see Table 2.6). Most of the biggest lobbyists are not company staffers or lawyers, but independent lobbying firms called contract lobbyists. Some of these are purely lobbying organizations, while others also manage trade associations, publish newsletters, set up conventions, and provide public relations. Sullivan & LeShane, the top lobbying group, is an example of the first, while Carroll Hughes, number four, is an example of the second. In 1987 Sullivan & LeShane represented twenty-four clients, primarily "black hats," or profit-making businesses, as opposed to "white hats," the nonprofit public-interest and health-care groups. Patricia LeShane points out, "You can't say we have to protect the consumers at the expense of having a viable economy. A strong business environment makes a better way of life in Connecticut."[34]

This view is not shared by Connecticut Citizens Action Group (CCAG),

Table 2.6.   Top Communicator Lobbyists in Connecticut, 1986

Lobbyist / Organization	Amount Received	No. of Clients (1987)
1. Sullivan & LeShane	$497,464	24
2. Updike, Kelly & Spellacy	248,849	16
3. Gaffney, Bennett & Associates	231,372	13
4. Carroll Hughes	176,852	24
5. Rome, Case, Kennelly & Klebanoff, P.C.	153,000	13
6. Elizabeth Martin Gallo Gov't Relations	100,148	17
7. Linda Kowalski	97,544	10
8. S&S Management Service Inc.	89,233	12
9. Louis Cutillo	89,013	5

Source: Connecticut State Ethics Commission.

34. Quoted in Steve Kemper, "Conversations: Patricia R. LeShane," *Hartford Courant*, April 3, 1988, Northeast Section, 4.

which has only one full-time lobbyist. The CCAG has tried to blunt the impact of big-money lobbying by using a "people-power" tactic: It buses scores of concerned constituents to attend or speak at hearings. The concern remains that most of the growth in the numbers of lobbyists is among those representing corporations and trade associations, who can thus advocate more effectively than the less well financed and underrepresented consumer groups and public-interest organizations. Alan Plofsky, executive director of the State Ethics Commission, said that top lobbyists representing banks and insurance companies will charge as much as $70,000 in fees for one session.[35]

Multiple Clients

Carroll Hughes, with twenty-four clients, runs both an association management company and a lobbying firm. He and his staff of seven provide all the services required by seven different trade associations. His clients include both "white hats" and "black hats," from the Connecticut Catholic Hospital Council to the Connecticut Package Stores Association. He tries to keep his clients compatible, turning down some who come to him because they would conflict with those he has on his list. Hughes recalls the time a printer's error had him representing the bar association instead of the bus association—at the time tort reform was an issue, and his insurance agency client "went crazy" and asked how he could represent the lawyers, who were seen as the enemy.[36]

Some say that lobbying is not a business for true believers. The techniques are transferable, and many lobbyists move to different clients as easily as moves in the game of musical chairs. The movement from association to association, and private client to state agency, reveals this conveyance of expertise, but I discovered a tendency for lobbyists to stay within certain parameters of interests in their moves. For instance, in 1986 there was a three-way transfer among lobbyists for labor and "white hats" involving the Community Action Program agencies, the AFL-CIO, and the Connecticut State Federation of Teachers. Another four-way exchange involved lobbyists for the Connecticut Business & Industry Association, the Insurance Association of Connecticut, Travelers Corporation, and the

35. See Reginald Johnson, "Even with Controls," 1.
36. William Weir, "Catching the Big Ones in Shark Alley," *Connecticut*, April 1988, 180.

Hartford Insurance Group. However, Elizabeth Gallo, who ranks sixth among communicator lobbyists (Table 2.6), is a true believer. She claims that all her clients are "white hats," including the American School for the Deaf, the Clean Water Coalition, and the New Haven Legal Assistance Association and declares she won't take a client whose cause she cannot support.[37]

Lobbying involves style, commitment, knowledge, contacts, and techniques. Access is so important that some firms will hire both an issues person and a professional lobbyist to provide the contacts. We turn now to the techniques and skills that lobbyists employ.

Skills and Techniques

Imparting information is the most important job of the lobbyist. Legislators need information about the impact a proposed piece of legislation will have on their constituents and on the public at large, and the source of the information is crucial to how the legislator will analyze the impact, and hence to his or her response. If a legislator has several sources of information, he or she can be confident of making an informed decision on how to vote. Fortunately, Connecticut legislators have adequate legislative support services. Since 1969 the General Assembly has made tremendous strides in improving the quality of its professional staff and the amount of information available to legislators. Because of this, legislators are not dependent on the executive agencies or the lobbyists as their only source of information.

Legislators in Connecticut now have an elegant new five-story office building, which was dedicated on April 8, 1988. For the first time, all Senators and Representatives have offices with up-to-date equipment, including a monitor that permits them to hear debate in House or Senate chambers or to follow a hearing and a communications system that serves as both telephone and computer, carrying voice messages and data simultaneously. Ten hearing rooms of different sizes are equipped with circular hearing tables surrounded by chairs for the public. This $63 million tribute may make the legislators feel important and confident and imbue them with the proper dedication to the public, which provided these amenities.

With alternative sources of information and efficient facilities, the legislators can interact confidently with lobbyists. The lobbyists devote most of

37. See ibid., 182.

their time to party leaders and committee chairs, who have the most control over legislation. When individual legislators are confronted, it is by lobbyists interested in their response to issues that are before their committees. Both legislators and lobbyists agree that the communication of information is the most important function of lobbying. However, information is imparted by those who have a significant interest in the passage or defeat of certain pieces of legislation. Legislators must separate the motives from the symbolism. For instance, in the 1988 session of the General Assembly, lobbyist Carroll Hughes represented the Restaurant Association, which was pushing a bill that would allow fifteen-year-olds to work in restaurants, as they now can in retail stores. The restaurant owners wanted the bill because of the shortage of unskilled labor in the state, but Hughes developed the Horatio Alger argument, stressing the self-discipline, cleanliness, and respect for others that young people would learn from part-time work. Opposing the bill were the union lobbyists, who did not want to see the jobs go to part-time underpaid youngsters. The unions stressed the value of school homework, contending that what young people learn from their studies is more useful than what they learn from washing dishes. The unions won.

Interest groups and their lobbyists appear to be a permanent part of the legislative process. It is not unusual for a lobbyist to write the first draft of a bill and give it to the co-chair of a committee or its ranking members. Eventually it is submitted to the Legislative Commissioner's Office, which produces the finished bill.

Lobbyists are prepared to help the legislators make compromises. In the case of the plastics association confronted with the issue of solid-waste disposal, Carroll Hughes, lobbyist for the plastics industry, said about the Environment Committee hearing and its co-chair: "I want to get inside Mary Mushinsky's head. I want to know what she really thinks about the bills that have been introduced. Does she want to preserve the environment, or does she want to punish people who make things out of plastic?"[38] Fearing that the co-chair might be dedicated, Hughes offered to compromise with the environmentalists. He found a firm that would recycle heavy-gauge plastic.

Lobbyists will arrange research missions for legislators. One lobbyist, Linda Kowalski, representing the optometrists, arranged an educational trip for members of the Joint Public Health Committee to the Pennsylvania

38. Quoted in ibid., 181.

College of Optometry, where they witnessed the training optometrists receive. This was crowned with success when the legislators passed a previously defeated bill, allowing optometrists to use diagnostic drugs.

Public opinion on the local level was so important to lobbyists for the Connecticut State Medical Society that they helped administer a voluntary program to treat low-income seniors. If the program proved successful, the legislature would not enact legislation to force physicians to accept Medicare as full payment on medical bills. Sullivan & LeShane helped the medical society design a public relations program to get the physicians signed on. At the local level, it kept the newspapers and other media informed about the success of the program. This would inform the legislators that there was no need to enact a mandatory program. The outcome was a compromise, as usual in Connecticut: The voluntary program did not meet its goals, but the mandatory regulations on the doctors were limited by income level and the ability to decline patients.

Socializing is a technique whose purpose is to develop friendship and trust, according to Patricia LeShane. Patrick Sullivan and LeShane entertain frequently, occasionally at their home. They discovered that if they did not spend more than $15 a person they did not have to report who came to the festivities, and this appealed to some of the legislators. According to LeShane, the only way to have the legislators feel comfortable and trust your motives and your information is to let them know you. "So whether it's having a reception that a client sponsors so you can introduce your client to a legislator, whether it's going to a UConn basketball game with a group of legislators, whether it's attending a seminar around a specific issue where you get to spend time with that legislator—its important to spend that kind of time."[39] This undoubtedly reflects the view of most lobbyists.

Legislators, however, may not be as comfortable with developing personal friendships, according to a survey by Wayne Swanson. The most common criticism of lobbying expressed by legislators is the tendency for personal relationships between lobbyists and legislators to influence voting behavior. Several legislators alleged that friendships get in the way of sound decision-making and deflect attention from the merits of pending legislation.[40] This tension is well known and will continue as long as legislators and lobbyists interact in the legislative process. Generally, in Con-

39. Quoted in Kemper, "Conversations," 4.
40. Swanson, *Lawmaking in Connecticut*, 61.

necticut, lobbyists target the party leaders and committee chairs for enter-taining—those are legislators who can hold their own and who must con-sider the balance of many pressures before they can take a stand.

In the final few days of the 1988 legislative session, several people—the "governor's men," as they were called—appeared on the floor of the legis-lature. They were there to see that the governor's bills were passed. Every-one knew that, and the party rallied behind its governor. This, in the final analysis, was the ultimate clout. The governor's program was passed. The leadership of the party was behind it, the whips were behind it, and the legislators knew that help in the election year would be forthcoming if they were behind it.

LOBBYISTS AND THE ADMINISTRATION

When interest groups register with the Ethics Commission, they report the amounts they spend lobbying the administration as well as the legislature. The two lists differ with regard to interests as well as spending (Table 2.7). Two familiar groups, the Insurance Association and the Connecticut Busi-ness & Industry Association (CBIA) appear on both lists, but they spend far less on administrative lobbying than on legislative lobbying. The ad-ministrative lobbyists appear to be those primarily interested in regulation. The Connecticut Industrial Energy Consumers claim their major concern is

Table 2.7.   Top Ten Administrative Lobbying Groups in Connecticut, 1985

Group	Amount Spent
1. Connecticut Industrial Energy Consumers	$85,855
2. Motor Transport Assn	26,018
3. Connecticut Citizens Action Group	18,846
4. Connecticut Conference of Municipalities	16,336
5. Insurance Assn of Connecticut	15,838
6. Connecticut Natural Gas	15,015
7. Connecticut Business & Industry Assn	14,543
8. Yale University	13,775
9. Connecticut Farm Bureau	10,705
10. Union Carbide	9,855

Source: Connecticut State Ethics Commission, *Registered Lobbyists and Their Expendi-tures and Receipts for Calendar Year 1985.*

the Department of Public Utility Control, which has primary regulatory responsibility for rates and quality of service for public-service companies. John Rathgeber of the CBIA lobbies the Department of Environmental Protection on behalf of businesses concerned with air emissions. Generally, about 82 percent of all lobbying expenditures are on legislative as opposed to administrative lobbying.[41] But here in the administration, far from public opinion, there may be a systematic bias in favor of business and industry. Here interests are well organized and may prevail over complicated regulatory issues, fair trade, occupational licensing, and the like.

THE POWER OF INTEREST GROUPS IN CONNECTICUT

The resources, skills, and incentives of interest groups are the bases of their power. Because Connecticut has competitive parties, which means officeholders must worry about their next election, the size, and hence votes, of an interest group bring power. Because incumbents need money for their next election, the monetary resources of a group are important. The seven most powerful interest groups in Connecticut have the greatest number of members or monetary strength. The AFL-CIO, the Connecticut Education Association, the American Association of University Professors, and the Connecticut Conference of Municipalities have many members and a powerful impact on the vote back home and are four of the most powerful lobbies. The Connecticut Conference of Municipalities was consistently one of the top ten spenders among the lobbying groups (in six out of seven years). In this affluent, business-oriented state, the Connecticut Business & Industry Association, the Insurance Association of Connecticut, and Northeast Utilities are among the top ten spenders every year. Following hard on the heels of the top seven are three banking groups: Northeast Bancorp, Connecticut National, and the Connecticut Bankers Association. Two health agencies with large memberships come next: the Connecticut Hospital Association and the Connecticut Association of Health Care Facilities. Three other powerful groups are the Tobacco Institute, the Connecticut Beer Wholesalers, and the Connecticut Retail Merchants.

But more is also involved in the power of an interest group. The vast

41. See ibid., 58.

bulk of lobbying involves straightforward communication of information and points of view that legislators need to make informed decisions. Legislators have cited education and health lobbies, as well as the business, insurance, and bank lobbies, as being skillful in presenting information.[42]

Of those fifteen most powerful groups, business interests make up nine, or 60 percent. This accords with the designation of Connecticut as a weak-interest-group state, one in which businesses are influential but do not dominate. Interest groups play a major role in the legislative process, but it is primarily a complementary one. Groups compete for the attention of legislators in the larger context of partisan politics. Two recent issues illustrate this hypothesis.

Late one Friday afternoon in mid-July 1983, Governor O'Neill signed H.B. 6810, the bill to remove tolls on the Connecticut Turnpike. There were no exclamations of triumph, no pens distributed. A notice was sent to the newspapers. Clearly the governor was not enthusiastic about signing the legislation: The state had a deficit of $240 million, and a section of a bridge on Interstate 95 had recently collapsed, sending three people to their deaths and injuring three others. The news media had called this an example of decaying infrastructure and the need for major repairs. The governor's budget director and transportation commissioner urged him to veto the bill. His own party was divided, with more in opposition than in favor. Those upstate did not want to lose $45 million a year in revenue. Why did the Toll Removal Bill become law? Was it the work of the powerful Southwest Area Commerce & Industry Association (SACIA) representing five hundred member companies in the wealthiest section of the state? Those who are impressed with lobbyist skills and resources would argue that the SACIA triumphed over the wishes of the governor and a majority of his party.

It is true that the Association used all the skills of modern lobbying. They set up an organization called "Banish All Tolls" (BAT) to give the appearance of a citizens movement, but the number involved was actually small but very committed. Testimony at hearings, mailgrams, brochures, lobbying, personal contacts, luncheons with legislators were all brought to bear. Grass-roots pressure was engineered by means of a portable toll booth carted off to oyster festivals along the coast. Signatures were collected from revelers who had no reason to object. But resources, skills, and incentives do not create success. It takes votes.

42. Ibid., 59.

In January 1983 a tragic and symbolic event occurred. A tractor-trailer truck crashed into several cars at the Stratford toll station, killing seven. Legislators heard from their districts as people showed up at hearings, probably not more than a few hundred but symbolic of many others. The legislators in the county and the governor could not take the chance that the people who spoke at the hearings were not representative of the majority in a county that contains 26 percent of the population of the state. The governor signed the bill. This case study shows that the SACIA used traditional methods, and skillfully, but they were not enough. The decisionmakers had to be convinced that the people wanted the tolls removed.

The second issue involves the personal income tax, another case where the essential decision was based not on interest-group pressure but on the relationship between the political parties and the people. Traditionally the businesses in Connecticut opposed the tax, and it was generally believed that their influence prevented the tax from passing. Governor O'Neill campaigned against the income tax in 1982, as had his predecessor, Ella Grasso. In that recession year, many of the leaders of the Democratic party favored the tax, including the Senate president and the majority leader. On the House side, the Speaker and chair of the Finance Committee favored the tax, while the majority leader was opposed. It was estimated that 13–15 Senate Democrats and 50–60 House Democrats wanted the tax. However, after agonizing hours of negotiation, the governor asked the Democratic legislators not to pass the income tax and received support from more than 80 percent from his party in both chambers.[43] This was clearly a party loyalty vote, since the majority of the party favored the tax.

As economic times became more favorable and the sales tax, corporate income tax, and countless other taxes were able to provide the state with sufficient revenues, the income tax receded as an issue. But in 1989 hard times hit the state again, and again the Governor asked the Democratic party not to pass the personal income tax. This time the tax proposal was not even reported out of committee.

By 1990 Connecticut faced the largest budget deficit as a proportion of its total budget of any state. Well over $2 billion out of a projected $7.9 billion budget could not be raised by the existing tax structure. The voters of Connecticut elected former Republican Senator Lowell Weicker, running as an independent, by 40 percent of the vote and barely kept the

43. Connecticut Poll 114 (July 31, 1991), University of Connecticut, Hartford Courant / Institute for Social Inquiry.

Democrats a major state party by providing them with 21 percent. Democrats continued to hold comfortable majorities in both chambers of the legislature. Weicker had run an antiparty campaign, claiming that both parties were obsessed with self-interest, hindered effective government, and perpetuated themselves through patronage. His party, called "A Connecticut Party" and created to meet the requirements of electoral law, did not hold a single seat in the legislature.

This was not the way to run a state government, as Lowell Weicker and leaders in both parties discovered. The governor had no governing coalition in place when he assumed office. Building a coalition was costly and cumbersome because he did not have the currency of party loyalty and party discipline. The Republicans thought him a traitor, and the Democrats had little reason to cooperate, having been called irresponsible.

Into this milieu the governor proposed a personal income tax as the only solution to the state's fiscal woes. For six brutal months of budget deadlock, the governor faced hostility in the General Assembly. This included three full-year budget vetoes and a partial shutdown of the state government. Finally, in August, both chambers passed a 4.5 percent flat-rate income tax with a system of tax credits that would reduce the burden on the poor and the middle class. The sales tax was lowered from 8 to 6 percent but extended to many new items.

Can the results of this struggle be credited to the efforts of the business lobbyists who favored an income tax as a condition for lowering the corporate tax? Can the AFL-CIO claim the credit as a traditional defender of the income tax? I think not. The real participants in this struggle are the parties and the voters of Connecticut. A majority of the Democrats in the House backed the income tax throughout and finally provided the momentum and votes that passed it (75-73). In the Senate, with the leadership opposed, sixteen out of twenty Democrats voted in favor, providing the critical votes necessary for the lieutenant governor to break an 18–18 tie. In the last analysis, this was party voting, but devoid of Senate leadership. A coalition of a governor and legislative leadership working in unity was missing.

Did the voters of Connecticut inform their representatives? How did the legislators interpret their messages? The will of the people was uppermost in the minds of the legislators. There was no governor to help either ticket, no one with whom to cooperate or oppose. No coalition, no coattails. In the Senate there was no majority-party leadership. Legislators were on their own.

Hence, public opinion was very important, and the public was divided. But there was more opposition to the amount than to the form of taxation. Those who expressed a preference for an income tax (32 percent) outnumbered those who wanted to raise other taxes instead (21 percent). But the key was the large number who said they liked neither (41 percent). Some 61 percent expressed the feeling that "it is possible to both maintain essential services and keep taxes down." However, when asked to assign priorities to a number of areas to aid spending restraint, there was not a single area where the public overall felt the priority should drop. With public opinion divided, as it was, strong leadership was necessary, but it was not there. The public simply did not agree with the assumption underlying all the budget plans seriously considered by the governor and the legislature that substantial tax increases were necessary. Building on this confusion, the Republicans immediately organized a taxpayers' revolt following passage of the measure. This is a case where an upset and confused public needed a strong governing party, a party that stood for tax reform and that was willing to lead and explain its position. At such a time, no interest group or combination could influence the results.

The case has been made that Connecticut is a "strong-party–weak-pressure-group" state, but this may overstate and oversimplify the situation. There is no question, however, that the parties are able to respond to the wishes of the public on issues that are important and where real public opinion exists, such as on tax matters, welfare policies, and education funding. Parties are able to control the nomination process on the town and state levels, and the two levels are linked at election time. The governor's platform is expected to become the focus for the governor's program, and cohesion within the legislature is strong enough to pass it. Legislative leaders control electoral funds through the caucus PACs to aid legislators' campaigns. Hence, the dynamic of electoral politics, played through the political parties, controls the influence of pressure groups.

But interest groups are a major force in the policy-making process. They are numerous and sophisticated. Labor is strong, and so are some "white hat" and consumer groups. But most of the money and most of the contract lobbyists are associated with "black hat" interests. The tables in this chapter reveal that most of the top-ten spending lobbyists represent the banks, insurance companies, businesses, and manufacturers of Connecticut. They also combine the "cozy triangle" of power, meaning the lobbyist-PAC relationship, where the lobbyist directs the money to legislators who support their interest. In view of this concentration of the power of business, it is remarkable that these interests are contained.

In this regard, a recent development within the House Democrats is worth watching for its potential impact on party cohesion. In 1988 the business lobbyists identified a group of Democrats who were to the right of center in their party and encouraged them to form a "moderate caucus." Although the caucus claimed as many as forty-six members (out of ninety-one Democrats), it generally rallied about twenty votes on issues it supported during its first session. The Moderate Caucus leaders claim that it was established as a counterweight to the Progressive Caucus, which supported liberal issues and was favored by the party leadership. In January 1989 the Moderate Caucus leaders conspired to join with the minority Republicans to defeat the House Speaker, who was seeking a third term. Thirty-one Democrats joined all sixty-three Republicans to oust Irving J. Stolberg, a liberal and a powerful leader. Such a split within the majority party had not occurred in Connecticut since 1943. The new Speaker, middle-of-the-road Democrat Richard Balducci, claimed that he had not made any concessions to his Republican supporters and that the Democratic Caucus would continue to unite and bind its members. Ideological differences within the party were evident during 1991, but leaders of both the Moderate and the Progressive caucuses supported an income tax, and voting did not reflect this moderate-liberal division.

More time is needed to assess the impact of the Moderate Caucus. So far, the Democratic majority leaders have been able to contain the threat to party cohesion by a group initiated and backed by business. It is an uneasy relationship, as in any courtship, but the parties continue to have the upper hand.

3

Delaware: Friends and Neighbors Politics

Janet B. Johnson and Joseph A. Pika

Nestled a little less than halfway between Capitol Hill and Wall Street, Delaware consists for most East Coast travelers of two toll plazas barely twenty minutes apart. What passersby miss, however, is the surprisingly diverse political life of a state more easily caricatured than characterized. One well-known study portrayed Delaware politics as largely shaped by the interests of the DuPont Corporation and the DuPont family,[1] a portrait with considerable accuracy in the past. But the full picture of group politics in Delaware has become increasingly complex. Corporate interests remain of paramount importance but extend well beyond the concerns of DuPont, particularly since passage of the Financial Center Development Act in 1981 and subsequent changes in the business community. DuPont's principal interests are seldom harmed, but the company no longer dominates such a wide range of issues, as was once the case.

Delaware's political system is accessible but quiescent. Elected officials are readily available, so that a small group, sufficiently mobilized to visit and lobby the General Assembly, can find considerable responsiveness. But there are substantial limits to political discourse. The media produce only a modest amount of investigative journalism, and public-interest groups are few in number and not very influential. The small political elite, low turnover among legislators and lobbyists, and commanding presence of corporate interests produces a pattern of "clubby," old-boy politics operating within consensual constraints. Groups enjoy special influence with the part-time legislature that devotes only modest resources to professional

1. James Phelan and Robert Pozen, *The Company State* (New York: Grossman, 1973).

staffing. These same legislative characteristics give the Governor's Office, and to a lesser extent government agencies, an especially powerful role in state policy-making. Political parties remain an influential force in state-wide politics—quite possibly the most influential.

Delaware's diminutive size masks diversity in its socioeconomic base as well as an enduring geographic division. As its tourism motto proclaims, the state is indeed "a small wonder." Delaware ranks 47th in population (1990 population 666,168) and 49th in area (2,056 square miles). In contrast to other eastern states, Delaware has relatively few local governments. Consequently, its three counties (New Castle, Kent, and Sussex) are important political and geographic entities. New Castle, the northernmost county, accounts for roughly two-thirds of the state's population, with the remainder almost equally divided between the other two counties. Wilmington, the state's largest city (1990 population 71,529) and site of DuPont's corporate headquarters, is located in New Castle County and has attained stature in the nation's legal and financial circles.

The Chesapeake & Delaware Canal, which runs across southern New Castle County, divides the state's diverse economic base into unequal halves. Industrial manufacturing, financial services, and corporate headquarters dominate northern New Castle County ("Upstate") while agriculture (particularly poultry farming) and recreational interests are paramount in the two southern counties ("Downstate"). In 1989 the per capita income for the state was $15,854 and the median family income was $40,252. Per capita and median family incomes were considerably higher in New Castle County ($17,442, and $45,216) than in Kent ($12,726 and $33,954) and Sussex ($12,723 and $31,112). The economic difference between the two sections of the state is partially obscured by the inclusion of Wilmington in New Castle County. Wilmington's 1989 median family income was only $31,140, indicating that the rest of the county is even more affluent relative to downstate Delaware. These contemporary economic divisions reinforce traditional differences dating to the Civil War, when the state remained in the Union but found many downstate residents siding with the Confederacy.

Racial composition is similar in all three counties. The state is 16.9 percent African American, although Wilmington has a higher concentration of African Americans (52.9 percent). Wilmington accounts for 33.3 percent of the state's total African American population, down from 37 percent in 1979.

DELAWARE'S ECONOMY

Delaware amply deserves its reputation as a probusiness state, and it has parlayed that image into a source of national influence. Although Delaware's economy felt the impact of the national recession, the number of jobs in the state grew by 1,900 in 1990, bringing the total number of jobs created since 1982 to 87,200. Per capita income grew by 8 percent between 1989 and 1990. The state's economy and employment is more heavily concentrated in manufacturing than in other regions and in the nation as a whole. In 1990 nearly 21 percent of Delaware's jobs were in manufacturing, compared with the national average of 17 percent. Of particular importance, however, is chemical manufacturing, which constituted 46 percent of the state's manufacturing jobs, compared with 6 percent nationally. Nearly half of the chemical manufacturing jobs are in home office and research operations, which accounts for considerably higher-than-average wages in this sector. Delaware's two largest employment sectors are Services and Trade, employing 24.5 percent and 21.9 percent of Delaware's workers respectively. These sectors represent a slightly smaller percentage of employment than the national average.[2]

Finance and the construction industry are important employment sectors, compared with national averages. Finance employs 9.2 percent of Delaware's jobs, compared with 6.3 percent for the nation, and has been the fastest growing sector of Delaware's economy. Stimulated by the 1981 Financial Center Development Act (FCDA), employment in Finance increased from 12,300 in 1980 to 31,700 in 1990, or by 158 percent.[3] Following a long tradition of encouraging business relocation to Delaware, the 1981 law sought to compete with favorable conditions then being created in South Dakota: the FCDA removed interest-rate ceilings on credit-card loans and provided major tax advantages. Out-of-state banks generating more than $30 million in income would pay only 2.7 percent on income over that amount, while banks generating less than $20 million faced a tax rate of 8.7 percent. The law restricted new banks from engaging in retail banking (thereby prohibiting competition with existing banks) and required them to hire at least 100 employees and to bring in at least $25 million in capital within their first year of operation. As a result, thirty

2. Delaware Development Office, *Delaware Databook 1991*.
3. Ibid.

major banks have established credit-card operations in Delaware.[4] More than 80 percent of this activity is located in the city of Wilmington and in surrounding New Castle County.

Success in attracting banks, however, is only the latest chapter in Delaware's long history of carefully calculated economic development. Since passage of the state's General Corporation Law in 1899, Delaware has provided an especially congenial economic environment for business. The law was initially designed to encourage corporations to relocate to Delaware away from neighboring states, particularly New Jersey.[5] Not only is it easy and relatively cheap for businesses to incorporate in Delaware, but there are also numerous tax and legal advantages, probably the foremost of which being a thoroughly tested body of case law interpreted by an experienced judiciary. As Columbia University Professor of Law Marvin Chirelstein explained, "Delaware is the most important base of corporate law in the country, exceeding even the U.S. Supreme Court. It's the author of corporate jurisprudence for the country, and in many ways for the world."[6]

The benefits accruing to the state from all this are substantial. In 1990 the number of firms chartered in Delaware grew by 6,000 to a total of 203,000, including more than half of the firms included in the Fortune 500 and half of all firms listed on the New York Stock Exchange.[7] Corporate franchise taxes and charter fees are projected to constitute more than 17 percent of the state's 1992 revenues, a very high proportion compared with other states[8] and ranked second only to personal income taxes as a source of state revenue. The General Assembly seeks to maintain the state's preeminence by adopting probusiness statutes—as in 1986, when limits were placed on the financial liability of corporate board members. One lobbyist commented on the success of different kinds of legislation in the General Assembly: "Nothing goes through as fast as business [legislation]. Business can't always stop something but they can generally get through what they need to get through."[9]

Nor do business interests take anything for granted. In a 1986 survey of

4. Ibid.
5. *New York Times Magazine*, June 5, 1988, 32.
6. Quoted in *New York Times*, June 1, 1986, F-6.
7. Delaware Development Office, *Delaware Databook 1991*.
8. Ibid.
9. Personal interview, May 16, 1988.

state legislators, business groups received the highest cumulative score in frequency of contact with legislators, although civic groups received more first-place mentions (see Table 3.1).[10]

DUPONT

Looming over Delaware's group landscape is the long shadow of the Du-Pont Corporation, which employs nearly 25,000 people in Delaware alone, making it by far the state's largest employer. This work force includes a high proportion of researchers, chemists, and executives, whose educational backgrounds and income make them more likely to be politically active. The corporation retains a full-time lobbyist to monitor business in Dover, but it also takes an active role in the state Chamber of Commerce and the Business Roundtable. The latter includes representatives from major corporate and banking interests centered in Wilmington and was reorganized in 1980 when it was discovered that its predecessor, the Governor's Business Advisory Group, was subject to provisions of the state Sunshine Law. Delaware's chemical industry includes two other major firms with

Table 3.1.   Frequency of Delaware Interest Groups Contacting Legislators, 1987 (Percentage of Respondents Ranking Frequency of Contact, $N = 38$)

Interest Group	1st	2nd	3rd	1st–3rd
Business	21.1%	34.2%	28.9%	84.2%
Civic	52.6	10.5	13.2	76.3
Labor	10.5	13.2	21.1	44.8
Farm	7.9	10.5	18.4	36.8

Source: Authors' 1987 survey of state legislators.

10. Questionnaires were mailed to 61 legislators in 1986. Some 38 were returned, for an overall response rate of 62.5 percent. By chamber, response rates were 52.4 percent for the Senate and 67.5 percent for the House. Although the 134th General Assembly was split fairly evenly along party lines (32 Democrats and 30 Republicans), 60.5 percent of the respondents to our survey were Republicans.

6,000 additional employees, Hercules (a pre–World War I spin-off of Du-Pont) and ICI Americas. Hercules, in particular, has led the charge on some issues, as in 1979, when its chairman threatened to relocate corporate headquarters unless the state lowered its top income-tax rates.[11] In the aftermath, personal income-tax rates have been lowered from a high of 19.8 percent to 7.7 percent. Despite its enormous financial resources, DuPont's political action committee, organized in 1984, follows a policy of not contributing to candidates in Delaware races, although some might argue that, given its other sources of leverage, such obvious methods of wielding influence are unnecessary.[12]

An examination of major legislative battles over the last two decades shows that DuPont's successes have been mixed. Corporate attorneys virtually drafted the state's right-to-know laws governing employee rights to information on workplace hazards, an especially important concern of the chemical industry. But the company has so far lost in efforts to set restrictive insurance liability limits, a similar issue. On another issue uniquely related to its operations, DuPont obtained legislation in the mid-1970s that voided a county facilities tax on the pipes, pumps, and fixtures at its manufacturing sites.[13] However, DuPont has lost on a number of issues not directly related to its operations. It unsuccessfully sought adoption of a state sales tax and repeal of the state's strong statute limiting coastal development, and it had to settle for a compromise on a state bottle bill. Thus, the corporation's record is far from perfect, and because DuPont has allies on most issues, it is difficult to attribute victory to its efforts alone.

DuPont, in fact, has been very much a "team player" within the corporate community. It participates in all appropriate trade associations (including the Oilmen's Association, which gained new relevance when DuPont acquired Conoco in 1981) and has led the fight on several important issues for economic development. DuPont's chairman reportedly played an instrumental role in negotiating favorable terms that attracted out-of-state banks to relocate operations since 1981, and the corporation was on the winning side in urging adoption of legislation severely restricting takeovers of Delaware-chartered corporations.

11. *Wilmington News Journal*, April 12, 1987, E6.
12. *Wilmington News Journal*, February 27, 1985, B2.
13. *Wilmington News Journal*, April 12, 1987, E6.

GROUP INFLUENCE AND POLITICAL STYLE IN DELAWARE

Beyond the high-stakes battle for corporate preeminence and the highly visible activities of DuPont, Delaware reveals an active pattern of interest-group politics. Three contextual features are particularly critical for understanding group influence in Delaware: state size, a simple media structure, and a part-time legislature with very few professional staff. The style of politics in Delaware is highly personalized. This can be attributed to the smallness of the state, to the longevity of the members of the General Assembly, and to a lobbying community that has among its most influential members former legislators and state administrators as well as long-time lobbyists.

The General Assembly consists of forty-one representatives and twenty-one senators. In 1991 the average number of years served in the Senate was more than eleven, and fifteen senators had served ten or more years. In the House the average length of service was just over nine years and twenty-seven of the House members had served four or more terms. Despite party competitiveness in the state generally, there is a strong incumbency factor. For example, five of the ten incumbent senators seeking reelection in 1986 were unopposed by a major-party candidate and in the House, and seventeen of thirty-nine incumbents ran unopposed.

Group Access

Face-to-face contact is both possible and effective in Delaware politics. The state capital, Dover, is within easy driving distance of all parts of the state, providing citizens with easy access to officials. As one lobbyist told us, "It's small and I think the smallness is good in a lot of ways and I think you can be effective. You can know a lot of different legislators. Legislative Hall is the most open place in the world. Citizens can go in there and see anybody they want. The politicians are always available for their constituents when they come in."[14] Data from our survey bear out interview materials (Table 3.2). State legislators regarded sending group members to Dover as the single most effective means for interest groups to get their message across. The effort to influence legislators does not have to be massive. As the same lobbyist put it, "In Delaware, if somebody gets five calls

14. Personal interview, March 17, 1988.

Table 3.2.   Effective Methods for Delaware Interest Groups to Get Message Across (Percentage of Respondents Selecting, $N = 38$)

Method	Percent[a]
Sending members to Dover	68.4%
Mobilizing public opinion	52.6
Letter writing	47.4
Forming coalition	31.6
Using skillful lobbyist	28.9
Using the press	10.5
Support at elections	7.9
Powerful group, able to hurt respondent	5.3

Source: Authors' 1987 survey of state legislators.

[a]Percentages total more than 100; multiple responses were allowed.

on an issue they think they're being flooded."[15] But the effort may be worthwhile, as a former legislative aide suggests: "My rule of thumb is if you want something passed get twenty-five or fifty constituents to write about it, and I don't care how many lobbyists talk to the legislators about it—they'll vote the way their constituents want them to. . . . Personal contact with constituents will outweigh lobbyists any day."[16]

Legislators are willing to support interest-group initiatives when they are consistent with broader public purposes. Thus, 97.4 percent of the legislators responding to our survey reported supporting particular policies promoted by interest groups "[when] it is supported by a majority of my constituents," and 71.1 percent "[when] it has general public support" (Table 3.3). It is less clear, of course, how closely particular and general interests coincide.

The apparent openness of legislative politics and its consequences are summarized by one legislative staff person:

> For better or for worse, Delaware is a state where you can pick up the phone and you can get through—not to the secretary of your representative or senator—you talk to *them*. They talk to you. You come down to Dover, you meet with them in their office. They

15. Ibid.
16. Personal interview, May 16, 1988.

don't shuttle you aside. There's a lot to be said for that. But there's a problem with that too—and that is, the people who come down there are the ones who have figured out how the game is played.[17]

Table 3.3. Delaware Legislators' Reasons for Supporting Legislation Promoted by Interest Group (N = 38)

Reason	Percent[a]
Supported by constituents	97.4%
General public support	71.1
In tune with philosophy	57.9
Supported by governor	13.2
Majority of legislators support it	7.9
Several groups support it	7.9
Supported by affected agency	5.3
Group is united	5.3

Source: Authors' 1987 survey of state legislators.

[a]Percentages total more than 100; multiple responses were allowed.

Thus, whereas one person we interviewed recalled the successful effort of well-dressed Wilmington Junior Leaguers to gain legislator support for improved services for foster children, another recalled how a bus carrying chief executive officers from major corporations unloaded in front of Legislative Hall as they prepared to lobby for additional benefits for business.

Public and Media Quiescence

Citizen activism is not ordinarily at high levels in Delaware. Participation in "public-interest groups" is limited. Common Cause and the League of Women Voters are persistent actors, though each has weaknesses. Some consider Common Cause to be too narrowly focused on procedural rather than substantive issues, and others see the League playing a diminished role as more and more women enter the work force. Consumer and environmental groups are active only intermittently.

An example of the weak role public-interest groups have in Delaware

17. Personal interview, April 5, 1988.

politics is the operation of the Joint Sunset Committee, which was established in 1981 with impetus from Common Cause. The purpose of the committee is to review the operation of state agencies and professional and occupational licensing boards to make sure they are operating in the public interest. According to one especially close and sympathetic observer of the committee, special interests are highly influential in the review process: "There is an inverse relationship between the power of a profession and the degree of reform we are able to effect through the sunset process."[18] Common Cause continues to monitor the committee's activities but now gives these problems lower priority. Some legislators are reportedly reluctant to serve on the committee because of the possibility of alienating professional organizations and losing campaign contributions. While there are legislators interested in making the committee work, there appears to be little consistent support from the public or from consumer groups for their efforts. The "logic of collective action" dictates that members of licensed groups have the greatest incentive to show up at public hearings. Legislators, highly responsive to the physical presence of constituents at hearings and legislative sessions, are much more likely to look out and see representatives of regulated groups rather than consumers.

A recent illustration of this was the successful effort of optometrists to prohibit large optical equipment retailers like Sears and Pearle Vision from providing optometric services. The professional association argued that the quality of services was lower in such large operations and that optometrists connected with them would seek to enhance sales. Research available to the committee indicated that the quality of services in such large operations was no different from that in the smaller ones typical in Delaware, but prices were substantially lower. Nonetheless, Delaware remains one of only five states to prohibit such affiliations. Absent an effective voice for consumers, and facing an audience of optometrists and opticians, legislators overwhelmingly rejected the idea of on-site optometrists.

Several interview subjects pointed to the small number of media outlets as a partial explanation for public quiescence. As one put it, "It's tough to have a public process when the public picks up a paper and they don't even know what's going on."[19] And another was more explicit:

18. Ibid.
19. Ibid.

> In Delaware, we're hurt by the fact that as far as the General As-
> sembly is concerned you really only have two players, two news-
> papers. . . . That isn't a great universe from which to draw investi-
> gative reporters. . . . In other states, the press would be much more
> heavily into it, and they would create the scandals or the questions
> which lead to groups like Common Cause requesting hearings or
> investigations or changes in the law.[20]

There are numerous radio outlets (nineteen in 1991) but no VHF television channel broadcasts within the state. Delaware is only a modest part of
the Philadelphia television market (8 percent), which devotes only limited
attention to Delaware news, although the state's two major cable systems
have sought to fill that gap. Debate is also constrained by the consensual
nature of Delaware politics as well as by the consciously cultivated, probusiness climate that is carefully sustained.

LEGISLATIVE STRUCTURE

Some believe that organized groups wield substantial influence because of
the Delaware General Assembly's part-time structure and modest investment in professional staff. In one sense, relying on legislators with other
principal jobs creates something approaching a "Jeffersonian concept of the
citizen legislature." But the legislators' part-time involvement may also
inhibit development of expertise in policy areas, a particularly important
resource in the absence of more extensive professional staffing resources.
Furthermore, the relative lack of professionalism in the legislature may partially explain the low level of public involvement and low profile of public-
interest groups. A recent study of state interest-group politics by Hrebenar
and Thomas indicates that more professionalized states tend to encourage
the development of social-interest groups.[21]

Since the mid-1970s, staffs working with the party caucuses have grown

20. Personal interview, March 30, 1988.
21. Clive S. Thomas and Ronald J. Hrebenar, "Interest Groups in the States," chap.
4 in Virginia Gray, Herbert Jacob, and Robert Albritton, *Politics in the American States:
A Comparative Analysis*, 5th ed. (Glenview, Ill: Scott, Foresman / Little, Brown, 1990).

gradually but remain small; with the close partisan division in the House (22–19 during 1987–88; 23–18 during 1989–90; 24–17 in 1991–92), almost half the representatives are at a distinct disadvantage. Only one committee has full-time professional assistance, although others are helped by per diem employees. The Legislative Council, the General Assembly's nonpartisan research arm, employs only four full-time professionals, none of whom is a program specialist. The Office of the Controller General provides primarily fiscal analysis for the legislature. The House, and more recently the Senate, has sought additional research capacity through a legislative-intern program operated jointly with the University of Delaware, but such opportunities do not provide continuity.

Under these conditions, lobbyists are an important part of the legislative process. Data from the survey of state legislators indicate that most Delaware lawmakers regard lobbyists favorably and interact with them frequently. More than 60 percent of the responding legislators said they can rely on lobbyists "most of the time," while 34 percent said they could rely on them "some of the time," which indicates a remarkably high level of confidence. Only 10.5 percent believed that lobbyists' activities constitute a form of improper pressure. Nonetheless, relations with lobbyists are sometimes strained: legislators objected to threats involving campaign contributions, attempts to change a legislator's mind after a clear position has been taken, efforts to cultivate "friendships," and hanging around all the time.

The prominent role of lobbyists is reflected in the frequency of their contact with legislators while the General Assembly is in session. Some 71.1 percent of the legislators surveyed reported at least daily contact with lobbyists. Only 5.3 percent reported they seldom had contact with lobbyists. Between sessions there is less contact, with 10.5 percent reporting no contact and 28.9 percent reporting monthly contact. However, 60.5 percent of the legislators reported having contact at least a few times a month.

According to legislators, an important function of lobbyists is providing research and technical information. Legislators ranked the provision of information about an organization and its policy goals as the most important function of lobbyists. Keeping legislators informed about pending bills was also important (see Table 3.4). Lobbyists are rarely seen as providing information about constituents, building support for bills, or keeping legislators informed about the attitudes of government agencies or other legislators and groups.

Table 3.4. Importance of Services Provided by Delaware Lobbyists
(Percentage Giving Rank, $N = 38$)

Service	Rank			
	1	2	3	1–3
Information on organizations and policy goals	31.6%	23.7%	7.9%	63.2%
Research and technical information	23.7	18.4	13.2	55.3
Keep informed about pending bills	18.4	28.9	15.8	63.1
Build support for my bills	13.2	13.2	13.2	44.8
Attitudes of other groups	2.6	5.3	15.8	23.7
Information about constituents	2.6	5.3	10.5	18.4
Other legislators' attitudes	0.0	5.3	10.5	15.8
Attitudes of gov't agencies	0.0	5.3	5.3	10.6

Source: Authors' 1987 survey of state legislators.

Lobby Regulation

Lobbying in Delaware is conducted within a weak regulatory framework. Current regulations were adopted in 1976 after a five-year effort during which the initial proposals were weakened considerably by floor amendments. Changes made during implementation make them little more than annoyances today. Provisions of the law require that lobbyists and their employers register with the General Assembly's Legislative Council and file quarterly reports of expenditures broken down for food and refreshment, entertainment, gifts, and expenses paid for legislators' lodging, travel and recreation. Members of the General Assembly who are recipients of such lobbyist largesse need not be identified unless expenditures exceed $50 a day, a figure somehow seldom reached. Penalties for failure to register or for filing a false report include a fine of up to $500 and imprisonment for a maximum of three months. Failure to file a report could result in loss of registration until the report is filed. No penalties, however, have ever been assessed.

Oversight and enforcement of even these modest requirements are weak, and compliance by lobbyists is lax. During the system's first year of operation, 30 percent of lobbyists missed the initial filing deadlines, and a year later nearly 40 percent did so, despite pressure from the state's largest newspaper. There are penalties for failure to file or for providing false information, but the staff arm charged with overseeing the files is small and relatively nonprofessional. Receipts and records necessary to verify reports need not be submitted, and at the time the law was implemented more detailed questions were deleted from the quarterly reporting form after lobbyists complained of the heavy paper load.[22]

To gain a better understanding of the lobbying community and the scale of its activities, quarterly spending reports for the first and second quarters from 1977 to 1986 (excluding 1979 reports, which could not be located) and the 1987 lobby registration list were examined. This was followed by later examination of the 1991 list of legislative agents and second-quarter filing reports. The picture is one of considerable stability in the lobbying community.

About 140 different lobbyists, some representing more than one organization, filed spending reports between 1977 and 1986. Eleven lobbyists filed reports in each year between 1977 and 1986. Thirty-three filed reports in five or more years. Thus, almost one-third of the lobbyists who filed spending reports were lobbyists in at least five out of the ten years. Eighty-five lobbyists filed reports in only one or two years. Spending in the second quarter, while the legislature is in session, is roughly three times as high as spending in the first quarter, when the legislature meets only briefly. Reported spending by lobbyists totaled $26,277 in the second quarter of 1986; thirty-eight lobbyists representing sixty-three organizations filed spending reports.

State legislators surveyed were asked to name the five most effective lobbyists in Delaware. Twenty-three lobbyists were mentioned, although eleven received only one mention. Table 3.5 shows the lobbyists Delaware legislators mentioned as influential, their clients, and the number of mentions each received. Contract and in-house lobbyists predominate. The top lobbyist, Ned Davis, who represents a variety of clients, was mentioned by almost 40 percent of the respondents. Robert Byrd of the Delaware Chamber of Commerce was mentioned second most often, followed by George Jarvis, who lobbied for Delmarva Power.

Table 3.6 shows the reporting and spending activity between 1977 and 1986 of the lobbyists legislators mentioned as most effective. In general, the top lobbyists have been active for some time: seven of the top twelve lobbyists have filed reports every year since 1977. A subsequent review of

Table 3.5.   Top Delaware Lobbyists and Their Clients

Name (No. of Mentions) (Name of Lobbying Firm)	Clients or Organizations
Ned Davis (15) (Ned Davis Associates)	Brandywine Raceway; Del. Academy of Ophthalmology; Del. Alcohol Beverage Distributors; Del. Assn of Professional Engineers; Del. Bottlers Assn; Del. Dietetic Assn; Del. Malt Beverage Distributors Assn; Del. Motor Transport Assn; Del. State Bar Assn; Dover Downs; Medical Society of Del. Inc.; Motion Picture Assn of America Inc.; Owens-Illinois Inc.; RLC Corp.; Rollins Inc.; Del. State Dental Society
Robert Byrd (9)	Del. State Chamber of Commerce
George Jarvis (8)	Delmarva Power & Light
Francis Biondi (5)	Bellevue Park Associates; Chase Manhattan; Del. Bankers Assn; Del. River & Bay Authority; J. P. Morgan & Co.; M Bank U.S.A.
John Brook (5)	University of Delaware
Ned Hankins (5)	Diamond State Telephone
David Swayze (5)	Anheuser-Busch; Baltimore & Ohio Railroad; Barclays Bank PLC; CSX Transportation; Del. State Chamber of Commerce; Del. Trust Co.; New Castle Economic Development Council; Quality Kitchen Corp.; Second National Building & Loan
Gary Patterson (3)	Delaware Petroleum Council
Dennis Crowley (2)	Delaware State Education Association
Gary Hildebrand (2)	Public Employee Council 81
Ronald Jefferson (2)	Pilots' Association for the Delaware Bay & River
William Wood (2)	Blue Cross & Blue Shield of Delaware; Duane, Morris & Heckscher; The Delaware Roundtable
Raymond Buttacovoli (1)	General Motors Corporation
Bill Freeborn (1)	Governor's Office
Clifford Hearn (1)	American Family Life Assurance; American Insurance Assn; Delaware Occupational Therapy Assn; Delaware Physical Therapists

Table 3.5. *Continued*

Name (No. of Mentions) (Name of Lobbying Firm)	Clients or Organizations
	Assn; Prudential Insurance Co.; Utility Contractors Assn
Jan Konesy (1)	Common Cause of Delaware
Joseph Kotula (1)	Delaware Technical & Community College
Joseph M. Moran (1)	Wilmington Trust Co.
Francis Morris (1)	Delaware Bankers Assn
Edward Peterson (1)	Del. State Labor Council AFL-CIO
David Poffenberger (1)	Del. Society of Certified Public Accountants; Occidental Chemical Corp.; Wine Institute; New Castle County Chamber of Commerce
Bruce Ralston (1) (Legislative Services Inc.)	Alliance of American Insurers; Assn of Delaware Hospitals Inc.; Commerce Clearing House Inc.; Conrail; Del. Alliance for Litter Control; Del. Salvage Dealers Assn; Glass Packaging Institute; National Soft Drink Assn.
Paula Roy (1)	Del. Retail Assn

Sources: Authors' 1987 survey of state legislators and the 1987 Legislative Agent List.

the 1991 legislative agent list and spending reports showed that not much had changed in five years. In 1991, twenty out of the twenty-three lobbyists identified as most effective in the earlier survey were still active as legislative agents. The number of organizations registering legislative agents increased from 171 in 1987 to 222 in 1991. There were 185 legislative agents who filed spending reports in the second quarter of 1991, although the vast majority reported that no money had been spent.

Of particular interest for an examination of lobbyist activity is the relationship between spending and reported influence. The most frequently mentioned lobbyist, Ned Davis, always exceeded the average amount spent by lobbyists during the second quarter. The 1987 legislative agent list also shows that he represented the greatest number of clients, sixteen. Other contract lobbyists—David Poffenberger, Bruce Ralston, and Clifford Hearn —filed spending reports for almost every year between 1977 and 1986 and were consistently among the top second-quarter spenders, but they each received only one mention. Conversely, some influential lobbyists filed no

Table 3.6.   Filing of Financial Reports and Spending by Most Effective
Lobbyists Mentioned by Delaware Legislators, 1977–1986

Name (No. of Mentions)	2nd Quarter Reports Filed	Above Avg. Spent[a]	No. of Years Filed	Percentage Reports Above Avg.[b]
Davis (15)	8	8	9	100.00%
Byrd (9)	7	5	7	71.43
Jarvis (8)	7	3	7	42.86
Biondi (5)	1	0	1	00.00
Brook (5)	9	3	9	33.33
Hankins (5)	9	2	9	22.22
Swayze (5)	4	2	4	50.00
Governor's (4)	0	0	0	—
Patterson (3)	2	1	2	50.00
Jefferson (2)	6	2	6	33.33
Crowley (2)	2	0	5	00.00
Hildebrand (2)	0	0	0	—
Wood (2)	7	4	9	57.14
Buttacovoli (1)	2	1	2	50.00
Freeborn (1)	0	0	0	—
Hearn (1)	8	6	9	75.00
Konesy (1)	0	0	0	—
Kotula (1)	0	0	0	—
Moran (1)	1	0	1	00.00
Morris (1)	1	0	1	00.00
Petterson (1)	0	0	0	—
Poffenberger (1)	8	8	9	100.00
Ralston (1)	9	9	9	100.00
Roy (1)	7	1	7	14.29

Source: Authors' 1987 survey of state legislators and second-quarter (April 1–June 30) lobbying expenditure reports filed by lobbyists for 1977–86, excluding 1979.

[a]Number of times a lobbyist spent above the average amount spent by lobbyists who filed financial reports in the second quarter.
[b]Percentage of second quarter financial reports in which lobbyist spent above the second quarter average for all lobbyists.

or only very few reports. This is partly accounted for by the fact that the Governor's Office, including Bill Freeborn, is not required to file spending reports, and that another lobbyist, Jan Konesy, the representative of Common Cause, is prohibited by organization policy from spending money on legislators. Finally, some highly effective lobbyists (John Brook, for University of Delaware, and Ned Hankins of Diamond State Telephone) have filed reports consistently but are infrequently above-average spenders. A highly effective lobbyist does not consistently have to outspend other lobbyists. Rather, spending by lobbyists is one way to establish and maintain personal relationships with legislators, something that in Delaware is relatively easy to do anyway.

Lobbying Among Friends and Neighbors

Personalized relationships characterizing the state capital are an important feature of lobbying in Delaware. Dover is a small community; lobbyists, legislators, and state officials constitute a small group of activists interested in public issues who interact not only in Legislative Hall but also in supermarkets and at social events. In fact, the major social occasions of the spring legislative session (when the fiscal year budget is adopted) are the receptions, cocktail parties, and brunches (more than forty in 1987) sponsored by major professional and industry associations. Every other year this season culminates in a cruise across the Delaware Bay sponsored by the River Pilots' Association for the Delaware Bay and River; the next year, increases in the pilots' rates are customarily approved.

Low turnover among legislators and lobbyists contributes to the development of personal ties. Furthermore, six of the twenty-two lobbyists mentioned as effective are either former legislators (Robert Byrd, George Jarvis, and Clifford Hearn) or administrative officials (David Swayze, chief of staff for former Governor Pete DuPont).[23] Bill Freeborn, a representative of Governor Michael Castle's office in 1987, became a private lobbyist by 1991. Political connections are important but by no means uniform: Ned Davis, once a reporter covering state politics, later served as a Democratic national committeeman; Gary Patterson was an administrative assistant for Republican U.S. Senator William Roth; and Bobby Byrd, named the second most influential lobbyist in our survey, gained a reputation as a pro-labor Democrat while serving in the legislature from a blue-collar district, but he readily switched sides by joining the state Chamber of Commerce as director of government relations shortly after a primary defeat in 1978.

23. There are now no limitations in Delaware on elected or appointed officials or state employees becoming lobbyists immediately after leaving public service, despite efforts to adopt such guidelines.

Familiarity is a distinct plus in Delaware politics, and several respondents mentioned that being from out of state is one of the greatest disadvantages a lobbyist can bring to the job.

The same factors contribute to a relaxed atmosphere surrounding lobbyist contacts within Legislative Hall. Not until the mid-1970s was action taken to exclude lobbyists from the floor of the House while in session. The Senate still allows lobbyists to occupy chairs that ring the chamber while it is in session, though they no longer perch on legislators' desks or chair arms, as reportedly happened in the past. Lobbyists can be observed sitting at desks and using the telephones in the hardly spacious offices of legislators. In some respects, lobbyists are as much a fixture of the legislature as the elected officials themselves. The product is a "clubby" atmosphere that one respondent characterized simply as "an old-boys' network" with an occasional woman participant. While lobbyist styles no doubt vary, the lobbyists identified as the most influential were consistently described as those relying primarily on personal friendships developed through past associations in government, or through entertaining at local restaurants and watering holes, or on the golf course. This pattern stands in marked contrast to the legislative survey, where meeting socially was judged to be only moderately effective as a means to gain access (see Table 3.7). But the reputational data is quite consistent with the view of one close observer: "The real influence that lobbyists have is camaraderie. It's

Table 3.7. Effective Methods for Lobbyists to Get Access to Delaware Legislators (Percentage of Respondents Selecting, N = 38)

Method	Percent[a]
Meeting in legislator's office	92.1%
Attend committee meetings	71.1
Telephone calls	39.5
Formal submissions (reports)	39.5
Meeting socially	28.9
Working through other groups / legislators	7.9
Working through aides	2.6
Chance meeting	2.6

Source: Authors' 1987 survey of state legislators.

[a]Percentages total more than 100; multiple responses were allowed.

such a small legislature, it's such a small state, that they're all friends."[24] There may be exceptions among both legislators and lobbyists, but the tone is set by leading figures on both sides.

It is not surprising that there is only moderate legislative support for strengthening lobbying regulations: 57.9 percent of the legislators surveyed believed the current regulations were fair; 31.6 percent believed they were not strict enough.

Opinions are mixed about the consequences of a legislative process in which lobbyists play such an active role. The *Wilmington News Journal* editorialized: "If people realized the extent to which the legislators are forced to rely for information on people with vested interests in legislation rather than on independent evaluations, we think they would support an improved legislative staff."[25] Another close observer of the legislature assessed the situation more bluntly:

> Because our legislature is there part-time and essentially the whole operation is part-time—they have very little staff—on any sophisticated issue they're going to rely heavily on lobbyists and outsiders to provide information to them. . . . They're being fed information, background, justifications for legislation from competing sides, along with the wine and steak dinners and probably the call girls and whatever else.[26]

A longtime participant in legislative politics, however, argued that Delaware's size limits the incidence of corruption and lobbying abuses: "You know how small Delaware is. You just can't do anything wrong for a real long time and not get caught in Delaware. Everybody, if they don't know everybody else, seems to know somebody who knows that person."[27] However, the real issue is not scandalous behavior, but rather the pervasive influence of organized interests and the relatively poor access of legislators to independent investigation of policy proposals.

24. Personal interview, May 16, 1988.
25. *Wilmington News Journal*, January 20, 1988, A10.
26. Personal interview, March 30, 1988.
27. Personal interview, May 16, 1988.

ELECTIONS AND CAMPAIGN CONTRIBUTIONS

Lobbyists and interest groups actively use contributions and other forms of campaign assistance as a means to influence the legislature. Legislators ranked election support very low among effective methods interest groups use to communicate their message (only 7.9 percent of respondents; see Table 3.2), but three-fourths of surveyed legislators reported receiving financial contributions from lobbyists or groups during their campaigns (see Table 3.8). Only 5.3 percent claimed that groups had provided no aid during their election campaigns.

Campaign contributions have recently been a contentious issue in Delaware. As in many states, Delaware's statute governing campaign contributions was adopted in the wake of Watergate. Despite many ambiguities and admitted deficiencies, the law was not amended until 1990. Dissatisfaction with the existing law, concern about rising election costs, and scandals that received considerable media coverage in 1986 and 1988 combined to produce a major effort to reduce the influence of PAC contributions and plug many of the current law's loopholes. Several changes were made, but a few significant loopholes remain.

Under the law, individuals, PACs, corporations, and unions operate under the same contribution limits of $1,200 to statewide candidates and $600 for nonstatewide candidates per election. (These limits reflect increases of $200 and $100, respectively. Primary and general election contests count separately.) Contributions of $100 or more must be reported, as

Table 3.8.   Percentage of Delaware Legislators Mentioning Ways Lobbyists or Interest Groups Helped During Election Campaigns ($N = 38$)

How Helped	Percent[a]
Financial contributions	76.3%
Endorsements	55.3
Campaign workers	18.4
Research and campaign strategy	7.9
No aid	5.3

Source: Authors' 1987 survey of state legislators.

[a]Percentages total more than 100; multiple responses were allowed.

well as all in-kind contributions. Currency contributions are discouraged by limiting them to $50. All PAC contributions must be by check. Candidates' financial reports are to be filed with the state election commissioner twenty days before the general election and on the last day of each year until a candidate's debts have been paid. A new feature of the amended law is that limits have been placed on contributions from political parties: a $75,000 limit to a candidate for governor; $25,000 for candidates to other statewide offices; $5,000 for the state Senate and $3,000 for the state House. Party expenditures made to benefit an entire ticket or a group of at least five candidates are not counted against these limits. Individuals may give up to $20,000 to any political party in a two-year election cycle. Political parties are expressly prohibited from contributing to PACs.

The 1986 scandal that triggered the reform process involved campaign contributions made by LAWPAC, a committee of the Trial Lawyers Association, to a Republican candidate for the state House of Representatives. LAWPAC's chief lobbyist, Bruce Hudson, asked four incumbent Republican legislators to funnel additional money from their own campaigns to a candidate whose contribution limit had been reached. The race was considered critical because the Republican was challenging a Democratic supporter of tort reform, an issue the Trial Lawyers had opposed for several legislative sessions. LAWPAC offered to replace the funds the other Republicans would funnel to the challenger. As it happened, the challenger lost and, after an involved process, no charges were brought against either the legislators or the lobbyist involved in the incident, although prosecution of the latter had been recommended by a grand jury.

In the election aftermath, Republican Governor Michael Castle proposed a number of changes in Delaware's campaign law and appointed a reform commission composed of the two party chairmen, representatives of Common Cause and the League of Women Voters, and Grover Brown, a highly respected member of the state bar association. Many dissatisfactions with the law were identified. Some reporting requirements were considered onerous by candidates, some provisions were described as confusing, and others were said to be ambiguous. Party leaders objected to operating under the same contribution limits as PACs (a provision that has since been changed) and saw this feature of the law as a prime cause for their declining influence. Well-known abuses were also uncovered: Reporting twenty days before the election—the least restrictive requirement among the forty-seven states requiring preelection disclosure[28]—means that many con-

28. *Wilmington News Journal*, January 22, 1987, A1.

tributions are made during the last three weeks of a campaign and escape public detection until contests are decided; funneling campaign contributions occurs, if not frequently; candidates are accepting contributions designed to retire old campaign debts (sometimes made in the form of personal loans to themselves) while conducting new campaigns and thereby expanding the contribution limits. Both the election commissioner and the attorney general have experienced problems in attempting to implement and enforce the law, partly explaining why no one had ever been found guilty of a violation.

Despite the governor's support and momentum from the election scandal, no reforms were adopted after the commission's report was submitted. Republicans, who enjoyed a slim majority in the House, sought to raise the party contribution limits substantially more than Democrats, who formed the Senate majority, were willing to accept. The impasse was never broken, and the effort died at the conclusion of the legislative session in 1988, despite another mini-scandal, when it was revealed that the state insurance commissioner, David Levinson, an elected Democrat, received contributions from many of the auditors contracted to monitor insurance records. (Insurance companies are the only businesses prohibited by law from contributing to campaigns in Delaware.)

The reform effort received renewed impetus with the revelation of financial violations in the race for president of the New Castle County council in 1988. This scandal involved illegal contributions to a Democratic candidate and ultimately produced a series of significant party reforms as well as the first convictions for violations of the campaign finance law. In the wake of this second scandal and the public outcry about corrupt politics, both political parties, the governor, and the legislature saw that completing the reform process would be in their interest. Most of the major shortcomings targeted in the original reform proposal have been corrected, with the exception of the early filing deadline; the position of political parties has been substantially strengthened; and the election commissioner has been given additional power to develop regulations. The new provisions became effective January 1, 1991.

The initial delay in undertaking campaign finance reform reflected the intensity of party competition and the divided party outcomes that typified the 1980s. Although Republicans held the governorship from 1977 to 1993, each party has a multiterm incumbent in the U.S. Senate and has shared control of other elected positions. The state's single House seat switched to the Democrats in 1982 after being held by three Republicans since 1966. A maverick Democrat won election to the separately elected lieutenant governorship in 1984, but the post reverted back to the Republicans in 1988 after a campaign that involved yet another alleged violation of financial regulations. The General Assembly has had divided party majorities since 1984, when Republicans regained control of the House by a single vote, although they have gradually extended their advantage. The close competition for legislative seats saw new records established in campaign expenditures, with party committees carefully targeting funds on pivotal contests.

Thus, the role of group contributions in Delaware election contests is problematic. Interparty competition has produced enhanced financial efforts by the political parties. Delaware races are relatively low-cost affairs, given the state's small size and the absence of major television markets. Nonetheless, party officials expressed concern about the growing role of PACs and the steady growth of campaign expenditures. The new reforms may have reclaimed some territory lost to PACs and plugged a variety of other loopholes. The future remains unclear, although the direction of change may have been altered.

EFFECTIVE INTERESTS IN DELAWARE

The discussion so far has indicated that business and professional organizations wield considerable influence in Delaware. Data from the legislative survey, and lobbying disclosure information, support this conclusion and give us more information about which specific interests are most influential in the legislature and how they achieve their influence.

Of the twenty-two individuals mentioned as effective lobbyists, six were contract lobbyists representing business and professional organizations. Other individuals are in-house lobbyists representing utilities, the Chamber of Commerce, major industries, a major bank, and the insurance industry. Two of the twenty-two represented labor interests, and three represented educational interests, including the University of Delaware. Only one represented a public-interest group.

The list of effective lobbyists corresponded fairly well with the groups mentioned as the most effective during legislative sessions (shown in Table 3.9) and at election time (Table 3.10). Some exceptions include the elderly, environmental interests and volunteer firefighters, none of whom was clearly associated with effective individual lobbyists. The last mention

Table 3.9. Most Effective Interest Groups During
Delaware Legislative Session

Group	No. of Mentions
Education	19
Chamber of Commerce	14
Banking	10
Labor	9
Lawyer	9
Business	3
Environmental	3
Volunteer firefighters	2
Constituents	2

Source: Authors' 1987 survey of state legislators.

reflects the fact that an issue concerning volunteer firefighters had recently been before the legislature and was undoubtedly fresh in the minds of legislators at the time of the survey.

The strongest group interests in Delaware, according to legislators, are education and business followed by labor. The state Chamber of Commerce, the Delaware State Education Association (DSEA), and the Delaware Trial Lawyers Association are particularly important interest-group organizations, both during the legislative session and at election time. Legislators report frequent contact by those representing business, labor, and farm interests (see Table 3.1), although they report being contacted most frequently by civic groups.

Discussion of interest-group influence and representation in Delaware is not complete without mentioning the legislators' own economic and professional interests. The General Assembly elected in fall 1986 included three farmers, five DuPont employees, nine educators, and only one lawyer. In this way, farm interests have retained an important influence, as does the DuPont Corporation, which encourages employee political activism.

Legislators consider interest groups to have considerable influence on public policy in the state. Nearly one-fourth of survey respondents rated interest-group influence as crucial or very important, and an additional 63 percent ranked it as important (Table 3.11). Moreover, nearly half considered interest-group influence to have grown over the last decade; less than

Table 3.10. Effective Delaware Interest Groups at Election Time

Group or Interest	No. of Mentions
Education, DSEA, teachers	17
Labor	15
Chamber of Commerce	10
Del. Trial Lawyers Assn, lawyers	8
Business	5
Civic and community groups	5
Political parties	4
Volunteer fire companies	4
NRA	4
Farm interests	4
LWV	4
Realtors, real estate	4
Constituents	3
Press, media	3
Environmentalists	3
Elderly	2
Builders	2
Common Cause	2
Banking	2
Issues	2
Delaware Mobile Home Assn	1
Veterans	1
F.O.P.	1
AAUW	1
Insurance	1
Churches	1
Political group	1
Local government	1
Governor's Office	1

Source: Authors' 1987 survey of state legislators.

10 percent considered it weaker (Table 3.12). A majority of legislators view interest groups as necessary and valuable (Table 3.13).

Administrative Branch Lobbying

Compared with other sources of influence on public policy in the state, however, interest groups are seen by legislators as far from dominant.

Table 3.11. Legislators' Assessment of Influence of Interest Groups on Public Policy in Delaware ($N = 38$)

Type of Influence	Percent
Crucial	2.6%
Very important	21.1
Important	63.2
Little importance	10.5
Insignificant	0.0
Don't know	2.6
Total	100.0

Source: Authors' 1987 survey of state legislators.

Table 3.12. Delaware Legislators' Opinions on Change in Interest-Group Power During 1978–1987 Period ($N = 38$)

Opinion on Change	Percent
Much more powerful	7.9%
More powerful	39.5
About the same	44.7
Less powerful	7.9
Much less powerful	0.0
Total	100.0

Source: Authors' 1987 survey of state legislators.

While lobbyists for interest groups may contact legislators frequently (see Table 3.14), the legislators are also lobbied by the Governor's Office and state administrators. The governor's chief lobbyist was mentioned among the most effective individual lobbyists. As is expected in a state with a part-time legislature, the executive branch is a dominant force in state policy-making. The governor and his staff were ranked most influential by more than 40 percent of the legislators surveyed (Table 3.15). Government departments and agencies received few top mentions although they ranked third in influence behind the legislature and the governor when the rankings were determined.

Table 3.13. Delaware Legislators' Responses to "Which of the Following Generalizations Best Reflects Your Own Judgment?" (*N* = 38)

Response	Percent
Interest groups are a necessary and valuable part of our political system.	52.6%
Such groups are sometimes useful in providing information and service otherwise unattainable.	34.2
Such groups probably reduce the rationality of the legislative process.	0.0
Such groups are generally ineffectual and are probably unnecessary.	2.6
Interest groups often act contrary to the public interest.	7.9
Don't know, no response	2.6

Source: Authors' 1987 survey of state legislators.

Table 3.14. Frequency of Contacting by Various Types of Delaware Lobbyists (Percentage of Respondents Ranking Frequency of Contact, *N* = 38)

Type of Lobbyist	1st	2nd	3rd	1st–3rd
Interest groups and organizations	55.3%	28.9%	13.2%	97.4%
State agencies and departments	7.9	26.3	39.5	73.7
Governor's Office	13.2	23.7	31.6	68.5
Individual pursuing pet project	26.3	21.1	21.1	94.9

Source: Authors' 1987 survey of state legislators.

Table 3.15. Sources of Influence on Delaware Public-Policy-Making Not Including Constituents (Percentage Giving Rank, *N* = 38)

Source of Influence	1st	2nd	3rd	1st–3rd
Governor and staff	42.1%	18.4%	10.5%	71.0%
Legislature	26.3	36.8	18.4	81.5
Gov't departments & agencies	2.6	21.1	36.8	60.5
Interest groups	10.5	10.5	15.8	36.8
Press	13.2	10.5	7.9	31.6
Judiciary	0.0	0.0	10.5	10.5

Source: Authors' 1987 survey of state legislators.

Contributing to the influence of the governor and the executive branch are weekly meetings that include the governor, legislative leaders from both parties, key staff, and selected department secretaries. This practice began in the DuPont administration and was used with increasing effectiveness by Governor Castle. The result was bipartisan and consensual decision-making generally favoring the governor's position. This pattern of decision-making has two important implications for politics and political influence in Delaware. First, it limits the active involvement of most legislators in the analysis and discussion of policy issues. Legislative leaders carry the position of the governor back to their caucuses and frequently urge its support. Second, insofar as interest groups focus their lobbying efforts on the governor, much interest accommodation may take place long before budgets and policies are debated in the legislature.[29] There is considerable evidence that this has been the pattern during 1990–92 in dealing with the state's fiscal problems. Executive branch officials consulted widely with those business interests likely to be affected by revenue decisions. In policy areas where group interests diverge more sharply from those of the governor (for example, education), battles were fought in the legislative arena. Castle's departure in January 1993, necessitated by a constitutional term limitation, could test these consensual practices, particularly because his successor is a Democrat, Thomas Carper.

Thus, those groups with favorable access to administration officials take advantage of this means to advance their interests. This avenue proved all the more significant because of the mechanism for bipartisan legislative-executive collaboration that operated for more than a decade.

THE TAKEOVER SAGA

Several central features of Delaware's group system are illustrated by the politics that surrounded adoption of Delaware's new guidelines on corporate takeovers adopted in January 1988. State legislators were the object of far more extensive press attention and lobbying efforts than anyone in the state capital could remember.

Action was triggered by the none-too-subtle hints from several major corporations that they were considering a shift of their corporate charter to

29. Personal interview, September 9, 1991.

a more protected legal environment. By year's end, twenty-seven states had adopted some version of antitakeover legislation, and Governor Michael Castle and his administration were convinced Delaware needed stronger provisions in order to squash the relocation threat. An effort was launched in the spring of 1987 to draft such legislation, with principal reliance on the Delaware Bar Association's corporate law section, a group of specialists operating in the preeminent arena for their profession. The decision would have national significance. As the *New York Times* suggested in its discussion of the issue, "Delaware . . . is to corporate law what Switzerland is to banking secrecy,"[30] and the *Wall Street Journal*, in one of several editorials opposing the legislation, argued, "As Delaware goes, so goes the nation."[31] Accordingly, drafts of the proposed statute were circulated to lawyers throughout the country. Virtually all substantive features of the law were determined by the bar association committee, whose deliberations were covered by the press in much the same way legislative committee sessions are covered elsewhere.

Corporate chief executive officers and their representatives descended on the state in unprecedented numbers, particularly during a twenty-four-hour period in January when the principal legislative committees from both houses held joint hearings on several competing proposals. Nearly fifty witnesses appeared during the marathon sessions, including Commissioner Joseph Grundfest of the Federal Securities and Exchange Commission, one of three commissioners who publicly opposed the proposed statute; it was the first time he had offered testimony on any state's legislation. T. Boone Pickens, noted "corporate raider" and founder of the United Shareholders Association and an opponent of the legislation, delayed his visit until the eve of floor votes taken the following week.

United Shareholders launched a massive publicity and letter-writing campaign of a sort largely unknown in Delaware. Radio spots, full-page newspaper ads, and a mass mailing to 40,000 of the state's 625,000 residents were coordinated by a Washington political consultant.[32] Legislators heard a great deal about how takeover restrictions would protect inefficient corporate managers and reduce the stock value of firms chartered in the state. But the campaign appears to have backfired. During his appearance in the Senate, Pickens was peppered with hostile questions about how

30. *New York Times*, June 1, 1987, D2.
31. *Wall Street Journal*, December 31, 1987, 6.
32. *Wall Street Journal*, January 14, 1988, 8.

much money had been spent on the effort. (His best guess was something in excess of $30,000—not large by the standards of some states, but enormous in Delaware.) Legislators largely discounted the letter-writing campaign generated by United Shareholders but deeply resented the tactics directed at state pensioners, who had been told their retirement was in jeopardy. Trustees of the state pension fund sent a reassuring letter to 9,000 retired state employees to ease their fears.

Given all the attention, the final votes were anticlimactic. Passed by votes of 39 to 0 in the House and 19 to 1 in the Senate, the new legislation imposed significant restrictions on corporate takeover efforts. Investors acquiring 15 percent of a company's stock would have to wait three years before completing a takeover bid, unless they acquired 85 percent of the stock at one time. Alternatively, if stockholders voted to waive restrictions (that is, agreed to the bid), a merger could proceed. Although opinions vary within the corporate community, many regard the statute as deliberately moderate, with provisions less restrictive than statutes already adopted in several states but principally designed to discourage poorly financed, hostile bids. The bar committee, in fact, had carefully modified its original draft of the statute to provide more opportunities for merger bids in response to concerns voiced by some attorneys. Literally hours after being signed by the governor, the statute's constitutionality was challenged in federal court, an effort joined by the Securities and Exchange Commission several months later.

Although the lobbying effort was atypical, many features of this case were vintage Delaware. Administrators and legislators responded quickly to a threat to the state's national preeminence in chartering corporations. Heavy reliance was placed on the state's professional community to draft the public response, and when confronted with criticisms that its actions were hasty and ill-considered given the lack of legislative staff expertise, the Senate hired a former head of the state's Chancery Court to provide counsel. Both sides to the issue hired local lobbyists to buttress their persuasive efforts, though the lineup of major forces behind the new legislation was overwhelming.

Interview and survey data demonstrate the moderately powerful role interest groups play in Delaware. They also reveal the limited range of the interests active in Delaware; public-interest and social-issue groups are particularly weak and inactive. Unlike many states, Delaware's compact area and small population give its citizens unusual access to state legislators, but the citizenry is no match for the governor and executive officials, or for well-organized and well-financed groups, when it comes to issue analysis and formulation of policy initiatives. Public engagement in policy debates is further limited by media noncompetitiveness, the national significance of Delaware's corporate laws, and the strength of major business interests. The legislature is best able to respond to issues when the affected interests provide much of the material (information and draft legislation) necessary for legislative action. Overall, Delaware interest-group politics fit the pattern observed by Hrebenar and Thomas: Less professionalized and more conservative state governments tend to have less pluralistic and varied group life than more professionalized and liberal states.[33]

What does the future hold for interest-group politics in Delaware? As they have in the past, business interests are likely to remain predominant, although no one company or industry dominates political life in the state, as once was the case. DuPont remains a towering influence, but the corporation's impact has declined with recent diversification in the business community. Barring a scandal of exceptional proportions, there does not appear to be enough concern about key features of interest-group politics to generate any additional reforms of lobby regulation in the near future.

There are, however, some signs of change. As a result of rapid economic growth in some areas of the state, quality-of-life issues have surfaced. Environmental issues are potentially explosive, given the presence of toxic dumps (twenty-one Superfund sites, including two of the ten worst in the United States) and problems associated with rapid coastal development. Concern over maintaining and improving the quality of the work force reveals continued attention to stimulating economic growth, a tradition nearly a century old. It is interesting that the problems of public education have increasingly been cast in terms of a "quality work force," which may enhance the probability of significant reform. These issues have the potential to increase the number and diversity of interests making demands on the legislature. Some legislators already believe that their ability to address complex and long-term issues is sorely limited by insufficient staff resources and their part-time status, and these concerns are likely to become more widely noticed if the public demands action on the emerging issues. In short, Delaware politics reveal an unusual degree of continuity, but the state's surprising economic and social complexity, recently fueled by rapid

33. Thomas and Hrebenar, "Interest Groups in the States."

economic growth, provides the basis for substantial tension and potential change. The political norms familiar to friends and neighbors are likely to come under increased pressure as new patterns of interest-group politics emerge.

4

Maine: From the Big Three to Diversity

Douglas I. Hodgkin

Three decades ago three interests allegedly dominated Maine politics: power, timber, and manufacturing of textiles and shoes. "There are other groups involved," wrote Duane Lockard, "but the power of the Big Three economic interests is such that the other elements seem to fade into the background, or else at times they become appendages of the Big Three."[1] A recent text continues to list the Big Three along with the Farm Bureau, the Grange, the liquor and beer lobby, the horse-racing lobby, and conservation groups.[2] Today, however, as a consequence of reforms and greater economic and political diversity, the unity and dominance of the Big Three have dissolved. A far more diverse array of interests are active and influential in Maine politics.

Two recent incidents illustrate the decline of Big Three interests. After lengthy regulatory proceedings and defeat in the legislature, the Great Northern Paper Company abandoned attempts to build a dam at Big Ambejackmockamus Falls, West Branch of the Penobscot River. "The death of Big A is viewed by industry spokesmen and environmentalists as yet another sign that the paper companies . . . are not all-powerful."[3] That was a highly visible battle, pitting a coalition of organized environmentalists against a major company. The second incident involved a handful of unorganized woodcutters and their wives, who told their stories of abuses by the timber companies and who successfully lobbied for a bill changing the

1. Duane Lockard, *New England State Politics* (Princeton: Princeton University Press, 1959), 107.
2. Sarah McCally Morehouse, *State Politics, Parties, and Policy* (New York: Holt, Rinehart & Winston, 1981), 110.
3. Paul Carrier, "Out of the Woods: Ailing Industry Tries to Polish Image," *Sunday Sun-Journal* (Lewiston), April 13, 1986, 12A.

wood measurement formula and regulating the payment and accounting procedures. Without publicity, money, or any of the other usual resources, their one-on-one lobbying defeated a phalanx of professional lobbyists.[4]

Trends in Maine group activity are similar to those in the rest of the nation. The number of groups has grown, the range of interests represented has expanded, and the intensity of lobbying has increased.[5]

SOCIOECONOMIC AND POLITICAL ENVIRONMENT

During the last few decades, Maine's economic, social, and political systems have become more heterogeneous.[6] While competition from elsewhere has undermined the shoe, textile, and lumber industries, the state's low labor costs and appealing lifestyle have attracted other manufacturing enterprises. Compared with the days when a few old-guard business executives of Maine-based companies dominated the state, business is now managed largely by professional managers for national and international corporations.[7] The service sector has grown rapidly, including substantial increases in government employment. Although the state still produces food and raw materials, agriculture has declined, especially potatoes and broilers. Urban and professional migrants into southern Maine and along the coast have created a boom in the southern and coastal regions centering on Portland, the largest city. However, economic decline and outmigration from the west and north have led to some rivalry between "the two Maines." Moreover, strong environmental concerns have emerged to compete with developmental pressures.

4. Abby Zimet, "Lobbying Drama Pits Cutters vs. Industry Pros," *Maine Sunday Telegram* (Portland), May 6, 1984, 14A.

5. Clive S. Thomas and Ronald J. Hrebenar, "Interest Groups in the States," in Virginia Gray, Herbert Jacob, and Robert Albritton, eds., *Politics in the American States: A Comparative Analysis* 5th ed. (Glenview, Ill.: Scott, Foresman / Little, Brown, 1990), chap. 4.

6. This paragraph summarizes findings in Allen Pease and Wilfred Richard, eds., *Maine: Fifty Years of Change 1940–1990* (Orono: University of Maine Press, 1983), 1–86. See also Phyllis Austin, "Who Runs Maine?" *Maine Times* (Brunswick), July 22, 1988, 8–13.

7. Austin, "Who Runs Maine?" 8.

Traditionally, the most politically relevant social cleavage in Maine was between rural Yankees and the Franco-Americans who had migrated from Canada and settled in textile-manufacturing cities, such as Lewiston and Biddeford. These two ethnic groups found representation electorally through the Republican and Democratic parties, respectively, rather than through active lobbying groups. Recently, however, new interests representing women, the aged, the handicapped, gays, and Native Americans have sought improved legal and social status through direct lobbying activity.

Greater two-party competition also has transformed the political system. Lockard concluded his analysis of Maine by predicting that "only when the opposition party can move into the legislative arena to affect basic policies will the predominant authority of the Big Three be successfully challenged."[8] During the 1950s, Maine began its realignment from one-party Republican dominance to a recent classification as the most competitive state in the nation.[9] Interest groups have had to adapt to these changed conditions. Rather than operate within the multifactionalism of a single party, groups now must gain access to both parties. As they compete for votes, the parties themselves must beware of appearing to be captive to a set of particular interests.

Business interests now must seek access to Democratic party leaders. Lobbyists with Democratic connections have long lists of business clients. The law firm of Preti, Flaherty, Beliveau & Pachios, which boasts three former Democratic party chairmen, is a premier lobbying operation in Augusta. Many clients are "business and professional interests that previously had used Republican lobbyists. For instance, the firm picked up the Hospital Association, which had used Republican lobbyists for years."[10] Another example is Central Maine Power Company's employment of David Flanagan, former Democratic governor Joseph Brennan's special counsel. Then company president John W. Rowe noted that Flanagan was "somebody who really understands state government, who knows the people and how

8. Lockard, *New England State Politics*, 118.

9. John F. Bibby et al., "Parties in State Politics," in Gray et al., *Politics in the American States*, 4th ed. (Boston: Little, Brown, 1983), 66. For the early stages of realignment, see Douglas I. Hodgkin, "Breakthrough Elections: Elements of Large and Durable Minority Party Gains in Selected States Since 1944" Ph.D. diss., Duke University, 1966).

10. Scott Allen, "From Lobbyist to Candidate," *Maine Times*, May 23, 1986, 18.

they think."[11] Another instance is the decision of Blue Cross & Blue Shield of Maine to hire Jadine O'Brien, former state personnel director in the Brennan administration, in addition to other lobbyists with strong Republican connections.[12] Major lobbying firms that have partisan leanings also are increasingly hiring people who identify with the opposite party, in a process described as "cross-pollenization."[13]

Political action committees donate freely to Democratic candidates and committees. Moreover, the Democrats have aggressively pursued contributions. In 1983 then Senate Majority Leader Charles P. Pray (later Senate president) sent lobbyists an invitation to a fund-raising dinner that read as follows:

> With a new party controlling the Senate, many of you are not familiar with some of the newer members of the majority. This gathering will allow you to get to know us, and we will have a chance to chat with you.
>
> With the new majority, we can also expect new issues during this session. Hopefully, this will provide a relaxed but productive setting for discussion.[14]

Lobbyists with Republican sympathies complained about "extortion," but most attended anyway.

In 1984 the Democratic legislature conducted an investigation of the political activities of the utilities, expecting to find close connections with the Republican party. To their embarrassment, Governor Brennan and other Democratic stalwarts were the prime beneficiaries of shared polling information. While some Democratic leaders claim that the utilities "are running away from politics," the evidence suggests that "the partisan barriers have broken down. The utilities not only deal with the Democrats, but even court them."[15]

11. Jeff Clark, "Conflict of Interest," *Maine Times*, May 11, 1984, 16.

12. Nancy Perry, "Ex-Legislators in Great Demand as Lobbyists," *Kennebec Journal* (Augusta), April 13, 1988, 7.

13. Francis X. Quinn, "Lobbyists' Power Has Waned, but They Find Ways to Adapt," *Lewiston Sun-Journal*, June 28, 1990, 25.

14. Associated Press, "Lobbyists Grumble over 'Party,'" *Portland Press Herald*, February 25, 1983, 6.

15. Scott Allen, "The Utilities Probe," *Maine Times*, January 11, 1985, 28.

Although party competition may check the power of groups, Maine political parties must at the same time operate in a candidate-centered political system. The decline of party politics[16] allows more latitude for interest-group activity.

THE GOVERNMENTAL AND LEGAL ENVIRONMENT

Just as competition in the political system has made life more complex for interest groups, the state's governmental institutions have become more professional, and there has been new legislation aimed at designing the policy-making process to be more resistant to special interests.

Reorganization of the executive branch during the 1960s and 1970s to emphasize gubernatorial direction included a lengthened four-year term, abolition of the appointment-confirming Executive Council, and consolidation into fewer departments. The governor also has an increased staff and a State Planning Office to provide research and policy-planning assistance.[17] No other officer is popularly elected statewide, although the legislature's election of the attorney general, secretary of state, state treasurer, and state auditor place these departments outside the chief executive's purview.

The legislature has become more diverse and more professional.[18] Diversity is most evident in better representation of urban areas, women, and a range of occupations. Some argue that the large number of women among both legislators and lobbyists tempers the "social lobby." The old Augusta House, a hotel that used to sit near the Capitol, used to be where lobbyists and legislators cut deals in after-hours sessions at card tables and in the bars, but fraternizing appears to be much less frequent now. As Assistant

16. Christian Potholm, "Maine's Changing Politics," in Richard Barringer, ed., *Changing Maine* (Portland, Me.: Edmund S. Muskie Institute of Public Affairs, University of Southern Maine, 1990), 72–75. The decline of local party capability and the increase of state party capability are described in Douglas I. Hodgkin, "State and Local Party Capability: Maine Republicans," *Party Line*, no. 17 (September 1984), 13–16.

17. In Pease and Richard, *Maine*, 104–5.

18. Ibid., 106–8; Kenneth T. Palmer, "Changing Government," in Barringer, *Changing Maine*, 53–54.

Republican Senate Leader Pamela Cahill noted, "Nothing really can go on that can't go on in mixed company."[19]

The legislature increased its capabilities with some reduction in member turnover due to enhanced salaries as well as with the creation of a professional staff in 1973. Kenneth Allen, an aide to House Speaker John L. Martin, was reported as saying that, although still small in number, the "objective" performance of the professional staff "constitutes 'the greatest single thing that has reduced the dependence on lobbying in this town'"[20]

Certain legislative rules also have implications for interest-group access, largely by reducing the chances for impermeable "iron triangles" to develop. Legislative leaders control the appointment of committee members and chairs; all bills must be reported to the floor. A Senate Appropriations Table, where all bills requiring spending are held until the end of the session, permits central determination of priorities.

The judicial branch has been reorganized to create full-time district courts, state financing of the court system, and establishment of an Administrative Office of the Courts to serve the entire judiciary. New rules of procedure have also been adopted, as well as codes of ethical standards. Finally, "to make clear the needs of the Judiciary, a 'State of the Judiciary' speech by the Chief Justice to the Legislature has been instituted as well as more open appearances before committees of the Legislature."[21]

Policy-making in Maine also occurs through popular vote on the ratification of constitutional amendments, all bond issues, referenda, and initiatives. The increased use of the latter reflects the rise of active citizens groups in the state.[22] The antinuclear forces have managed to mobilize petitions signed by the required 10 percent of the previous gubernatorial vote no less than five times in less than a decade, three times to close the nuclear power plant, once to seek popular election of the Public Utilities Commission, and once to require a popular vote on future nuclear waste disposal plans.

Laws passed in the 1970s on lobbying, conflict of interest, and campaign financing attempt to regulate the impact of special interests. A lobbyist is

19. Francis X. Quinn, "Back-room Dealings Emerge into the Light of Regulated Day," *Lewiston Sun-Journal*, June 27, 1990, 21.

20. Quinn, "Lobbyists' Power Has Waned," 25. Palmer, "Changing Government," 58, agrees that staff capacity and more stable membership lessen the power of organized interest groups.

21. Entire paragraph from Pease and Richard, *Maine*, 108–11; quotation at 110–11.

22. Palmer, "Changing Government," 60, notes only seven initiated statutes in the 1909–70 period but fifteen such measures for 1971–88.

defined by law[23] as any person who is employed for lobbying or a regular employee of a business or organization who spends more than eight hours lobbying in a calendar month, therefore not covering unpaid lobbyists. Specifically excluded from the definition are state agencies, the University of Maine, and the Maine Maritime Academy. Because lobbying itself is defined as communicating directly with the legislature, it does not include grass-roots lobbying or attempts to influence other branches of government (except the governor in connection with his veto power). Moreover, it excludes from the definition appearances before legislative committees or responses to requests for information from any official of the executive branch.

Lobbyists must register with the secretary of state within seven days of commencing activity and then must submit monthly reports detailing compensation, expenditures, and names of legislative officials or their immediate family on whose behalf expenditures totaling more than $25 are made. Some lobbyists assert that this record-keeping enhances the role of professional lobbyists.[24]

However, some consider the law deficient in its coverage, implementation, and enforcement. In addition to those exemptions noted above, coalitions of groups need not identify their membership or funding sources, no reports are required for months the legislature is not in session, detailed reports are required only when the lobbyist expects compensation or expenses of more than $1,000 on a bill, and lobbyists need to report only bill numbers on which they worked, not the titles or topics. The data reported are often vague, particularly for in-house lobbyists for whom lobbying is only one part of their job and for contract lobbyists who charge an annual fee for a variety of services. Many lobbyists file late or fail to provide the information required. Enforcement is weak: nonfilers are fined only $50, and there is no penalty for incomplete or vague reports.[25]

Because legislator salaries in Maine are low, despite recent increases, sessions are limited and few legislators make a lengthy career out of public service. Most maintain private businesses or employment concurrent with legislative service. Not only does this citizen legislature become reliant on outside interests and the bureaucracy for information, but frequently when

23. Lobbyist disclosure legislation is at 3 M.R.S.A. 311–26.

24. Christopher Callahan, "Banking Industry Big Spender on Statehouse Lobbying in 1982," *Kennebec Journal*, February 8, 1983, 1.

25. Paul Carrier, "Lobbyist Reports Give Little Insight," *Maine Sunday Telegram*, September 22, 1991, 1B, 8B.

legislation is considered affecting the insurance industry or the teaching profession, for example, the substantial representation of those interests within the legislature raises charges of conflict of interest. Although the law does prohibit action by a legislator where there is "a direct substantial personal financial interest," the benefit must be "unique and distinct from that of the general public or persons engaged in similar professions, trades, businesses or employment."[26] In practice, it is extremely rare for the presiding officer or the Commission on Governmental Ethics and Election Practices to rule that a conflict exists.

State executive branch employees may not participate in their official capacity in proceedings in which they and others closely associated with them have a direct and substantial financial interest. Former employees may not represent a firm in a proceeding before their state agency for a year after departure if the state is a party or has a substantial interest and if "the particular matter at issue was pending before his agency and was directly within his official responsibilities . . . within one year prior to the termination of his employment."[27]

Regulation of campaign financing was tightened in 1975 with adoption of reporting requirements for candidates, for their committees, and for the parties. However, information on political action committees (PACs) was available only from these individual reports until 1985, when specific legislation required that PACs too must register with the Commission on Governmental Ethics and Election Practices and report all contributions received and given over $50. Individuals may contribute up to $1,000, while corporations, associations, PACs, and other groups may contribute up to $5,000 per election per candidate or political committee.[28]

GROUPS AND LOBBYISTS IN MAINE

Individuals and groups desiring to contact legislators and executive officials find it easy to do so in Maine. Legislators in particular, who have no pri-

26. 1 M.R.S.A. 1014, sub A, sub F.
27. 5 M.R.S.A. 18. Although a legislative committee found no major conflict-of-interest problem in Maine state government, the current laws were deemed somewhat limited and provided a potential for such a problem. Maine Legislature, Joint Standing Committee on State Government, *An Evaluation of Maine's Conflict of Interest Laws* (Augusta, Me., 1988).
28. 21-A M.R.S.A. 1011–62.

vate offices, may be approached easily in the lobby under the capitol rotunda. Individual citizens can and do appear to testify at committee hearings without prior arrangement. In 1987 an elementary school class was able to lobby for a bill requiring a picture of a lobster on motor vehicle license plates. Legislators frequently emphasize that the most effective lobbying is contact by letter or telephone from their constituents.[29]

Formally registered lobbyists do constitute an enduring and influential presence in Augusta. The numbers have increased sharply,[30] and the proportional distribution of the types of interests represented has changed in some categories (Table 4.1). Local governments and consumer groups have declined notably, in addition to some decline of labor union representation. Professional and religious or civic organizations show significant increases.

Full-time employees of the organization increasingly find contact with the state government part of their responsibilities as in-house lobbyists. Corporations use their executives, such as James McGregor of the Bath Iron Works, and trade associations and other groups use their executive directors and other staff, such as Floyd Rutherford of the Paper Industry Information Office and Everett "Brownie" Carson of the Natural Resources Council.

Groups may also hire contract lobbyists, some of whom may be former legislators or others who through long experience have built familiarity with legislators, the legislative process, and administrative personnel. Their value increases "as the volume and complexity of state legislation and regulation grows."[31] The leading example, former State Senate President Kenneth MacLeod, grossed roughly $76,550 in 1991 while representing eleven interests, including Maine Beer & Wine Wholesalers, American Cyanamid Company, Illinois Tool Works, Sawyer Management Services (solid waste), and the Flexible Packaging Association.[32]

Corporations also may hire former bureaucrats as lobbyists and consul-

29. See, e.g., Michael McGuire, "Lobbying—Political Clout Not Limited to Big Guns," *Courier-Gazette* (Rockland), February 5, 1987, 1; Ronald D. Deprez, "Internal Characteristics and Effectiveness of Lobbying Organizations in the State of Maine" (Ph.D. diss., Rutgers University, 1977), 133.

30. For 1991 there were 298 individuals registered as lobbyists. Secretary of State, Lobbyist Registrar, "Individual Active Lobbyists in Maine," August 1991.

31. Perry, "Ex-legislators," 7.

32. Compiled from reports in the files of the Lobbyist Registrar, Office of Maine Secretary of State, for the 115th Legislature, First Regular Session 1991.

Table 4.1. Distribution of Types of Interest Groups Registered in Maine (Selected Years)

Group Type	1971 No.	1971 %	1979 No.	1979 %	1985 No.	1985 %	1991 No.	1991 %
Single business	85	37.0	74	36.2	82	37.8	108	39.0
Trade association	53	23.0	60	29.4	69	31.8	78	28.2
Local governments	22	9.6	14	6.9	8	3.7	12	4.3
Professional	16	7.0	15	7.4	18	8.3	37	13.4
Labor	10	4.3	11	5.4	7	3.2	7	2.5
Religious, civic	9	3.9	15	7.4	17	7.8	18	6.5
Consumer	8	3.5	3	1.5	1	0.5	1	0.4
Farm	6	2.6	5	2.5	3	1.4	5	1.8
Environmental	5	2.2	3	1.5	6	2.8	6	2.2
Veteran, military	2	0.9	1	0.5	2	0.9	0	0.0
Retiree	2	0.9	0	0.0	0	0.0	0	0.0
Miscellaneous	12	5.2	3	1.5	4	1.8	5	1.8
Total	230		204		217		277	

Sources: For 1971, James F. Horan et al., *Downeast Politics: The Government of the State of Maine* (Dubuque, Iowa: Kendall / Hunt, 1975), 49; for 1979, compiled from lobbyist registrations in Office of the Secretary of State; for 1985, compiled from Secretary of State, "Joint Lobbyist / Employer Registration 112th Legislature: First Regular Session," 1985; for 1991, compiled from Secretary of State, "Joint Lobbyist / Employer Registration Listing 115th Legislature—First Regular Session" and "Addendum to Lobbyist List," 1991.

tants. Phyllis Austin, a writer for the *Maine Times*, found that many members of the Brennan administration from the agencies related to the environment are now working for developers. She noted that they all had valuable knowledge about the inner workings of state government and strong past environmentalist credentials that gave them a credibility with regulators and legislators.[33]

More and more, organized interests are hiring professional lobbying firms to represent them (see Table 4.2). Most are law firms, some of whose partners or staff specialize in lobbying. Many are well connected politically. The best known and probably the most powerful is Preti, Flaherty, Be-

33. Phyllis Austin, "Greener Pastures," *Maine Times*, June 10, 1988, 2–4.

Table 4.2. Maine's Largest Contract Lobbyists, 1991 Regular Legislative Session

Lobbyist Firm	Total Fees[a]	No. of Clients[b]
Preti, Flaherty, Beliveau & Pachios (L)	$316,992	43
Eaton, Peabody, Bradford & Veague (L)	182,772	9
Public Policy Associates (C)	122,800	10
Doyle & Nelson (L)	117,153	12
Weil & Howe Inc. (C)	107,556	13
Dyer, Goodall & LaRouche (L)	105,638	11
Public Affairs Group (C)	105,128	14
Bernstein, Shur, Sawyer & Nelson (L)	86,512	5
Marden, Dubord, Bernier & Stevens (L)	83,984	7
Kenneth MacLeod (I)	76,550	11
J. Oliver Associates (C)	71,644	8
Capitol Consultants Inc. (C)	67,621	5
Pierce, Atwood, Scribner, Allen, et al. (L)	60,205	18
Verrill & Dana (L)	56,775	20
Curtis, Thaxter, Stevens, et al. (L)	51,655	10

Sources: Lobby registrations and monthly reports filed through August 1991 with the Maine Lobbyist Registrar, Office of the Secretary of State.

[a]Includes retainer fees that may cover more services than lobbying, particularly for consulting firms and for MacLeod.
[b]Includes all clients for whom the lobbyist registered; some reports indicated no lobbying and no payments.

(L) Law firm; (C) Consulting firm; (I) Individual.

liveau & Pachios, whose clients include the Tobacco Institute, Anheuser-Busch, the American Insurance Association, Cumberland Farms, the Environmental and Economic Council of Maine,[34] the Industrial Energy Consumer Group, the New England Cable TV Association, and Maine associations of automobile dealers, hospitals, and optometrists.

Indeed, Severin Beliveau, a former Democratic party chairman and a

34. This is a business trade association that is not merely another client; apparently it was established by the law firm as another vehicle to focus on the regulatory difficulties of many of the firm's other clients. Randy Wilson, "More on Beliveau," *Maine Times*, May 17, 1991, 21.

candidate for the 1986 Democratic gubernatorial nomination, is featured in many news accounts concerning lobbying in Maine.[35] Two legislators listed Beliveau on questionnaires distributed by the author as one of the most powerful "organizations" in Maine. His influence derives from his access to the Democratic leadership of the legislature, his ability to provide information and to recruit important constituents to accompany him in his lobbying, and his influence on the distribution of PAC money. Beliveau, however, "attributes his success neither to Democratic ties nor to control over PACs. He says he has been successful over the long run because he has been honest and persuasive."[36]

A strongly Republican firm is Verrill & Dana, with whom Governor John R. McKernan Jr. was associated before his election to the U.S. Congress in 1982. Banks, utilities, paper, insurance companies, and hospitals are among their clients. But they declined sharply in their level of lobbying activity from 1989 to 1991,[37] possibly reflecting the judgments of potential clients that a Republican firm is not useful in influencing a heavily Democratic legislature.

Legislators perceive lawyers as very powerful, as we shall see, probably on the basis of the important role they play in the lobbying process. One legislator who rated lawyers as the most effective group before the legislature attributed their influence to "their ability to assist in wording of amendments" and "by generally confusing everyone not a lawyer."

Increasingly, clients are turning to consulting firms for their sometimes lower fees, particularly when highly technical legal work is not involved.[38] The Public Affairs Group (formerly Cohen-Herman Associates and then Cohen & Green) is the first and most prominent of the consulting firms.

35. See esp. Scott Allen, "From Lobbyist to Candidate," 16–19; and Randy Wilson, "Who's Really Pulling the Strings?" *Maine Times*, May 3, 1991, 21. Beliveau also was featured in John Weiss et al., *A Citizen's Guide to the Maine Legislature* (Augusta: Maine People's Resource Center and Maine Common Cause, 1985), 88–89.

36. Allen, "From Lobbyist to Candidate," 18.

37. They had 24 clients paying a total of $193,106 in 1989, but 20 clients paying a total of only $56,775 in 1991, and of the latter only 11 paid more than $500. Totals for 1989 derived from Paul Carrier, "Lobbyists Proliferate in Augusta," *Maine Sunday Telegram*, July 23, 1989, 36A, plus July reports filed with the Lobbyist Registrar, Office of the Secretary of State. Data for 1991 are derived from monthly reports filed that year with the Lobbyist Registrar.

38. Mary Ellen Matava, "Lobbyists Taking on New Identity in Augusta," *Kennebec Journal*, April 12, 1988, 1, 10.

Marshall Cohen came to Maine as administrative director of Pine Tree Legal Assistance in 1973 and served as the state's chief lobbyist for the poor. In 1981 he went into lobbying on his own and found a considerable market among nonprofit groups. The firm's clients in 1991 have a generally different cast from those of the firms described above and include Maine Community Action Agencies, the Maine Association of Substance Abuse Programs, the Sweetser Children's Home, and associations of physical therapists, psychologists, and radiologists. The anomaly seems to be Cohen's representation of Central Maine Power Company "to provide advice . . . on how best to serve the needs of low-income, elderly and other client groups . . . and to represent the views and concerns of the Company in connection with such programs and initiatives before public bodies."[39] Critics say the power company co-opted him and gained favorable public relations.

Public Policy Associates, one of several new firms, was formed in 1990 and immediately attracted several lucrative clients, including the Aseptic Packaging Council, the Champion International Corporation, the Maine Gaming Association, and Multi-State Associates, which represents three national firms.[40]

GOVERNMENT AS A LOBBY

A set of lobbyists about whom there is little systematic evidence are the liaison personnel of the executive branch. The governor has staff whose

39. Scott Allen, "Switching Sides?" *Maine Times*, February 22, 1985, 36. See also Nancy Perry, "The Lobbyists," *Portland Press Herald*, January 3, 1983, 11; and Francis X. Quinn, "Longtime Lobbyist Heads for Washington," *Kennebec Journal*, March 29, 1988, 8. After fifteen years in Augusta, Cohen has taken a position as strategist and PAC director for the American Psychological Association in Washington, D.C.

40. The firm's partners are former Democratic State Representative Gregory Nadeau, who served on the legislature's Appropriations Committee and then chaired the Housing and Economic Development Committee; Richard S. Davies, former Democratic representative and then director of government and public affairs for the Maine State Housing Authority; and Republican John C. Turner, former development director for the city of Auburn.

prime responsibility is monitoring the progress of legislation and representing gubernatorial interests in legislative negotiations. Governor McKernan's present finance commissioner, H. Sawin Millett, was the governor's top aide in dealing with the legislature during his first two and a half years. Millett had previously served as a legislator, as executive director of the Maine School Management Association, and as education commissioner under Governor James B. Longley.

The same functions are performed by personnel in each of the executive departments. Douglas M. Smith, a former legislator who now serves as a lobbyist, stated, "Bureaucrats are the unregistered lobbyists of state government. There are hordes of them and they can easily outgun you."[41] Department personnel are also active in grass-roots lobbying for bond issues subject to popular vote. Department of Transportation personnel are concerned with highway bonds, vocational technical institutes back frequent bonds affecting one or more campuses, and the commissioner of corrections touted recent prison bond issues.[42] Legislators rate the executive departments among the most influential of Maine's interest groups (see Table 4.4).

A prime source of influence for the bureaucracy is its ability to provide information and expertise to legislators, but that information must be trusted. One study found that members of the Agriculture Committee in 1986 distrusted the Department of Agriculture as politically charged and providing distorted information.[43] Beyond its lobbying clout, the bureaucracy now has pervasive regulatory and decision-making authority to implement legislation. For example, the Conservation Department issued draft rules to implement the 1989 Forest Practices Act. Believing that the rules actually undercut the goals of the legislation, environmentalists made their own specific recommendations.[44]

41. Quoted in John Hale, "Legislative Lobbying an Art and a Business," *Bangor Daily News*, January 16, 1986, 21.

42. David D. Platt, "Bureaucrats as Campaigners," *Maine Times*, November 10, 1989, 14.

43. Kenneth R. Liebman, "Subsystem Government: A Case Study of Agriculture Policy-Making in Maine" (senior thesis, Bates College, 1986), 70–71.

44. Phyllis Austin, "Forest Rules: A Coalition Seeks Clear-Cut Controls," *Maine Times*, September 21, 1990, 4.

INTEREST-GROUP TACTICS

Elections and PACs

Groups are active in campaigns in many traditional ways. They circulate questionnaires to candidates to determine their stands and to extract commitments, if possible. They contribute money and in-kind assistance, such as use of membership lists, telephones, postage, envelope-stuffing machines, and printing. Of course, the candidate must report the value of these as campaign contributions. Groups with large and/or committed memberships, such as unions or antinuclear groups, may also provide volunteers to help candidates favorable to their causes.

A major development in Maine interest-group activity is rapid expansion of the financial role of interest groups in state legislative elections.[45] As one reporter put it, "There were no significant Maine-based PACs until 1976, when the Maine Merchants' Association set one up. Today [1986], there are 36 and PAC money is increasingly available to bottom-of-the-ticket candidates for the 151 House seats."[46] Most PAC contributions to legislative candidates are in the $50 to $500 range,[47] but some observers worry that contribution amounts may escalate as campaigns become more expensive. Total expenditures of the forty-eight interest-group PACs contributing in the 1990 candidate elections were $470,127. Those contributing the most were the Maine AFL-CIO COPE ($57,291.24), the Maine Business PAC ($34,620.76), and the Maine Teachers Association ($30,600.57).[48]

45. "The increased role of groups in the financing of elections . . . has been largely responsible for their increased prominence and power over the last decade or so" in states throughout the nation (Thomas and Hrebenar, *Interest Groups in the States*, 128).

46. Scott Allen, "Money, the Mother's Milk of Politics," *Maine Times*, December 5, 1986, 4A.

47. Mary Lou Wendell, ed., *Citizen's Guide to the Maine Legislature* (Portland Maine People's Resource Center, 1988), 86–94, contains a listing of contributions in 1986 by selected PACs.

48. Compiled by the author from Commission on Governmental Ethics and Election Practices, *Annual Report 1990*, 31–35. The commission reports a total of 88 PACs spending $1,670,198. This includes PACs administered by legislative leaders and other individual politicians as well as those involved only in ballot-question campaigns. The dollar figure includes duplicative transfers among PACs. All figures represent only contributions made by PACs, which are required by law to report. Maine law permits

Gubernatorial campaigns already attract large contributions; in 1986 three of the four major candidates in the general election spent more than $1 million.[49] In 1990 Governor John McKernan and former governor Joseph Brennan each spent approximately, $1.5 million. Their respective receipts from businesses and corporations were 39 percent and 35 percent; from unions receipts were 0 percent and 2 percent; and from PACs, 3 percent and 10 percent.[50]

Large amounts have also been spent in initiative and referendum campaigns, such as successful efforts to defeat a state Equal Rights Amendment and closing the nuclear power plant. The greatest PAC spending on a ballot question in 1990 was on the issue of Sunday shopping in large stores, including the Retail Federation of Maine PAC ($323,674.71) and Citizens for Choice on Sunday ($153,054.09), in favor of Sunday shopping, versus Citizens to Save Maine's Heritage ($90,441.54) and Save Our Sundays ($53,547.92), opposed.[51] As has been frequently the case in Maine, the side spending the larger amount won.[52] Big-spending failures were the attempts to block and then repeal the bottle bill and the attempt to block a ban on local measured telephone service.

PACs are becoming increasingly sophisticated in their operations. Some provide services to groups of candidates; Dirigo Alliance, a coalition of eight groups seeking to elect "progressives," sponsors training seminars and strategy sessions for their targeted candidates. Energypac, of the Maine Oil Dealers Association, conducted polling to assess the chances of two favored candidates. Fleet Bank and Local 1253 of the International Brotherhood of Electrical Workers raise funds through payroll deduction plans.[53]

Many PACs contribute without regard to party affiliation, indicating a general attempt to gain access. Most contributions seem to be in support of candidates whose past voting record or questionnaire responses indicate

---

individual corporations to make contributions without submitting reports; records of these contributions are found only in the reports that the individual candidates file.

49. Maine Common Cause placed an initiative on the November 1989 ballot that would have provided partial public funding and would have limited spending in gubernatorial campaigns, but it was defeated by the voters.

50. Commission on Governmental Ethics and Election Practices, *Annual Report 1990*, 11–12. Percentages computed by the author.

51. Ibid., 36.

52. William H. Coogan, "Comment," in Richard Barringer, *Changing Maine*, 64–65.

53. Nancy Perry, "PACs Bring Efficiency to Campaign Spending," *Maine Sunday Telegram*, July 15, 1990, 11A.

they are sympathetic and who have a chance to win. The Maine Teachers Association includes an elaborate interview process. Ideological PACs, such as the Committee for Maine's Future and the Maine Impact Coalition PAC, are more likely than others to give to challengers.[54] During recent elections, many PACs have required the candidate to request the contribution, thereby resulting in some self-selection in applications to congenial PACs. The parties also engage in some direction of PAC money to compatible and competitive candidates.[55]

There are no available studies on whether contributions affect Maine legislative voting. The Legislature's Committee on Election Laws concluded: "There is nothing to indicate that campaign contributions have influenced the actions of elected officials at any level."[56] On the other hand, political scientist and former state senator Ken Hayes has asserted, "Lobbyists tell you, 'This vote is going to hurt you.'"[57] A few studies do show that there are simple correlations between contribution patterns and selected roll-call votes.[58] PACs also give strategically to relevant committee members and legislative leadership,[59] as well as to candidates in close contests.[60]

Increasing amounts of money are disbursed by PACs controlled by legislative leaders and ranking members to which interest-group PACs and lob-

---

54. The operations of selected PACs in raising and distributing funds are described in Alexandra C. Messore, "Political Action Committees in Maine," in Douglas I. Hodgkin, ed., *Groups and PACs in Maine Politics: Short Term Studies*, 50–54 (Lewiston, Me.: Department of Political Science, Bates College, 1990), and in Paul Ippolito and Andrew Mullen, "The Organization and Operation of Maine PACs," in Hodgkin, ed., *Groups and PACs*, 55–58.

55. Information based on the author's involvement in state legislative campaigns.

56. Maine Legislature, Joint Standing Committee on Election Laws, *Campaign Finance and Ballot Question Reform* (Augusta, Me., March 1984), 5.

57. Allen, "Money, the Mother's Milk of Politics," 3A.

58. Mark Burnett, "Is There an Iron Triangle in Maine's Labor Committee?" 9–12; Elizabeth Weimer, "Women's Groups Influencing the Legislature: On the National Level and in Maine," 40; Russell T. Jaquith, "Sportsman's Alliance of Maine: An In-Depth Look at the Local Level and the NRA," in Hodgkin, *Groups and PACs in Maine Politics*, 46–48.

59. Paul Cooper, "The Maine Banking Industry: A Case Study of Political Action Committees," 20–25; Jaquith, "Sportsman's Alliance of Maine," 46, both in Hodgkin, *Groups and PACs*.

60. Jeffery Bochenek and Abraham Grayzel, "Maine PACs: A Level Playing Field," in Hodgkin, *Groups and PACs*, 62.

byists contribute.[61] House Speaker Martin controls the Aroostook PAC to pay for his campaigning and unofficial duties as Speaker, as well as the Legislative House Campaign Fund. Counterparts of the latter exist for each party in each chamber. The head of the Taxation Committee, Representative John A. Cashman, sponsors JACPAC to support progrowth Democrats. Candidates for legislatively elected posts, such as attorney general, secretary of state, and state treasurer, raise funds to distribute to legislative candidates. Although these PACs may further the ambitions of their sponsors and provide access to leadership for their contributors, it can also be argued that the money distributed by these PACs to candidates strengthens the party role. The total contributions to 1988 Maine Senate contests by legislative leadership PACs and by party committees amounted to about $225,000 or about 25 percent of all receipts. The total for PAC and corporate contributions, at about $163,000, constituted about 18 percent. Although much of the party money may have originated with PACs, legislative candidates may be more grateful to the party than to special interests.[62] Of course, candidates may simply consider party support their due, and some contributions from individuals may be identified with special interests.

Legislative Lobbying

Maine groups employ all the traditional techniques to influence legislation. In a newspaper interview, lobbyist Donald H. Marden detailed his typical ten- to fourteen-hour working day as beginning with a stop at his Waterville law office, followed by meetings in Augusta with clients. Before the legislative session begins, he checks the posted bills and the legislative calendar and consults with legislative leaders and staff members about what information they may need. During the session, he compares notes with other lobbyists and meets with clients. In Maine, committees usually hold hearings and work sessions in the afternoon, and Marden juggles his attendance at these meetings or arranges for a client to attend. Then he returns

61. Nancy Perry, "PACs Bring Efficiency," 11A; Nancy Perry "Martin Uses Three Funds for Many Purposes," *Maine Sunday Telegram*, July 15, 1990, 11A; Quinn, "Lobbyists' Power Has Waned," 25.

62. Compilation of data for individual candidates and this interpretation are found in Brian Cleasby, "The Electoral Connection: The Importance of Party Campaign Contributions in Maine," in Hodgkin, *Groups and PACs*, 64–72.

to his Waterville office to do his paperwork and to prepare material for the next day. The reporter summarized,

> He says a good lobbyist needs to know the legislative process, to have political instincts, to know which legislators are effective and which aren't, to be able to keep track of bills and assess their ramifications for CMP or grocers.
>
> Half of a lobbyist's time, Marden says, is spent relaying information about legislation back to a client, rather than airing the client's views.[63]

A study conducted in the 1970s concluded that Maine organizations whose lobbying staff and membership interacted most with legislators were judged as most effective in the sense that they provided useful information. This conveyed legitimacy that translated into influence.[64]

Assessment of the actual influence of lobbying is anecdotal. Sometimes it seems to get results; at other times it fails. The *Maine Times* cited one instance: "Just how much pressure the lobbyists are applying can be seen by the 24-hour flip-flops on bills after a night of working the phones. The House flip-flop-flipped on a sales tax exemption for snow-making fuel and electricity [for ski-slope operators], 81–56 against, 70–68 for, and 81–49 against, on three consecutive days."[65]

Most Maine legislators do make a positive assessment of the role of organized interests in general. In a 1987 survey,[66] a strong majority (59 percent) believe that interest groups have the right amount of power and that the legislature would be worse (57 percent) or the same (23 percent) without interest groups. Legislators agree that lobbyists provide valuable specialized information about issues (96 percent), provide help in drafting bills and amendments (64 percent), and help line up support for bills (79 percent). On the other hand, 41 percent of the responding legislators did state that interest groups have been a problem in some way (Table 4.3).

---

63. Gerry Boyle, "Lobbyist Owes His Success to Patience and Long Hours," *Morning Sentinel* (Waterville), February 15, 1985, (annual business edition).

64. Deprez, "Internal Characteristics . . .," 133–135, 198.

65. "The Political Season," *Maine Times*, April 1, 1988, 12.

66. The questionnaire was mailed to all members of the 113th Legislature. Of 183 members (three vacancies), 79 responded, for a return rate of 43 percent.

Table 4.3. Maine Legislators' Perceptions of Groups as a Problem, 1987

Legislators' Perceptions	Percent (N = 79)
Groups have been a problem	39.2%
Too demanding, take too much time (15.2%)	
Too rigid and uncompromising (8.9)	
Deceitful, partial information (5.1)	
Oppose in election or misinform constituents (2.5)	
Cause legislators to misrepresent constituents (3.8)	
Other (1.3)	
No reason given (2.4)	
Groups have not been a problem	39.2
No response to the item (unusually high)	21.5
Total	100.0

Source: Questionnaire distributed by the author in 1987.

Probably the most significant change in lobbying techniques is the establishment of extensive networks or coalitions to coordinate their activities
and to extend their access, similar to Washington lobbying.[67] A Workers
Compensation Reform Committee included thirty-nine business organizations, such as the Maine Hospital Association, the Maine Restaurant Asso-
ciation, the National Federation of Independent Businesses, and the Maine
Grocers Association.[68] Among the dozen organizations in the Penobscot
Coalition to Save the West Branch (of the Penobscot River from the Big
A dam) were several environmental groups: the Sportsman's Alliance, the
Maine Council of Trout Unlimited, the Eastern Professional River Outfit-
ters Association, and rafting and boating organizations.[69] The Women's
Legislative Agenda Coalition includes thirty-two organizations, among
which are the Maine Women's Lobby; the League of Women Voters; the

67. Kay Lehman Schlozman and John T. Tierney, *Organized Interests and American
Democracy* (New York: Harper & Row, 1986), 278–79.

68. John Lovell, "Business Learns to Lobby," *Maine Sunday Telegram*, December
14, 1986, 44A; Nancy Perry, "Lobbyists Thrive on Comp Crisis," *Portland Press Herald*,
July 10, 1991, 1A, 8A.

69. Phyllis Austin, "Big A Strategies," *Maine Times*, March 1, 1985, 12.

National Organization for Women (NOW); organizations of university women, labor union women, displaced homemakers, nurses, the handicapped, and veterans; the Maine Coalition on Rape; the Alliance to Preserve Reproductive Choice; and the Maine Council of Churches.[70]

Group members themselves may be called on to join the lobbying effort. During the state government shutdown in July 1991, when the governor and the legislature were deadlocked on a budget and on workers' compensation, the state employees and other union members engaged in activities ranging from telephoning legislators to pounding on the governor's office door. They crammed the hallways of the statehouse, waving signs, chanting, and harassing Republican senators in particular. Their tent city in the park in front of the capitol building, and pickets along the streets, attracted national news coverage.

Administrative Lobbying

While lobbying organizations have traditionally focused on the legislature rather than on executive agencies to obtain their objectives,[71] now such bodies as the Public Utilities Commission, the Milk Commission, and the Board of Environmental Protection are more important policy-making arenas. Moreover, the decisions of regulatory agencies are no longer predictably sympathetic to business. As agency powers have developed, new procedures are put in place, and environmental and other competing lobbies take advantage of these, business lobbyists are paying more attention to "the Wednesday government"—the departments and agencies that publish proposed rules and regulations on that day.

The conditions for group influence in the bureaucracy are suggested in the Committee on State Government report on the Bureau of Insurance. There is little public input on insurance rates, and the required data are extremely complex and inaccessible. The resources of insurance companies are drawn from national companies, but interveners are limited to local resources. As a result,

70. Nancy Perry, "Women's Groups Unite on Money Issues," *Portland Press Herald*, January 13, 1984, 16; Kenneth Z. Chutchian, "Coalition to Fight Parental Consent Bill," *Kennebec Journal*, January 31, 1989, 5.

71. Deprez, "Internal Characteristics . . .," 244–45; James F. Horan et al., *Downeast Politics: The Government of the State of Maine* (Dubuque, Iowa: Kendall/Hunt, 1975), 68–69.

the Superintendent of Insurance is obligated to protect the solvency of the insurance industry. The evidence and perspective which the Superintendent evaluates are provided primarily from one very biased source, the insurance companies. With respect to all rate filings before the Superintendent, very seldom are perspectives and evidence provided by interveners in opposition to those of the insurance companies.[72]

On the other hand, the committee found environmental groups to be effective in hearings before the Board of Environmental Protection and the Land Use Regulation Commission: "Specifically the Natural Resources Council, the Audubon Society, local interest groups, and other public interest organizations actively participate in proceedings before these agencies. In addition, these 'intervenor organizations' are effective and perform a role very similar to that of the Public Advocate."[73]

Successful lobbying of the bureaucracy has indirect payoffs in the legislative process as well. A study of the forest management issue in the late 1970s revealed close relationships among the personnel of the timber industry, the Forestry Department, and the Forestry School at the University of Maine at Orono. A united front was maintained, and the industry was able to prevent transmittal of information to the legislature in a classic illustration of "non-decision-making." Thus, "policy decisions are removed from the Legislature by value judgments made within the bureaucracy."[74]

On the other hand, lobbyists who have difficulty with the bureaucracy may seek redress in the legislature. Business groups, complaining that the Department of Environmental Protection takes too long to process applications for projects, sought to streamline the process, with legislation setting deadlines for each stage.[75]

One pervasive problem may be conflicts of interest caused by service of industry representatives on some business and professional regulatory boards. For example, by state law, the seven-member Pesticides Control

72. Maine Legislature, Joint Standing Committee on State Government, *An Expanded Role for the Public Advocate* (Augusta, Me., January 1984), 8.

73. Ibid., 3.

74. Todd Anthony Robinson, "Policy Formation of Timber Industry Related Bills in the Maine State Legislature," (Honors thesis, Bates College, 1979), 121–36; quotation at 132.

75. Randy Wilson, "Who's Really Pulling the Strings?" 21.

Board includes a pesticides applicator, two pesticide users, and an expert on insects and pesticides. Although a legislative report suggested reorganization, the legislative oversight committee is the Agriculture Committee, itself composed of many pesticide and herbicide users.[76]

The Courts

Undoubtedly, groups are interested in the policy-making of the courts, but their activity in that arena is much less visible than elsewhere. One group that is relatively ineffective before the legislature, but with some chance in the courts, is the Maine Civil Liberties Union. "[It] persuaded a Superior Court justice that the wholesale practice of searching canoeists on the Saco River for drugs is unconstitutional. . . .The MCLU is also involved in a class-action suit over conditions at the Augusta Mental Health Institute."[77]

The Conservation Law Foundation, the Island Institute, and the Maine Audubon Society recently sued the city of Westbrook and the Portland Water District for discharges into Casco Bay under Section 505 of the Clean Water Act. Jeff Thaler, an environmental attorney, believed the suit would prompt the state Department of Environmental Protection to stiffen its resolve in regulating these units, as well as to clamp down on other smaller communities that were violating their discharge permits. Such suits are viewed as an important form of citizen access.[78]

Mothers Against Drunk Driving (MADD) seems to have been particularly effective in Maine with its program of monitoring drunk-driving cases. According to a National Highway Traffic Safety Administration study of Maine cases, where MADD's monitors have been present, "there is a higher conviction rate, sentences and fines are slightly higher, and there are fewer plea bargains to lesser charges, such as driving to endanger."[79]

76. Christine Kukka, "Conflict of Interest: Can You Get Expertise Without Bias?" *Maine Times*, October 6, 1989, 16–18.

77. "More Card Carriers in Maine," *Maine Times*, April 21, 1989, 2.

78. David D. Platt, "If Environmental Protection Falters, Citizen Lawsuits Will Fill the Gap," *Maine Times*, May 24, 1991, 8–9.

79. Randy Wilson, "Getting MADD Means Going to Court," *Maine Times*, October 19, 1990, 13.

INTEREST-GROUP POWER

As the interest-group system in Maine has become more diverse, has influence on policy-making itself become more dispersed? What is the relative influence of individual groups?

Legislators are in a strategic position to make such assessments. Although these estimates are subjective and may rely on group reputations, members can subject these reputations to a reality test as they observe and participate in legislative outcomes. Maine legislators in 1987 were asked which groups were most influential and how much influence each of several listed groups had in the Maine Legislature (a lot, some, a little, or none). The results are presented in Table 4.4: the groups with the lowest average scores are deemed most influential.[80]

Economic Interests

Of the old Big Three, only paper and power fare well in the responses. Spontaneous mention of the paper companies seems relatively low, although legislators did give them the fourth strongest rating when asked directly. The forest products industry accounted for twenty-three lobbyist registrations in 1991, including such individual companies as International Paper, Boise Cascade, and Scott Paper, as well as trade associations, such as the Maine Forest Products Council and the Paper Industry Information Office. The industry seems to have declined in visibility with diversification of the state's economy, stronger environmental safeguards, and foreign (particularly Canadian) competition for markets. Because the perception of the "omnipotence" of the paper companies lingers,[81] the Maine Forest Products Council recently mounted public relations activities and more visible participation in the political process to com-

80. Republican and Democratic legislators differ on estimation of the influence of groups; see Horan et al., *Downeast Politics*, 58. Because Republicans are overrepresented among the respondents in the 1987 survey, the average power rating in Table 4.4 is weighted for party. On no other data reported here did the parties differ significantly.

81. There is an extensive literature that details the power the paper industry has wielded in Maine politics. See, e.g., Lockard, *New England State Politics*, 107–10; Neal R. Peirce, *The New England States* (New York: W. W. Norton, 1976), 406–11; and a Ralph Nader study, William C. Osborn, *The Paper Plantation* (New York: Grossman, 1974).

Table 4.4. Interest Groups Most Frequently Named by Legislators as Very Influential in Maine Politics, 1974 and 1987

Interest Group	No. of Mentions 1974	No. of Mentions 1987	Weighted Avg. Power Score 1987
Labor (including AFL-CIO)	21	54	1.51
Maine Teachers Assn	24	40	1.50
Environmentalists (also Maine Audubon & Natural Resources Council)	13	30	1.50
Sportsmen	11	27	—
Utilities (also CMP and telephone)	18	21	1.73
(Big) Business (also Chamber of Commerce / Industry and Maine Merchants)	7	21	2.04
Maine Municipal Assn (local gov'ts)	4	18	1.70
Insurance (also Blue Cross / Shield)	19	17	1.86
Paper companies	20	16	1.59
Maine State Employees Assn	16	15	1.90
Medicine (also hospitals)	7	14	2.07
Banks	15	10	1.87
Low-income / human services	3	8	2.37
Christian Civic League	—	7	—
Elderly, retired	3	7	2.03
Highways and truckers	29	6	2.01
Antinuclear groups	—	6	—
Women's groups	12	6	1.95
Real estate	—	6	2.31
Liquor	19	5	2.12
Farmers	5	5	2.42
School management	—	5	—
Veterans	4	3	—
Maine Impact Coalition	—	3	—
Lawyers	5	2	1.84
Churches	9	1	2.66

Table 4.4. *Continued*

Interest Group	No. of Mentions 1974	No. of Mentions 1987	Weighted Avg. Power Score 1987
Executive departments	3	1	1.70
Railroads	3	0	2.65

Sources: For 1974, James F. Horan et al., *Downeast Politics: The Government of the State of Maine* (Dubuque, Iowa: Kendall / Hunt, 1975), 57; for 1987, a questionnaire distributed by the author.

Notes: Included are groups or categories with three or more mentions in either year. Not included for both years are several mentions of "MMA," which could stand for Maine Municipal Association, Maine Medical Association, or Maine Merchants Association, all of which were mentioned by other legislators. The 1987 average power score is weighted by party to adjust for different response rates and is based on 1 = "a lot," 2 = "some," 3 = "a little," and 4 = "none."

bat "widespread ignorance of forestry's complexity and indifference to its needs."[82]

Many paper companies now are controlled by national or international corporations, and none of them is solely owned within the state. Whereas the former in-state leadership was vitally interested in state policies and monitored government actions closely, more distant executives now are less likely to take a direct interest. They hire professional lobbyists where necessary and may have substantial impact there, but they leave a vacuum on many issues for other interests to occupy.

Legislators also perceived the utilities as a powerful segment, with Central Maine Power Company (CMP) and New England Telephone receiving individual mention. Each has been involved in visible, expensive campaigns against initiative questions to close the Maine Yankee nuclear power plant and to prohibit local measured telephone service, respectively. CMP and Maine Yankee accounted for eight lobby registrations in 1991, with other utilities contributing twenty-three more. Their lobbyists are considered among the most prestigious and skillful.[83]

Changes in the economy have undermined the lobbying coalitions be-

82. Carrier, "Out of the Woods," 12A.
83. For more on the past power of the utilities, see Lockard, *New England State Politics*, 110–12; and Peirce, *The New England States*, 392–95.

tween the paper companies and utilities, however. For example, the energy crisis created opposing interests between them. Whereas the paper companies benefited from cheap power, and the utilities welcomed trouble-free volume business, this changed as energy prices soared and paper companies began generating their own power. "The paper companies are now interveners, if not adversaries, in utility CMP cases involving general rate increases, cogeneration and small power producer rates, dam development projects and CMP corporate rate reorganization."[84]

Legislators mentioned neither the textile nor the shoe manufacturing industries as major interests. They no longer are major employers in the state; plants have been established elsewhere in the country, and foreign competition absorbed much of the domestic market. These industries had no direct lobbying representation in 1985 and 1991. This element of the Big Three seems to have virtually disappeared from the political scene.

"Business" is mentioned as an important interest, with most references specifically to the Maine Chamber of Commerce and Industry. Increasingly, however, individual businesses are hiring their own lobbyists rather than relying solely on trade associations; in addition, their own executives spend more time lobbying. Business lobbyists are becoming more sophisticated, and their presence is more regular. They are also involved in a greater variety of issues. As reporter John Lovell put it,

> Legislators, legislative aides, business leaders and lobbyists all agree that business interests are spending more money, as well as more time, on lawmaking. They say there are more lobbyists than there were a few years ago, that the lobbyists are spending more, and that corporate political action committees are increasing in number and contributing more to legislative candidates.[85]

Business claims that its power is limited, however, by dispersal of power from leadership and committee chairs, by the hostility of a Democratic-controlled legislature, and by the counterlobbying by environmental interests.[86]

Other specific business interests have been influential. Although highway interests were ranked first in 1974, they are hardly mentioned in 1987

84. Phyllis Austin, "Paper and Power," *Maine Times*, March 22, 1985, 30.
85. Lovell, "Business Learns to Lobby," 44A.
86. Quinn, "Lobbyists' Power Has Waned," 25.

(Table 4.4). In 1991 they were represented by the Maine Better Transportation Association, the Maine Motor Transport Association, Merrill Industries, and indirectly by Associated General Contractors. The Maine Good Roads Association has been active in support of bond issues for highway construction. The banking and insurance industries continue to receive prominent mention as influential interests. In 1991 banking accounted for only seven lobby registrations; insurance contributed twenty-nine, a jump from the seventeen of 1985. A notable array of thirty-three lobby registrations in 1991 represent the health community, including the variety of professionals, hospitals, and other providers. Hospital involvement was stimulated by recent legislation and regulations aimed at cost containment.

Three interests that are notable for their absence from assessments of powerful groups, given the nature of the state's economy, are fishing, tourism, and agriculture. To some extent, each is plagued by smallness of scale, diversity, and rivalries. A former commissioner of the Department of Marine Resources illustrated this with a description of fishing industry conflicts: "You've got the lobstermen versus the scallopers, the autotrawlers versus the gillnetters and the shrimpers, the seiners versus the gillnetters, the clammers versus the musselmen, the lobstermen versus the draggers and the purse seiners. There's the charter boats versus the gillnetters, the lobstermen versus the musselmen. . . ."[87] Nevertheless, the strong leadership provided by Edward A. Blackmore as executive director of the Maine Lobstermen's Association enabled that group to win a few victories on issues of direct interest.[88]

Farmers rate few mentions among the powerful interests and receive the third weakest average rating in 1987 (Table 4.4). Some legislators do seem to be conscious of farm interests among their constituents and attempt to represent them. Opposition, however, comes from wholesale and retail interests, whom some see as providing indirect representation of consumer interests. For example, "There was a time, back before there was any such thing as Cumberland Farms or store brand milk, when Maine's dairies told the Maine Milk Commission they needed a price hike and got it," but no longer.[89] The Grange, once a powerful force, now has only its chief elected

87. Jeff Clark, "Gear Conflicts," *Maine Times*, May 18, 1984, 18.
88. Clarke Canfield, "State Lobstermen Lose Their Powerful Voice," *Maine Sunday Telegram*, July 28, 1991, 1B, 12B. Blackmore has announced his retirement.
89. Scott Allen, "The Commission Keeps Trying," *Maine Times*, September 7, 1984, 16. See also Maine Legislature, Joint Standing Committee on State Govern-

officer as a part-time lobbyist. No longer serving as the social and civic center of rural communities, its membership has declined significantly.[90]

A study of agricultural policy-making in Maine concludes that farm lobbyists do develop close relationships with Agriculture Committee members and provide valuable information in work sessions. However, farm lobbyists tend to be part-time or to represent a multiplicity of interests, agriculture being only one. Moreover, agriculture does not participate in the electoral process.[91]

A striking finding is the power attributed to labor unions (see Table 4.4). Listed among the top groups in 1974, labor (including the AFL-CIO) now is most frequently mentioned, with additional specific mentions of the Maine State Employees Association (MSEA) and the Maine Teachers Association (MTA). Labor, the MTA, and environmentalists were in a virtual three-way tie for the strongest average power rating among the groups listed. This comes despite a slight decline in the number of unions registering lobbyists (Table 4.1).

Despite a changing economy that might have undermined the unions' role, union power seems to survive. Thirty years ago, one-third of Maine workers were members, but in 1986 only about 15 percent were organized.[92] As noted, the textile and shoe industries have cut back sharply. The paper companies are adopting laborsaving machinery; some intense battles, including extended strikes and public relations campaigns, have emerged as managements seek wage cuts and more authority to assign workers. The rapidly expanding service economy is unorganized. Reporter Scott Allen noted:

> Increasingly, organized labor is an object of criticism. The left criticizes labor for being undemocratic while the right sees unions as archaic. In the middle, the general public has turned on the unions, having little sympathy for people who make $15 an hour

---

ment, *An Expanded Role for the Public Advocate*, 4.

90. Karen Hamilton, "Granges Are Sowing New Seeds," *Sunday Sun-Journal*, October 8, 1989, 1E, 7E.

91. Liebman, "Subsystem Government," 70–76.

92. Union membership of 81,935 in 1990 is minimally changed from the 80,848 in 1986. See John W. Porter, "Crystal Ball on Labor," *Maine Sunday Telegram*, September 1, 1991, 5F.

and then go on strike. Consequently, labor's issues have become politically unpopular.[93]

Labor has adapted by forging alliances with other liberal groups, including low-income groups, women, and environmentalists, according to the nature of the issue. Moreover, a strong bond with the Democratic party legislative leadership provides special advantages in legislative decision-making. Questionnaire comments of two Republican legislators as to why they believed labor interests to be strong illustrate this assessment:

> The Democrats control both the House and Senate. Past and present legislative sessions have demonstrated a willingness on the part of the Democrats to assume a prolabor posture.

> The current leadership of the House and Senate. Labor through leadership sees to it the members vote the party line on workers comp. no matter what the issue.

On the other hand, a Republican Governor McKernan now serves as a check by vetoing some labor-backed bills to the point that in labor circles he has become known as "Governor McVeto." Moreover, legislative Republicans and the governor refused to approve a budget containing tax increases for the 1991–92 fiscal year until Democrats made concessions on workers compensation legislation. President Charles O'Leary of the state AFL-CIO was so angry that the Democrats did make compromises that he called for a new party.[94]

The Maine Teachers Association has achieved a powerful rating, as have teachers in many states. They have respected lobbyists and they have a large, active, skillful membership. In election campaigns, their endorsement seems most valuable as a source of workers and votes, and they are becoming an important source of financial contributions.

93. Scott Allen, "Adjusting to a Hostile World," Maine Times, September 5, 1986, 2. See also Clark T. Irwin Jr., "Labor Unions Fighting for New Life," Maine Sunday Telegram, September 6, 1987, 1C, 4C.

94. Associated Press, "AFL-CIO Calls for Third Party," Maine Sunday Telegram, July 28, 1991, 3B. O'Leary later backed off from this threat. Patrick McTeague, legal counsel for the AFL-CIO, has suggested that, to put pressure on Democrats, labor might become more active in Democratic primaries and even back some Republican candidates. Porter, "Crystal Ball on Labor," 1F.

Citizen and Public-Interest Groups

Environmental and antinuclear groups have emerged as influential actors in Maine politics. The two leading organizations of the environmental lobby, the Maine Audubon Society and the Natural Resources Council, now have substantial memberships and budgets. The two organizations seem to have divided issue responsibilities. "The NRCM has focused on growth management, solid waste, toxics, and energy policy, among others, while Maine Audubon has targeted forest practices, pesticides, sand dunes, ocean pollution, and protection of endangered species."[95]

Both groups have developed considerable corporate and business connections, both on their boards and in funding. They claim that they need such resources for "staff-based legal and scientific research that can no longer be funded solely from the nickels and dimes of members" and that they prefer to focus resources on major issues. Their critics claim they have lost touch with citizen activists and "have abdicated leadership on key issues such as nuclear power, forest practices and pesticides, issues closely identified with strong corporate interests in Maine."[96] Recently, budget constraints have required Maine Audubon to cut back its lobbying, litigation, and research in favor of more traditional activities, "such as education, field trips, wildlife sanctuaries, and 'environmental citizenship' that emphasizes recycling and other 'lifestyle changes.'"[97]

The most prominent antinuclear power group is the Maine Nuclear Referendum Committee, which, as noted above, has sponsored five petition drives to place initiatives on the ballot. Other groups emerged in response to the U.S. Department of Energy's proposal to locate nuclear waste dumps in Maine, the most prominent being Citizens Against Nuclear Trash (CANT). These groups were able to raise substantial funds, turn out supporters at hearings, and convince several state politicians to change their positions on nuclear issues.[98]

On the legislator survey, environmental groups received large numbers of mentions as influential groups and achieved the strongest average influ-

95. Randy Wilson, "Retrenchment or Redirection? Maine Audubon Copes with a Budget Shortfall," *Maine Times*, July 6, 1990, 14.

96. Randy Wilson, "The Perils of Success," *Maine Times*, March 13, 1987, 2, 4. Everett B. Carson, executive director of the NRCM responded in a letter, "Clear Conscience," *Maine Times*, April 3, 1987, 12.

97. Wilson, "Retrenchment or Redirection?" 14.

98. Scott Allen, "The Nuclear Debate," *Maine Times*, March 21, 1986, 3–5.

ence rating (see Table 4.4). They are respected in part for well-researched positions presented in legislative and administrative hearings, but the most important factor seems to be a broad consensus in Maine in support of environmental issues. "Independent polls and legislators' own constituent surveys that showed upwards of 80 percent of Mainers supporting strong recycling laws helped win passage of a comprehensive solid waste bill with an expansion of the state's bottle law to cover juice, wine and liquor bottles."[99]

The environmentalist position now has a powerful ally in the Sportsman's Alliance of Maine (SAM), a large and growing organization dedicated to preserving the rights of hunters and fishermen, including the right to own and use guns. The group has served as the state's gun lobby, but it has also emphasized its conservationist goals by aligning with environmentalists on construction of dams and usually on the preservation of wildlife. When they do enter such an alliance, they constitute a powerful force, for legislators perceive SAM as representing "a more rural, less affluent sector of Maine's population" than Maine Audubon and the Nuclear Referendum Committee. "So when all three groups line up behind a bill, legislators obviously feel it has wide support."[100]

Sportsmen received only eleven mentions in the 1974 survey, but by 1987 they were much more prominent. SAM was founded in 1975 and has provided organization, the resources of mass membership, and a skillful full-time lobbyist. Many members are active and contact their legislators. The group also rates legislators' voting records and endorses candidates, while its national affiliate, the National Rifle Association Political Victory Fund, makes campaign contributions. Its membership doubled when it fought an initiative to ban moose hunting, and its image was enhanced with defeat of the proposal. It also successfully backed a state constitutional amendment to clarify the right to keep and bear arms, and legislation for the state to preempt local governments from adopting their own gun regulations. They also receive backing from the Democratic House Speaker and Senate president, both representing rural, northern districts.[101]

Consumers have little specific lobbying representation among Maine in-

99. Joe Rankin, "Environmental Lobby Is Small but Effective," *Kennebec Journal,* July 7, 1989, 7.

100. Dennis Bailey, "Maine Sportsmen Take Their Case to Augusta," *Maine Sunday Telegram,* May 22, 1983, 27A.

101. Randy Wilson, "Taking Aim: The Gun Lobby Still Calls the Shots in Maine," *Maine Times,* April 13, 1990, 8.

terest groups: "Maine's consumer lobby is all but non-existent in the State House, Northeast COMBAT and the Public Interest Research Group having abandoned their Augusta operations years ago. And Pine Tree Legal, the law firm that represents low income clients, has been one advocate short in Augusta since 1981, because of federal budget cuts."[102] The Maine People's Alliance is concerned with a variety of issues, including consumer problems. The only "consumer" organization to register as such during the 1985 legislative session was the Maine Telephone Users Association, which emerged during the contest concerning the adoption of local measured service. It turned out to be connected with the Savings Bank Association, indicating it represented large consumers. The "consumer" organization registered in 1991 was the Industrial Energy Consumer Group.

As alternatives to specific consumer organization, the consumer movement now seems to work through two devices. First, it may be represented by coalitions of groups, such as Consumers for Affordable Health Care, a coalition of twenty-six health, labor, women's, and senior groups.[103] Second, the state bureaucracy now has institutions dedicated to consumer interests, including the Consumer Credit Protection Bureau and a public advocate in the Public Utilities Commission. In addition, "citizen advisory groups oversee various parts of the government. The Administrative Procedures Act, setting out guidelines for the conduct of regulatory business, has 'had a tremendous effect on the state,' according to Lance Tapley, the former director of Common Cause."[104]

The number of specific civic and religious organizations registering lobbyists has expanded greatly (Table 4.1), although many of the organizations registered in 1985 were not in 1991. Those with some continuity include such groups as the Christian Civic League, the Family Planning Association, the United Way, the Maine People's Alliance, and the Maine Women's Lobby.

The Maine Women's Lobby provides the only full-time paid lobbyist on women's issues, although the Maine League of Women Voters has also initiated active lobbying recently. Both are active in the Women's Legislative Agenda Coalition, an umbrella group of about thirty-two organizations. The Maine NOW PAC gives election campaign contributions.

At the conservative end of the spectrum on such social issues as abortion

102. Allen, "Money, the Mother's Milk of Politics," 3A.
103. "The Political Season," *Maine Times*, May 19, 1989, 5.
104. Allen, "Money, the Mother's Milk of Politics," 7A.

and gay rights is the Christian Civic League (CCL), claiming about 8,000 members. Under its current executive director, Jasper Wyman, the group has deemphasized its historical liquor prohibition stand and broadened its legislative agenda, such as support for funding for rape-counseling centers and for prisons.[105] The organization achieved a reputation for influence with the defeat of a state equal-rights amendment but then lost its initiative to ban obscene materials. A few legislators did cite the League as among the state's powerful interests.

At the other end of the religious spectrum, the Maine Council of Churches takes liberal positions on issues. Its most visible achievement was its two successful campaigns against maximum-security-prison bond issues.[106]

THE DISPERSAL OF INFLUENCE

This review demonstrates that the influence of Maine interest groups does not depend solely on money and skilled lobbyists. Legislators mentioned a broad distribution of reasons for the influence of various organizations (Table 4.5). Because no single resource is necessary for influence, many kinds of interests may play the game.

A few legislators emphasized that interest-group influence not only is derived from a variety of resources but also is issue-specific. Some qualified their responses by noting that they observed groups only in connection with their own committee assignments or with bills they had sponsored, indicating that other groups were active in other areas. One legislator summarized this view by noting, "Lobbies are effective on some issues, ineffective on others, depending on a host of factors."

Certainly some groups are more influential than others. The paper companies and labor unions can marshal substantial resources to gain access and to shape policy. Legislators noted other groups, such as gay-rights advocates and the poor, that lack much influence. Nevertheless, the collection of powerful voices in Maine's capital now includes not only the paper

105. Scott Evan Allen, "A New Vision," Maine Times, March 2, 1984, 16–17; Glenn Adams, "Civic League Works on Conciliatory Image," Kennebec Journal, February 10, 1987, 10.

106. Randy Wilson, "Churches Find Outlet for Social Conscience," Maine Times, October 19, 1990, 12.

Table 4.5. Maine Legislators' Explanations for Group Influence, 1987

Explanations	Percent of Responses	Percent of Legislators
Number of members	11.2%	16.7%
Membership commitment, activity	9.3	13.9
Constituency pressure, elections	10.3	15.3
Money for campaign contributions and lobbyists	15.0	22.2
Well-organized	5.6	8.3
Lobbyist skills, effort, presence	20.6	30.6
Lobbyist provision of information	6.5	9.7
Issue popular, clear, emotional	7.5	11.1
Access to legislative leadership or members	14.0	20.8
Total	100.0	148.6

Source: Questionnaire distributed by the author in 1987.

Note: $N = 107$ responses from 72 legislators.

companies, utilities, and other business interests but also labor, teachers, environmentalists, sportsmen, local governments, and many others.

As indicated in Table 1.1 of this book, myriad factors influence the interest-group system in Maine and elsewhere. The state policy domain affects which groups are active; when Maine sought to contain medical costs or extended the bottle bill to juice containers, lobbies for the hospitals and for aseptic packaging interests entered the fray. As policy-making decentralized from the national government and centralized from local governments, Maine government grew with a concomitant intensification of lobbying in the state capitol building.

Lobbying activity is somewhat restrained by the state's moralistic culture as well as by strong environmentalism and suspicion about concentrated power. Government restructuring and professionalization, as well as increased party competition, provide other constraints. The state has tightened its public-disclosure laws. On the other hand, the parties are weaker in the face of voter independence and candidate-centered campaigning, while the costs of gubernatorial and state legislative campaigns are rising sharply. These trends allow more group access, and the lobbies are becoming more sophisticated.

Therefore, while interest groups remain moderately influential in Maine, the lobbying system has been transformed. No longer do the Big Three dominate the policy-making process. Increased economic and social pluralism have provided the base for a broader representation of interests. The Big Three themselves have changed with internal competition and economic setbacks. A competitive party system and a more volatile electorate keep power relationships fluid. It is apparent that the Maine political system now is characterized by substantial diversity.

Funds from a Roger C. Schmutz Faculty Research Grant at Bates College supported the collection of questionnaire data used in this chapter. Research assistants Ross H. Josephson and Peter F. Carr II gathered other information.

5

Maryland: The Struggle for Power in the Midst of Change, Complexity, and Institutional Constraints

Ronald C. Lippincott and Larry W. Thomas

In its development, Maryland has reflected some of the major changes in the broader American society. As one of the original thirteen colonies, Maryland was founded as a religious refuge for Catholics. Its early economy was basically agricultural, although Baltimore City provided the basis for port commerce. While technically a "Northern state" during the Civil War, numerous Maryland landowners were slaveholders. Maryland participated in the urbanization and industrialization of the nation, with large numbers of European immigrants and Southern blacks moving into the state and working in its rapidly developing manufacturing economy. Currently, Maryland is coping with a new set of national trends—basic decisions about the level of taxation and the scope of government services, structural shifts in its economy, the growth of suburbia, the continued degradation of its environment (particularly the Chesapeake Bay), and the threatened decline of Baltimore, its aging major city.

The complexity of a state's socioeconomic system, the structure of its political institutions, and the character of the decision-making processes affect interest-group domination of the policy process. The greater the economic and social diversity of a state, the more competitive its political parties, the more professional its bureaucracy, and the more centralized the decision-making process of the legislative and executive branches of government, the less likely that any one group (or small number of groups) can dominate the policy process.[1] This chapter examines interest groups in this diverse, complex state by analyzing how (1) the socioeconomic and

---

1. L. Harmon Zeigler, "Interest Groups in the States," in Virginia Gray, Herbert Jacob, and Kenneth N. Vines, eds., *Politics in the American States*, 4th ed. (Boston: Little, Brown, 1983), 111–23.

political environment of the state, (2) the institutional rules for lobbying, (3) the kinds of interest groups and their lobbying expenditures, (4) the characteristics of the state's lobbyists, (5) lobbying techniques and their effectiveness, (6) perceptions about the functioning of the interest-group system, and (7) interest-group power in Maryland affect interest-group activity.

THE SOCIOECONOMIC AND POLITICAL ENVIRONMENT

Maryland is a small state geographically (ranking 42nd), but its dense population (ranking 6th) manifests an important characteristic: social heterogeneity and religious diversity. Whites, who constitute approximately 75 percent of the population, exhibit significant ethnic diversity (for example, Polish, Italian, Greek), while the percentage of blacks (23 percent) is nearly double the national average. In terms of religion, the state is largely Protestant, with a significant Roman Catholic minority and one of the largest Jewish populations (4.8 percent) of any state in the nation. The social heterogeneity often provides the basis for the formation of single-issue interest groups that lobby on such topics as abortion, gun control, and capital punishment.

A second important dimension of the environment is the structure of Maryland's economy. Employment in the state is distributed across diverse categories: service-related (27 percent); trade (26 percent); government (18.6 percent); manufacturing (10.4 percent); construction (7.5 percent); finance, insurance, and real estate (6 percent); and transportation and communications (4.5 percent).[2] This heterogeneity has spawned a variety of interest groups that frequently exert countervailing pressures against one another.

This economic diversity was once considered to be a safeguard against a sharp downturn, but Maryland is currently emerging from a severe recession, which spanned 1990 and 1991. Causes of the economic slump included a decline in defense contracts, a contracting federal work force, a glut of commercial real estate, and a downturn in the construction indus-

---

2. Maryland Department of Community and Economic Development, *Maryland Statistical Abstract 1990–1991*, 16.

try.[3] The recession touched even white-collar workers—their taxable income went down[4] and their unemployment rate went up[5]—a sector of the economy previously considered relatively insulated. This poor economic performance intersected a structural transformation in Maryland's economy, particularly the growth in the service sector, which generates relatively few high-paying jobs.[6] Moreover, the shift in consumer spending from goods to services has continually narrowed state sales tax revenue, because most professional services—that is, legal, medical, and educational—are exempt from the state's taxing authority. The fiscal consequences of this situation are clear: declining tax revenue.

The economic situation has combined with Maryland's liberal "social contract"[7] to produce the foremost policy issue confronting the state—budget deficits. Traditionally, many citizens have expected the state to "provide a social safety net for the poorest and neediest and an array of services for middle-class Marylanders, especially a vast infusion of funds for public schools."[8] The services were supported by Maryland's prosperous economy in past years, but with tax revenues falling and expenditures rising in the areas of aid to local government, public assistance, Medicaid, other health and social programs, and public safety,[9] the governor's budget cuts in fiscal years 1991 and 1992 totaled approximately $1 billion.[10] Approval of the most recent state budget (fiscal year 1993) involved a cut of approximately $487 million in the governor's original budget proposal and approval of a package of taxes that presumably will increase revenues by nearly half a billion dollars.[11]

Despite the budget cuts and tax increases made for fiscal year 1993,

3. Barry Rascovar, "In Maryland, It Is the Worst of Times," *Baltimore Sun*, August 11, 1991, 3G.

4. "Maryland: Now the Cuts Hit Home" *Washington Post*, October 20, 1991, C-6.

5. Timothy J. Mullaney, "Sliding Off the Fast Track," *Baltimore Sun–Maryland Business Weekly*, October 21, 1991, 8–10.

6. Barry Rascovar, "Still, Marylanders Just Don't Get It," *Baltimore Sun*, October 6, 1991, 3G.

7. Barry Rascovar, "Renegotiating Maryland's Social Contract," *Baltimore Sun*, October 20, 1991, 3G.

8. Ibid.

9. John W. Frece, "Maryland Deficits May Trigger Cuts, Taxes," *Baltimore Sun*, August 2, 1991, 1C–2C.

10. Frederick W. Derrick and Charles E. Scott, "A Better Way to Close Maryland's Budget Gap," *Baltimore Sun*, October 15, 1991, 11A.

11. John W. Free and Marina Sarris, "Budget Passes But Tax Boosts Will Jolt Many," *Baltimore Sun*, April 11, 1992, 1A.

Maryland's fiscal problems persist. An additional $56.5 million had to be cut from the state budget in order to end fiscal year 1992 in balance, and estimates of the state deficit for the current fiscal year (1993) already range from $170 million to $240 million.[12] The state's recovery from the recession, which has been uneven,[13] may be contributing to the state's continuing fiscal problems. While the Governor's Commission on Efficiency and Economy in Government is currently attempting to find savings in state government, it is likely that the recurrence of a major deficit in the state budget will again confront Maryland citizens with fundamental decisions about the future scope of government and the level of taxes.

Regardless of Maryland's budget situation, the link between the economic structure of the state and the fiscal situation is ironic, because economic development has been a recent policy emphasis in the state government. With decreasing employment in the area of traditional mass manufacturing, and increasing awareness that much economic growth involves small and medium-size firms in advanced manufacturing, biotechnology, computer software, and other high-tech sectors of the economy, the state has attempted to stimulate high-tech development by establishing an Office of Technology, creating a privately managed seed venture capital industry, and attempting to reorganize and increase the funding for the state's higher education system.[14] Such a restructuring of the state's economy would, it is hoped, help replace the high-income mass-manufacturing jobs that have been lost, thereby providing more substantial employment for the state's citizens and a firmer tax base to fund state services. Unfortunately, the capacity of the higher education system to provide the institutional basis for training a high-tech work force is in doubt, because of recent severe budget cuts.

The state's fiscal situation is likely to exacerbate other policy issues related to another major characteristic of the state's environment—its disparity in wealth. While Maryland has one of the highest per capita incomes (in 1987, $18,174) in the United States, regional per capita income differences within the state are significant: the suburbs of Baltimore City and Washington, D.C. ($18,679); Baltimore City ($14,549); Eastern

12. Marina Sarris, "Schaefer Complains Local Jurisdictions May Be Wasteful with Funds from State," *Baltimore Sun*, July 23, 1992, 3B.

13. Kim Clark, "Marylander's Income Outpaces Inflation," *Baltimore Sun*, July 23, 1992, 13C.

14. Tim Baker, "Needed: A High-Tech Council," *Baltimore Sun*, November 21, 1988, 7A.

Shore / Southern Maryland ($14,459); and Western Maryland ($12,388).[15] Moreover, the percentage of poor families in the suburbs (4.3 percent) is very low, compared with Baltimore City (18.9 percent).[16]

The regional income data suggest a basic cleavage between the "haves" and the "have-nots." State generosity concerning the needy has been an ongoing area of dispute,[17] and conflicts over welfare policy will likely intensify in light of recent cuts in family welfare programs and General Program Assistance. A basic political reality is symbolized by the "Baltimore-bashing" that has involved some suburban legislators representing Montgomery County, the fifth richest county, per capita, in the United States.[18] State aid to local governments, which accounts for 40 percent of the state's budget,[19] was recently cut, resulting in reductions of varying amounts for Maryland counties and Baltimore City. This situation may intensify concerns about the relative contributions the various localities make to state revenues and about the formulas that determine the return of money in the form of state aid. Of course, underlying any such conflict is the variation in wealth between the state's regions.

In addition to socioeconomic factors, Maryland has certain political characteristics that affect interest groups. First, executive and legislative decision-making is relatively centralized. The governor plays a significant role in the policy process through the power to appoint cabinet members, through the legislative veto, and through an executive budget process.[20] In

15. Maryland Department of Community and Economic Development, *Maryland Statistical Abstract*, 1990–91, 14.

16. Ibid., 152.

17. Robert Barnes and John Lancaster, "For Wealthy State, the Question Is How Well It Takes Care of Its Own," *Washington Post*, January 8, 1989, D-1, D-5.

18. Barry Rascovar, "A Technician Departs," *Baltimore Sun*, November 21, 1988, 7A.

19. "Cutting School Budgets," *Baltimore Sun*, October 24, 1990, 8A.

20. In Maryland the state constitution authorizes the governor to submit a budget, which the legislature can cut but not add to. However, the budget process has become enmeshed in conflict. In response to California Proposition 13, the legislature approved a law (in 1982) that established the Spending Affordability Committee, the function of which is to formulate an advisory limit on government spending by the state. The committee has pursued this objective by tying growth of the state budget to growth in personal income. In addition to methodological issues concerning estimates of personal income growth and calculations about "base" budget figures, the law has caused a conflict over budgetary authority between the current governor and the legislature. The dispute has also touched a long-standing issue in Maryland politics: funding programs

the legislature the Speaker of the House and the president of the Senate, who are elected by a caucus of the majority party in each house, have the power to appoint all committee members, to designate committee chairpersons, and to control the schedule of legislation in their respective chambers. Also, committee chairs exercise significant control over both the content of bills and the determination of which bills are ultimately considered by the committee. This centralization not only causes interest groups to focus on the legislative leadership and relevant committee members in their lobbying, but also presents a formidable obstacle to interest-group dominance of the political system in Maryland.

A second political characteristic of the state is its large bureaucracy. Approximately 89,300 people (11 percent of the state's work force) are employed by state agencies, and about half of these people hold managerial, technical, or professional positions, indicating a relatively high degree of professionalism among state employees. Finally, state agencies are quite active in lobbying, a situation that is likely to intensify in response to recent cuts in the state work force.

A third political characteristic is Maryland's electoral tendencies. With the exception of a few moderate-to-liberal Republican governors and U.S. senators, the Democratic party has dominated the state. Recently, however, Maryland has begun to exhibit "split-level" electoral tendencies, shifting to the Republicans at the presidential level but voting strongly Democratic for other offices. A significant Republican vote in the state's growing suburbs provided the basis for Reagan and Bush victories in the last two presidential elections. However, both U.S. senators are liberal Democrats, and the state's congressional delegation, five of whom are Democrats, has a relatively liberal orientation. The top elected executive officials—the governor, lieutenant governor, attorney general, and comptroller—are all Democrats, and the Democratic party controls the state Senate (38–9) and the House of Delegates (116–25) by significant margins.

While the Democratic predominance in state and electoral offices indicates that Maryland is a one-party state, this situation may be in flux. Republican voter registration in the suburbs is rising, and in the 1990 election the Republicans won county executive offices in three of the largest

for the underprivileged. For an analysis of these issues, see John W. Price, "Schaefer, Lawmakers Square Off on Spending," *Baltimore Sun*, December 18, 1988, 1A; Barry Rascovar, "Political Affordability," *Baltimore Sun*, January 5, 1989, 7E; and Robert Barnes and John Lancaster, *Washington Post*, January 8, 1989, D-1, D-5.

counties (Anne Arundel, Baltimore, and Howard) and gained nine seats in the House of Delegates. While these types of grass-roots gains are necessary to establish a two-party system in the state, similar Republican gains in past Maryland history have faded. The basic question is whether the current political context—that is, voter resentment about taxes and the increase in certain kinds of state spending (for example, public assistance)— will provide the basis for a Republican breakthrough at the state level. Perhaps a continuing decline in the overall economy (that is, "double-dip" recession) will enhance support for the Democrats, but in the meantime many Democratic state legislators see resistance to tax increases as essential to their political survival. While this Democratic stance may blunt larger Republican victories, it could mean that adaptation to growing suburban political power makes the Democratic party a vehicle for a Republican policy perspective—retrenchment of government and holding the line on, if not lowering, taxes.

Corruption is another aspect of Maryland's political culture.[21] During the late 1960s and early 1970s, two successive governors (Spiro Agnew and Marvin Mandel), one U.S. senator (Daniel B. Brewster), two U.S. congressmen (Thomas F. Johnson and William O. Mills), four members of the state Senate, five members of the Maryland House of Delegates, as well as numerous other state and county officials were indicted for crimes such as bribery, tax fraud, kickbacks, and mail fraud.[22] In the late 1970s the Maryland General Assembly passed an enhanced ethics law, required lobbyist registration, adopted "sunshine laws," and mandated full financial disclosure by candidates and elected officials. The elections of Harry Hughes and William Donald Schaefer as governor in 1979 and 1987, respectively, demonstrated that civic virtue and ethical behavior had become necessary qualifications for holding high public office in the state.[23]

LOBBYING IN MARYLAND: THE INSTITUTIONAL RULES

One aspect of the environment with particular importance for lobbyists is state lobbying laws. Maryland's laws, which are implemented by the State

21. Robert J. Brugger, *Maryland: A Middle Temperament, 1934–1980* (Baltimore: Johns Hopkins University Press, 1988), chap. 12.

22. George H. Callcott, *Maryland and America, 1940 to 1980* (Baltimore: Johns Hopkins University Press, 1985), 296–99.

23. Ibid., 300.

Ethics Commission, emphasize the disclosure of such information as the name of a lobbyist's employer (if any), the topic of lobbying activity, and the amount of expenditures. One major regulatory provision is the prohibition against contingent compensation, while certain kinds of political activities (campaign contributions, for example) by lobbyists are controlled through statutes that cover all of the state's citizens.

The great proportion of individuals who register under the lobbying laws in Maryland file as "legislative branch" and/or "executive branch" lobbyists.[24] A "legislative lobbyist" is a person who incurs expenses of $100 or more or receives $500 or more as compensation (in a reporting period) in an effort to influence legislative action. An "executive lobbyist" is a person who spends $100 or more "for meals, beverages, special events, or gifts" in an attempt to influence executive action. Typically, these lobbyists have an "employer-employee" relationship with an organizational entity, as either contract or in-house lobbyists.[25]

A prominent exemption to registration under the Maryland law concerns lobbying by individuals affiliated with governmental institutions. One exemption concerns officials (elected, appointed, or employees) of the national government, state government, or political subdivisions of the state acting in an official capacity, while another involves officials (officers, members, employees) of an "association engaged exclusively in lobbying for counties and municipalities." The latter exemption essentially applies to the Maryland Association of Counties and the Maryland Municipal League. The number of unregistered lobbyists falling into the "governmental" category has been estimated to exceed 150 individuals, but conceptual

24. In addition to "legislative" and "executive" lobbyists, there are three other kinds of registrants: (1) an "individual registrant," a person who spends $100 or more to represent his or her *own* views, not the views of an organizational entity; (2) a "grass-roots" lobbyist, a person who spends $2,000 in an effort to get other individuals "to communicate with any official to influence any legislative or executive action"; (3) "non-exempt employers" (an "employer"—that is, an individual who spends $500 or more to compensate a legislative and/or executive lobbyist—is exempt from registration if all lobbyist expenditures are reported by the "lobbyist employee" and if the employer "engages in no other act which requires registration"; failure to meet these criteria makes an "employer" "non-exempt," triggering a requirement to register). The number of lobbying registrants falling into these three categories is very small in Maryland.

25. The description of the "executive" and "legislative" lobbyists delineates the basic characteristics of each group. Additional details may be obtained from the Maryland State Ethics Commission, Ethics Commission Form No. 4 (Baltimore, Maryland), August 1987.

ambiguity about the application of "lobbyist" to government officials generally makes such estimates unreliable.

Additional exemptions from Maryland's lobbying laws include members of the press, radio, and television involved in disseminating the news; representatives of religious organizations who are protecting their right to practice their religious doctrine; individuals who limit their activity to drafting bills and advising clients about proposed legislation; persons who appear before the legislature at its specific invitation; and individuals who limit their activities to testifying before a legislative committee at the stated request of a registered lobbyist.

THE NUMBER AND TYPES OF INTEREST GROUPS ACTIVE IN MARYLAND

The number of groups active in Maryland increased by 144 (47.2 percent) between 1980 and 1987, from 305 in the 1980 legislative session to 449 in the 1987 session (see Table 5.1). The number of different lobbyists grew at a slower pace, expanding by 34 individuals (11.4 percent) between 1980 and 1987. In addition, there were 191 more lobbying registrations in 1987 than 1980, a growth rate of 44.9 percent.[26] Two factors that facilitated this growth in interest-group activity were the increase in policy activism at the state level during a conservative administration in the national government and attempts by groups to influence the allocations of a state budget, which expanded during this period. While the growth in interest groups may slow during the current retrenchment in Maryland state government, the intensity of lobbying may increase as groups attempt to protect their program interests from cutbacks.

The diversity of interest groups in Maryland reflects the underlying complexity of the state's economy (see Table 5.2). In the 1987 lobbying year, the categories with the highest proportion of groups were banking, finance,

26. Because lobbyists can represent more than one group, and because groups sometimes have more than one lobbyist, the number of registrations was greater than the number of lobbyists and the number of groups in 1980 and 1987. The fact that the absolute increase in registrations was greater than both the number of new groups and the number of new lobbyists suggests that the phenomenon of multiple representation among both groups and lobbyists increased between the 1980 and 1987 legislative sessions.

Table 5.1. Growth in Maryland Interest Groups, Lobbyists, and Lobbying Registration, 1980–1987

	No. in 1980 Session	No. in 1987 Session	Absolute Change 1980–87	Percent Change 1980–87
Interest groups	305	449	+144	+47.2%
Lobbyists	298	332	+34	+11.4
Lobbying registrations	425	616	+191	+44.9

Source: Data provided by the Maryland State Ethics Commission. The 1980 data is based on Lists 2–12 of Legislative Agents for the 1980 Legislative Session. The 1987 data is based on lobbying activity reports submitted for the first reporting period (November 1, 1986–April 30, 1987) for the 1987 Legislative Session.

insurance (13.5 percent), trade associations (9.8 percent), health (9.2 percent), miscellaneous commerce (6.3 percent), and building and construction (5.1 percent). For the 1980–87 period, most of the changes in the proportion of groups within each category were relatively small; the major exception was the "health" category, which grew approximately 7 percent.

Data on lobbying registrations and total lobbying expenditures by group category provide additional perspectives on Maryland's interest groups. It is not surprising that the percentage of groups in a category has a strong, positive correlation with the number of lobbying registrations and total lobbying expenditures. Banking, finance and insurance, health, trade associations, and building and construction had the highest percentage of lobbyist contracts (see Table 5.2), and these same groups also had the highest share of total lobbying expenditures (see Table 5.3). However, "miscellaneous commerce," ranked fourth in proportion of groups in a category, is replaced by "business associations" with regard to proportion of lobbying contracts and share of total lobbying expenditures.

Breaking down the data in the group categories offers a more detailed view of the interest groups. Table 5.4 shows specific interest groups by number of lobbyists. Maryland Elected Small Business Advocates had the largest number of lobbyists (eight) of any group in the state, while ten groups tied with four lobbyists. Moreover, the list appears to exhibit a modest pattern. Six of the sixteen groups—Baltimore Gas & Electric, Citibank, First National Bank of Maryland, James T. Lewis Enterprises, Maryland Natural Gas, and Medical Mutual Liability Insurance Society of Maryland—were specific businesses that have retained multiple lobbyist representation. However, the remaining organizations—which are larger in

Table 5.2. Interest Groups and Lobbying Registrations in Maryland by Category, November 1, 1986–October 31, 1987 (Ranked by Number of Groups in Category)

Rank	Type of Group	No. in Category	No. of Lobbying Registrations[a]	Approximate Group Representation	Total Lobbying Registrations
1	Banking, finance, insurance	66	99	13.5%	14.7%
2	Trade associations[b]	48	57	9.8	8.5
3	Health groups[c]	45	59	9.2	8.8
4	Commerce (misc.)	31	32	6.3	4.8
5	Building and construction companies	25	37	5.1	5.5
6	Professional and occupational groups, health	21	30	4.3	4.5
7	Professional and occupational groups, nonhealth	18	19	3.7	2.8
8	Business associations[d]	17	33	3.5	4.9
8	Citizens groups	17	24	3.5	3.6
8	Petroleum, coal, and chemical companies	17	20	3.5	3.0
9	Manufacturing (misc.)	14	19	2.9	2.8
9	Social welfare and community service groups	14	17	2.9	2.5
10	Auto companies and related services	13	20	2.7	3.0
10	Public-employee groups (includes unions)	13	27	2.7	4.0
11	Educational groups	11	12	2.2	1.8
11	Local government groups	11	11	2.2	1.6
12	Private-sector unions	10	15	2.0	2.2
12	Utilities	10	22	2.0	3.3
13	Racing and track groups	9	12	1.8	1.8
14	Airline and transportation companies	8	10	1.6	1.5
14	Alcoholic beverage companies	8	11	1.6	1.6
15	Food and nonalcoholic beverage companies	7	11	1.4	1.6

Table 5.2. *Continued*

Rank	Type of Group	No. in Category	No. of Lobbying Registrations[a]	Approximate Group Representation	Total Lobbying Registrations
15	Pharmaceutical companies	7	7	1.4	1.0
15	Real-estate companies	7	10	1.4	1.5
16	Communications companies	6	10	1.2	1.5
16	Motorist organizations (e.g., AAA)	6	10	1.2	1.5
16	Women's groups	6	7	1.2	1.0
17	Environmental groups	5	7	1.0	1.0
17	Religious groups	5	6	1.0	0.9
18	Agricultural groups	4	5	0.8	0.7
18	Cemetery and mortuary groups	4	5	0.8	0.7
18	Day-care companies (adult and child)	4	4	0.8	0.6
19	Tobacco companies	3	4	0.6	0.6
	Total	490	672		

Source: Compiled from List 5 of Registrants / Lobbyists (July 31, 1987) of the State Ethics Commission.

Note: Due to rounding off, total percentages may not be exactly 100.

[a]Total lobbying registrations is essentially the number of contracts between employers and lobbyists. Because some groups in a given category hire more than one lobbyist, registration is considered a better indicator of the lobbying representation retained by a group category.

[b]"Trade associations" for a specifically identified group category have been counted in the specific group category. For example, the building trade associations have been counted in the "building and construction companies" category.

[c]"Health groups" does not include health occupation groups.

[d]"Business associations" refers to umbrella organizations composed of diverse types of businesses whose major interest is to promote the economic development of a particular geographic area (e.g., Maryland Chamber of Commerce).

Table 5.3. Lobbying Expenditures in Maryland by Category, November 1, 1986–October 31, 1987 (Ranked by Lobbying Expenditures)

Rank	Type of Group	Lobbying Expenditures	Percent of Lobbying Expenditures (approx.)
1	Banking, finance, insurance	$1,286,536	17.1%
2	Health groups[a]	683,473	9.1
3	Trade associations[b]	479,232	6.4
4	Building and construction companies	420,163	5.6
5	Business associations[c]	409,018	5.4
6	Professional and occupational groups, health	390,268	5.2
7	Utilities	364,445	4.8
8	Citizens groups	336,551	4.5
9	Petroleum, coal, and chemical companies	304,187	4.0
10	Communications companies	244,855	3.3
11	Commerce (misc.)	223,634	3.0
12	Public-employee groups (includes unions)	218,375	2.9
13	Auto companies and related services	207,683	2.8
14	Professional and occupational groups, nonhealth	193,838	2.6
15	Educational groups	177,727	2.4
16	Alcoholic beverage companies	169,853	2.3
17	Manufacturing (misc.)	160,944	2.1
18	Private-sector unions	156,752	2.1
19	Local government groups	121,141	1.6
20	Real-estate companies	116,505	1.6
21	Airline and transportation companies	109,086	1.5
22	Social welfare and community service groups	107,226	1.4
23	Food and nonalcoholic beverage companies	96,876	1.3
24	Tobacco companies	92,358	1.2

Table 5.3. *Continued*

Rank	Type of Group	Lobbying Expenditures	Percent of Lobbying Expenditures (approx.)
25	Religious groups	82,998	1.1
26	Racing and track groups	75,690	1.0
27	Cemetery and mortuary groups	64,962	0.9
28	Pharmaceutical companies	57,925	0.8
29	Motorist organizations (e.g., AAA)	54,196	0.7
30	Environmental groups	42,254	0.6
31	Agricultural groups	38,990	0.5
32	Women's groups	31,643	0.4
33	Day-care companies (adult and child)	10,637	0.1
	Total	$7,530,021	100.0%

Source: Compiled from List 5 of Registrants / Lobbyists (July 31, 1987) of the State Ethics Commission.

[a]"Health groups" does not include health occupation groups.
[b]"Trade associations" for a specifically identified group category have been counted in the specific group category. For example, the building trade associations have been counted in the "building and construction companies" category.
[c]"Business associations" refers to umbrella organizations composed of diverse types of businesses whose major interest is to promote the economic development of a particular geographic area (e.g., Maryland Chamber of Commerce).

number (ten)—were "umbrella" organizations, suggesting that their broad-based membership provided a more substantial basis for supporting a cadre of lobbyists.

The top twenty interest groups in Maryland by lobbying expenditures (see Table 5.5) can be classified as "economic" or "occupational" groups,[27] and as such their expenditures can be viewed as an "investment" in obtaining a desired legislative outcome in the political marketplace. The outcome—either blocking an undesirable bill or getting a desired bill passed—will presumably result in a "yield" exceeding the lobbying costs. If the

27. L. Harmon Zeigler and G. Wayne Peak, *Interest Groups in American Society* (Englewood Cliffs, N.J.: Prentice Hall, 1972).

Table 5.4. Maryland Interest Groups with Four or More Lobbyists,
November 1, 1986–October 31, 1987

Interest Groups	No. of Lobbyists
Maryland Elected Small Business Advocates	8
AAA Potomac	5
Greater Washington / Maryland Service State & Auto Repair Assn	5
Maryland State and D.C. AFL-CIO	5
Maryland State / D.C. Professional Fire Fighters Assn	5
Maryland Chamber of Commerce	5
Medical and Chirurgical Faculty of Maryland	4
Baltimore Gas & Electric Co.	4
Citibank of Maryland	4
First National Bank of Maryland	4
Home Builders Assn of Maryland	4
James T. Lewis Enterprises	4
Maryland Natural Gas	4
Maryland State Teachers Assn	4
Maryland Classified Employees Assn	4
Medical Mutual Liability Insurance Society of Maryland	4

Source: Compiled from List 5 of Registrants/Lobbyists (July 31, 1987) of the Maryland
State Ethics Commission.

group fails to achieve its objective, the "loss" is not particularly significant
because the sums of money are probably insignificant relative to the extensive resources presumably possessed by the top twenty groups. In this view,
a "loss" does not pose tremendous risk, and the possible payoff makes the
effort worthwhile.

From another perspective, these expenditures are quite significant.
While each group in the top twenty group did not by itself expend a high
proportion of the total lobbying money for 1987 ($7,530,021), they each
clearly spent more than the mean ($15,367) and median ($8,100) expenditure figures for groups in the state. Moreover, analysis indicates that fourteen of the organizations in Table 5.5 fall into group categories that are
judged to be the most powerful with the legislature. This suggests that
power follows money, thereby establishing a possible bias in the functioning of the political system.

Table 5.5. Top Twenty Maryland Interest Groups by Lobbying Expenditures, November 1, 1986–October 31, 1987

Interest Groups	Lobbying Expenditures
Maryland Chamber of Commerce	$182,631
Health Facilities Assn of Maryland	133,649
Medical Mutual Liability Insurance Society of Maryland	112,889
Citibank of Maryland	108,274
Maryland State and D.C. AFL-CIO	100,390
Maryland Classified Employees Assn	95,730
Maryland Hospital Assn	93,623
Chesapeake and Potomac Telephone Co. of Maryland	92,026
Maryland Bankers Assn	91,501
Perpetual Savings Bank, FSB	91,463
Medical and Chirurgical Faculty of Maryland	90,543
AT&T	89,766
Baltimore Gas & Electric Co.	80,383
Marylanders for Malpractice Liability Reform	78,016
Maryland National Bank	74,346
Cable T.V. Assn, Maryland, Delaware, D.C.	73,025
Potomac Edison Co.	72,072
Tobacco Institute	71,468
State of Maryland Institute of Homebuilders	70,704
Bethesda Chevy Chase Chamber of Commerce	66,864

Source: Compiled from List 5 of Registrants / Lobbyists (July 31, 1987) of the Maryland State Ethics Commission.

PROFILE OF MARYLAND LOBBYISTS

Lobbyists in Maryland have manifested distinctive demographic characteristics.[28] In addition to being overwhelmingly white (97 percent) and disproportionately male (77 percent) in 1987, they were relatively young, with 28 percent falling in the 30–39 age category and 37 percent in the 40–49 age interval. Finally, the lobbying corps was particularly well edu-

---

28. The analysis in this section is based on a fall 1987 survey of lobbyists in Maryland. Respondents' names were obtained from State Ethics Commission List No. 5 of Registrants/Lobbyists (1986–87), dated July 31, 1987. Some 58 percent of the registered lobbyists responded to a four-page questionnaire. Percentages in the analysis have been rounded off.

cated; 25 percent had an undergraduate degree, and 61 percent had a graduate or professional degree.

Because a large proportion of the lobbyists had served short tenures, lacked prior legislative and public administrative experience, and had non-legal occupations, the lobbying corps as a whole does not fit a stereotyped image of lawyers with a strong political background and lengthy lobbying experience. Approximately 50 percent of the lobbyists had served four years or less, another 25 percent had served between 5 and 10 years, and the remaining 25 percent had more than 10 years of service. Only 7 percent were former state legislators, while a greater proportion (31 percent) have held administrative positions in local, state, or federal government. In terms of occupation, the lobbyists fell into five basic occupational groups,[29] the largest proportion (27 percent) being "executive/managers." While 21 percent were attorneys and 14 percent were "government relations" specialists within their organizations, the two smallest occupational groups were "public affairs" contract consultants (9 percent) and "employees" (6 percent) of an organization.

Classifying lobbyists as "in-house" or "contract" provides further perspective on the legal-profession background of Maryland's lobbyists. Approximately 72 percent of the lobbyists were employees of the organizations they represented (that is, "in-house"), while 28 percent were retained to represent the interests of one or more client organizations (that is, "contract"). The great proportion of contract lobbyists were attorneys (58 percent) or public-affairs consultants (21 percent), while 77 percent of the in-house lobbyists held the following organizational positions: executive/manager (38 percent), government relations specialist (19 percent), employee (13 percent), and attorney (7 percent).[30] This data suggests that although the legal profession did not dominate the set of *all* lobbyists, it was predominant among contract lobbyists.

29. Data concerning lobbyists' occupations are from the activity reports submitted to the Maryland State Ethics Commission by each lobbyist. Unfortunately, the occupational designations were not always clear, particularly for lobbyists who fall into two occupational groups: executive/managers and employees of an organization. As a result, the proportion of lobbyists in these two groups may have been understated. Because some of the registered lobbyists did not indicate an occupation in their activity reports, the results do not total 100 percent.

30. Because some contact and in-house lobbyists did not indicate an occupation in their activity reports, the categories do not total 100 percent. See note 29 for an explanation of the underestimation of in-house lobbyists in the "executive/manager" and "employee" categories.

The distinction between in-house and contract lobbyists also highlights important differences in background experiences. Approximately 49 percent of contract lobbyists had previous legislative or public administrative experience, while only 28 percent of in-house lobbyists had such experience. Apparently, the credibility of contract lobbyists hinges on such factors as personal relationships with legislators and agency officials, familiarity with the policy-making process, and knowledge of policy issues. In contrast, in-house lobbyists relied on their private administrative experience and organizational position to legitimate themselves with legislators.

The personal entree of contract lobbyists into the political system, as well as their capacity to represent multiple clients, had implications for another important characteristic of Maryland lobbyists—compensation. As noted earlier, contract lobbyists were a relatively small percentage (28 percent) of the total lobbyists, but their representation of multiple clients meant that they represented a disproportionately large share of the *interest groups* in Maryland. For example, contract lobbyists represented 60 percent of the organizations with lobbyists in this study's sample. The top ten lobbyists in terms of compensation (see Table 5.6) represented multiple clients; indeed, seven of them were ranked in the top ten among lobbyists with more than one client. Only Burridge was a contract lobbyist who was *not* an attorney, and these individuals, who formed approximately 3 percent of the total registered lobbyists in this period, accounted for approx-

Table 5.6. Top Ten Maryland Lobbyists by Compensation, November 1, 1986–October 31, 1987

Lobbyist	Total Compensation	No. of Groups Represented
1. Bruce Bereano	$776,967	61
2. James Doyle	229,222	15
3. Franklin Goldstein	194,253	11
4. Caroline Burridge	185,929	9
5. Ira Cooke	182,569	19
6. Devin Doolin	141,020	8
7. George Manis	141,000	13
8. Dennis McCoy	130,955	6
9. Frederick Rummage	122,499	6
10. Joseph Swartz	110,000	12

Source: Compiled from List 5 of Registrants / Lobbyists (July 31, 1987) of the Maryland State Ethics Commission.

imately 37 percent of the total dollar compensation paid to the state's lobbyists.

Finally, data about lobbying hours worked during the legislative session
do not fit another stereotype: the "full-time" lobbyist. Using "twenty hours
or less" to define "part-time" lobbyists, we found that 46 percent of the
respondents fell into this category, while "full-time" lobbyists (working
more than thirty hours a week) composed 35 percent of the sample. Approximately 18 percent of the lobbyists fell into the transitional category of
working 21–30 hours a week.

LOBBYING TECHNIQUES IN MARYLAND

Given the characteristics of lobbyists in Maryland, how do they perform
their function of lobbying? In the legislative arena, personal contact between legislators and lobbyists is an important aspect of lobbying. Effective
lobbyists develop relationships with legislators wherein they are well-
known, liked, a trustworthy source of information, and helpful in solving
policy conflicts. Because legislators are unable to study all the bills introduced in a legislative session, these relationships can be an important
source of influence in the policy process. John O'Donnell, director of the
State Ethics Commission, notes: "Usually, if bills don't directly affect their
constituents or attract undue attention, most lawmakers are ambivalent
about them. If that's the case, they are more likely to vote based on their
personal relationship with a lobbyist."[31] With 84 percent of the lobbyists in
the survey indicating that they initiated 70 percent or more of their contacts with legislators, lobbyists clearly assume major responsibility for developing relationships with legislators.[32]

The nature of the legislative system in Maryland strongly affects which
legislators get the attention of lobbyists. A highly centralized legislative
system, and the high approval rate by each legislative body of bills passed
in their respective committees, lead lobbyists to focus on the legislative
leaders and members of legislative committees. Approximately 64 percent

31. Quoted in Keith F. Girard, "The Connection Machine," *Warfield's* 4 (May
1989), 85.
32. The lobbyists' views about the initiation of contact with legislators are based on
a survey of Maryland state lobbyists, on which see note 28.

of the lobbyists[33] and 50 percent of the legislators[34] indicated that "gaining access to legislative leadership" was a "very effective" lobbying technique, making it one of the most effective of the lobbying techniques used in the state. Moreover, Democratic monopolization of legislative leadership positions and heavy Democratic majorities on the legislative committees strongly influences the interaction of interest groups with the political parties. While interest groups seeking votes may lobby members of both political parties, groups logically focus attention on the Democrats and know that strong identification of a policy with the Republicans is an obvious political liability.

Lobbyists use a variety of techniques in order to facilitate the development of personal relationships with legislators. One technique is expenditures for meals and "special events." Spending on meals for "officials (primarily legislators) or employees and their families" has had an average growth rate of 13.5 percent across three years (1984–87), while the average growth rate for "special-event" spending is an even more dramatic 28.3 percent.[35] While all lobbyists do not incur these expenses, it is apparent that the stereotype of "wining and dining" as a lobbying technique has validity in Maryland. Lobbyists have used sixteen other techniques in lobbying legislators (see Table 5.7). Eleven of the techniques were used by more than 80 percent of the respondents, four fell in the 70 percent range, and one was in the 60 percent interval, suggesting that a relatively high proportion of Maryland's lobbyists have used each of these techniques.

The data also revealed a modest relationship between the use of different lobbying techniques and the full-time or part-time status of a lobbyist. As summarized by the mean percentage figures, use of the techniques tended to rise as the kind of lobbyist changed from part-time (79.7 percent) to transitional (86.9 percent) to full-time (91.5 percent). Most noteworthy were the differences between full-time and part-time lobbyists in the use of "talking to the press and media" and "communicating opinions of legislators," two techniques whose use entails a relatively large investment of

33. The lobbyists' views about the effectiveness of "access to legislative leadership" as a lobbying technique are based on a survey of Maryland state lobbyists, about which see note 28.

34. The legislators' views about the effectiveness of "access to legislative leadership" as a lobbying technique are based on a survey of Maryland state legislators undertaken in fall 1987; the response rate to the four-page questionnaire was 67 percent.

35. The source for the data on expenditures for meals and "special events" was the Eighth Annual Report (January 1, 1986–December 31, 1986) and the Ninth Annual Report (January 1, 1987–December 31, 1987) of the State Ethics Commission.

Table 5.7. Lobbying Techniques Used by Maryland Lobbyists, 1987

	Percent Using Techniques	Part-Time (20 hrs. or less)	Transitional (21–30 hrs.)	Full-Time (31+ hrs.)
1. Alerting legislators to implications of a bill	99.5%	98.9%	100.0%	100.0%
2. Providing technical information / answering questions about legislation	97.9	96.6	100.0	98.5
3. Presenting testimony at formal committee hearings	97.4	94.3	100.0	100.0
4. Presenting research results to legislators	92.7	88.6	97.1	95.5
5. Getting interest-group members to lobby legislators directly	91.1	92.0	91.2	89.7
6. Building a coalition with other groups to develop support for a bill	90.1	85.2	91.2	95.6
7. Suggesting compromise positions to legislators in cases of conflict on a bill	89.6	84.3	94.1	94.0
8. Having prominent constituents contact legislators	88.5	85.4	91.2	91.0
9. Helping to draft legislation	86.5	78.4	88.2	95.6
10. Prompting letter-writing campaigns	86.5	83.9	85.3	89.7
11. Planning strategies with legislators to get bills passed	81.2	71.9	85.3	91.2
12. Communicating opinions of other legislators to a legislator	78.6	64.8	91.2	89.7

Table 5.7. *Continued*

	Percent Using Techniques	Part-Time (20 hrs. or less)	Transitional (21–30 hrs.)	Full-Time (31 + hrs.)
13. Talking to the press and media	75.9	64.4	72.7	91.2
14. Building public opinion in support of a bill	75.0	67.0	73.5	85.3
15. Providing campaign contributions	72.9	67.0	67.6	82.1
16. Getting interest-group members to participate in elections	63.0	52.8	61.8	75.0
Mean percent		79.7	86.9	91.5

Source: Authors' survey of Maryland state lobbyists in fall 1987.

time around the legislature. These differences suggest that the resources available to full-time and part-time lobbyists vary, thereby affecting the range of techniques each group has the capacity to use.

The relationship between use of lobbying techniques and the years of lobbying experience revealed two basic groups.[36] One group included the first ten techniques in Table 5.7, except for "helping to draft legislation." Differences in the use of these techniques varied relatively little with the lobbyists' years of experience. For example, the highest utilization rate difference between "low" (0–5 years) and "high" (+ 15 years) experience lobbyists was 13 percent, ("prominent constituent contact," "suggesting compromise positions"), while the lowest was 1 percent ("alerting legislators"). These techniques are commonly used to convey a group's position and to exert pressure, a basic reason that utilization would vary little by the years of experience of the lobbyists.

The second group of techniques showed much wider variation in utilization by lobbyists. It included the last six items in Table 5.7 and "helping to draft legislation." The highest utilization-rate difference between "low" and "high" experience lobbyists was 32 percent ("group member participation in

36. The data about lobbying techniques and the level of experience of the lobbyists are based on a survey of Maryland state lobbyists, on which see note 28.

elections"), while the lowest was 20 percent ("draft legislation"). Over time, a lobbyist becomes familiar with the needs and viewpoints of various participants in the legislative system (for example, legislators, the press), making use of these techniques more likely. For instance, highly experienced lobbyists have worked through more election cycles, which gives them knowledge and experience about using such techniques as "campaign contributions" and "getting interest group members to participate in elections."

Organizing lobbying techniques into four categories—lobbyist informational, lobbyist influencing, organizational contact, and external community—provides additional insights.[37] Most noteworthy is that four of the techniques with the highest utilization rate ("alerting legislators about a bill," 99.5 percent; "providing technical information," 97.9 percent; "presenting committee testimony," 97.4 percent; and "presenting research results," 92.7 percent)—fell into the "lobbyist informational" category. A fifth technique, "helping draft legislation" (86.5 percent), also fell in this group. The high use of these techniques, which essentially involve transfer of information about a group's legislative positions and interests from a lobbyist to legislators, supports the view that a basic role of lobbyists is the provision of information, particularly at the state level, where there is a relative paucity of information compared with the federal level.

The three other categories of lobbying techniques differentiate ways that lobbyists influence legislators toward a particular policy outcome. The "lobbyist influencing" category concerns efforts by lobbyists to influence legislators through direct contact. It involves such interactions with legislators as "suggesting compromise positions on a bill" (89.6 percent), "planning strategies to pass bills" (81.2 percent), and "communicating the opinions of other legislators" (78.6 percent). Instead of direct lobbyist-legislator interaction, the "organizational contact" category stresses efforts by lobbyists to pressure legislators by stimulating interest-group members. It includes "getting interest group members to lobby legislators" (91.1 percent), "prompting letter writing" (86.5 percent), "providing campaign contributions" (72.9 percent), and "getting interest group members to participate in elec-

37. The types of lobbying techniques are derived from a modification of a typology used in Ronald J. Hrebenar, Melanee Cheery, and Kathanne Green, "Utah: Church and Corporate Power in the Nation's Most Conservative State," in Ronald J. Hrebenar and Clive S. Thomas, *Interest Group Politics in the American West* (Salt Lake City: University of Utah Press, 1987). The utilization rate data for the various techniques are contained in Table 5.7.

tions" (63 percent). Finally, the "external community" category contains techniques to influence legislators through establishing favorable relationships with individuals, organizations, and institutions in the broader political environment of the legislative system. It involves such techniques as "building coalitions with other groups" (90.1 percent), "having prominent citizens contact legislators" (88.5 percent), "talking to the media" (75.9 percent), and "building public opinion for a bill" (75 percent).

Two general points emerge from this data. First, compared with the "lobbying informational" category, there was greater variation in the utilization rate between the techniques composing the other three groups—a finding that reinforces the importance of information in lobbying at the state level. Second, there was a pattern that cuts across all four categories: the most highly used lobbying techniques usually involved direct contact with legislators. This pattern supports the often-noted point about the importance of personal relationships and contacts in lobbying.

The relative effectiveness of different lobbying techniques, according to the four categories mentioned above, varies considerably (see Table 5.8). As a group, "lobbyist informational" techniques tend to be rated as the most effective. Additional support about the importance of information was provided by the survey of legislators.[38] An evaluation of the effectiveness of various characteristics of interest groups in achieving legislative objectives shows that the characteristic with the highest combined rating (88 percent) of "very effective" (45.6 percent) and "effective" (42.4 percent) was "provision of trustworthy information" by a group's lobbyist. Interviews with lobbyists and legislators revealed that legislators particularly desired information that outlined a proposal's past legislative history (if any), defined the problem, explained how proposed legislation would solve the problem, and answered technical questions and clarified the meaning of the proposal in order to avoid any "unexpected" negative fall-out from the proposal.

THE FUNCTIONING OF THE INTEREST-GROUP SYSTEM IN MARYLAND

To attain desired policy outcomes, interest groups must be perceived as legitimate participants in the political process. Approximately 64 percent

---

38. For details about the survey, see note 34.

Table 5.8. Effectiveness of Lobbying Techniques Used by Maryland Lobbyists, by Type of Technique, 1987

Technique Category	Percent of Lobbyists Rating Technique				Effec. Index[a]
	Very Effective	Effective	Somewhat Effective	Ineffective	
Lobbyist Informational Techniques					
Alerting legislators to implications of a bill	47.9%	42.1%	9.5%	0.5%	1.6
Providing technical information / answering questions about pieces of legislation	51.6	38.2	9.1	1.6	1.6
Presenting testimony at formal committee hearings	21.5	45.7	30.6	2.2	2.1
Presenting research results to legislators	21.0	46.0	30.7	2.3	2.1
Helping to draft legislation	38.2	40.0	18.8	3.0	1.9
Lobbying Influencing Techniques					
Suggesting compromise positions to legislators in case of conflict on a bill	32.2	46.2	20.5	1.2	1.9
Planning strategies with legislators to get bills passed	46.2	38.5	13.5	1.9	1.7
Communicating opinions of other legislators to a legislator	9.3	35.3	46.7	8.7	2.5
Organizational Contact Techniques					
Getting interest-group members to lobby legislators directly	40.2	31.6	24.7	3.4	1.9
Prompting letter-writing campaigns	20.1	32.9	40.9	6.1	2.3
Providing campaign contributions	16.7	31.2	46.4	5.8	2.4
Getting interest-group members to participate in elections	25.8	37.5	33.3	3.3	2.1

Table 5.8. *Continued*

Technique Category	Percent of Lobbyists Rating Technique				Effec. Index[a]
	Very Effective	Effective	Somewhat Effective	Ineffective	
External Community Techniques					
Building a coalition with other groups to develop support for a bill	36.6	47.1	15.7	0.6	1.8
Having prominent constituents contact legislators	39.1	38.5	21.3	1.2	1.8
Talking to the press and media	7.0	18.9	54.5	19.6	2.9
Building public opinion in support of a bill	32.2	31.5	33.6	2.8	2.1

Source: Authors' survey of Maryland state lobbyists in fall 1987.

[a]The effectiveness scale ran from "1" through "4," with "1" being "very effective" and "4" being "ineffective." As a result, the closer a mean value is to "1," the more effective the technique is.

of the legislators believed the legislature would function "somewhat worse" (40.2 percent) or "much worse" (23.9 percent) if there were no interest groups, while about (13 percent) thought it would function "somewhat better" (8.5 percent) or "much better" (4.3 percent).[39] The remainder (23.2 percent) believed it would function "about the same." From the *lobbyists'* perspective, approximately 95 percent felt that the legislators were "generally open" (40.8 percent) or "very open" (54.5 percent) to the lobbyists' viewpoint.[40] These data clearly indicate that legislators accept interest groups as an important part of the political process, and lobbyists express the complementary attitude that the legislators are accessible in their efforts on behalf of interest groups.

Legitimacy facilitates the access of lobbyists to the legislative system, but certain qualitative characteristics of lobbyists, such as trustworthiness and accuracy of information, affect the degree to which they gain meaningful entree into the system. While a sizable minority of the legislators believe that lobbyists are "very trustworthy" (36.8 percent) and provide "very accurate" information (38.7 percent), approximately half of the legislators found lobbyists to be only "somewhat trustworthy" and "somewhat accurate."[41] Lobbyists thus appear to have a relatively high degree of credibility, but the predominance of "somewhat" in the responses suggests that many legislators may discount the information of lobbyists to a certain degree because it comes from advocates of particular interests.

Although legitimacy and credibility are important, the ultimate purpose of interest groups and their lobbyists is to influence public policy. There was some tendency for lobbyists to rate their importance more highly than legislators, but it is striking that the proportion of legislators (77.3 percent) who believed interest groups were "very important" or "important" in determining public policy in Maryland approximated the proportion of lobbyists (79.2 percent) with this perception (see Table 5.9).

Another indication of the relative importance of interest groups in the formation of public policy is how often contact by lobbyists causes legisla-

39. The legislators' views about how well the legislature would function without interest groups and lobbyists are based on a survey of Maryland state legislators, on which see note 34.

40. The lobbyists' views about the "openness" of legislators to the viewpoint of lobbyists are based on a survey of lobbyists in Maryland, on which see note 28.

41. The legislators' views about the trustworthiness of lobbyists and the accuracy of lobbyist information are from a survey of Maryland state legislators, on which see note 34.

Table 5.9. Perceptions of Legislators and Lobbyists About Importance of Interest Groups in Determining Public Policy in Maryland, 1987

Degree of Importance	Legislators ($N = 123$)	Lobbyists ($N = 187$)
Crucial	8.9%	13.3%
Very important	36.6	44.4
Important	40.7	34.8
Somewhat important	12.2	7.0
Of little importance	1.6	0.5

Source: Authors' survey of Maryland state lobbyists and legislators in fall 1987.

tors to change their positions on a bill.[42] Such a measure is particularly revealing because changing a legislator's position is one of the most difficult tasks confronting a lobbyist. A majority of legislators (67.5 percent) and lobbyists (52.1 percent) reported that change "sometimes" occurred, but a higher percentage of lobbyists (25 percent) than legislators (9.8 percent) believed that such a change was "infrequent." Assuming that legislators would be inclined to underestimate the occurrence of such change, lobbyists may be underestimating their capacity to shift the position taken by legislators in Maryland. In any case, the data indicate a degree of flexibility on the part of legislators under conditions where exerting lobbying influence is probably most difficult.

LOBBYING IN THE COURTS AND BUREAUCRACY

The focus of this study has been on the functioning of interest groups in the legislature, but it is important to acknowledge two other possible arenas for lobbying—administrative agencies and the courts. The large percentage of legislators who indicated that they were lobbied either "very frequently" (29 percent) or "frequently" (31.5 percent) by state agencies reveals that the state bureaucracy is an active lobbying force,[43] but other

42. The comparative data about how frequently contact by lobbyists causes legislators to change their positions are based on survey data of Maryland legislators and lobbyists, on which see notes 28 and 34.

43. The legislators' perceptions about the frequency of lobbying by state agencies are based on a survey of legislators in Maryland, on which see note 34.

data raise questions about its ultimate influence in the policy process. Legislators ranked two contextual factors (state revenue level, ranked first, and objective needs of the policy arena, ranked third) and two institutions (the governor, ranked second, and the Department of Budget and Fiscal Planning, ranked fourth) as the most important influences on a state agency's appropriations. An agency's achievements and lobbying efforts were ranked fifth and sixth, respectively.[44] Furthermore, lobbyists ranked state agencies last among six institutions in influence on public-policy-making in Maryland, a perspective that offers a possible explanation for why lobbyists devoted only approximately 15 percent of their time lobbying these agencies during the entire year.[45]

As for the courts as an interest-group arena, the data indicate that while they were not widely used they were perceived as more powerful than state agencies. While lobbyists devoted an average of 57.6 percent of their time lobbying the legislature during the entire year, they devoted only 2.6 percent of their time to lobbying the courts.[46] Data from the Maryland Court of Appeals (1987–90) reveal that only 14 of 874 cases (1.6 percent) involved interest-group attempts to influence policy.[47] This provides additional evidence that the courts were infrequently used by interest groups to attain policy goals. However, lobbyists ranked the judiciary third behind the governor (ranked first) and the legislature (ranked second) in influence on the policy process in Maryland, suggesting that although groups may not often use the judiciary they perceive its potential to influence policy.[48]

44. The legislators' views of factors that affect a state agency's appropriations are based on a survey of legislators in Maryland, on which see note 34.

45. The lobbyists' perceptions about the influence of different institutions on public-policy-making in Maryland and the amount of time devoted to lobbying certain institutions are based on a survey of lobbyists in Maryland, on which see note 28.

46. The lobbyists' perceptions about the amount of time devoted to lobbying certain institutions are based on a survey of lobbyists in Maryland, on which see note 28.

47. The data about interest-group cases in the Maryland Court of Appeals were collected from *Maryland Appellate Reports*, vol. 69–85 (St. Paul, Minn: West Publishing Co., 1987–91).

48. The lobbyists' perceptions about the influence of different institutions on public-policy-making in Maryland are based on a survey of lobbyists in Maryland, on which see note 28.

INTEREST-GROUP STRENGTH IN MARYLAND

The above analysis suggests that lobbyists and interest groups in general are influential within the legislative system, but what particular groups are perceived as powerful? In *State Politics, Parties, and Policy*, Sarah McCally Morehouse concluded that the most powerful interest groups in Maryland were banks, industrialists, the AFL-CIO, and the liquor lobby.[49] The ranking of the top ten interest groups by legislators and lobbyists (see Table 5.10) partially supports this view. "Banking, finance, and insurance" was the lobby most frequently ranked in the top five by both legislators and lobbyists. Maryland has regulatory responsibility over state-chartered banks, state-chartered savings and loans institutions, and insurance companies that write policies in the state. These groups therefore have a clear financial interest in attempting to develop a legislative environment responsive to their concerns, particularly in light of the instability recently exhibited by the state's savings and loan industry and the recent crisis in medical malpractice insurance. The banking, finance, and insurance lobby accounted for 17 percent of the total 1987 lobbying expenditures in the

Table 5.10.   Ranking of Effectiveness of Maryland Interest Groups by Lobbyists and Legislators, 1987

Lobbyists	Legislators
1. Banking, finance, insurance	1. Banking, finance, insurance
2. Business associations	2. Business associations
3. Labor unions	3. Local government
4. Local government	4. Citizens groups
5. Health organizations	5. Labor unions
6. Education	6. Professional / occupational groups
7. Professional / occupational groups	7. Health professionals
8. Environmental groups	8. Health organizations
9. Public utilities	9. Environmental groups
10. Citizens groups	10. Racing
11. Transportation	

Source: Authors' survey of Maryland state legislators and lobbyists in fall 1987.

49. Sarah McCally Morehouse, *State Politics, Parties, and Policy* (New York: Holt, Rinehart & Winston, 1981), 110.

state (see Table 5.3), indicating a significant effort to pursue its political interests.

The second most frequently mentioned "top five" lobby was "business associations." Defined as organizations composed of diverse types of businesses whose major interest is to promote the economic development of a particular geographical area, this category is broader than Morehouse's "industrialists." In recent years, these associations have waged an effort to create a favorable business climate in Maryland, particularly with regard to governmental regulation and the state's tax structure.

As with Morehouse's findings, both legislators and lobbyists ranked labor unions relatively high in influence. Partially an outgrowth of the period in which Maryland's economy emphasized mass manufacturing, labor unions (particularly the AFL-CIO) have been powerful in state politics since before World War II. While the influence of private-sector unions has been weakened by the structural changes in Maryland's economy, the current retrenchment of state government will severely test whether the state's public sector unions can protect the interests of the state's employees as effectively as such unions have in other states.[50]

The remaining groups in Table 5.10 were not mentioned by Morehouse. For example, "local governments" was a lobby mentioned prominently by both legislators and lobbyists. Because the state is responsible for supervising the local administration of programs, overseeing federal programs being implemented at the local level, and providing funds for approximately one-third of local government expenditures, it is a major influence on local government affairs. As noted earlier, cuts in state aid to local governments, which essentially shifts part of the state fiscal burden to the localities, will intensify and sorely test lobbying by this group.

Two additional lobbies, "health" and "environmental" groups, were less frequently mentioned as influential, possibly because of their relatively narrow concerns. Maryland's Atlantic coastline, as well as the condition of the Chesapeake Bay, have prompted the concern of environmental groups. While the "health professional" group is technically a subset of "professional/occupational" groups, it was analyzed separately because the number of professional/occupational health groups (twenty-one) exceeds all the other professional/occupational groups combined (eighteen). The large number of professional/occupational groups reflects Maryland's complex urban economy, and mention of these groups as influential probably reflects

50. Andrew Bates, "Blame Game," *The New Republic*, November 4, 1991, 11–12.

the state government's historical responsibility for occupational licensure. The particular prominence of health groups in lobbying, whether occupational or institutional (hospitals, for example), reflects that the relatively high income in the state supports a significant health-care industry.

The respondents, legislators more than lobbyists, also indicated that citizen groups are adept at achieving their legislative objectives. Many citizens groups have organized around single issues, and they appear when the legislature deals with "their issue." For example, the influence of groups such as Mothers Against Drunk Driving and the Stephanie Ann Roper Commission have resulted in the legislature passing stringent drunk-driving laws and stiffer legislation for persons committing violent crimes.

Finally, in contrast to the findings in other states, education groups and farm organizations in Maryland did not appear to be highly effective in achieving their legislative objectives. Education groups ranked sixth with lobbyists but were not ranked by legislators. The large local government responsibility for primary and secondary education, as well as the divisiveness of state education-funding formulas, may have influenced legislative perceptions of educational groups. "Farmers" do not appear in the ranking for either legislators or lobbyists. This largely reflects the movement of the state away from an agrarian economy, but it is still somewhat surprising given the truck and poultry farms located on Maryland's Eastern Shore and the tobacco farms located in southern Maryland.

While certain groups may be viewed as more powerful than others, a major theoretical issue is the relative power of interest groups within the political system of a state. Zeigler asserts that the power of interest groups within a political system is a function of whether groups encounter competition in performance of the "input function."[51] In a similar argument, Morehouse asserts that interest-group power depends on the degree of "counteractivity" within the political system.[52] Legislators and lobbyists in Maryland clearly believe that interest groups are influential, but whether such groups dominate the system is a broader, more basic issue whose assessment requires examining the state's interest groups in the context of a complex set of conflicting factors.

One set of forces in Maryland is clearly conducive to a strong interest-group system. As noted earlier, Maryland is a one-party state, which means that two-party competition, a major institutional barrier to interest-group

51. Zeigler, "Interest Groups in the States," in *Politics in the American States*, 111.
52. Morehouse, *State Politics, Parties and Policy*, 114.

dominance, according to Morehouse, does not exist in Maryland.[53] The continuing growth of the state budget has attracted increasing interest-group activity at the state level. Analysis of lobbying techniques has shown that information is a prime resource in the relationship between legislators and lobbyists. Indeed, the importance of information to lobbyists and interest groups as a political resource is accentuated by the relative lack of support services for legislators and by the "part-time" orientation of most state legislators in Maryland.

On the other hand, a set of factors mitigate interest-group strength. Maryland's socioeconomic complexity has led to a large number of different groups, thereby enhancing the possibility that groups exert countervailing pressures against themselves. Group competition over policy demand in Maryland is best symbolized by the fact that legislators and lobbyists ranked business associations and labor as relatively high in power. While party competition is relatively insignificant, a strong governor, a centralized legislature, and a large, active state bureaucracy present institutional obstacles to interest-group dominance of the political system. Finally, incumbency apparently has begun to increase among state legislators in Maryland; with their increase in experience and professionalism, they may become less dependent on interest groups for information.

In light of these complex factors, Maryland is best categorized as "moderate" in terms of its interest-group strength. In making this claim, however, it is important to note a basic distinction. While one group, or a small number of groups, does not dominate the state's political system, it is quite possible for a group, or a small number of groups, to be quite powerful within a particular policy domain in the political system. A policy domain is a particular area of specialized policy, a phenomenon best exemplified in Maryland by the power banks and insurance companies have to influence public policy in these particular areas of finance. In effect, the relative power of a group or groups depends on the level of analysis examined.

Interest groups are an active, significant aspect of the political system in Maryland. Not surprisingly, the activism of a large number of different groups in the state has resulted in the expenditure of a relatively large amount of resources on lobbying activities. Interest groups and lobbying are clearly viewed as legitimate elements of the political process, and a rela-

53. Ibid., 95.

tively high mutual respect exists between the lobbyists and legislators. In developing good relationships with legislators, effective lobbyists attempt to become well known, liked, a trustworthy source of information, and helpful in solving policy conflicts. Beyond personal relationships, information, access to the legislative leadership, and direct lobbying by interest-group members are effective techniques in lobbying. Ultimately, lobbying activities appear to be worthwhile, for both legislators and lobbyists report that interest groups and lobbyists are influential in the political process.

Interest groups in Maryland, however, attempt to exercise power in a complex environment. The history of Maryland reflects many of the major changes experienced by the broader American society, and from this dynamism has emerged the state's complex socioeconomic environment. This complexity has decreased the possibility that one group, or small number of groups, can dominate the state's political system. Moreover, interest groups must function in the context of a political environment composed of powerful "countervailing institutions," such as a strong governor, a large, active bureaucracy, and a centralized legislature.

Speculation about future trends involves the implications of the retrenchment state government is currently undergoing. The growth rate in the number of interest groups, which has been partially spurred by past expansions of the state budget, is likely to slow as the budget is cut. However, the intensity of conflict among groups will probably increase as the fiscal reductions cause the budgetary process to assume a zero-sum character. Exemplary of this situation is that the Maryland State Police avoided proposed cutbacks while local governments absorbed large reductions. Moreover, this conflict may assume a significant class dimension, because certain rapidly growing parts of the state budget—Medicaid and public assistance—benefit the poor. If growth in these programs is perceived as a major reason for a squeeze on middle-class services, conflicts over welfare policy may become prominent.

Additional state revenues could decrease the interest-group conflict over resources. An increase in state revenues due to stronger growth in the state economy is the optimal solution to the fiscal situation. Absent this development, an increase in taxes is a source of additional revenues, but this poses great political risks. A major increase in taxes was passed in 1992, so legislators will probably be reluctant to approve another large tax increase, even if it is supported by interest groups. The state's Democratic legislators are well aware that continued tax increases could provoke a backlash in the electorate, thereby providing an opening for major gains by the Republican party, which is already benefiting from rising Republican voter registration in the state's growing suburbs. These forces could ultimately prompt the emergence of another formidable "countervailing institution"—a two-party political system.

Essentially, a difficult structural situation appears to confront Maryland's citizens. Given the recent performance of the state's economy and the present nature of the state's revenue system, the budget deficits suggest that the state cannot afford the level of services currently provided. Closing this gap by continuing to reduce state programs will clearly produce a difficult political environment in which interest groups must function. However the fiscal situation is finally resolved, interest groups in Maryland must continue to struggle for power in the midst of change, complexity, and institutional constraints.

6

Massachusetts: Citizen Power and Corporate Power

John C. Berg

"Unfair to those who care!" "Gov's Bill Hazardous to Health." About fifty picketers marched in an oval in front of the Massachusetts State House, while 6,500 more gathered across Beacon Street on Boston Common. Other signs bore the names of hospitals or indicated the target of the crowd's displeasure: the new proposal by Governor Michael Dukakis to provide some form of health insurance to every resident of the state. Despite the grass-roots aura of the demonstrators, their appearance had been arranged by the Massachusetts Hospital Association (MHA), one of the state's most powerful lobbying groups. According to the *Boston Globe*, hospitals paid their workers to attend the rally.

The governor's plan would have limited hospital revenues to $190 million more than they were currently receiving, while the MHA argued that an additional $540 million was needed.[1] By mobilizing their employees, the hospitals hoped to give a popular slant to the testimony they were presenting in a committee room inside the State House. But the hospitals didn't put their trust in demonstrations and testimony alone; they also spent more than $500,000 on lobbying efforts in 1987.[2] This strategy was successful; the governor's proposal rapidly lost its initial momentum and failed to pass until the next year, after it had been modified to meet the hospitals' objections.

This incident illustrates two important points about Massachusetts interest-group politics. First, the rules of the game have changed. It used to be played in smoke-filled rooms, with campaign contributions and patronage

---

1. Bonnie V. Winston, "Hospital Workers Rally Against Health Proposal," *Boston Globe*, September 17, 1987, 56.
2. *Boston Globe*, January 16, 1988.

jobs as the major playing pieces. Except for the smoke, it is still played that way today—sometimes. But sometimes it is played in the streets, in the voting booths, or in the courtrooms, with mass demonstrations, referenda, and lawsuits as significant new playing pieces.

The new rules have been fought for and won by new players, but the old players are still in the game. Hospitals are one of the state's major industries, and because they are greatly affected by state policies they have been heavily involved in politics for decades. They are well able to play with the traditional pieces; as tax-exempt nonprofit institutions, they cannot make political contributions, but their executives and board members can. However, they have mastered the use of the new ones as well.

The rise of new groups and new tactics is among the most important recent changes in Massachusetts politics. Other important changes include administrative reform, the partial professionalization of the legislature, and the long-term decline in both the voting strength of the Republican party and the organizational coherence of the Democrats. In order to understand these developments more clearly, we must first take a brief look at the state's history and at the basic structure of its government.

POLITICAL AND LEGAL ENVIRONMENT

Constitution

The constitution of the Commonwealth of Massachusetts is seven years older than that of the United States. It is also three times as long, containing a thirty-article declaration of rights, six chapters on the frame of government, and 116 articles of amendment. However, much of this length comes from the detailed provision for such things as the governance of Harvard University, not from the inherent complexity of the form of government. Massachusetts government does have some peculiarities, though, and two of these are particularly important for interest groups.

The constitution provides for six statewide elected officials: a governor, a lieutenant governor, a secretary of the commonwealth, an attorney general, a treasurer, and an auditor.[3] There is a bicameral legislature, with a

---

3. It might be more accurate to say 5.5 statewide elected officials; voters get to cast ballots for lieutenant governor in the party primaries, but in the general election they

40-member Senate and a 160-member House of Representatives. Voters also elect eight members to the Executive Council, the major function of which is to confirm certain gubernatorial appointments, mainly those of state judges. At times the Executive Council has been seen as a center of corruption, but for the last several years it has confirmed most appointments rather routinely.

The constitution also provides citizens with two ways to get involved in legislation. First, the right of free petition lets any citizen submit a bill. Legally, all such bills must have public hearings and be reported to the House and Senate, but this is generally done in only a *pro forma* way, so that the right of free petition is of limited significance. The initiative petition is much more important. By collecting signatures from registered voters equal to 3 percent of the total vote for governor in the last election (in 1990 about 73,000 signatures were required), a group can compel the legislature to vote on any proposed new law. Moreover, if the law is not enacted exactly as written, the group can have it placed on the ballot for the next general election by submitting additional signatures equal to 0.5 percent of the gubernatorial vote. If approved by a majority of voters, the measure will become law. In recent years, initiative petitions have led to a deposit requirement on beverage bottles and cans, to severe restrictions on the establishment of nuclear waste dumps, and to a limit on property taxes—and have altered the political scene in the process.

Interest Groups and Parties

Past studies of Massachusetts interest groups have generally found that these groups are relatively weak, and this weakness has usually been attributed to the presence of a strong state two-party system.[4] However, the most recent of these studies was published in 1969; the 1981 book by Sarah Mc-

---

can only choose among governor / lieutenant governor tickets. This can lead to interesting results. In 1978 incumbent Governor Michael Dukakis was upset in the primary by an ultraconservative challenger, Edward J. King. Dukakis's lieutenant governor, Thomas P. O'Neill III, retained the nomination. O'Neill stayed in the race but refused to endorse his own ticket. King won, carrying O'Neill with him, but was ousted in turn by Dukakis in 1982.

4. Duane Lockard, *New England State Politics* (Princeton: Princeton University Press, 1959); Harmon Zeigler and Michael A. Baer, *Lobbying: Interaction and Influence in American State Legislatures* (Belmont, Mass.: Wadsworth, 1969); Sarah McCally Morehouse, *State Politics, Parties, and Policy* (New York: Holt, Rinehart & Winston, 1981).

Cally Morehouse, simply reports the conclusions of the earlier studies. Things have changed a great deal in the last two decades.

The most dramatic change has been the rise in Democratic party dominance of the legislature. The Democrats won control of both houses for the first time ever in 1958 and have not lost it since. In the 1976 election, Republican numbers in the state Senate dropped below the level needed to force a roll call vote (eight members) and continued to hover just above or below this line until 1990.[5] During the 1970s the Republicans failed to contest most seats. If every Republican candidate in the 1986 election had won (and only 58 percent of the Republicans did), the Democrats would still have retained control of both houses by virtue of the 114 uncontested seats (see Table 6.1). Although Ronald Reagan carried the state in both

Table 6.1. Party Competition in Massachusetts Legislative Elections, House of Representatives, 1986–1990

Type of Contest	1986	1988	1990
Uncontested Democratic seats	92	84	34
Uncontested Republican seats	16	14	16
Two-way contest with independent			
Democratic victor	11	5	6
Republican victor	3	0	1
Independent victor	0	0	1
Party contest (with or without third candidate)			
Democratic victor	23	39	80
Republican victor	14	18	22
Independent victor	1	0	0
Total seats won			
Democrats	126	128	120
Republicans	33	32	39
Independents	1	0	1

Sources: Calculated from *Massachusetts Election Statistics 1986*, 198–357; *Massachusetts Election Statistics 1988*, 348–510; *Massachusetts Election Statistics 1990*, 202–361.

5. Cornelius Dalton, John Wirkkala, and Anne Thomas, *Leading the Way: A History of the Massachusetts General Court, 1629–1980* (Boston: Office of the Massachusetts Secretary of State, 1984), 277–78; Alec Barbrook, *God Save the Commonwealth: An Electoral History of Massachusetts* (Amherst: University of Massachusetts Press, 1973), 104–5.

1980 and 1984, Republicans did not win a statewide elected office, either state or federal, from 1978 to 1990. Party competition in Massachusetts reached a low point in 1986. The first two Republican candidates for governor withdrew from the ballot in the face of scandal, while the Republicans failed to contest 7 of the 10 Democratic seats in the U.S. House of Representatives, 6 of the 8 seats in the all-Democratic Executive Council, 22 of the 29 Democratic seats in the state Senate, and 103 of the 126 Democratic seats in the House of Representatives.[6]

But 1990 saw a big change. Taking advantage of a state budget crisis, the Republicans won the elections for governor / lieutenant governor and for treasurer. Led by an aggressive chairman, Ray Shamie, the Republican state committee increased its paid staff to twenty-eight and recruited legislative candidates energetically. Republicans contested 37 of the 40 state senate seats and won 16, doubling their strength. They raised the number of House seats they contested from 71 to 119, and the number they won from 33 to 39. The Republicans seem determined to bring two-party competition back to Massachusetts. However, at this writing the Democrats continue to dominate the legislature, hold all the congressional seats, and tend to dismiss the Republican victories of 1990 as a fluke. In 1992 Republicans won two congressional seats but lost ground in the legislature; their strength in the Senate fell to eleven, no longer enough to uphold a veto.[7]

One result of the Democrats' electoral prosperity in the 1970s and 1980s was the loss of any internal coherence the party may have had. Massachusetts developed an electoral pattern similar to that traditional for the one-party South. In both the state legislature and the U.S. House of Representatives, the renomination of incumbents was rarely challenged, but when a vacancy occurred, there would be a mad primary scramble among six, seven, or more candidates. The primary winner—who often had far less than a majority of the vote—would then face only token or no opposition from the Republicans and would generally be able to retain the seat for as long as he or she chose. A similar pattern prevailed among the Republicans in the few strongholds they retained, except that there were likely to

6. *Massachusetts Election Statistics 1986.*

7. Agnes S. Bain and John C. Berg, "Redistricting and Endangered Incumbents: The 1990 Massachusetts State Senate Elections" (Paper presented at the New England Political Science Association, Worcester, Massachusetts, 1991); John C. Berg, "The Gerrymander Comes Home: Redistricting the Massachusetts General Court in the 1980s," in Leroy C. Hardy, ed., *Gerrymandering in the 1980s* (Claremont, Calif.: The Rose Institute, forthcoming).

be fewer primary contestants. There are preprimary endorsement conventions for statewide offices, but these have little effect, because any candidate who gets as much as 15 percent of the delegate vote can and does go
on to the primary.

Despite the recent Republican upsurge, the pattern of individualism and
disunity still dominates the Democratic party. Individual Democratic politicians may have strong organizations, but these are purely personal. Such
organizations work hard for their leader but have little or no effect on
nominations for other offices. This is especially true in the downward direction: a local official may call on his or her troops to work for a gubernatorial candidate, but any attempt by a governor to influence the outcome of a local primary contest is likely to be deeply resented and
counterproductive. Thus, Governor Dukakis, who had one of the strongest
personal organizations of any Massachusetts politician, chose to stay out of
contests for lieutenant governor in 1984 and 1988 even though he then
had to run on a joint ticket with the victor in November.

The absence of a strong Democratic party organization might have led to
a disorganized, chaotic legislature, but it does not, because power in the
General Court is highly centralized in the hands of the Senate president
and the Speaker of the House. The two presiding officers are chosen
by majority vote of the members of their respective chambers, but once
elected, each possesses a multitude of resources for consolidating his (or
potentially her) power. Unlike the U.S. Congress, the Massachusetts General Court has no seniority system. Committee memberships and chairman-
ships, office space, additional staff support beyond the one aide to which
each member is entitled, patronage jobs in the State House, and even
parking space in the state garages are all under the control of the two
presiding officers. Legislative leaders also control significant patronage in
the state's executive branch, due to another peculiarity of the state constitution, which permits the legislature to define the terms of office—including terms for life—of all executive officials other than judges and elected
constitutional officers. Until 1967, governors were often not able to choose
major department heads.[8]

The privileges and positions of legislators can be conferred or taken away
at any time by the leadership. Moreover, many leadership positions carry
salary increments, so that members' pocketbooks as well as their power
depend on the leaders' will. Leaders who wield this power too willfully risk

8. *Massachusetts Constitution*, chap. 1, sec. 1, art. 4; Dalton et al., *Leading the Way*,
146, 329.

being deposed by the membership, as happened in 1985 when Speaker Thomas McGee was ousted by George Keverian; but challenges to sitting leaders are rare, and leaders have a good deal of leeway in legislative matters.

Because the Democrats held the governorship and the two legislative leadership positions from 1975 to 1990, strong party coordination of policy might have been possible. But in practice the Democrats' numerical strength was so great that much of the pressure for unity was removed, and disputes among the three powerful Democrats were brought to the center of the stage, so that the level of fragmentation of the policy process remained relatively high (see Table 1.1). This tendency has survived the loss of the governor's chair to Republican William Weld; despite efforts at party unity, House Speaker Charles Flaherty (Cambridge) and Senate President William Bulger (Boston) do not find it easy to reach agreement. The conclusions of Doyle and Milburn in 1981 still apply strongly to Massachusetts today: "Because of the fluid party organizational structures within most of the New England states, the general influence on governmental policy in all six states comes from organized interests. Factions appear within the parties of the legislatures and from one gubernatorial officer (often of the same party) to another."[9]

This increase in interest-group activity is consistent with many past studies, which find an inverse relationship between the strength of interest groups and that of political parties.[10] However, interest groups can be dominant in two different ways. On the one hand, one or two particular interests may dominate a state's politics, getting their way on all issues important to them. Morehouse found this to be the case with the Farm Bureau in Alabama, for example.[11] On the other hand, interest groups taken collectively may serve as the main vehicle for political conflict, but with powerful groups opposed to each other, so that no single interest can count on dominating. The situation in Massachusetts is closer to the latter, but the evenness of the balance is rendered lopsided by what Lindblom has called

9. William Doyle and Josephine F. Milburn, "Citizen Participation in New England Politics: Town Meetings, Political Parties, and Interest Groups," in Josephine F. Milburn and Victoria Schuck, eds., New England Politics (Cambridge, Mass.: Schenkman, 1981), 49.

10. Morehouse, State Politics, Parties, and Policy, 116–18; Doyle and Milburn, "Citizen Participation," 49; Lockard, New England State Politics, 162; V. O. Key Jr., Politics, Parties, and Pressure Groups, 5th ed. (New York: Thomas Y. Crowell, 1964), 154–61.

11. Morehouse, State Politics, Parties, and Policy, 106.

"the privileged position of business."[12] While interest groups are now more likely than political parties to define the terms of political conflict, groups are likely to find themselves opposed by other groups, so that no single interest can be seen as all-powerful. But because groups do not all enter this conflict with the same resources, some find it easier than others to win.

Regulation of Lobbyists

Massachusetts began to regulate lobbyists in 1890, after an investigation initiated by representative George Fred Williams (D–Dedham), a leading reformer. One witness in the investigative hearings described the efforts by the Fitchburg Railroad to win a state subsidy for construction of a tunnel, "when legislators were carted in droves from one end of this state to the other, and feasted and feted day and night; when even wine wasn't good enough for them, and they invoked the nectar from above, I suppose, or below, and sought for nightingales' tongues on which to feed them."[13] Financier Henry M. Whitney, who had hired thirty-seven lobbyists and hosted legislators at elaborate private dinners in his quest for a charter for the West End Street Railway, concurred with an investigator who described lobbyists as "a venal body of men, whose services are for sale to anyone who will pay them, which stands between the petitioner for legislation and the Legislature."[14]

Some legislators feared that to register lobbyists would put the stamp of legitimacy on their activities, but the majority agreed with J. Otis Wardwell of Haverhill that a bill was needed "to regulate and restrict an evil which cannot be done away with."[15] Lobbyists and those who employed them were required to register with the legislature's sergeant-at-arms and to file a full report of all lobbying expenses within thirty days of prorogation (as adjournment is known in Massachusetts) each year. Additional bills enacted over the next several years excluded lobbyists from the House and Senate chambers and the corridors outside them and prohibited corporations from contributing to campaigns.

12. Charles E. Lindblom, *The Policy-Making Process*, 2nd ed. (New Haven: Yale University Press, 1980), 71–82.

13. Testimony of George M. Stearns in *Report of the Committee to Investigate Methods Used for and Against Legislation Concerning Elevated Railroads*, House No. 585, June 1890, pp. 530–31, quoted in Dalton et al., *Leading the Way*, 181.

14. Ibid., 182.

15. Ibid., 183.

The lobbyist registration law was changed substantially in 1973. The new law formally established a formal definition of "legislative agent":

> any person who for compensation . . . does any act to . . . influence legislation . . . or to influence the decision of any member of the Executive branch [concerning legislation] . . . or the adoption, defeat or postponement of a . . . rule or regulation. . . . The term shall include persons who, as part of their regular and usual employment and not simply incidental thereto, attempt to . . . influence legislation . . ., whether or not any compensation in addition to the salary . . . is received for such services.[16]

In 1983 the law was extended to cover lobbyists for nonprofit organizations.

Responsibility for registering legislative agents was shifted from the sergeant-at-arms (chosen by the legislative leaders) to the secretary of the Commonwealth (independently elected). Lobbyists are now issued photo identification cards and are required to file reports of their expenditures twice a year. Payment of lobbyists' fees contingent on passage (or defeat) of particular bills is prohibited. Violation carries a fine of $100 to $5,000, and convicted lobbyists are disqualified for three years.[17]

The law applies to attempts to influence executive branch decisions as well as legislation, and organizations that do not employ lobbyists are still required to register if they spend more than $250 on lobbying activity. But there are still some loopholes. Government legislative liaisons are exempt from the requirement to register, and volunteer and "hobbyist" lobbyists are not covered because they do not receive compensation. In-house lobbying by corporate executives on their own companies' behalf need not be reported as long as it is "incidental" to their "regular and usual employment." Finally, many nonprofit issue-oriented organizations define their activities as "educational" in order to let their supporters deduct contributions from their federally taxable income. Such groups may hire staff members to educate their members, and the general public, about an issue. They may even endorse bills, as long as this constitutes less than about 5 percent of their total activity. Such staff members fit this book's definition of an in-house lobbyist, but the law covers them erratically. They must

16. Quoted in Ernest Winsor's "Registering as a Massachusetts Lobbyist," in Judith C. Meredith and Linda Myer, Lobbying on a Shoestring: How to Win in Massachusetts . . . and Other Places, Too (Boston: Massachusetts Poverty Law Center, 1982), 149.

17. Massachusetts Secretary of State, Lobbying: The Law, the Process, and You, 4; Dalton et al., Leading the Way, 347–48.

register as lobbyists if they make any attempt to influence state agency
regulations, but only "significant" amounts of effort seeking to influence
legislation require registration.[18]

MASSACHUSETTS LOBBYISTS

As interest groups grow more important, so do lobbyists. Contract lobbying
is a growth industry in Massachusetts. In 1984, registered lobbying groups
reported spending just under $5 million. By 1986 the total had reached
$8.9 million and by 1990 had grown to $15.4 million.[19]

Contract lobbyists come in many types. Some are retired politicians,
such as former Senate President Kevin Harrington, whose six-foot-six figure can often be seen around the State House. Harrington reported lobbying income of $123,015 in 1986, $199,336 in 1987, $252,149 in 1989, and
$135,316 in 1990, from sources including insurance interests, Shell Oil
Company, the Air-Conditioning and Refrigeration Institute, and the Association of Massachusetts Recyclers.[20] Some are professional lobbyists who
have worked their way up, based on their skill and contacts. A good example is William R. Delany, a retired police officer who launched a lobbying
firm, Delaney Associates, in 1980. In 1987 the firm earned $593,288 from
twenty-one business clients. Delaney learned his skills as president of the
Metropolitan Police Patrolmen's Union in the early 1970s, then decided to
go into business for himself.[21] Delaney's success has not been unmixed;
early in 1988 he was indicted for having failed to file state income tax
returns for the years 1982–84.[22] Nevertheless, the firm still had eighteen
clients and lobbying earnings of $532,000 in 1990.

18. Massachusetts Secretary of State, Lobbying, 11; Allan G. Rodgers, "Potential
Restrictions on Lobbying," in Meredith and Myer, Lobbying on a Shoestring, 147–48.

19. Massachusetts Secretary of State, Financial Statistics for Lobbyists 1986 and 1990.

20. Massachusetts Secretary of State, Legislative Agents and Employers 1986, Disclosed
Salaries—Cross Reference; Legislative Agents and Employers 1987, Disclosed Salaries—Cross
Reference; Legislative Agents and Employers, Disclosed Salaries 1989; Legislative Agents and
Employers, Disclosed Salaries 1990.

21. Frank Phillips, "Beacon Hill Lobbyists Bring Home More Bacon," Boston Globe,
February 1, 1988, 17–18; Renee Loth, "Lobbyist's Rise to Top," Boston Globe, February
23, 1988.

22. Renee Loth, "Top Lobbyist Charged with Tax Violations," Boston Globe, February 27, 1988. Earnings are from Massachusetts Secretary of State, Legislative Agents and
Employers 1987, Disclosed Salaries—Cross Reference, which includes income reported
through May 1, 1988.

Harrington and Delaney fit the traditional picture of the contract lobbyist who works for well-heeled special interests. Old-style lobbyists, aware of the high centralization of power in the Massachusetts General Court, cultivated personal relationships with the House Speaker, the Senate president, and a few other key legislators. Much of their work was done over a drink at the Golden Dome pub across the street from the State House, over lunch at Anthony's Pier 4 Restaurant on the Boston waterfront, or during conversations in the private offices of the leaders. Campaign contributions, along with occasional bribes, were a major source of influence, but knowledgeable intermediaries were needed to direct the money to the right place while avoiding scandal. Therefore, the ideal lobbyists were either former legislators or others who had built up networks of personal friendship with legislators over the years.

Lobbying of this sort was effective, but limited to those who could afford it. Because it was based on money, it was most useful for business interests. Labor unions also employed similar tactics and were successful at gaining limited objectives. Unions of state employees seeking legislated pay increases, and construction unions seeking public works projects, were particularly prominent in their use of lobbyists.

Over the last several years, a new and more populist style of lobbying has developed. Judy Meredith is a good example. Meredith began as a community activist, found that she enjoyed lobbying, and decided to go professional. In 1986 she reported earnings of $59,200 from such groups as the Council of Human Service Providers, the Coalition to License Acupuncturists, and Greater Boston Legal Services; she earned $63,000 and $57,792 in 1989, including $16,000 each year from the city of Boston. In 1990 her operations had grown so big that she filed in the name of her firm, Meredith & Associates Inc., which reported twenty clients and income of $219,065. Her clients were mostly social service agencies, but also included the Playtex Family Products Corporation.[23] Meredith and other lobbyists of this type have found that they can replace the power of money with the power of votes. They put more of their energy into educating their own client groups' membership about issues and legislative procedures and find ways to let legislators know that their constituents are watching how they vote. One such tactic, now become a State House fixture, is the

---

23. Massachusetts Secretary of State, *Legislative Agents and Employers 1986, Disclosed Salaries—Cross Reference; Legislative Agents & Employers 1987, Disclosed Salaries—Cross Reference; Legislative Agents and Employers, Disclosed Salaries 1989; Legislative Agents and Employers, Disclosed Salaries 1990.* See also Meredith and Myer, *Lobbying on a Shoestring.*

lobby day, where supporters of a cause from around the state come to the State House on the same day to meet with their representatives and senators.[24]

These new tactics have helped change the style of Massachusetts interest-group politics. Today, even business-oriented lobbyists find that demonstrations of grass-roots support help their cause, as with the Massachusetts Hospital Association campaign described at the beginning of the chapter.

Nevertheless, money is still of vast importance in lobbying, and more and more of this money is funneled through political action committees (PACs). In 1989, a year in which only a few local elections were held, 146 PACs gave a total of $912,250 to state and county candidates, while 15 PACs gave to only one candidate, the Beer Distributors PAC gave to 99. In 1990, with hotly contested statewide elections, 198 PACs gave $1,376,907; 17 gave to only one candidate; and the Professional Firefighters PAC gave to 109.[25] Most of the top ten PACs were based on an industry or a labor union (see Table 6.2).

THE CURRENT INTEREST-GROUP SCENE

In order to find out what legislators and legislative staff thought about various interest groups, a survey was drawn up and sent to every member of the legislature in 1987. Members were asked to fill out one survey form themselves and to give another one to a staff aide. Replies were received from 42 of the 200 legislators, and from 36 staff members. This response rate is not high enough to show significant patterns through statistical analysis, but the responses were suggestive in some areas. While it is possible that some important groups were not mentioned by the respondents, we can fairly conclude that any group that *was* mentioned frequently is of some importance.

By its nature, a survey of legislators and their aides does not provide any

24. Meredith and Myer, *Lobbying on a Shoestring*, 12–14.
25. Massachusetts Office of Campaign and Political Finance, "Report of Campaign Finance Activity by Multi-Candidate Committees (PACs) in Massachusetts During 1989 and 1990." PACs are limited to contributions of $1,000 per candidate per year, so making off-year contributions allows them to double the amount contributed.

Table 6.2.   Contributions by Ten Largest PACs to Massachusetts State and County Candidates, 1987–1990

Name of PAC	Amount Contributed		Amount Contributed	
	1987–88	Rank	1989–90	Rank
Coalition of Democrats Dedicated to				
Legislative Excellence (CODDLE)	$86,800	1	$107,000	1
Beer Distributors PAC	64,425	2	95,240	2
Massachusetts Banker PAC State				
Fund	61,700	3	64,850	4
Massachusetts Taxpayers Committee	58,250	4	NL	
Massachusetts DEAC (Auto Dealers)	49,450	5	49,800	5
Painters District Council #35 PAC	41,600	6	36,162	16
Committee to Elect Responsible				
Public Officials (Utility Interests)	41,100	7	40,300	13
Bay PAC/Bay State Physicians PAC	40,800	8	NL	
Massachusetts Realtors PAC	40,650	9	66,100	3
Local #7 Political Action League	40,470	10	34,375	20
Professional Firefighters of Massa-				
chusetts, AFL-CIO CLC	NL		49,777	6
Massachusetts Dentists Interested in				
Legislation	38,850	11	48,700	7
IPAC (eye doctors)	NL		48,000	8
State Police Assn of Massachusetts				
PAC	26,800	17	47,100	9
Lawyers for Action	NL		45,825	10

Sources: Commonwealth of Massachusetts, Office of Campaign and Political Finance, "Report of Campaign Finance Activity by Multi-Candidate Committees (PACs) in Massachusetts During 1987 and 1988" and "Report of Campaign Finance Activity by Multi-Candidate Committees (PACs) in Massachusetts During 1989 and 1990."

NL = Not listed among largest twenty contributors.

information about interest-group activity lobbying the executive branch or in the courts. Nevertheless, these are important areas of interest-group influence. Some major issues are played out almost entirely within the executive branch. For example, in the ongoing controversy about the design of the relocated Central Artery (a major highway through downtown Boston), Executive Secretary of Transportation Fred Salvucci was both the main decision-maker and the focus of lobbying efforts. Before leaving office at the end of the Dukakis administration, Salvucci signed an agreement with one environmental interest group, the Conservation Law Foundation (CLF), in an attempt to bind his successors to the result of these negotiations. Other groups, dissatisfied with this bargain, later announced that they would take the issue to court on the ground that the project's environmental impact review had not been conducted properly; and the CLF also decided to sue when federal highway officials declared that its agreement with Salvucci was not legally binding. The CLF is an important environmental interest group, but it does not show up as such in the survey results because its focus is on action in the courts, not in the legislature.[26]

In other cases, interest groups seek the governor's support in getting their proposals through the legislature. When such support is not forthcoming, as with the plant-closing bill described below, the group's position is weaker.

Business

A discussion of interest-group resources usually includes the topics of votes, money, and information.[27] Business, taken collectively, has an additional resource: without its cooperation, the economy will cease to function. Labor too can bring the system to a halt by striking. But when union members strike it is an extraordinary event; for a corporation to decide to close a plant in Massachusetts and open a new one elsewhere is simply an everyday business decision. This is what Charles Lindblom calls "the privileged position of business."[28] Political leaders must meet the needs of the business community regardless of their lobbying effort. Voters hold the governor responsible for economic prosperity, so this type of influence is often applied directly to the executive. Since business leaders are often effective in-house legislative lobbyists as well, their power is maximized.

A recent example of this privileged position came in 1975–76. With the state facing a recession and a budget crisis, a group of large financial institutions, led by the First National Bank of Boston (as it was then), informed

26. "DeVillars Gives Major OK to Artery Project," *Boston Globe*, January 3, 1991; "Six Parties to Sue Artery Project," *Boston Globe*, January 25, 1991; "Group Will Seek Halt to Artery; Environmental Grounds Are Basis of Lawsuit," *Boston Globe*, May 29, 1991.

27. Key, *Politics, Parties, and Pressure Groups*, 132–38.

28. Ibid.

Governor Dukakis that it would not buy any of several forthcoming state debt offerings unless several conditions were met. Some of these conditions were economic in the narrow sense. So-called "moral obligation" notes had to be replaced by those backed with the full faith and credit of the state, and short-term notes backed with long-term bonds, and the new bonds were sold with above-market interest rates. But other conditions were more political. In November 1975 the banks insisted that a "credible" state budget be passed before they would purchase $131 million in notes. The budget that resulted cut 8,000 cases from the general relief category of welfare, reduced social-service programs by $300 million, eliminated planned cost-of-living increases for welfare clients and state workers, and raised taxes by $350 million.[29] Should this bargaining be considered a simple banking transaction, or was it a very successful case of lobbying the executive branch? However we choose to classify it, the incident is evidence of the special power business can sometimes wield.

In an effort to determine which formally organized groups were the most active, the survey asked legislators and aides to list the groups from which they heard most frequently. The results are in Table 6.3, along with some other information about those groups. However, while some specific groups do stand out—the Associated Industries of Massachusetts (AIM), the Massachusetts High Technology Council, and the Business Round Table, in particular—in other cases the interest group tends to blend together with the broader interest, or even with the lobby, in respondents' perceptions. Thus, the Massachusetts Hospital Association (MHA) was mentioned by name six times, but "hospitals" and the "health-care industry" received five additional mentions. This indicates that the MHA has chosen an effective lobbying strategy, not that it is weak. One state senator, dissatisfied with the survey form, added a written comment: "Your survey fails to delineate the type of lobbying which is effective. If groups have members who are my constituents who contact me—especially on a personal level as opposed to petition or preprinted letter—I listen. Otherwise 'groups' don't influence me very much other than local groups." This statement would apply to many legislators, and the MHA accordingly seeks to present its cause through representatives of local hospitals, not just in its own name.

29. Michael Stone and Emily Achtenberg, *Hostage! Housing and the Massachusetts Fiscal Crisis* (Boston: Boston Community School, 1977), 28–30. See also John Kifner, "Massachusetts Raises Taxes Sharply Under Pressure of Banks," *New York Times,* November 10, 1975.

Table 6.3. Business Groups Most Commonly Heard from by Massachusetts Legislators and Staff

Group	No. of Legislator Mentions	No. of Staff Mentions	No. of Paid Agents, 1990	Reported Spending, 1990
AIM	26	16	8	$188,683
Massachusetts Business Round Table	11	4	1	3,705
Chambers of Commerce[a]	10	11	9	75,671
Massachusetts High Tech Council	10	5	2	12,803
MHA	5	6	3	61,969
Life Insurance Assn of Massachusetts (LIAM)[b]	5	5	3	249,675
"Small business"[c]	10	8	—	—

Sources: Calculated from survey by author, November–December 1987, and from Massachusetts Secretary of State, *Financial Statistics for Lobbyists 1990*, and *Legislative Agents and Employers 1990, Disclosed Salaries—Cross Reference*.

[a]"Chambers of Commerce" includes seven local Chamber of Commerce organizations.
[b]"LIAM" includes mentions of "insurance" or "insurance lobby."
[c]Most mentions were to generic "small business"; no one organization stood out, although several received a mention.

The most prominent group by far is the Associated Industries of Massachusetts (AIM), the umbrella group for Massachusetts manufacturers. It concerns itself with the overall business climate, seeking to lower taxes, limit regulation, and counterbalance the influence of labor unions on such issues as worker compensation and plant-closing legislation. With eight paid agents, AIM is active and visible to legislators and their aides. However, much business lobbying focuses on the specific concerns of such regulated industries as health care, banking, insurance, and utilities. Groups representing each industry are active when that industry's interests are at stake, so that the relative prominence of any particular group is more an indication of what the legislature is doing that year than of that group's inherent influence.

Professional groups were listed separately on the survey form but might better be considered as a subset of business groups. Respondents mentioned doctors (the Massachusetts Medical Society) and lawyers (the Massachusetts Bar Association) most prominently.[30] These groups are strongest when they are defending their professional jurisdiction against incursions by nurses or paralegals. The two groups have also confronted each other recently over the issue of medical malpractice, with doctors seeking to limit liability, and lawyers upholding the sovereignty of juries. The result has been a lack of state action, with the costs adding to health-care inflation.

Organized Labor

Legislators rated labor as the most powerful interest in the state, while aides paired it with business in first position. Like business, labor has economic power to back up its political efforts, but that power is more difficult to use. Business decisions about investment, plant location, and layoffs or new hiring are everyday matters. On the other hand, a strike or other work action by labor provokes an immediate crisis and so can be used only rarely. Collective bargaining is an effective means of pursuing economic goals, but with the important exception of public employees, for whom decisions about wages and working conditions are simultaneously political and economic, it is difficult to use collective bargaining for political ends. Hence, unions in Massachusetts have developed sizable lobbying operations. Groups classified as "labor unions" by the secretary of state reported spending $430,661 on lobbying activities in 1990. If we add the $130,854 reported by the Massachusetts Teachers Association, which is classified as an "education affairs and services" group but which holds numerous union contracts with local school committees, the total rises to $561,515. Police and fire unions lobby so intensively that the secretary of state gives them their own category; these groups reported spending $93,814.[31]

Lockard and Morehouse both found that Massachusetts unions were tied closely to the Democratic party.[32] This remains true today, although some leading Democratic politicians, such as former Governor Dukakis and former U.S. Senator Paul Tsongas, have been hesitant to identify themselves with unions too closely. Given the overwhelming Democratic dominance of the legislature, unions have seen little need to seek Republican votes.

30. Teachers also got some mentions, but their organizations were more likely to be considered labor unions.

31. Massachusetts Secretary of State, *Financial Statistics for Lobbyists 1990.*

32. Lockard, *New England State Politics*, 163; Morehouse, *State Politics, Parties, and Policy*, 115.

However, the influence of the unions is limited by the equally significant power of business. Rather than wage intensive conflict for broad social change, labor in Massachusetts has generally chosen to narrow its focus. In addition, some unions are more influential than others. As a result of both these factors, much of labor's lobbying effort is devoted either to winning approval for job-creating public-works projects or to improvement of the pay and working conditions of public employees. On the first, labor is as likely as not to find itself allied with business. On the second, its power is limited by budgetary constraints and opposed by antitax groups, but such opposition is normally subdued.

Of the labor groups that respondents reported hearing from most commonly (see Table 6.4)—except for the umbrella AFL—CIO, which leads the list—public-employee unions dominate; the AFL-CIO Building Trades Council is the only other group to receive significant mention. In recent years the AFL-CIO has pursued interests ranging from the reform of workers compensation to the defeat of a bottle-deposit law. It has also worked to support the aims of the other unions listed in the table. But despite some internal dissent, the AFL-CIO has not pursued a broad working-class agenda. When it has done so, its efforts have met with only limited success.

In 1984, for example, unions endorsed a bill sponsored by the then-state representative Thomas Gallagher, a Boston Democrat, to protect workers from plant closings. Basic industry in Massachusetts has been declining, and several of the state's smaller cities have seen the closing of factories that were the mainstay of the local economy. This industrial decline was counterbalanced in the 1980s by the growth of jobs in the service sector and in the high-technology industries, so that the statewide unemployment rate remained low until the beginning of the recession of 1989. But even during the years of prosperity the new jobs either paid less than the old ones or went to different people; hence, members of the unskilled industrial work force suffered, and locally depressed areas persisted even during the statewide boom of the 1980s.

Gallagher's bill would have required advance notice of layoffs on a graduated scale, from one month for layoffs of 50–99 employees to one year for layoffs of 1,000 workers or more. Companies that failed to give notice would have had to provide severance pay for each employee in proportion to the notice not given. It would also have helped community-based non-profit organizations take over the operation of closed plants. Although the bill was co-sponsored by 81 of the 160 state representatives, and 11 of the

Table 6.4. Labor Groups Most Commonly Heard from by Massachusetts
Legislators and Staff, 1990

Group	No. of Legislator Mentions	No. of Staff Mentions	No. of Paid Agents, 1990	Reported Spending, 1990
AFL-CIO	30	15	1	$ 54,068
Teachers				
Massachusetts Teachers Assn	10	8	9	130,854
Massachusetts Federation of Teachers	2	2	2	81,854
"MTA and MFT"	2	1	—	—
Firefighters				
IAFF, Boston	10	4	2	1,800
"Police and Fire" (6 police unions)[a]	1	1	11	166,120
AFL-CIO Building Trades Council	7	3	1	3,666
AFSCME	6	4	2	85,000
SEIU (includes locals #254, 285, 509)	6	5	1	51,344

Sources: Calculated from survey by author, November–December 1987, and from Massachusetts Secretary of State, *Financial Statistics for Lobbyists 1990*, and *Legislative Agents and Employers 1990, Disclosed Salaries—Cross Reference*.

[a]Police Alliance of Boston, Boston Police Patrolmen's Association, Massachusetts Police Association, Metropolitan Police Patrolman's Union, International Brotherhood of Police Officers / NAGE, and State Police Association of Massachusetts.

40 senators, it was blocked by the insistence of the Massachusetts High Technology Council that its members would refuse to expand their operations in Massachusetts if the bill passed. Both sides lobbied Governor Dukakis for his support; instead, he called all parties together to try for a compromise. After protracted negotiations, a much-weakened version of the bill was enacted, making advance notice voluntary and providing some funds for retraining of workers. Despite intense dissatisfaction with the law as passed, Gallagher and the unions ultimately supported it as the best they could hope to get.

The most dramatic recent labor political victories have not been in the legislature. The unions made a dramatic move at the Massachusetts Democratic Convention in 1983. They had not yet endorsed a presidential candidate for the 1984 election and wanted to demonstrate their importance to the Democrats, so they asked delegates to write in the word "JOBS" for a presidential straw poll taken at the state convention. "JOBS" came in second to Walter Mondale, with 25.6 percent of the vote. While this reaffirmed labor's importance to the party, however, it is difficult to trace any specific policy results to it.[33]

Labor won a more substantial victory in the 1988 general election. The Associated Builders and Contractors (ABC), an interest group of builders that employ nonunion workers, had placed repeal of the Massachusetts prevailing wage law on the ballot by initiative petition. The ABC portrayed the law as helping only highly paid construction workers while driving up the cost of local government. The unions might have been vulnerable to these arguments, but they successfully defined the issue as one of broad class solidarity. Most of their campaign shunned debate on the specifics for such broad slogans as "Question 2—Bad For You" and, on a suitably illustrated billboard, "Listen to Mama—Vote No on 2." All members of AFL-CIO Building Trades Councils in Massachusetts were assessed $50 for the campaign fund, and thousands worked the polls on election day. Despite one serious gaffe—a worker used in a television advertisement was found to have made $70,000 in the past year—the unions won by a landslide. Its victory was defensive, but the new level of rank-and-file mobilization obtained carries the possibility of growing strength in the future.[34]

As stated above, most labor lobbying is done by public-employee unions, which have grown larger in recent years, in Massachusetts as elsewhere. Moreover, these unions devote more of their resources to lobbying than private-sector unions do, which is understandable because, unlike private-sector unions, their pay and working conditions are part of the state policy domain. Public-employee unions lobby executive officials for better contracts and lobby the legislature for the funds to pay for them. They may also seek to legislate pay raises and job security directly. Unions of teachers, police officers, and firefighters have been particularly effective in

33. Chris Black, "Mondale Wins Mass. Straw Poll," *Boston Globe*, April 10, 1983, 1, 46; Robert Healy, "The Mondale Vote and Labor's Clout," *Boston Globe*, April 10, 1983, 44.

34. Clyde W. Barrow, "Organized Labor and Community Mobilization: The 1988 Massachusetts Prevailing Wage Initiative" (Paper presented at the New England Political Science Association, Cambridge, Massachusetts, April 1989).

influencing legislation. In return, they are able to deliver campaign contri-butions and the votes of their members in the district. Normally the result is a classic case of what Theodore Lowi has called "interest group liberal-ism";[35] public-employee unions press strongly for particularized benefits and are opposed only by diffuse taxpayer resistance, so the unions normally win. This has often been the case in Massachusetts—but not always, as we shall see.

Grass-roots Lobbying

The civil rights and campus protest movements of the 1960s and 1970s spawned a host of community organizations all across Massachusetts. Some were launched by former campus activists seeking to broaden their base, others were initiated by local residents who saw and admired the successes of groups elsewhere. All shared some relation to the New Left tenet that all people have a right to participate in making decisions that affect their lives. These local groups developed a wide repertory of political tactics, from civil disobedience, to picketing of officials' homes, to mass attendance at legislative hearings. While many such groups were unable to sustain grass-roots involvement and burned themselves out after a few years, a few have developed funding mechanisms and membership structures that have enabled them to become more permanent. A typical example of such a group is the Massachusetts Public Interest Research Group, more com-monly known as MassPIRG, which was cited both by legislators (tied for tenth place) and by the legislative staff (tied for sixth place) as among the most powerful groups in the state (see Table 6.7 below).

MassPIRG is part of a national PIRG network, inspired by and still affili-ated with Ralph Nader. Nader's idea was that college students vote to have a per capita fee added to their tuition bills, either as a portion of the student activities fee or as an additional levy, and paid in a lump sum to a state PIRG, which would do research and lobby in the public interest—at least, as the PIRG conceived it. The idea caught on at several campuses, providing MassPIRG with a stable membership and source of funds.

This official campus funding arrangement is unique to the state PIRGs. In addition, MassPIRG uses a technique that it shares with a number of similar organizations: the professional canvass. Full-time and part-time can-

35. Theodore J. Lowi, *The End of Liberalism: The Second Republic of the United States*, 2nd ed. (New York: W. W. Norton, 1979), 50–61.

vassers, many of them students, are hired on commission to go door-to-door talking about PIRG's current campaigns and asking for contributions. No canvasser is likely to grow rich under this arrangement, but many young people find it rewarding to pick up some ready cash while contributing to a cause they believe in. The canvass produces new dues-paying members, occasional activists, and a steady source of funds to pay the expenses of organizing, research, and lobbying.

MassPIRG has sought to represent the diverse interests of citizens and consumers, counteracting the tendency toward "interest group liberalism" mentioned above. Typical MassPIRG legislative goals over the years have included mail-in voter registration, the closing of nuclear power plants, more rigorous testing of drinking water, and requiring developers to include child-care facilities in large commercial or industrial properties.[36]

MassPIRG, together with a group of similar grass-roots organizations, played a central role in developing the initiative petition as a lobbying tool. Article 48 of the amendments to the Massachusetts Convention, which provides for the right of initiative, was ratified in 1918 but had fallen into relative disuse by the early 1960s. However, the initiative has seen a revival in the last two decades. Early efforts included unsuccessful attempts to regulate utility rates and to enact a bottle-deposit law, and a successful one to allow cities and towns to tax business property at a higher rate than residential property. By the late 1970s, citizen-originated referenda often dominated the otherwise uninteresting ballot in statewide elections, further fragmenting the policy process.

Such groups as MassPIRG and Massachusetts Fair Share liked the initiative because it not only gave them a chance to defeat better-financed interests but also provided the kind of organizing tactic they needed to maintain their mass-membership base. These advantages soon became apparent to another group that felt excluded form the state's power structure, the far right. Following the well-publicized victory of the Jarvis-Gann tax-cutting initiative, "Proposition 13," in California, conservative activist Barbara Anderson launched an initiative drive to enact "Proposition 2½." In this case, the number referred not to the measure's position on the referendum ballot (it was actually Question 2) but to its central provision: With certain qualifications and modifications, no city or town would be permitted to set its property-tax rate at more than 2.5 percent of fair market value.

Anderson's action touched off a protracted battle. Proposition 2½ threatened the vital interests of public employees, who feared that passage

36. *MassPIRG Report* 21 (1988), no. 1.

would deprive local government of the money to pay them. If that wasn't enough, it also contained provisions repealing all state mandates for spending by local school authorities and abolishing compulsory arbitration of labor disputes involving police and fire departments. These provisions had been important past victories of the teachers and of the police and fire unions, respectively. Advocates of improved welfare, health care, and housing also opposed Proposition 2½; although their programs were state-funded, they realized the state would have to make up some of the local governments' fiscal losses, leaving less for other state functions. Local governments themselves opposed the referendum almost unanimously, as did most other elected officials. On the other side, Anderson and her group, Citizens for Limited Taxation (CLT), received major support from the Massachusetts High Technology Council, from real-estate interests, and to a less visible extent from other business groups. Because the state's voters were to decide, both sides had to go beyond the usual lobbying tactics. Media advertising, bumper stickers, leafleting, and grass-roots meetings burgeoned. But ultimately the chance to vote for lower taxes proved irresistible. Proposition 2½ was enacted—1,438,768 to 998,839—in the 1980 general election.

The initiative and referendum process leads to the enactment of a state statute. Like any statute, Proposition 2½ could have been amended or repealed by the legislature, but CLT was able to combine grass-roots pressure with lobbying to rule this out almost immediately. State legislators and local elected officials alike, almost all of whom had opposed the referendum beforehand, scrambled to get back in step with their constituents by announcing that they had gotten the message and would try their best to make the new law work. State aid to local government was increased, but not enough to make up for the loss in local revenues; public employees were laid off and services were cut back. The sense of crisis wore off after two or three years, but the unions had learned that there were new limits on their influence, and both left and right had learned that the initiative process could be used by either side.

Both MassPIRG and CLT remain active. In 1990 the CLT employed two paid agents and reported spending $14,163 on lobbying, while MassPIRG employed eleven agents and spent $130,266.[37] While the CLT is still influential, it no longer succeeds in presenting itself as the voice of the tax revolt; it never managed to develop an organized mass base out of those

37. Massachusetts Secretary of State, *Financial Statistics for Lobbyists 1990* and *Legislative Agents and Employers, Disclosed Salaries 1990.*

who voted for Proposition 2½, and in 1990 it was defeated in a referendum campaign to cut the state income tax rate. In the survey, it was mentioned twenty times as one of the groups most commonly heard from, but only fifteen of those who mentioned it considered it to be a "grass-roots citizens group," while the other five listed it as a "business group." MassPIRG's condition has been more stable. While it never reached the height of power once attained by the CLT, it does have a mass base on the campuses and in individual members obtained through canvassing. It continues to enjoy mixed success as it tackles controversial issues, as in its recent campaign to require the use of recyclable packaging materials for retail merchandise.

Environmental protection organizations in Massachusetts comprise a hybrid category. On some issues they resort to grass-roots mobilization; this has been particularly true of the long battle over nuclear power and of the successful effort to pass a bottle-deposit law. But much of the environmentalists' concern has been with preserving open space or protecting the state's wetlands and coastline from destructive development. There has been grass-roots involvement on these issues too, but the tactics have centered on education and persuasion of policymakers rather than on mass mobilization and initiative petitions. These tactics have been fairly successful; Massachusetts now has strong coastal-zone management and wetlands protection laws, and the environmental interest has encouraged executive officials to make use of them. This success may have come more easily in part because the areas protected are found in towns inhabited by the states's social elite. Success in cleaning up Boston Harbor, where untreated sewage washes up on beaches used by the working class, has been harder to come by.

The Catholic Church

In 1958 Duane Lockard declared, "A good deal of foolishness has been written about the relationship between the Catholic church and the Democratic party in Massachusetts."[38] Much of this foolishness is still believed, yet legislators and staff in the survey were nearly unanimous in rating religious groups as the least influential of the types of group included. The Roman Catholic church does try to influence politics and legislation, as do Protestant churches to a lesser extent. Twenty-two legislators mentioned

38. Lockard, New England State Politics, 164.

the Catholic church, and thirteen mentioned the Massachusetts Council of Churches among the religious groups most commonly heard from. Eleven aides also mentioned the Catholic church, the only group mentioned more than three times.[39] But only three respondents considered "religious groups" to have "a great deal" of influence on legislation. Moreover, the Catholic church has not been very successful in battles over policy. Its highest priorities have been restricting abortions, gaining state financial support for parochial schools, reducing access to birth-control information, and preventing use of the death penalty. Only on the last issue has it been successful, and here it has been joined by the liberal groups that have opposed it on the first three.

However, the Catholic church has won more often in the legislature itself; its final defeats have come in the courts, or from the voters. Abortion policy provides a good example. While the right of a pregnant woman to have an abortion is protected by the U.S. Constitution and the federal courts, states are not required to pay for abortions through the Medicaid program, and no federal matching funds are provided to states that choose to pay for abortions. The Massachusetts legislature voted in 1979 not to pay for abortions with state funds, either for Medicaid patients or for state employees. This law was revoked by the state's Supreme Judicial Court, which found it to be unconstitutionally discriminatory against women, and the state resumed paying for abortions. Antiabortion forces, which included the Catholic church, then sought to amend the state constitution. Amendments must be approved by two successive biennial legislatures, which meet in joint session as Constitutional Conventions ("ConCons") for this purpose, and then submitted to the voters at the next general elections. Advocates of abortion rights were able to slow down but not halt passage of the amendment by the "ConCon." In 1986 a question appeared on the ballot that would amend the constitution to "allow the legislature to prohibit or regulate abortions to the extent permitted by the United States Constitution," except for "abortions required to prevent the death of the mother." The ensuing referendum campaign was hard-fought but not particularly close; the proposed amendment was defeated by a 42–58 percent margin.[40] It was a bad election for the Catholic church, as a second proposed amendment, which would have permitted state aid to religious and

---

39. It may be relevant that fourteen of the legislators surveyed, but only five of the aides, identified themselves as Protestants.

40. *Election Statistics 1986*, 450.

other private elementary and secondary schools, was defeated even more badly, 30–70 percent.

These events show that the Catholic church does not control Massachusetts, but they do raise a question about the survey results. Is the low influence reported for religious groups inconsistent with the success of the Catholic church in the legislature on these two issues? While the available evidence does not allow a definitive answer, I do not believe that the legislators and aides were responding dishonestly. Rather, many legislators are personally opposed to the right to abortion. While many of these are Catholics and see their position as part of their Catholic beliefs, they also see it as coming from within, from their own consciences, rather than from without, from pressure by church leaders. While we cannot tell what would happen in the unlikely event that the Catholic church were to change its official position, the legislators themselves believe that they are not responding to influence when they vote on abortion.

This interpretation is reinforced by the knowledge that the Catholic church as an organization does not represent the views of its members. While the church has made opposition to abortion rights the centerpiece of its political program, opinion surveys have shown consistently that a majority of Catholic voters are on the other side. This has been reflected in the church's inability to deliver votes. The antiabortion amendment lost in every county in the state, but came closest to winning in Berkshire County, one of the most Protestant. And when the archbishop of Boston called on the faithful to vote against U.S. representatives Barney Frank and James Shannon in 1982, both won the election.

Women's Groups

As is true in every state, women are underrepresented among elected officials in Massachusetts. Women make up 52.4 percent of the population of Massachusetts, but only 19.4 percent of the House of Representatives and 17.5 percent of the state Senate. The percentage of women in both houses is 19 percent, which places Massachusetts twenty-first among the fifty states.[41] As of 1992 there were no women in the state's congressional dele-

41. National Conference of State Legislators, "Women Legislators Following the 1990 Election" (Denver: National Conference of State Legislatures, 1991).

gation.[42] The former lieutenant governor, Evelyn Murphy, is the only woman to have held statewide elected office. While seeking to increase the number of women in politics, political feminists have also sought to compensate for their underrepresentation through lobbying efforts.

Survey respondents ranked women's groups one step from the bottom in frequency of contact and influence on legislation. They were ranked somewhat higher in influence on the respondent's own vote, but even here were only fourth. However, women legislators scored women's groups markedly higher than their colleagues did on frequency of contact and on influence on their own vote (Table 6.5).

Legislators of both genders concur in assigning women's groups less-than-average influence on the outcome of legislation, but these groups are both heard from more often and given a better reception by women legislators than by their male colleagues. No doubt the selective lobbying of the most receptive representatives is a necessity, given the resource constraints faced by women's groups. Of the four women's organizations mentioned most frequently by survey respondents, only two reported spending any money at

Table 6.5. Mean Ratings of Women's Group Activity and Effectiveness by Women Legislators and All Legislators, Massachusetts, 1987

Characteristic Rated	Mean Rating by Women Legislators ($N = 12$)	Mean Rating by All Legislators ($N = 38$)
Groups most often heard from (from 1, never, to 5, very frequently)	3.83	3.29
Influence on own vote (from 1, none, to 5, a great deal)	3.92	3.26
Influence on outcome of legislation (from 1, none, to 5, a great deal)	2.92	2.89

Source: Calculated by author from November–December 1987 survey.

42. There have been two women representatives from Massachusetts, Louise Day Hicks, a conservative Democrat, and Margaret Heckler, a moderate Republican. Both were defeated for reelection, Hicks after one term, Heckler after eight.

all on lobbying. The National Organization for Women (NOW) reported spending of $6,093, with one paid agent, but did not report in 1989 or 1990. The League of Women Voters spent $526 and had no paid agents. "Mass Choice" and the Massachusetts Women's Political Caucus each received at least ten mentions, but neither is registered as a lobbying organization. Mass Choice is legally a political action committee; presumably the Massachusetts Women's Political Caucus relies on volunteer efforts by their members for any lobbying they do.

Despite their shortage of money, women's groups have had some success. Massachusetts has both ratified the Equal Rights Amendment and adopted a similar amendment to its own constitution. The women's lobby has also won passage of a bill to change sentencing practices to make the laws against rape more enforceable and of various measures to improve the enforcement of child-support orders. The feminist movement has done much to increase awareness of the problems of battered women and has been able to force the removal or censure of some judges who have been notably insensitive on this issue.

But women's groups have met with markedly less success on issues that require spending money. Every year a broad coalition of women's groups, social service agencies, and welfare advocates launches the latest round in the "Up to Poverty" campaign, seeking to bring the income of AFDC recipients up to the official poverty level. The coalition lobbies the governor and the executive secretary of human services to ask for more money and then lobbies to raise the amount of the governor's request. Nevertheless, every year the shortfall between benefits and the poverty line increases. The "Up to Poverty" coalition is not able to overcome the constraints imposed on the budget by those who support other spending programs or oppose higher taxes.

THE MOST POWERFUL INTEREST GROUPS

Along with questions about different types of groups, respondents were asked to rate the seven types separately by three different criteria: how often they heard from each type of group; how likely their own vote (or their boss's, in the case of aides) was to be influenced by that type of group; and how much influence that type of group had on the outcome of legislation. The responses were averaged, and interest-group types were ranked (see Table 6.6). The data show a certain amount of cynicism on the part of the respondents. While they report that their own votes are influenced most by environmentalist and grass-roots citizens groups, which are popularly seen as more benign and democratic, they perceive business and labor, traditionally viewed as narrower "special interests," as having the most influence on the votes of their colleagues. Similarly, respondents see themselves as more responsive than the legislature as a whole to women's groups. In part, this may show that the sample is unrepresentative; in particular, proportionately more women than men responded (12 female and 26 male legislators filled out questionnaires; of the 200 members in 1987, 37 were female), but it may also represent a recognition of what one respondent wrote on the questionnaire: "Most high-powered lobby efforts are really geared toward the House Speaker, the Senate president, and a few key committee chairmen because the rank-and-file legislators rarely vote against what these people say."

The specific groups most often mentioned by both legislators and staff members in response to a request to list by name the groups which are "the most powerful in Massachusetts" include business (AIM), local government (MMA), labor (AFL-CIO, MTA, Firefighters), and citizens groups of left MassPIRG) and right (CLT) (see Table 6.7). On most major issues, powerful groups are likely to be opposed to each other, yet every group listed as powerful has some issues over which it is the dominant influence.

Table 6.6. Composite Rankings (by Legislators and Staffs) of Interest-Group Influence, Massachusetts, 1987

Type of Group	Frequency of Contact		Influence on Personal Vote		Influence on Outcome of Legislation	
	Leg.	Staff	Leg.	Staff	Leg.	Staff
Labor	4th	5th	3rd	6th	1st	1st (tie)
Business	2nd	1st	5th	5th	2nd	1st (tie)
Environmentalist	1st	3rd	1st	2nd	3rd	5th
Grass-roots citizens	3rd	2nd	2nd	1st	4th	3rd
Professional	5th	4th	6th	3rd	5th	4th
Women's	6th	6th	4th	4th	6th	6th
Religious	7th	7th	7th	7th	7th	7th

Source: Calculated from author's November–December 1987 survey.

Table 6.7. Legislator and Staff Mentions of Groups as Among the Most Powerful in Massachusetts, 1987

Group	Legislator Mentions	Staff Mentions
Association Industries of Massachusetts (AIM)	12	7
Citizens for Limited Taxation (CLT)	12	7
Insurance Industry	11	6
Massachusetts Teachers Assn (MTA)	12	7
AFL-CIO	8	5
Massachusetts Hospital Assn (MHA)	6	6
Professional Firefighters of Massachusetts	6	3
Massachusetts Bar Assn	5	3
Massachusetts High Tech Council	4	2
Massachusetts Municipal Assn	7	3
Massachusetts Public Interest Research Group (PIRG)	4	5
Gun Owners Action League	4	2
League of Women Voters	1	3
Chamber of Commerce	0	3
Massachusetts Medical Society	1	4

Source: Calculated from author's November–December 1987 survey.

Interest groups are a big and growing business in Massachusetts. The number of registered lobbyists continues to rise, as do both interest-group spending and campaign contributions. During the 1980s, as the Republicans failed to convert their two presidential victories into organizational strength, Massachusetts seemed to be developing a traditional one-party system.

But Massachusetts differed from the one-party states of the Old South in having strong labor unions, environmental organizations, women's groups, and such grass-roots groups as MassPIRG. These interests were not strong enough, singly or collectively, to overcome the economic weight and political power of the state's businesses, but they were strong enough to prevent the development of the kind of single-interest business dominance common in the Old South and the West. Moreover, there were and are important divisions within the business community—for example, the huge health-care industry depends on third-party payments, which are paid through taxes and premiums assessed in part on other industries. Such divisions acted to prevent single-interest dominance. Interest groups are also constrained by powerful elected officials, particularly the governor, the senate president, and the Speaker of the House. At the end of the decade, Massachusetts interest-group strength could best be described as dominant/complementary.

Recent events suggest that party competition may return. The Republican party made a significant comeback in the 1990 election, winning the governorship and the treasurer's office and doubling the size of its state Senate bloc. The new governor, William Weld, is a Republican in the mold of John Volpe and Francis Sargent, and his victory would have done no more than theirs did to change the balance of party strength. But the Republican legislative gains may have more lasting importance. The Republican state committee, which in the last few elections had run talented neophytes for U.S. Congress (and seen them obliterated) while virtually ignoring the state legislature, reversed its strategy; it made a strong effort to find legislative candidates, and the party gained seats as a result. It also made a serious effort to shed its previous antiabortion label; Weld, Cellucci, and several successful Republican legislative candidates in 1990 took strong positions in favor of the right to reproductive choice.

If the Republicans can sustain their efforts for the next few elections, Massachusetts may come to have a real two-party system.[43] If this happens, it may lead the Democratic party to gain more policy coherence as well; some interest groups may then find themselves forced into partisan coalitions. Labor unions, citizens groups of the left and right, and the Massachusetts High Tech Council already show signs of partisan sympathy.

However, environmentalist groups, women's groups, and other business groups—particularly the life-insurance and health-care interests, but also AIM—seem determined to work with members of both parties. Unless the parties unify themselves much more strongly than they have to date, these groups will probably succeed in remaining neutral. The next election will show whether the Republicans can sustain their momentum. If they do, Massachusetts interest-group politics may move all the way into our complementary category, with policy-making dominated by party-centered coalitions.

---

43. On the other hand, Weld may find—as Volpe and Sargent did in their time— that he can govern best by cooperating with the legislature's Democratic leaders. If so, this may undercut his party's ability to make a strong partisan appeal to the voters.

Earlier versions of this chapter were presented in 1989 at the New York State Political Science Association and at the New England Political Science Association, and portions of it appeared in the *New England Journal of Public Policy*, vol. 7 (Fall–Winter 1991). The author wishes to thank the editors of this volume; discussants Edmund Beard, Jerome Mileur, and Stewart Shapiro; reviewer Robert Friedman; and Frances Burke, Donald Levitan, Richard McDowell, Garrison Nelson, David Pfeiffer, Padraig O'Malley, and Gerry Morse, for their comments and suggestions on earlier drafts. The survey would have been impossible without the help of Jean Walsh and the student assistants of the Suffolk University Department of Government. The staff of the Research Desk of Suffolk University's Sawyer Library and of the Office of the Massachusetts Secretary of State and the Office of Campaign and Political Finance; Mary F. Renstrom of the National Conference of State Legislatures; and Mark Cheffro gave invaluable help in obtaining documents.

7

New Hampshire: Tradition and the Challenge of Growth

Robert Egbert and Michelle Anne Fistek

New Hampshire is perhaps best known for holding the first primary in presidential election years, the flamboyant conservative style of its only statewide daily newspaper, its tradition of resisting broad-based taxes, its inexpensive liquor stores on major highways, and its hard-nosed conservatism expressed in the state motto, "Live Free or Die." Challenging the granite traditions of people who revel in being different is the advance of real change in the state's economic, social, and political environments. Growth is the central feature of New Hampshire politics today, redefining the parameters of political conflict in the state. Growth has expanded the scope of group conflict and has changed power relationships among groups.

Rapid change is unusual in the state. Its institutions and culture have always resisted pressures of modernization, industrialization, and postindustrial society. Perhaps the major attraction to new residents in the state is the folksy, common-man, practical, nonimposing lifestyle of another era. Ironically, it is that very attraction that has created an atmosphere in which the former flavor of public and private life may no longer be possible. The invasion from "Taxachusetts" and other northeastern states has brought elements of a new lifestyle and new expectations about the role of government in today's society.

Population growth in the state is at explosive levels. From a modest 491,524 in 1940, the state's population grew to 1,109,117 by 1990. The decades of the 1940s and 1950s saw a growth rate of about 12 percent; the 1960s brought a 20 percent increase in population; the 1970s, 22 percent; and the 1980s, about 21 percent. The two southeastern counties on the Massachusetts border have absorbed much of this new population. The decade from 1970 to 1980 saw 23 percent and 37 percent population increases in Hillsborough and Rockingham counties. New Hampshire has become much more prosperous over the same period. For example, the gross state product nearly doubled during the 1960s. Some of the consequences of growth have been very welcome: New Hampshire had one of the lowest unemployment rates in the nation during the 1980s, dropping to below 3 percent from 1986 through 1988. It is yet too early to predict with certainty the duration and severity of the 1991–92 recession, but it clearly will have a strong impact on employment and population growth.

NEW HAMPSHIRE POLITICS AND GOVERNMENT

To understand interest-group activity in New Hampshire, we first need to outline some of the general characteristics of the unusual structure and spirit of the state's politics. One of the original thirteen states, and the ninth to ratify the U.S. Constitution, New Hampshire has always seen itself as special. Its state constitution dates from 1783 and, though voters may call for a constitutional convention every ten years, it has retained the essentials of the original form. Attempts to reduce the size of the legislature and increase legislative salaries, to reorganize the executive branch, and to eliminate the Governor's Council have failed. Even the recent institution of annual sessions of the legislature is under serious attack by legislative leaders. It appears that for the near future the state will meet its challenges with its traditional structure of government intact.

The New Hampshire legislature, the General Court, consists of a House of Representatives with 400 members and a Senate of 24 members. By far the largest state legislature, it is also perhaps the most amateur by commonly used standards.[1] Salaries, by constitutional mandate, are $200 per biennium plus a small per diem for up to fifteen days a term and mileage, and $250 per biennium with per diem and mileage for the presiding officers of each house. Only legislative leaders and a few committees enjoy staff assistance. No office space is available to House members except leadership; instead, each member has a mailbox under his or her seat in the chambers. Senate members share office space. The small Legislative Research and Committee Research Offices respond to requests from legislative

---

1. Thomas R. Dye, *Politics in States and Communities*, 5th ed. (Englewood Cliffs, N.J.: Prentice-Hall, 1985), 157.

leaders and committees only. Meeting annually from January through April, The General Court accomplishes its formal work on Tuesday through Thursday. It is extremely unlikely that this "citizen legislature" will change significantly; most observers in the state view it with pride.

Several attempts to restructure the executive branch have failed. The governor is elected for a two-year term with no limitation on succession, has no item veto, has direct legal authority over only a few major executive offices, and shares some powers with the Executive Council. The Executive Council, the last such functioning body in the nation, consists of five members elected by district for terms of two years. It has power to advise the governor, to approve all gubernatorial appointments, to approve all sizable state contracts, and to approve the exercise of the pardon. State administration is performed by at least 160 departments, boards, and advisory and regulatory commissions. Officers in these are selected by such various means as appointment by the governor with Council approval, election by the General Court, and election by the State Supreme Court.

The state court system consists of a Supreme Court, Superior Courts in each county, and special jurisdiction courts, such as the town District Courts. There are no intermediate courts of appeals. The Supreme Court has supervisory power over all other courts and power to establish procedural guidelines and rules of practice therein. All judges are appointed and can be removed for reasonable cause by the governor and Council. In addition to its usual judicial powers, the Supreme Court may give advisory opinions at the request of the governor or either house of the General Court.

The subject of taxes is central to political discussion in the state. Eschewing broad-based income taxes and sales taxes, voters reject any candidate who fails to subscribe to the "no broad-base tax" pledge. New Hampshire state revenues are raised primarily in the form of "sin" taxes, taxes on visitors, several kinds of lotteries and pari-mutuel gambling, some very narrowly based income and sales taxes, and state liquor sales. The state contributes very little to local governments such as school districts; consequently, the local governments tax property extremely heavily. The recession of the early 1990s, state revenue shortfalls, and rebellion against increasing and unfair property taxes have combined to prompt the first serious discussion of tax reform in many years. A few incumbent officials and several candidates for 1992 have endorsed tax reform but carefully couch such discussion in terms of "property tax relief" or "making the business profits tax more fair." Drastic change is unlikely in the near future.

New Hampshire is a modified one-party Republican state.[2] Only in four cities in the state do Democrats consistently enjoy electoral success: Nashua, Manchester, Portsmouth, and Berlin. The Republican party is a loose coalition of extreme conservatives, moderates, and Democrats who use the Republican label in areas inhospitable to the Democratic party. The Republican majority in the legislature is not cohesive. Voter registration favored the Republican party for a long time, but the number of independent registrants now exceeds Republican registration. The electoral fate of the Republican party is unlikely to be seriously challenged in the near future in spite of recent energetic attempts to rejuvenate the state Democratic party.

The political culture of New Hampshire has been primarily "moralistic," with some elements of the "individualistic" culture in the most southern part of the state.[3] Unlike a "traditionalistic" political culture in which citizens defer to the political judgment of elites, and unlike an "individualistic" culture in which political participation is seen as a means to satisfy group and individual interests, the "moralistic" culture expects widespread participation with an eye to the good of the community as a whole. Article 1 of Part the First of the New Hampshire constitution declares that government is instituted for "the general good." Participation in the affairs of the community and the state is expected of and provided for all adults. In the 1988 presidential primary, voter turnout was higher than 50 percent, much higher than in other primary states. The public does not accept the idea that their elected officials should be in office for personal gain, as illustrated by the token salaries of legislators and the amateur nature of the legislature. With the exception of localities designated as cities, citizens possess the legislative power of the community through the town meeting. Many large cities even continue to hold "town meetings" for resolution of the most serious and controversial of local issues. Although attendance at such meetings is not extremely high, the meeting has important symbolic meaning as ordinary citizens assume leadership roles, politely consider each others' positions, and demand that all details of town management be made available for their scrutiny. Such interest extends to state affairs. Since 1784, Article 8 of Part the First of the state constitution has required that all public meetings and public records be open to the public. New

2. Ibid., 116.
3. See Daniel J. Elazar, *American Federalism: A View From the States* (New York: Thomas Y. Crowell, 1966), 107.

Hampshire people have a clear sense that the business of government is their business, that one should not hesitate to demand open disclosure of official acts, and that public business should be accomplished as a public service with few perquisites and little or no remuneration. This sense is reflected in the structure of government described above.

Long ago, consistent with its preference for open government, the General Court enacted several "sunshine" laws of importance to interest groups and political committees. Since 1909, legislative lobbyists have been required to register with the secretary of state and report related expenditures. Each lobbyist must pay a $50 annual fee for each group represented. The law does not clearly require agency and other governmental lobbyists to register, and they do not do so. Political committees that spend in excess of $200 in election campaigns have been required to file receipt and expenditure reports since 1911. The law treats individual campaign committees and PACs in the same manner. While these laws do not greatly limit the activities of interest groups or PACs, big spenders are subject to adverse public scrutiny when the *Union Leader* publishes this information.

New Hampshire's peculiar brand of conservatism is not, as reputed, simply a reflection of citizens' desire to be left alone. State government is expected to be active in providing for the common good but to do so frugally. It is not intolerant. The habit of hearing all opinions and leaving most personal decisions to individuals may prompt gossip about some individuals but not their exclusion or persecution. New Hampshire is one of few states whose constitution prohibits discrimination on the basis of sex. While clearly conservative in fiscal and international affairs, there is a somewhat more moderate view on social and class issues.

Within this context, organized interests compete for influence in the government of New Hampshire. The state's highly porous and accessible political system encourages public and private groups in many ways to further their view of the public interest.

THE ISSUE CONTEXT

Most salient and persistent issues in New Hampshire are somehow related to growth. Gubernatorial election campaigns have recently focused on the issue of the state's considerable need for additional electric power. The Seabrook nuclear power plant has been seen by recent governors as the only realistic solution. Among the plant's strongest supporters was former Governor John Sununu. His opponents, calling him a "nuclear theologist," were numerous environmental and public-interest groups, residents and local towns near the seacoast site of the plant, and state and local governments in Massachusetts and Maine. The plant was finally licensed after years of delays caused by construction and safety problems, inspection requirements, and confusion about its funding. Conflict continues to focus on the safety and financial issues. The plant is located in the center of a popular beach area subject to extreme congestion during the summer months. The possibility of evacuating the area in case of a nuclear accident is, at best, questionable. The Public Service Company of New Hampshire (PSNH), the principal owner of the facility, has sought debt protection, and only the purchase of a large share of the plant by Northeast Utilities has averted a complete disaster for PSNH. A related but less internally divisive issue was the selection of a Hillsborough, New Hampshire, site by the Nuclear Regulatory Commission as a possible nuclear-waste depository. Although it appears that the issue has been resolved happily from the state's perspective, there lurks some sense of a need to maintain vigilance.

Housing problems have also emerged as a result of growth. The state has not acted to offset the virtual abandonment of federal programs in this area by the Reagan and Bush administrations. While a glut of condominiums has emerged in some areas of the state, low-cost housing has been largely ignored. According to the Office of State Planning, during the mid-1980s the average price of a home more than doubled, to $140,000, excluding many families from the homeowners' market and creating demand-push inflation in the rental market. The present recession has seen some moderation of prices, but few sales have resulted and repossessions are plentiful. Legislation was introduced in the House of Representatives in 1988 to provide incentives to build low-cost housing and to assist buyers with interest relief, but the Senate and the governor managed to cut the modest authorizations by one-half.

Highways create conflict in New Hampshire as growth taxes the capacity of existing roads and demands new construction. The north-south corridors are served by three interstate highways, but east-west highways are extremely inadequate. In the southern portion of the state, increased development and commuters to and from employment in Massachusetts have resulted in serious air-pollution problems in Nashua, the state's largest urban area. The state's current plan is to require inspection of vehicle emissions in the Nashua area and to expand freeway capacity, charging tolls to finance the expansion.

Several law-and-order issues surfaced during the 1980s. The state prison and Youth Development Center are overextended in terms of capacity. Drug problems have attracted considerable attention, due in part to heightened national publicity and to increased drug-marketing activities moving from Massachusetts to the southern part of New Hampshire. The age at which minors may be tried as adults for serious crimes was lowered to thirteen years in 1988.

Although the state pays little of the cost of education, it actively supervises local districts and administrative units. Educational concerns include an increasing dropout rate, layoffs of teachers so local districts can balance their budgets, provision of kindergarten by fewer than half of the school districts, and funding to meet federal requirements for special education. Recent revenue shortfalls reduce the probability that increased state funding of education will be a high priority. Because the constitution requires the state to fund mandated programs, localities will be left to support education the best way they can. This occurs at a time when cities are experiencing a popular revolt against rising property taxes. For example, the Laconia school budget was slashed by independent city councilors calling themselves the "Straight Arrows."

One of the issues recently attracting widespread group activity was interstate banking. The legislature passed a regional interstate banking bill in 1987 after several years of debate. But it did not provide the bank commissioner with much guidance regarding implementation criteria, so a new round of conflict ensued. Following a series of outside acquisitions, mergers, and the more recent failure of several banks, the state is left with only three major banks and a few small local ones.

PATTERNS OF INTEREST INVOLVEMENT

New Hampshire's earliest history is of three fairly isolated peoples inhabiting separate geographical areas. The western people in the Connecticut River valley, who had strong ties to Connecticut, and the central Merrimack River people, who had migrated from Massachusetts, were mostly farmers. The early Portsmouth population relied on shipping and trade for their livelihood. Portsmouth, the earliest state capital, had been one of the most active shipping ports in America during the colonial period. It was largely the Federalist influence of the trading interests that resulted in New Hampshire's ratification of the U.S. constitution. Growth of the central area of the state, and placement of the state capital in Concord, followed the decline of the importance of Portsmouth shipping. Agriculture, always marginal, also suffered serious decline in importance, as textile mills, lumbering, paper mills, and railroads became the primary industries of the state in the nineteenth century.

Interest-group power in New Hampshire has typically resulted from development of coalitions among the major business interests of the state. Although they did not include New Hampshire in their study, Harmon Zeigler and Hendrick van Dalen's category of "alliance of dominant groups" best describes the state's pattern.[4] By the middle of the nineteenth century, water-powered textile mills were being built along the major rivers of the state and soon joined with the Democratic party in protecting industrial interests. These became a major focus of industrial growth in the United States, strongly influencing state and national policy.

During the latter half of the 1800s, textile mills and lumber and railroad interests formed a coalition with the Republican party and established hegemony in New Hampshire politics. Operating in the manner of the political machine, the coalition controlled state government by patronage and informal bargaining among the party elite and the dominant interests of the time. For years state legislators were routinely given Boston & Maine Railroad passes. This alliance was weakened in 1909 when primary nominations were established in the state parties. Diversification of industry, dissolution of the Republican party machinery, and moderate growth of Democratic voting strength among Irish and French-Canadian immigrants introduced a new era of interest control of state politics.

Beginning in the last decades of the nineteenth century and continuing to the present, growth in tourism has prompted recognition of the importance of maintaining a hospitable and attractive environment. Before their eventual demise, textile mills began to side with progressive and conservation groups against the lumber and paper interests, which were effectively destroying much scenic beauty and watershed by denuding entire areas of

4. L. Harmon Zeigler and Hendrik van Dalen, "Interest Groups in State Politics," in Herbert Jacob and Kenneth N. Vines, eds., *Politics in the American States: A Comparative Analysis*, 3rd ed. (Boston: Little, Brown, 1976), 96.

the state of their forest cover. Railroads, supporting tourism as well as the other major economic interests, were caught in the middle. Expansion of highway transportation has since rendered them insignificant in the state today. Small and medium-size businesses began to develop outside the traditional population centers in the river valleys. Particularly in the southern part of the state, immigration of factories and other businesses from Massachusetts began to occur. New Hampshire was seen as offering more favorable tax and labor climates than the more populous southern New England states.

By 1981 Sarah McCally Morehouse reported that New Hampshire had a strong interest-group system and that public utilities, paper manufacturing, lumber, and race track interests were dominant.[5] Comparing the states, she found that strong pressure systems correlated highly with a lack of "modern integrated cultures," single or few major economic enterprises, homogeneity, and rural, low population states.[6] Recent changes in New Hampshire, including growth, changing issues, and economic diversification, have brought an increased number and variety of interests to the fore.

INTEREST-GROUP POWER TODAY

Many interest groups do not actively participate in lobbying in every legislative term. Of 173 groups registered under New Hampshire statutes to lobby the legislature in 1988, some 58 did not register in 1987, and an equal number registered in 1987 did not register in 1988. Bills to be presented each year in the General Court are made available to legislators and the public before the beginning of the session, and groups seem to determine quite early whether they are interested in paying the required $50 registration fee. Most groups remain vigilant and engage in some other activities, whether or not they decide to lobby. The number of groups acting politically increases incrementally each year.

While exact numbers of organized interests in the state are elusive, those registered to lobby are probably somewhat representative (see Table 7.1). In 1988 and 1990 the most numerous groups were business- and develop-

5. Sarah McCally Morehouse, *State Politics, Parties, and Policy* (New York: Holt, Rinehart & Winston, 1981), 109.
6. Ibid., 112.

Table 7.1. Registered Lobby Groups, New Hampshire, 1987 and 1990

Category	1987	1990
Business / development	65	71
Banking / financial services	15	10
Insurance	13	15
Citizen / public interest	12	17
Medical / health	18	20
Professional (other than medical)	6	5
Conservation / environment	5	3
Public utilities	12	14
Tourism / hospitality	5	5
Intergovernmental	5	6
Labor	7	8
Civil rights / civil liberties	2	2
Educational institutions	1	2
Religious	0	1
Other and unclassifiable	7	11
Total	173	191

Source: Reports of income and expenditures of lobbyists, Office of the Secretary of State, State of New Hampshire.

ment-oriented. Distant runners-up were citizen and public-interest groups, insurance, medical and health, public utilities, and banking and financial services. Most interest groups spend modestly for lobbying in New Hampshire (see Table 7.2). In 1987 and 1990 about two-thirds of the groups spent less than $10,000 in salaries, fees, and expenses in their lobbying activities, and few groups spent more than $40,000. The big spenders in 1987 included the New Hampshire Bankers Association, $64,586; Hinsdale Race Track (pari-mutuel racing), $37,435; Free Access to the Courts (opposing tort liability limitation), $35,692; NEA-NH, $34,616; Rockingham Venture (pari-mutuel racing), $33,311; and Trust for New Hampshire Lands (land conservation), $33,280. Groups spent somewhat more in 1990, with fourteen spending more than $30,000. The highest expenditures included the Rockingham Venture, $62,630; the New Hampshire Municipal Association, $54,040; Wheelabrator Environmental System, $53,038; the New Hampshire Bankers Association, $52,800; the New Hampshire Wholesale Beverage Association, $50,160; and Kawasaki Motors, $45,416.

Table 7.2. Group Expenditures for Legislative Lobbying, New Hampshire, 1987 and 1990

	1987		1990	
Expenditures	No.	%	No.	%
$0–$9,999	116	67	122	64
$10,000–$19,999	33	19	38	20
$20,000–$29,999	18	10	16	8
$30,000–$39,999	5	3	8	4
$40,000–$49,999	0	0	1	1
$50,000 and above	1	1	5	3
Total	173	100	190	100

Source: Reports of income and expenditure of lobbyists, Office of the Secretary of State, State of New Hampshire.

Numbers of groups and the amounts they spend are not conclusive indicators of group strength. However, our interviews revealed a fairly clear consensus about group strength in the state, and recent policy outcomes confirm such perceptions. Most policy impacts seem to reflect the results of pressures by group lobbies rather than single groups, and the most powerful such lobbies can be ranked in two categories. The first, "most powerful," tier includes prodevelopment groups such as realtors, housing, the Business and Industry Association, the banking lobby, and the tourism/hospitality lobby. Important interests in the second, "powerful," tier include the medical professional lobby, the insurance industry, the conservation lobby, state and school employees, municipalities, fish and game interests, the *Manchester Union Leader*, the criminal-justice lobby, citizens groups, and public utilities.

Groups favoring development have the clear backing of state government and therefore frequently spend fewer resources to influence policy than many opponents. About one-quarter of the members of the General Court are realtors, and the vast majority are or have been engaged in prodevelopment employment. A favorable business climate in the state is a concern that faces little opposition. Even liberal and proenvironment citizens groups find it difficult to oppose growth in the housing industry, given the shortage of affordable housing. Banking interests have an important role and stake in development, but they were recently divided very visibly on the interstate banking controversy. The smaller and local banks opposed interstate banking, while the larger banks were strong supporters. Each side won in part as the law was passed in the form of regional interstate banking. Administrative rules set strict standards on incoming banks and protect many of the interests of local and small banks. Because many state revenues are generated from tourist- and travel-related sources, discouraging development in these areas is seen as self-defeating by those who fear broad-based taxes. These first-tier groups, then, are powerful because they have many resources and they get their way most of the time. More important, their interests are dear to those whom they must influence.

Several comments should be made about some second-tier interests. The *Manchester Union Leader* has long been thought to be the *prime mobil* of New Hampshire politics. If that was ever true, it is much less true today. While it manages to emotionalize an occasional issue, such as prohibition of homosexual foster parents, its influence is limited to a few issues. Its style has become considerably subdued since the death of William Loeb in 1981, and it faces serious competition for people's attention from several regional newspapers and television stations. The *Boston Globe* has introduced a New Hampshire section, "NH Weekly," in its Sunday edition and is, like the *New York Times*, becoming a newspaper of choice for the state's better-educated population. Among the groups mentioned most frequently by interviewees were medical and insurance groups. While most state employees are protected by Blue Cross & Blue Shield, and the prestigious Hitchcock Medical Center at Dartmouth College is highly regarded by officeholders, these and other such interests recently suffered serious defeat in their attempts to pass a limitation of tort liability law. Public utilities have lost status in the state, due in part to the earlier-mentioned problems of the Public Service Company. Citizen and public-interest groups are very successful on occasion. Most of these, including such groups as New Hampshire Citizen Action, Common Cause of New Hampshire, the New Hampshire Civil Liberties Union, and the New Hampshire Women's Lobby, act primarily as watchdog and veto groups rather than as agenda-setters.

ASSESSMENT OF GROUP STRENGTH

We believe that New Hampshire's interest groups now fall into the "complementary" category. In 1981 Sarah McCally Morehouse placed New

Hampshire in the "strong group" category. At that time, politics in New Hampshire was dominated by power, racetracks, lumber, and paper manufacturing. In the ensuing years, New Hampshire has undergone great changes in its economy and population. The number of groups vying for influence in the government has risen, new industries have moved into the state, and the southern tier of the state has become much more urban/suburban in character.

Although political parties remain rather weak and disorganized, the number of groups that fight one another has risen appreciably. This challenge has weakened the power of the groups listed as controlling the state in 1981. Morehouse points out: "As the number of competing groups increases, so do the opportunities for government officials to play the demands of one group against those of another. . . . No single group is likely to predominate."[7]

Although many of the characteristics of the strong interest-group model remain, such as unequal distribution of income and lack of a modern integrated culture, the changes the state is going through are affecting these characteristics. At least in the southern tier of the state, there is wealth, professionalism, and an urban/suburban lifestyle.[8] Another factor that moderates the influence of interest groups is the state's political culture, discussed earlier.

The number of interest groups rises and falls depending on the legislative agenda for any particular year. Groups are activated only by issues of immediate concern to them, not by all legislation. The coalitions they form are not permanent or monolithic but quite fluid, depending on the issues. Even the groups within each of the categories discussed earlier oppose one another frequently. As one contract lobbyist, David Minnis, pointed out, very few issues in the legislature are of a win-or-lose nature. There seems to be an effort made to give everyone something they can at least live with. None of the groups seems to have unlimited or even vast resources. The lobbyists with the greatest resources are contract lobbyists, who actually represent many groups, limiting the focus of their attention and resource utilization.

Interest groups in New Hampshire seem to resemble the national interest groups found by scholars in the 1950s and 1960s.[9] National interest groups

---

7. Ibid., 113.
8. Ibid., 112.
9. See Raymond A. Bauer, Ithiel de Sola Pool, and Lewis Anthony Dexter, *Ameri-*

at that time influenced the details of policies but rarely determined policy outcomes. As Kay Schlozman and John Tierney point out, however, determination of the details of policy should not be viewed as insignificant. Certainly the details of policy help determine how policy is implemented.

In trying to determine the amount of influence interest groups have, it is necessary to go beyond a simple calculation of wins and losses. Schlozman and Tierney point out:

> The appropriate standard for assessing policy impact should not be whether the organization sustained a victory or a defeat, but whether the resolution of a particular political conflict reflects the efforts of organized interests. Sometimes organized interests are able to ameliorate the extent of a defeat; the apparent loss thus masks the degree to which things would have been worse had the organization not gotten involved. Similarly, victories may be false evidence of organizational effectiveness, determined by other factors (such as support of key policymakers) rather than by organized interest activity. In short, in making inferences from cases about organized interest influence, what matters is not simply who won or lost, but whether the score would have been different had interest groups not been active.[10]

Interest groups in New Hampshire do matter. Their influence depends on the nature of the issue, the nature of the demand, the structure of political competition, and the distribution of resources, just as it does in the national legislature.[11]

LOBBYISTS

Lobbying is typically a part-time activity in New Hampshire; indeed, only about 13 percent of registered lobbyists reported earning $20,000 or more

---

can Business and Policy, 2nd ed. (Chicago: Aldine, 1972); Lester W. Milbrath, The Washington Lobbyists (Chicago: Rand McNally, 1963).

10. Kay Lehman Schlozman, and John T. Tierney, Organized Interests and American Democracy (New York: Harper & Row, 1986), 392.

11. Ibid., 317.

from their lobbying efforts in 1987 and 1990 (see Table 7.3). On average, only about ten lobbyists earned more than $40,000. About three-quarters of the lobbyists earned less than $10,000. The few who earn very high incomes are primarily contract lobbyists working on behalf of a variety of groups. The part-time nature of the legislature accounts partially for the low incomes, but the reporting process itself may omit income for some lobbyists. Lobbyists are required to register with the secretary of state and report income for lobbying the General Court only. In-house lobbyists report only a prorated salary for time spent on legislative lobbying, and lobbying other branches of government is not reported at all. Of necessity, therefore, the figures in Table 7.3 are incomplete and perhaps most useful only for making general comparisons.

Typical lobbyists in New Hampshire are employees or members of the groups they represent, call themselves public-relations or governmental-relations specialists, are part-time lobbyists, and earn little of their income from that activity. About 75 percent of New Hampshire lobbyists are male. Approximately 25 percent are attorneys, while others come from such varied backgrounds as education, economics, public relations, railroad labor, real estate, insurance, construction, and sales. In 1987 only thirty-nine were contract lobbyists; most of the remaining 61 percent were in-house lobbyists. There are a few volunteer and individual lobbyists, but they are not required to register, and most do not. There is no clear evidence that

Table 7.3. Lobbyists' Income, New Hampshire, 1987 and 1990

Income	1987		1990	
	No.	%	No.	%
$0–9,999	111	74	114	75
$10,000–$19,999	20	13	19	12
$20,000–$29,999	10	7	5	3
$30,000–$39,999	2	1	4	3
$40,000 and above	8	5	11	7
Total	151	100	153	100

Source: Reports of income and expenditures of lobbyists, Office of the Secretary of State, State of New Hampshire.

Note: Includes only funds expended in lobbying the General Court. New Hampshire law does not require reporting expenditures for other lobbying or activities.

lobbyists are becoming significantly more professional or that lobbying will soon be accomplished primarily by law firms and consulting firms. In general, this corps of part-time lobbyists resembles those with whom they most interact: a part-time legislature of ordinary people from a variety of backgrounds and possessing a variety of levels of experience and skill.

INTEREST-GROUP TACTICS

Interest groups in New Hampshire use a variety of techniques to influence decision-makers. Their most important function in the policy-making process is to provide information. The amateur nature of the legislature and the scarcity of staff in executive agencies enhances the importance of the ability of interest groups to research issues and provide the needed information to legislators and bureaucrats alike. They in effect take over the function of staffers in more professionalized state governments. Groups that can offer specialized information are most likely to prevail when they are the only reliable source.

The Legislature

Access, so necessary for interest-group influence, is easy in the New Hampshire legislature. The statehouse atmosphere is relaxed and personal. Staff members in the leadership offices are friendly and helpful. People in the statehouse seem to enjoy their work and their interaction with citizens and lobbyists. Legislators quickly learn to rely on lobbyists for needed information. One member asserted that legislators who are doing their jobs seek out lobbyists, and that the others do not.

Zeigler and Michael Baer found that "simply 'being around' helps quite a bit," and "the longer one has been lobbying the greater the likelihood of interaction initiated by a legislator,"[12] which seems to apply to the position of lobbyists in New Hampshire. Lobbyists must prove themselves before legislators trust them. Legislators frequently ask lobbyists, even those whose causes they do not support, for information if the lobbyists are well respected. According to one member, David Cote, the most respected lob-

12. L. Harmon Zeigler and Michael Baer, *Lobbying: Interaction and Influence in American State Legislatures* (Belmont, Calif.: Wadsworth, 1969), 136.

byists are those who keep their answers in hearings short and concise, personalize issues, take their time explaining issues to legislators, tell no lies, play no violins, do favors for legislators, have some "sex appeal," pat legislators on the back for their cooperation, and dress professionally. Militancy on the part of groups like the Clam Shell Alliance, an anti-Seabrook group, was seen with distrust. Mass demonstrations, slick campaigns, and civil disturbances do not influence the legislature positively. The most successful groups are those whose image is moderate. Private citizens who testify before legislative hearings are taken most seriously when they perform with the same professional decorum expected of lobbyists.

Many groups hire former legislative leaders or former government officials to do lobbying for them. In a state as small as New Hampshire, these links are important. Many legislators are more likely to trust familiar people than newcomers, so former leaders will have more influence in the body. New Hampshire has a relatively small community of political actives at the state level, and breaking into this tight network may take an outsider some time. Many legislators serve as town selectmen and school-board members in addition to attending to their legislative duties, so everyone knows everyone else.

Although not typical in all respects of contract lobbyists, Richard Bouley is one of the most successful and highly paid New Hampshire lobbyists. Presently representing such diverse groups as Teamsters Local 633, Developmental Disabilities Providers, Granite State Wine & Spirits Association, the New Hampshire Coalition of Senior Advocates, and New Hampshire Consulting Engineers, Bouley served as liaison to the Executive Council in the capacity of special assistant to Governor Hugh Gallen from 1979 to 1983. After briefly returning to his profession of teaching, he began working for George Roberts, the most highly paid lobbyist in the state and a former Speaker of the House. Bouley and Roberts dissolved their association in 1986, and Bouley opened his own political-consulting office. A New Hampshire native, Bouley attended a local high school and Plymouth State College, and his ties to many legislators and other government officials go back to his youth.

In a 1988 *Concord Monitor* profile, reporter Aaron Zitner followed Bouley's activities for more than a week. The reporter identified Bouley as utilizing at least fifteen of the twenty-seven interest-group techniques Schlozman and Tierney name as tactics used by national-level interest groups in their dealings with the U.S. Congress (Table 7.4).

Of the other twelve techniques, all were mentioned by those we inter-

Table 7.4. Techniques Used by Interest Groups, New Hampshire, 1987

1.*	Testify at hearings
2.*	Contact government officials directly
3.*	Informal contacts
4.*	Presenting research results or information
5.*	Send letters to members of the organization
6.	Entering coalitions with other organizations
7.	Attempting to shape the implementation of policies
8.*	Talking with people from the press and the media
9.*	Consulting with government officials to plan legislative strategy
10.*	Helping to draft legislation
11.*	Inspire letter-writing or telegram campaigns
12.*	Shaping the government's agenda
13.*	Mounting grass-roots lobbying efforts
14.*	Having influential constituents contact their U.S. Representative's office
15.*	Helping draft regulations, rules, or guidelines
16.	Serving on advisory commissions and boards
17.	Alerting representatives to the effects of a bill on their district
18.	Filing suit or otherwise engaging in litigation
19.	Making contributions to electoral campaigns
20.*	Doing favors for officials who need assistance
21.	Attempting to influence appointments to public office
22.	Publicizing candidate's voting records
23.	Engaging in direct-mail fund-raising
24.	Running advertisements
25.	Contributing work or personnel to election campaigns
26.*	Making public endorsements of candidates
27.	Taking part in protests or demonstrations

Source: Kay Lehman Schlozman and John T. Tierney, *Organized Interests and American Democracy* (New York: Harper & Row, 1986).

*Activities performed by R. Bouley in Aaron Zitner, "The Best or Just a Pest?" *Concord Monitor* 95 (April 21, 1988): A-1, A-12.

viewed, except service on advisory commissions or boards. Although lobbyists did not claim to be involved, many group members and other personally interested people are represented on boards and commissions. The ranking by frequency of use of these techniques by national groups seems to hold for New Hampshire groups as well.

One of the most successful tactics lobbyists use is that of forming coalitions within lobbies to strengthen their position on any given issue. These coalitions are by no means monolithic, and membership varies with the issue. A good example of breaking ranks occurred during the previously mentioned fight for interstate banking. Usually the groups representing banking issues band together, but in this instance many of the local, smaller banks opposed interstate banking.

Although some groups employ the tactic of packing hearings with their members, each of whom testifies, legislators dislike this tactic because it lengthens the hearing process and can be annoying and repetitious. Groups believe they are showing legislators that constituents are interested in the piece of legislation and that some action must be taken, but they risk a backlash from annoyed legislators.

One citizens group, New Hampshire Citizen Action, invited legislators to meetings in their various legislative districts. The group then packed the meetings with its own members, not necessarily from those districts, to make it appear that constituents were firmly behind the group's proposals. At the end of the meeting, the group brought out a list of their issue positions and attempted to get the legislators to sign before the crowd, indicating their support. Many legislators felt that this was a form of blackmail, and some who supported these positions almost balked at signing because of the blatant pressure placed on them. Tactics like this tend to alienate even supporters.

Many of the most respected lobbyists spend most of their lobbying time testifying at hearings. Claire Ebel, executive director of the New Hampshire Civil Liberties Union, rarely approaches legislators to lobby. Instead legislators seek her out for her expertise on how issues affect civil liberties and how the courts are likely to respond if legislation is later challenged. She maintains her credibility by giving straightforward responses, even when she wishes the courts would be more supportive of the Union's positions.

Even generally well-respected lobbyists, such as Richard Bouley run the risk of pressuring legislators too much. Thirty women legislators have twice given Bouley the "Voodoo Award" for being the most obnoxious lobbyist. They stated that he "needled" them too much, and some said he is "conniving and true to the most negative image of the lobbyist, willing to work for anyone for a buck."[13] Contract lobbyists must be careful not to gain this

13. Aaron Zitner, "The Best or Just a Pest?" *Concord Monitor* 95 (April 21, 1988), A-12.

type of image, which is quite unpopular with legislators. Lobbyists lose their credibility if they appear to be "hired guns" or switching sides on issues too often.

Because of the large size of the House, lobbying done there must be targeted, mostly toward leadership. Any wining and dining is aimed at the leadership. Such tactics are used on the "converted," to reinforce their support rather than to influence. Since committee recommendations are rarely overturned on the floor, committee leaders are key targets for lobbyists.

The small size of the Senate—twenty-four—allows for more direct contact by groups. The small number of senators leads to some unusual committee hearings. Because they serve on so many committees and cannot attend all hearings, some hearings consist of a tape deck set up in an otherwise empty room to record testimony. Committee recommendations are frequently overturned in the Senate, and there is no consent calendar in the Senate, as in the House. Furthermore, senators are less likely to be able to become specialized, so they debate each piece of legislation as a body, making the committee system almost redundant.

For the most part, legislators and lobbyists say they hold high opinions of one another and work hard to maintain their positive images. Politics tend to be "moralistic," and ethical behavior is expected by legislators and citizens alike.[14] Generally, lobbyists enjoy their jobs and feel the legislators are genuinely nice people to work with.

Some lobbyists hang around outside the legislative chamber during sessions hoping to talk with legislators as they drift in and out of the room. Only legislators are allowed on the floor, so lobbyists often use other legislators as messengers to contact legislators in the chamber. On the door jamb into the chamber there is a line beyond which lobbyists may not pass, but it is common to see lobbyists with their toes on the line leaning into the chamber trying to signal legislators during floor debates. When a legislator prefers, lobbyists can be easily avoided. Lobbyists are required to wear hunter-orange badges showing their names or group affiliations when in the state house.

Concord, New Hampshire, has many meeting places for lobbyists and legislators. For years the most popular bars were the Eagle Court Lounge, formerly called the Millstone Lounge and strategically located across the street from the statehouse, and the now-defunct Highway Hotel, a frequent campaign headquarters for Republican state and national candidates. Other

14. See Elazar, *American Federalism*, 97–99.

nearby establishments, such as Cheers and the Ramada Inn, have become popular. In the past, legislators frequently stayed in Concord during the legislative session, which gave them added opportunities to meet one another, and those seeking leadership positions took advantage of this to build support for themselves. Former Speakers of the House, such as Douglas Scammon, have employed this tactic to gain their positions. In the most recent sessions, many legislators who used to stay do not remain in Concord during the week, which makes it more difficult for lobbyists to ply their trade and for leaders to consolidate their strength.

Several legislators believe that interest groups are beginning to become interested in the recruitment of candidates for the legislature, but none could provide a specific example. Especially when seats are open, they may try to recruit candidates sympathetic to their interests. Interest groups lobby strongly during the beginning of the legislative term when the leadership is elected, supporting candidates and openly campaigning for them.

Interest-group activity in the funding of legislative races is almost negligible because of the large size of the legislature. Legislators spend little to run for their seats. They may buy a few ads in local newspapers and put up a few yard signs, but not much else in the way of campaign spending is done. Constituents and officeholders view spending a lot of money as wasteful and inappropriate. In our interviews and in compiling our financial data, we noted a clear pattern of pejorative comments about the "big spenders" and the "high-priced lobbyists."

Spending by interest groups and PACs in campaigns is difficult to gauge because of the disorganized way the state keeps financial and expense records. They are not cumulative, not computerized, and do not clearly distinguish between in-state and out-of-state income and expenditures. The small number of PACs has grown considerably in the past few years (Table 7.5). Discounting for the number of candidate and party PACs in which interest groups are likely to be involved incidentally or not at all, the total climbs from twelve in 1978 to forty-nine in 1990.

The Executive

The relationship between the executive and the legislative branches is not particularly friendly or cooperative. Most past governors have not been able to work with the legislature to come up with creative, bargaining relationships, and recent governors are no exceptions. Most legislators did not find John Sununu's liaison staff very helpful and considered him reactionary and abrasive. Nevertheless, the legislature passed most of his initia-

Table 7.5. Political Action Committees, New Hampshire, 1978–1990

	1978	1982	1986	1990
Business	6	9	11	10
Candidate	40(14)[a]	37	34	45
Education	0	3	2	1
Ideological	2	2	0	7
Labor	0	6	2	8
Political party	4	4	10	18
Professional	1	4	2	3
Public employee / intergovernmental	0	4	1	3
Public interest / good government	1	9	12	8
Other	2	4	8	9
Total	56(30)[a]	82	82	112

Source: Reports of political committees, Office of the Secretary of State, State of New Hampshire.

[a]Included are twenty-six PACs formed under an umbrella PAC to reelect former Governor Meldrim Thomson. The number in parentheses is the number of larger PACs only.

tives. By contrast, the present governor, Judd Gregg, and his staff have had much less influence on the legislature. Legislators report a somewhat less contentious relationship with Governor Gregg, but conflict remains high, which is perhaps best exemplified by the legislature twice passing legislation rescinding the presently unconstitutional antiabortion statues despite Gregg's vocal opposition and promised vetoes.

State agencies vary in their levels of activity and success in the legislature. Most have people designated to perform legislative liaison by tracking legislation, offering testimony in hearings, and informally contacting legislators. For example, Major Henry Mock of the State Fish and Game Commission is at the state house almost daily. Although these agency staff and liaison personnel rarely initiate legislation, the legislature seldom passes legislation over their strong objections. These people do not register as lobbyists and are frequently not seen as such by legislators. Rather, legislators see them as people who can help them understand agency needs and how to avoid future administrative problems. One state official we interviewed believed that the representative of the university system, Gene Savage, should register as a lobbyist but was surprised to be asked why personnel of other agencies were not registered.

One example of a state agency that is very active in lobbying the General Court is the Attorney General's Office. Former Attorney General Stephen Merrill testified frequently at legislative hearings and was particularly powerful in Senate judiciary hearings. The chair often looked to him for reactions to testimony being given. The shortage of staff in the Attorney General's Office was quite noticeable, as his opinions were frequently based on incomplete facts, giving power to lobbyists who did have concrete facts and figures to present to the legislative committees.

The influence of the Attorney General's Office should not be underestimated, however, as demonstrated by a March 30, 1988, Senate vote on a bill that would have given the attorney general the power to seize money, property, and vehicles without going through the courts in cases dealing with drugs. The lobbyist for the New Hampshire Civil Liberties Union had testified against the administrative procedure in the bill at a Senate Judiciary Committee hearing on the grounds that innocent people might be deprived of their property without due process of law in the courts. Based on this testimony, the Judiciary Committee cut the section from the bill. When the bill reached the floor, the chair of the committee, Senator Eleanor Podles, testified that the administrative procedure should be restored because of new information she had received from the Attorney General's Office. The "new information" to which Podles referred was a one-page handwritten note from Deputy Attorney General Jeff Howard that said simply that the procedure posed no constitutional problems. The procedure was restored to the bill, and the bill passed promptly.[15]

State agencies are as much in need of the information gathered by interest groups as legislators. Agencies are therefore subject to capture by interest groups. Along with the widely used practice of appointing people who have a personal or professional interest in decisions agencies and commissions make, appointments to such bodies sometimes become the object of intragroup conflict. For example, the "straight" and "mixed" chiropractors attempted for some time to use lobbyists to influence the Chiropractic Board of Examiners but have recently put their principal efforts into influencing appointments to the five-member board. One of the main responsibilities of the Executive Council is to approve gubernatorial appointments, so council members are constantly lobbied to advance or reject administrative appointments. Many groups influence the implementation

15. Bill Ibelle, "Senate Votes to Allow Seizures in Drug Cases Without a Court Hearing," *Concord Monitor* 95 (March 30, 1988), B-1.

process by alerting the agencies to practices they dislike. The agencies often are willing to change offensive practices rather than face possible litigation or bad publicity. Agency power is further constrained by the House Administrative Rules Committee, which takes its oversight responsibilities seriously. This committee is quick to overturn agency decisions if it believes the agencies have overstepped their bounds into areas of legislative prerogative.

The Courts

Only a few groups, such as New Hampshire Legal Assistance, the New Hampshire Civil Liberties Union, and the New Hampshire Ratepayers Association, use extensive resources on litigation and attempt to influence the courts through *amicus curiae* briefs. In these instances, they act as veto groups attempting to stop practices already being implemented. They may also try to retain statutes they view favorably that are under attack. Such groups find as much or more success in the courts as in the legislature.

Within a relatively static institutional and cultural context, growth and development have changed interest-group politics in New Hampshire significantly. New challenges have altered the number, sophistication, and power of groups. Economic diversity has brought many new interests to the fore, and competition among groups has increased. This has resulted in individual groups being less powerful and a sharing of power among a wider variety of interests. The pressures of growth have brought prodevelopment groups to the fore, but probably not permanently.

Interest groups will continue to be important in New Hampshire, but the forces that maintain the present state are unlikely to persist. Can the fragile environment of this small state long support rapid development? Can the state continue to satisfy a growing and changing population's needs by relying on visitor and sin taxes rather than on more reliable broad-based taxes, and can present economic growth be maintained by holding out the promise of low business and individual taxes? Will its political culture, which has been largely responsible for moderating the power of interests, remain unchanged in the face of a more diverse and growing population? Finally, can its amateur state government institutions avoid being captured in the long run if interest groups become more sophisticated and numerous? The answer to these questions is probably no.

8

New Jersey: From Political Hacks to Political Action Committees

Barbara G. Salmore and Stephen A. Salmore

To understand New Jersey today, it might seem best to ignore anything written about it before the late 1970s. In only a brief time the Garden State has experienced massive social, economic, and political changes. The shape of public opinion, the key players in campaigns and elections, the role of the governor and the legislature, the state economy, and the major state issues would all be almost unrecognizable to someone who understood the state well barely a decade ago. However, beneath all the real change, there are also some important continuities. This combination of change and continuity shapes the recent role of interest groups in New Jersey politics.

THE POLITICAL CONTEXT: CHANGE AND CONTINUITY

Demographic Change

New Jersey's traditional image is of the archetypical urban, industrial state, but if that characterization was ever true it is much less so today. Rather than being dominated by its cities, New Jersey is and long has been the most suburban state in the country. Its "Big Six" cities are not metropolises like New York or Chicago. Newark, the largest, had a peak population of under 500,000 and, like most of the others, has since shrunk in size by more than one-quarter. At their zenith in the Roosevelt era, the Big Six produced barely two-fifths of the state's jobs. By the early 1980s their share of both jobs and population hovered around one-tenth. As New Jerseyans and their jobs moved to the suburbs, the state's economic base shifted from heavy industry to service and trade. Three out of four jobs are now in the service sector, as compared with the 4–1 dominance of manufacturing jobs in 1946.

An unattractive part of New Jersey's conventional image is as a bedroom (and garbage dump) for New York City and Philadelphia, which sit astride the state's northeastern and southwestern borders. So enduring was New Jersey's plight that the first known allusion to it is Ben Franklin's famous depiction of the state as "a keg tapped at both ends." Yet in recent years New Jersey has gained much that its two huge urban neighbors have lost. Migration out of those two cities into the Garden State's burgeoning suburbs in the 1950s and 1960s was of such magnitude that New Jersey's in-migration was greater than any state's except California.[1]

Significant economic enterprises quickly followed. Wall Street firms transferred many "back office" jobs across the Hudson River. New York and Philadelphia department stores opened large branches in New Jersey's vast suburban shopping malls. And most visibly, several major-league sports franchises (notably the National Football League's Giants and Jets, and the National Basketball Association's Nets), moved their home games from New York to New Jersey's Meadowlands sports complex, perhaps symbolically built on the site of a former New York City landfill. Legalized casino gambling came to Atlantic City and lured large numbers of tourists. To add insult to injury, a congressman even filed suit to force New York to "return" Liberty Island and the Statue of Liberty to their original geographic home in New Jersey. As notable as these socioeconomic changes are, however, they pale in comparison to the recent political changes.

Traditional Politics

New Jersey was the home of some of the country's strongest traditional political machines, led by such colorful figures as Hudson County's "Boss" Hague. The strength of the county machines derived from the structure of state government. Until 1967 the state senate had only twenty-one members, one from each county. Counties representing as little as 15 percent of the state's population could capture majority control. Although less severely malapportioned, the sixty-person Assembly also provided for at least one member per county until 1947. The Assembly was up for

1. Neal R. Peirce, *The Megastates of America* (New York: W. W. Norton, 1972), 184.

election every year, and more than half its members left after two terms.

Nominations and legislative voting were tightly controlled by county bosses. The rural bias gave the Republicans virtually uninterrupted control of the state Senate for the first six decades of the twentieth century, and the strict discipline exerted in the party caucus—requiring a majority vote to release any bill or nomination—led Belle Zeller to call it "the most powerful majority party caucus in any state chamber."[2]

The ability of county bosses to deliver the vote in both parties' primaries also gave those bosses control over gubernatorial nominations. The state's practice of holding most state elections in odd-numbered years insulated them from the effects of national political tides. Until 1947 the New Jersey governor was one of the weakest in the nation. He could serve only non-consecutive terms of three years and could appoint only two of the heads of the more than 100 executive-branch agencies. The legislature appointed all the others, to terms noncoterminous with that of the governor. These agencies were therefore rich sources of patronage jobs for the county party organizations. Even after the 1947 state constitution created a governorship that was, on paper, the strongest in the nation, the chief executive's actual dependence on county leaders was such that the Republicans could "dump" their own sitting governor in their 1973 party primary because they felt he did not give them enough attention.

Fiscal power, and thus much policy-making power, also was concentrated at the county level. Until the legislature passed a state sales tax in 1966, New Jersey was one of only three states in the nation without a broad-based state tax. In 1962 almost two-thirds of all revenues were raised at the local level (principally from the property tax), compared with a national average of under one-half. Not only were the public schools financed almost entirely at the local level, but there was no state university until 1946—college students were one of New Jersey's leading exports.

Finally, localism was bolstered by the legislature's peculiar meeting schedule. The state is so geographically compact that the legislature met once or twice a week (generally Monday and Thursday, from January to June), and members returned home at night. Thus, instead of participating in the intense extrasession legislative life that characterizes most states' legislative sessions, representatives spent most session time in their individual constituencies.

2. Belle Zeller, ed., *American State Legislatures* (New York: Thomas Y. Crowell, 1954), 207.

The state's media patterns powerfully reinforced these structural sources of parochialism. Most notably, New Jersey was, until 1984, the only state without its own VHF television station.[3] Residents thus listened to out-of-state "local news" on television, as did more than half of those who used radio as a major source of political information. Print media did little to foster statewide concerns either. Of the ten newspapers with the largest circulations in New Jersey, four were published in New York or Philadelphia. The New Jersey–based papers were primarily locally oriented, serving small central cities and the surrounding areas, or covering sprawling suburbs. The leading papers in Newark—the largest city—circulated fairly widely but reached only a limited number of readers in the northern half of the state. Although they did reach much of the narrow political elite, they were not instruments for reflection or shaping of public opinion.[4]

The majority of state residents did not take an active interest in either local or state government. They learned little about state politics from either out-of-state television and radio or locally oriented newspapers. Many had only recently arrived from nearby states, where they still worked and had family connections. The rather frequent indictments and convictions of many local political figures for fraud, extortion, and "mob"-connected crimes helped create and reinforce a widespread cynicism toward local politics and politicians.

Thus, New Jerseyans were notoriously ignorant, apathetic, and cynical about state politics. In a 1980 survey barely half called themselves "very" or "somewhat" interested in state politics, compared with an average of three-quarters of the residents of six other states. In October 1973 more residents of the heavily populated northern part of the state could name a candidate in New York City's mayoral election than could identify a New Jersey gubernatorial candidate.[5] It would not be too much to say that *state* politics

---

3. In 1984 an independent television station in New York City, WWOR, was required to move its license to New Jersey. However, it did not have a studio in the state until 1986; it does not maintain a full-time correspondent in Trenton; and it still has one of the smallest audiences among the seven VHF stations in the New York metropolitan area.

4. See Stephen A. Salmore, "Public Opinion," in Alan Rosenthal and John Blydenburgh, eds., *Politics in New Jersey* (New Brunswick, N.J.: Eagleton Institute of Politics, Rutgers University, 1975).

5. Cliff Zukin, "Political Culture and Public Opinion," in Gerald M. Pomper, ed., *The Political State of New Jersey* (New Brunswick: Rutgers University Press, 1986), 15. The other states were Kentucky, Delaware, New Hampshire, Connecticut, Massa-

barely existed. Virtually the only important statewide issue from the 1950s on was vociferous public opposition to a state income tax that could provide the revenue for stronger state institutions and policies. An income tax was finally passed in 1976 because state Supreme Court rulings closed the public schools and gave the legislature no alternative.

Post-1970s Politics

As entrenched as this traditional political system was, it collapsed within a decade. Several events laid the groundwork for its disintegration. The 1947 constitution made the governor a very powerful official, if he or she could break loose of the county party organizations. Migration brought many new residents without ties to the old local machines. Perhaps most important, U.S. Supreme Court reapportionment decisions of the 1960s compelled a redrawing of legislative districts that crossed county and even municipal boundaries—a potentially lethal blow to the county-based machines. Since 1967 the legislature has been comprised of forty senators and eighty Assembly members, two from each state Senate district.

All the silent undermining came to a head in the 1977 gubernatorial election when Democratic county leaders, emulating the Republicans in 1973, decided to "dump" their sitting governor because of his identification with the newly enacted state income tax. The governor fought back by conducting an unprecedented primary campaign on television, emphasizing the themes of leadership, political independence, and the real need for the income tax. Such a media-based campaign, already commonplace in many states for years, was unprecedented because, as already noted, New Jersey was, and remains, the only state in the union without its own VHF television station.

Conducting a television-based campaign on New York and Philadelphia stations—two of the most expensive markets in the nation—is extremely costly. None of the five largely unknown candidates backed by various county organizations could match the governor's expenditures. In a crowded field, he won the primary with 30 percent of the vote, and the general election in a landslide.

This election was a watershed in New Jersey politics. First, it ended the party organizations' power forever. Based on the winning gubernatorial

chusetts, and Texas. The data were generated in a cooperative effort by the Network of State Polls.

candidate's proportion of the primary vote in the six elections between 1956 and 1978, Morehouse called New Jersey party strength moderate. When the same measure is applied to the six most recent elections (1969–89), New Jersey party strength slips well into the level Morehouse characterizes as weak.[6]

Second, the governor's success in winning what amounted to a referendum on the income tax guaranteed the state substantial revenues for the first time and permitted major state undertakings like the Meadowlands complex, the expansion of Rutgers (the state university), and the public financing of gubernatorial primaries and elections. Channeling the money through candidate committees further debilitated the severely weakened parties. Gubernatorial public financing also diverted traditional campaign contributors to the legislative races, where PAC contributions to individual candidates were unlimited. Candidates, particularly in competitive races, obviously welcomed the money—ten state Senate candidate committees spent more than $200,000 in 1987, and six assembly candidates spent over $100,000.[7]

Third, the legislature was transformed. The legislative budget rose from $500,000 in 1970 to $44.5 million in Fiscal Year 1990–91. Most of the increase went for "professionalization"—higher legislative salaries, the opening of legislative district offices, and professional and partisan staff to support the strengthened committee system that took over from the party caucuses. Turnover dropped sharply, and leadership rotation ended.[8] Incumbency became a more important campaign resource than party label.[9] With greater internal resources and new responsibilities the federal government imposed on state governments, Trenton was a busier and more exciting place to be.

These changes made state politics much more competitive and volatile

6. Sarah McCally Morehouse, *State Politics, Party, and Policy* (New York: Holt, Rinehart & Winston, 1981), 147. From 1969 to 1989 the governor's mean primary vote is 56 percent; if the 1965 and 1985 elections featuring popular incumbents are excluded, the average slips to 36 percent. Morehouse calls states with averages between 35 percent and 65 percent "weak party states."

7. ELEC news release, December 9, 1987.

8. Legislative turnover dropped from an average of 50 percent in the early 1970s to less than 25 percent in the 1980s.

9. In the 1985 legislative elections, for example, on average, a 1 percent increase in identification with their party resulted in a one-point increase in assembly candidates' votes, but incumbency was worth twelve points. Stephen A. Salmore and Barbara G. Salmore, "Determinants of State Legislative Elections: The Case of New Jersey" (Paper presented at the Annual Meeting of the American Political Science Association, Chicago, September 1987), 17.

and increased the number of relevant players. Party control of state government was split continuously between 1981 and 1989—half the time not only between governor and legislature but also between the two legislative houses. Furthermore, party labels became less useful predictors of the legislative vote, even on matters considered crucial by a strong and popular governor. As Joseph Gonzales, executive director of the New Jersey Business and Industry Association observes, "In the old days with the caucus, you needed a majority of the majority party. . . . Now you have to worry about committees and even second committees. There are a lot more players in the process with life and death power over your bill."[10]

Despite all this, there remain certain important elements of continuity in New Jersey politics, the most important of which has to do with the state's peculiar media patterns. Because New Jersey continues to have no major television station or statewide newspaper, it is still difficult for statewide issues to surface and be widely debated. Most of the time, the legislature still operates in obscurity, and support for home rule remains a major impediment to statewide and regional initiatives. Although the proportion of all tax revenues raised from the local property tax dropped to 34 percent in the 1980s, it is still one-third higher than the average for the rest of the country.[11] Finally, even though the number of legislative session meeting days has risen from the old average of twenty to thirty to around fifty in recent years, lawmakers continue to journey to Trenton twice a week and return home every evening. How has this mixture of change and continuity affected New Jersey's interest groups?

NEW JERSEY INTEREST GROUPS—
THEN AND NOW

As we have just described, two critical developments affecting interest groups occurred almost simultaneously in the 1970s—the local party organizations that shaped New Jersey state politics collapsed very suddenly, and the state government, as a result of both internal evolution and events in Washington, could newly inject itself into numerous areas of concern to interest groups.

10. Quoted in Dan Weissman, "Fourth Branch of Government: Lobbyists Play Pivotal Role in Legislative Action," *Newark Star-Ledger*, March 22, 1987.

11. Susan S. Lederman, "Financing the State," in Pomper, ed., *Political State*, 190.

A major tenet of the standard works on interest groups in the states is that they are weak where political parties are strong, and strong where parties are weak. All these studies describe New Jersey as a strong-party and weak-interest-group state. This research, done before the late 1970s or heavily reliant on the work of this earlier period, makes frequent reference to the power of the county party organizations and the legislative caucuses, as well as to the absence of a significant state policy agenda that would concern interest groups.[12] Governors through the 1950s and 1960s knew personally most of the players in the small political elite and needed to gain the assent of only a few key county leaders to effect policy—although that assent was not always simple to obtain.[13] With so little at stake, the major traditional interests had little incentive to lobby state capital politicians.

Although there is therefore some validity to the pre-1980s characterization of New Jersey as a weak-interest-group state, it is a remarkably anomalous case in all the major studies. Zeller, upon whose work many later writers relied, places New Jersey in a group of nine states with a majority party and a competitive minority party and comments, "In all nine states in this group except New Jersey, pressure politics seems to play a major role, and localism is strong."[14] Morehouse observes that states with weak pressure groups subject them to strict reporting requirements. Yet New Jersey's reporting requirements are of the most recent vintage. The study by Wahlke and his colleagues also characterizes New Jersey as an exemplar of the strong-party-weak-interest-group hypothesis, but their data also place New Jersey second highest on an index of potential pressure group influence.[15]

In contrast to the standard literature, contemporaneous local analyses

12. The standard studies making this assertion include Zeller, *American State Legislatures*, 206; Morehouse, *State Politics, Party, and Policy*, 117; L. Harmon Zeigler and Hendrik van Dalen, "Interest Groups in State Politics," in Herbert Jacob and Kenneth Vines, *Politics in the American States* (Boston: Little, Brown, 1976), 95; and John Wahlke et al., *The Legislative System* (New York: Wiley, 1962), 352–55. The Zeller study is particularly influential and often cited in later works.

13. For example, the new state constitution, proposed by a Republican governor in the 1940s, was held up by Republican bosses in Essex County who wanted changes in the state court system. The sales tax passed in the 1960s was a substitute proposed by legislative Democrats who opposed the Democratic governor's preference for an income tax. The income tax supported by another Democratic governor in the 1970s was passed by a Democratic legislature only after a virtual mandate by the state supreme court.

14. Zeller, *American State Legislatures*, 206.

15. Wahlke et al., *The Legislative System*, 321, 352, 355.

dispute the view that pressure groups in New Jersey were weak during the heyday of the party machines. A 1934 *Fortune* magazine study of the state's major power and public transportation utility concluded: "In the [unique] politics of New Jersey, Public Service to an extraordinary degree is the state; and the state, to an extraordinary degree, is Public Service."[16] Princeton University political scientist and sometime state legislator Dayton D. McKean estimated in 1938 that 90 percent of the floor action in the legislature was attributable to interest groups.[17] In 1979 another New Jersey political scientist ascribed the prevailing academic view of New Jersey as a weak-interest-group state to an original error by Zeller:

> In the early 1950s one multi-state survey claimed that pressure groups were relatively weak in New Jersey. However, this assertion, which has since been repeated in many other works, was based on the opinion of an extremely small number of respondents in each state and should not be considered an accurate appraisal of the strength of interest groups in New Jersey.[18]

The peculiar nature of the New Jersey political system before the late 1970s is the likely reason for this divergence in views. Although the county parties were very strong, the state parties and government were very weak and the state government's agenda was extremely narrow. If the measure of an interest group's influence is its ability to achieve goals defined by the group, most interests in New Jersey were successful in their goal of ensuring that the state left them alone.

In this sense, interest groups in the past profited from government's "nondecisions" and were granted "legitimized autonomy."[19] Much of the interest-group-generated legislation noted by McKean in the 1930s dealt with such items as the establishment of clientele-controlled licensing

16. *Fortune*, November 1934, 128.

17. Dayton D. McKean, *Pressures on the Legislature of New Jersey* (New York: Columbia University Press, 1938), 222.

18. Philip Burch, "Interest Groups," in Richard Lehne and Alan Rosenthal, eds., *Politics in New Jersey* (New Brunswick, N.J.: Eagleton Institute of Politics, Rutgers University, 1979), 131n.

19. The concept of "nondecisions" is developed by Peter Bachrach and Morton S. Baratz, *Power and Poverty* (New York: Oxford University Press, 1970); "legitimized autonomy" is developed in Michael T. Hayes, *Lobbyists and Legislators* (New Brunswick, N.J.: Rutgers University Press, 1981), 30.

boards and exclusive franchise grants. However, as Wahlke and colleagues observed in 1962, the *potential* for strong interest groups that could shape government "action" as well as "inaction" had been present for a long time. Even though the New Jersey legislators interviewed in their four-state study had the strongest perceptions of party conflict and party influence on members' behavior, they also ranked second in their ability to recognize, identify, and distinguish interest groups in the state. New Jersey respondents also ranked first in the diversity of interests legislators identified.[20]

Because of that diversity, in the current postparty era, proposed regulation of, for example, increased development pits not only builders and environmentalists but also builders and agricultural interests, or commercial and residential developers, against each other. Proposed health-care regulations feature changing coalitions of hospitals, health maintenance organizations, private physicians, nurses, optometrists, nursing homes, and physicians' assistants. As Lawrence Weiss, chair of the powerful Senate Finance and Appropriations Committee describes it, "Every issue around here has more than two sides. They are more a cube than a coin." From the point of view of Frank Capece, a leading lawyer lobbyist, "it's like eighteenth century Europe. There are no friends or enemies, just shifting alliances."[21] Against this backdrop, we can describe the types of groups and lobbyists that now operate in New Jersey, the extent to which they are regulated, what sort of political tactics they use, and the extent and nature of their power.[22]

THE INTEREST-GROUP UNIVERSE

In 1990 more than 600 individual businesses, industries, and associations employed 444 individual "legislative agents" or registered lobbyists in Trenton, as compared with 254 registrants in 1976. Although mutually exclusive categories are difficult to construct, interest-group sectors that each account for about 5 percent of the total number include banks and other financial institutions, pharmaceutical and chemical companies, educational groups, energy companies, health professions, other regulated oc-

20. Wahlke et al., *The Legislative System*, 317.

21. Both quoted in Weissman, "Fourth Branch of Government."

22. A revised version of much of the remainder of this chapter also appears in Barbara G. Salmore and Stephen A. Salmore, *New Jersey Politics and Government: Suburban Politics Comes of Age* (Lincoln: University of Nebraska Press, 1993), chap. 6.

cupations, insurance companies, labor unions, and "good government" groups. Other diverse business enterprises constituted another 40 percent. The small remainder are comprised chiefly of public utilities, alcohol-related interests, gambling casinos, builders, and local government representatives.[23]

Lists of groups tell little about relative salience or efficacy or how it has changed over time. Since the 1930s there have been four studies of varying precision that permit examination of this question. Although the findings are not directly comparable, there are interesting patterns over time.

In 1938 Dayton McKean offered his own informed if impressionistic judgment.[24] He named the New Jersey State Teachers Association (later renamed the New Jersey Education Association), the Chamber of Commerce, the New Jersey Manufacturers Association (later renamed the New Jersey Business & Industry Association), the Public Service Corporation, the New Jersey Taxpayers Association, and the American Federation of Labor as the state's most influential groups. These groups had different resources and sources of power.

The teachers, the Manufacturers Association (representing smaller companies than the Chamber of Commerce), and the unions were present in almost every legislative district. Unions confined themselves mostly to electoral reprisal or support, while teachers and business also spent time lobbying effectively in Trenton. The other three groups—large corporations or institutions representing them—contributed money to the parties and were rumored to have lawyer-legislators on retainer. McKean also noted that the state's business groups were more often fragmented and conflictful than mutually supportive. Finally, he praised the New Jersey Municipal Association for its useful information about the numerous technical ordinances on municipalities.

The more systematic survey by Wahlke and his colleagues (1962) confirms McKean's impressionistic analysis. Legislators were asked an open-ended question about "the most powerful groups" in their states (termed "generalized power") and which groups' advice *ought* to be considered whether they happen to be powerful or not (termed "group merit").[25] The results for New Jersey are in Table 8.1.

Although New Jersey legislators named thirty-eight different organiza-

23. This count is based on our analysis of the registered interests listed in the 1990 *Manual of the Legislature of New Jersey*.
24. McKean, *Pressures*, 52–120.
25. Wahlke et al., *The Legislative System*, Appendix 6, 498–500.

tions in response to these questions, only nine were mentioned by at least 1 percent of the respondents. Only the three groups with significant numbers of members in every legislative constituency—the state teachers organization and the largest business and labor groups—were fairly widely regarded as "powerful." New Jersey respondents were also least likely to assign generalized power to business groups, were most likely to say that educational groups were powerful in their own constituencies, and named the fewest total number of groups.[26] Results such as these led to the widespread conclusion that New Jersey was a weak-interest-group state.

In 1979 New Jersey political scientist Philip Burch conducted the next wide-ranging study of New Jersey interest groups, based on approximately sixty in-depth interviews with legislators, lobbyists, reporters, and high executive branch officials, including former governors and cabinet officers. Respondents were asked "a series of questions ranging from an appraisal of the strength of interest groups and an assessment of the various major kinds . . . to a more detailed evaluation of all organizations."[27]

Burch singled out the New Jersey Education Association (NJEA) for "[standing] out as unusually effective" and the Chamber of Commerce and the New Jersey Business & Industry Association (NJBIA) as the most im-

Table 8.1. Interest Groups Most Frequently Cited by New Jersey Legislators, 1962

Interest Group	Generalized Power	Group Merit
New Jersey Education Assn	30%	11%
Chamber(s) of Commerce	20	25
AFL-CIO	23	10
N.J. Municipal League	7	17
N.J. Taxpayers Assn	5	21
N.J. Manufacturers Assn	7	2
League of Women Voters	3	12
N.J. Farm Bureau	4	2
PTA(s)	1	—

Source: John Wahlke et al., *The Legislative System* (New York: John Wiley, 1962), 318–19.

Note: Numbers are the percentage of legislators interviewed who mentioned the group. All groups mentioned by at least one percent of the respondents are included.

26. Ibid., 315.
27. Burch, "Interest Groups," 111.

portant business groups. He described the AFL-CIO membership as so large that it "cannot help but be a major force in New Jersey politics," but "unlike the NJEA, it has never been able to translate most of its vast personnel and financial resources into any kind of equivalent political power." The League of Municipalities was again cited for technical expertise in its narrow domain. Burch also noted the latent influence of the legal profession because of its many legislative members rather than its organizational clout.

Burch also discussed a number of other groups that the earlier studies did not mention at all, including senior citizens, builders and realtors, and the health professions. Although he did not perceive them as particularly active or effective, their inclusion in the analysis signals the broadened scope and activity of New Jersey state government, which was just beginning at the time of his research.

Finally, in 1987, the Associated Press asked state legislators to name the "three most powerful lobbying groups in the state."[28] The results show the continuing dominance of the New Jersey Education Association (see Table 8.2), whose impressive five-story headquarters is located across the street from the state capitol building. As many as 84 percent of those responding place the NJEA among the three most powerful groups in the state. Legislators respect the NJEA both for its political clout and for its professionalism, as reflected in comments from two Assembly Democrats:

> They have good lobbyists. They stay on your back and explain the issues. They also have large memberships they can mobilize.

> They're the biggest union in the state. They're in everybody's district. They have money and keep a lobbying presence in the Statehouse at all times.[29]

The NJBIA is far back in second place, with 31 percent mentioning it. Like the NJEA, the Business & Industry Association is respected for its knowledge, presence, and ability to help in campaigns. Respondents describe it as "knowledgeable," "credible," and "having good contacts in both parties." As a Republican assemblywoman puts it, "They come across as having the support of all the businesses in the state."[30]

28. Joel Siegel, "Legislators Say Teachers' Union Has Most Clout," *Easton Express*, October 12, 1987. Siegel reports that 69 percent of legislators answered the question.

29. Ibid.

30. Ibid.

Table 8.2. Most Powerful Lobbying Groups in New Jersey According to New Jersey Legislators, 1987

Lobby	Percent of Mentions
N.J. Education Assn	84
N.J. Business and Industry Assn	31
Trial lawyers	27
Builders and developers	24
Organized labor	24
Public strategies (Harold Hodes)	15
Environmental groups	9
Banks	6
Utility companies	6
Joseph Katz	6
Police and firefighters	6
Insurance companies	5

Source: Associated Press survey of state legislators as reported in Joel Siegel, "Legislators Say Teachers Union Has Most Clout," *Easton Express*, October 12, 1987.

Another important similarity is the pervasive presence of both groups in legislators' districts. The NJEA has nineteen field offices and thirty-seven field representatives and sends all its members in each legislative district an endorsement letter. The NJBIA has employer legislative committees in twenty of the twenty-one counties; the county business leaders on these committees hold monthly meetings with the association's lobbyists to share information and concerns.

Trial lawyers, the third most frequently cited group, at 27 percent, were not even mentioned by Burch. Builders and developers, tied for fourth place at 24 percent, were also described by Burch as "having little political influence in New Jersey."[31] Their recent rise in importance is the result of both state government's expanding issue agenda and the power of political money.

Controlling growth and development and auto-insurance reform have been two of New Jersey's leading issues in recent years, in terms of both public concern and the legislative agenda. As debate on them has grown in intensity, both the builders and the trial lawyers have become campaign contributors. Legislators cited these contributions regularly in explaining

31. Burch, "Interest Groups," 117.

their rankings of the two groups. The trial lawyers also benefit from the presence of many lawyers in the legislature. An Assembly Republican summed it up: "They have the ear of legislators because many legislators are lawyers and because they contribute lots of campaign money."[32]

The Associated Press survey also shows the continuing (but relatively lesser) influence of the AFL-CIO, which also has large numbers of members in many districts, but most interesting is the appearance in Table 8.2 of many new groups, including several described by Burch as politically feeble in the late 1970s—environmental groups, banks, and utilities. The legislators responding to the survey also specifically named two contract lobbyists—Joseph Katz and Harold Hodes of Public Strategies Inc.—as among the ten most powerful groups in the state, reflecting their particular clout and that of contract lobbyists in general.

Thus, a few New Jersey groups have been continually influential over a period of at least fifty years—the largest business groups, the major labor federation, and the teachers organization. They have been joined recently by a number of others whose economic interests are now more affected by state action. With the establishment of political action committees (whose dramatic growth we discuss later) and the waning of strong local party organizations, they have greater access to legislators, who are both free of party discipline and more in need of campaign contributions. Large individual corporations, with the exception of those headquartered in the state, play a limited role because their major continuing concerns are not dealt with at the state level. Issues that do concern them are handled primarily by umbrella associations, such as the Chamber of Commerce. Large companies headquartered in New Jersey—particularly Johnson & Johnson and the Prudential Insurance Company—have been and continue to be important players in state politics.

Aside from the state's largest newspaper and the state Supreme Court (both of which we discuss below), most "interests" or "pressures" other than these formal and traditional interest groups do not play a significant role in New Jersey. Unlike many states in the west or south, the federal government is not a visible presence as landowner or source of employment, and the state sends more money to Washington than it gets back.

The larger religious organizations in the state are denominationally diverse and predominantly mainstream and liberally inclined. Although maintaining registered representatives in Trenton to lobby on narrow is-

32. Siegel, "Legislators Say. . . ."

sues, such as state aid to parochial schools, they generally adhere to the principle of separation of church and state and seldom get actively involved in broader social issues.[33]

"Good government" groups like the League of Women Voters and Common Cause often receive approving lip service for their activities but do not have either the numbers or the financial resources to lobby their issues effectively. Even organized environmentalists, whose issues often dominate the public agenda in New Jersey, are not at the forefront of the environmental battle. Rather, in a state that has the country's greatest population density and largest number of federally designated superfund cleanup sites, "impetus for all of New Jersey's activism came from the apprehension and impatience of the general public."[34]

Public clamor on an aggressive environmental policy and other visible state issues is often shaped as well as reflected by the *Star-Ledger*, the most widely read newspaper in New Jersey. The paper has recently opened a number of satellite printing plants and aggressively and successfully sought to expand its circulation area to include almost all of central and northern New Jersey. Its effective circulation area covers almost two-thirds of the state and an even larger portion of the population.

In addition to its large readership, the paper's Trenton bureau of ten full-time reporters dwarfs its competitors, and it publishes three times as much news about state government as any other paper. The size of its Trenton staff, which comprises one-fifth of the entire statehouse press corps, allows for considerable specialization. A number of its veteran reporters, particularly on the education and environmental beats, are regarded as extremely influential in their policy areas. The *Star-Ledger*'s style has been described as "crusading," "populist," and heavy on state "boosterism."[35] Typically, beat reporters write multipart front-page articles on what the paper regards as major current issues. The drumbeat is then taken up on the editorial page, and action, or at least talk, in Trenton follows.

The other important nontraditional "pressure" in New Jersey is the state's Supreme Court, which has a national reputation for judicial activism. To some extent, over the last twenty years, the court has served as the

33. Alice Chasan Edelman, "Church and State Street," *New Jersey Reporter*, November 1985.

34. Richard Sullivan, "Environmental Policy," in Pomper, ed., *Political State*, 224.

35. David Sachsman and Warren Sloat, "The *Star-Ledger*: Does Bigger Mean Better?" *New Jersey Reporter*, February 1983.

advocate of the powerless and unorganized, as seen in its two most contro-versial and well-known series of rulings. In the 1970s its rulings on public school finance led to the enactment of the state income tax and, like subsequent rulings in the early 1990s, were intended to help urban school districts with many poor students and dwindling local tax bases. Another series of decisions striking down exclusionary local zoning ordinances was just as clearly meant to increase the number of low-income housing units and minority residents in wealthy all-white suburbs. The court—five of whose seven current members were in high positions in the executive branch when appointed—has also repeatedly supported recent governors in power struggles with both the legislature and interest groups. For example, it has consistently defined union bargaining rights very narrowly, forced insurance companies leaving the state to place their policyholders else-where, and struck down the legislative veto.

The role of other elements of the state government has traditionally been fairly minimal. The governor's top staff lobby extensively for the chief executive's major priorities, but as in the past, support from his own parti-sans is by no means assured, as legislators with independent power bases still tend to vote their electoral and fund-raising constituencies. The gover-nor was further hampered in recent years by split partisan control, which requires continuous bargaining with shifting legislative coalitions.

Recent structural and political developments have somewhat enhanced the lobbying role of state agencies. State intervention in so many new areas has essentially forced agencies to develop their own agendas and ap-point legislative liaisons. The larger number of issues led most recent gov-ernors to choose a few high priorities on which to concentrate their lobby-ing efforts, leaving the agencies to deal with the others. Divided government and a more assertive legislature also often make the governor's office more reactive than proactive, with a need to turn to agency institu-tional memory and expertise. Governors also sometimes prefer to foist un-popular decisions on the agency so that they can avoid blame. For exam-ple, a recent solid-waste removal crisis forced some counties to accept trash from others with no facilities. It was no accident that the Department of Environmental Protection rather than the governor took the lead and was identified with this highly unpopular policy.

When left without direction from the top, cabinet officials and agencies' legislative liaisons often allied with their clientele groups and opposed each other. Pesticide legislation, for example, found the Department of Agricul-ture allied with the industry against the Department of Environmental Protection and the Office of the Public Advocate. The latter two agencies joined with unions in support of another controversial bill, regulating chemicals in the workplace. They were opposed by the chemical industry, the Chamber of Commerce, the NJBIA, and the Department of Commerce and Economic Development—whose commissioner was a major stockholder and former vice-president of American Cyanamid, a leading chemical company.

Although there is thus some increase, likely permanent, in the autonomous lobbying role of state agencies, two final points should be noted. First, the two governors who served through most of the 1970s and 1980s, Democrat Brendan Byrne and Republican Thomas Kean, both had managerial styles that encouraged gubernatorial focus on only a few issues. More interventionist chief executives could be more prone to consolidate lobbying operations in their own offices or to issue more directives to agencies, as did Kean's successor, Democrat James Florio. Second, some of the policy areas that generate extensive state government lobbying in other states are run by quasi-independent agencies in New Jersey, with their own lobbyists. These include, for example, Rutgers and New Jersey Public Transit, which deals with many transportation issues.

LOBBYISTS: A PORTRAIT

Most New Jersey lobbyists either are employed full-time as government affairs specialists by individual businesses or associations or are contract lobbyists representing several clients on a fee basis. The state's largest concerns often have sizable in-house lobby operations. Public Service Electric & Gas, the largest utility, has a twenty-person government affairs staff. Both the NJBIA and the NJEA have a half-dozen full-time lobbyists.

The role of contract lobbyists has recently increased dramatically. Joseph Katz, considered to be the first "hired gun," remains highly regarded. He left the administration of Democratic Governor Richard Hughes to set up shop in 1966. By 1983 there were twenty-two individuals or firms with multiple, unrelated clients, collectively representing 181 concerns. By 1990 this had mushroomed to forty-five different individuals or firms with 421 clients. Fifteen contract lobbyists had more than ten clients, and three had more than forty. Their clients are not confined to enterprises without their own legislative agents; a number of firms hire contract lobbyists to augment in-house staff. Some firms without in-house personnel also retain more than one contract lobbyist.

Almost all the leading contract lobbyists previously held high positions in the executive branch of government or on the legislative staff. Harold Hodes, a principal of Public Strategies Inc., was chief of staff to Governor Brendan Byrne. Joel Sterns, a partner in a law firm doing contract lobbying, was counsel for Governor Hughes. His partner, Richard Weinroth, served in the counsel's office under Republican Governor William Cahill.

Several other leading figures are former legislators or former reporters for the state's largest newspapers. Raymond Bateman was the Republican state Senate president before running unsuccessfully for governor in 1977. Joseph Katz was a reporter for the now-defunct *Newark News* before entering the Hughes administration. The executive director of the NJBIA, Joseph Gonzales, had served as executive director for the Assembly Republicans.

Most firms are also notably bipartisan, with principals who have served governors of both parties. In addition to Sterns and Weinroth, Harold Hodes and Raymond Bateman worked together for a time, and Hodes now counts among his partners Roger Bodman, who served as campaign manager and commissioner of labor for Republican Governor Thomas Kean. The only woman heading a major contract lobbying operation, Nancy Becker, is a rare exception to this vocational pattern; she began her Trenton career as executive director of New Jersey Common Cause.

A likely reason contract lobbyists doubled their client roster in the 1980s is that legislators tend to regard them favorably. A survey of legislators conducted in 1987 by the Gallup Organization asked whether "in general," contract, staff, or volunteer lobbyists from an organization's membership were "most effective in communicating issues to you." Of the three-fifths of respondents who indicated a preference, 47 percent chose contract lobbyists, 27 percent said staff lobbyists, and 26 percent picked the nonprofessionals.[36]

Another reason for contract lobbyists' growth is the increased use of transient multigroup alliances to lobby major issues. Sometimes one of the participants' lobbyists assumes the lead role. In a major "right-to know"

---

36. Calculated by the authors from the *1987 Gallup Survey of the New Jersey State Legislature* (Princeton, 1987), 7. This was a proprietary survey conducted for several major lobbying groups; partial results were made public.

controversy over what information chemical companies would be required to give to workers dealing with hazardous substances, the Chamber of Commerce, the NJBIA, and the Chemical Industry Council joined forces, led by the CIC's lobbyist. Opposing them was the New Jersey Right to Know Coalition, comprised of environmental groups and their lead player, an industrial union federation. More often, however, a contract lobbyist assembles the coalition or is hired to lead it, as in the case of the Federation of Advocates for Insurance Reform, known by its acronym, FAIR. FAIR is a joint effort of insurance companies, professional groups, and corporations that are frequent targets of liability lawsuits, to change the state's liability insurance laws.

REGULATION OF LOBBYISTS

New Jersey was one of the last states to regulate lobbyists. Not until 1971 were lobbyists required to register with the state Attorney General's Office, to disclose clients, to report their interest in bills quarterly, and to wear a badge while plying their trade in the capitol building. Technically, a lobbyist in New Jersey is someone who attempts to influence legislation and either does so on a regular basis or is paid at least $100 every three months to do so.

In 1973, when the Election Law Enforcement Commission (ELEC) was established to monitor party and campaign expenditures, the legislation included a proviso that lobbyists would have to file annual spending reports. This portion of the law was immediately challenged by twenty lobbyist plaintiffs, led by the Chamber of Commerce, and was tied up in legal wrangles for six years. The legislature took up the financial reporting requirement again in 1981, when it became the most heavily lobbied bill of the year.[37]

The lobbyists furiously objected to the bill's provision that expenditures be reported for *any* contacts with a legislator "without limitation." They argued not only that it was unreasonable to subject entertainment expenses

37. Neil Upmeyer, "The Sunshine Boys," *New Jersey Reporter*, June 1983, 12–17. For a full account of the battle, see that article and Dan Weissman, "Just One Little Word in Lobbyist Law Makes Big Difference on Disclosure," *Star-Ledger*, March 24, 1987.

unconnected to specific legislation—such as free meals, drinks, tickets, or convention trips—to reporting, but that the law was so vague it could include incalculable portions of office rent and utility bills and even threatened freedom of speech. As Prudential Insurance's lobbyist Joseph Frankel put it, "We were being drawn into a situation that was not intended. . . . If I am not talking to a legislator about an issue and I am just in his company, why report it? There are some First Amendment implications." Charles Stapleton, a lobbyist for the New Jersey Savings League and formerly executive director for the Senate Republicans, complained, "That is not lobbying as I understand it. It is building a relationship, not discussing legislation. . . . No other people in the world are asked to quantify that."[38]

The session-long battle came to an abrupt and mysterious end at literally the last moment. In the middle of the January 1982 night before a new governor and legislature were to take office, the outgoing legislature struck out the bill's "without limitation" wording and substituted language that only lobbying expenses connected "expressly" with discussions of specific legislation would have to be reported. Departing Governor Brendan Byrne, who had previously vetoed several similar wordings, signed it at 8:00 A.M. on his way to the inaugural. All the participants later claimed surprise that the final bill was so favorable to the lobbyists. Most legislators said they did not realize what they were voting on in the year-end legislative blizzard, and the Chamber of Commerce lobbyist, James Morford, who had led the fight for seven years, claimed it was a "Hail Mary" bill—one hoped for but never expected to happen.[39]

After a series of scandals during 1990, a blue-ribbon commission on legislative ethics and campaign finance, appointed by the Senate president and headed by the director of the Eagleton Institute of Politics at Rutgers University, recommended that lobbyists be required to reported all goodwill spending. In 1991 the legislature finally passed a reform package removing the "expressly" wording, extending reporting requirements to lobbying directed at executive branch agencies, and centralizing all reporting at the Election Law Enforcement Commission.

The new reforms could provide for more meaningful public disclosure. It has been difficult to get access to the information collected. The lobby reports submitted quarterly to the attorney general's office are filed by assigned numbers rather than by name. Numbers—more than 400 of them—

38. Quoted in Weissman, "Fourth Branch of Government."
39. Upmeyer, "The Sunshine Boys," 18.

were assigned by the date of an individual's or a firm's first registration rather than alphabetically or by clients. The data were compiled by hand and were not computer-retrievable. It was time-consuming to determine such simple facts as the names of all the lobbyists representing one organization or all those interested in a given issue.

Even worse, surmounting these hurdles yielded little useful information on the true scope of lobbying activity. Lobbyists were required to report only whether they support, oppose, or seek to amend a particular bill, not the nature of the amendments. As a result of the "expressly" wording, the spending reports filed annually with the ELEC since 1982 provided no information about "goodwill" expenditures, such as all-expense-paid legislative trips to business conventions at luxury resorts. Nor were lobbyists required to report either legal fees paid to lawyer-lobbyists or expenditures on issue-related public-relations campaigns.

The new law somewhat strengthens weak regulation of lobbyists and a law that was "notoriously weak by comparison," with other states.[40] The head of New Jersey Common Cause called it "a real reform" but still "not as complete as it needs to be."[41]

INTEREST-GROUP TACTICS

New Jersey's interest groups spend most of their time and resources cultivating access to legislators and executive branch officials. The two sure ways to gain access are providing these targets with campaign money and reliable technical information. Given the complex array of groups interested in almost any issue, seasoned lobbyists hope to delay action in the legislature or implementing agencies and maintain the status quo for as long as possible; to insert amendments in bills or regulations that make unwanted legislation more palatable; or to persuade the governor to exercise one of several different types of veto power.[42]

40. The quotation is from ELEC Executive Director Frederick Hermann, in Robert Schwaneberg, "Hired Guns Report Collecting Fees of $6.6 Million for Trenton Lobbying," *Star-Ledger*, February 21, 1990, 19.

41. Bob McHugh, "Tougher Ethics Rules Cleared by Assembly," *Star-Ledger*, June 18, 1991, 1.

42. In addition to the total veto and the line-item veto, New Jersey's governor may

Information

Technical information has long been the stock-in-trade of lobbyists. When the New Jersey legislature met only once a week for a few months a year, had almost no staff, and was populated by amateurs with high turnover rates, lobbyists practically had a monopoly on information and even bill-drafting.[43] More staff and a more professional legislature have not diminished the value of lobbyists' information, because of the great increase in the number of complex issues. As legislators' comments about the NJEA and the NJBIA indicate, they are quite willing to listen to lobbyists with reputations for knowledge and probity.[44] The same is true at the governor's office, which often requests information on a bill's impact. Governor Kean's chief counsel observed, "I believe my job is to give the governor every piece of information there is on a bill so he can make a judgment. No particular lobbyist has any particular influence, but certain ones have more credibility. We talk to both sides."[45] There is no doubt that, as legislation has become more complex, technical expertise has become more important for lobbyists. However, as our description of the leading contract lobbyists makes evident, political connections count for at least as much, and probably more, as technical knowledge. These leading players may depend on their own staff for data, but it is these former officeholders and high state government officials that do the important contact work.

Money

The newer development is the greatly increased reliance of lobbyists on political contributions to secure access to lawmakers. In the past, interest

---

exercise a conditional veto, which permits him to send a bill back to the legislature with suggestions for changes in wording.

43. McKean, *Pressures*, 204, estimated that two-thirds of all bills in the 1930s were written by lobbyists.

44. The Gallup survey found that more than 50 percent of legislators found such information "very useful." They were much less likely to appreciate lobbyists' organization of constituent support or opposition (18 percent) or working with party leadership (16 percent) as "very useful" (*Gallup Survey*, 17). About half said they relied on lobbyists "very" or "somewhat" frequently for information, and only 11 percent said "not frequently at all." Senior legislators were only slightly less likely to say they relied on lobbyists with some regularity (14).

45. Michael Cole, quoted in Weissman, *Star-Ledger*, March 22, 1987.

groups certainly contributed to campaigns, but the amounts were much smaller and were directed to the county party organizations. Campaigns in New Jersey's premedia age, which extended well into the 1970s, were relatively inexpensive. The collapse of the local party organizations and the era of high-tech candidate-centered campaigns dramatically escalated costs. Senate and assembly candidates raised $15 million and spent $11 million on their 1987 campaigns—a 69 percent increase in constant dollars from 1983, and in 1991 they spent $15 million.[46]

PACs are a particularly attractive target for legislative candidates seeking funds, because there are no limits on PAC or corporate contributions to individual candidates.[47] Thus, $10,000 individual contributions are not unusual and have ranged as high as $30,000. The thirty PACs that gave at least $1,000 and were therefore required to report in 1979 contributed 14 percent of all campaign money that year. In 1987 some 187 PACs met the new reporting threshold of $2,500 and accounted for 29 percent of all contributions.

In interpreting key data on the largest givers (Table 8.3), several factors must be kept in mind. New Jersey, as noted, places no limits on direct corporate or individual contributions except to gubernatorial candidates who accept public financing. Although most political contributions are funneled through PACs, some companies still make significant direct contributions. Several groups on the list—the Transportation Trust Fund II, for example—directed their contributions to campaigns concerned with ballot questions or bond issues. Even with these caveats, however, the similarities of this list to the rankings obtained by the Associated Press are striking. The top five groups in the AP study are well represented. Although some groups do not appear on both lists, there does seem to be a connection between perceived effectiveness by legislators and the amount contributed to election campaigns.

As a result of this apparent connection, the state's leading "good government" advocates accuse the PACs of "buying" elections. Not surprisingly, the givers and recipients do not see it quite that way. Legislators freely admit that they will indeed give "access" to "heavy hitters." John Russo, who as Senate president from 1985 to 1989 raised well over $1 million for

46. ELEC news release, December 9, 1987; *Bergen Record*, October 11, 1987.

47. Banks, insurance companies, railroads, casinos, and utilities are not permitted to contribute to campaigns, but they are permitted to contribute to trade association PACs (and do so heavily).

Table 8.3.   Twenty Largest Political Action Committee (PAC) Contributors
in New Jersey, 1987

1987 Rank	1985 Rank	Name	Amount
1	1	Education Assn PAC	$269,548
2	2	Builders PAC	211,765
3	8	Medical Action Committee (MEDAC)	190,173
4	3	Campaign Fund for Lawyers Encouraging Government	188,470
5	6	Realtors PAC	177,415
6	5	N.J. Dental PAC	144,750
7	15	Operating Engineers Local 825 Political Action & Education Committee	137,112
8	7	N.J. Conference of Auto Retailers (CAR)	134,424
9	4	N.J. Organization for a Better State (NEWJOBS—N.J. Business Industry Assn)	127,500
10	—	American Trial Lawyers Assn	119,336
11	12	N.J. CPA PAC	118,525
12	—	N.J. Council of Multi-Housing Industries	109,351
13	—	Transportation Trust Fund II	107,500
14	9	Savings Assn PAC	85,475
15	—	Greater Camden Committee	78,931
16	13	South Jersey Builders PAC	73,615
17	—	Midatlantic State Bank PAC	70,375
18	—	Private Enterprise PAC	64,000
19	20	Food Council Committee	63,650
20	—	Laborers' Union Local 172 PAC	63,586

Source: Election Law Enforcement Commission News Release, April 14, 1988.

Democratic Senate candidates, has said, "If you call me up and if you've been a substantial contributor and supporter, I'll say that I'd like to see you. They listened to my plea, I'll listen to theirs."[48] In a 1987 Gallup survey, 45 percent of legislators thought PAC contributions had a positive effect on their relationship with these groups, 7 percent thought it had a negative effect, and 48 percent expressed no opinion. They cited good

48. "Quotas and Blackjacks: How the System Works," *Bergen Record*, October 13, 1987.

personal relations, more awareness of issues, and support for their own personal positions as the major positive effects.[49]

However, legislators strenuously deny being "bought." Raymond Lesniak, the candid former chairman of a heavily lobbied senate committee, gives an example from his own experience: Out-of-state bankers offered him a free trip, which he accepted, to a Florida convention. Both before and after the trip, he led the opposition to the bankers' chief legislative priority—permission to open branch banks in New Jersey. After the bankers lost on the floor, Lesniak went back to them for a campaign contribution. Fearing loss of access, they gave it to him. He therefore argues, "It certainly doesn't get them what they want—their bills passed or not. What it does get them is time to build more support for their position if they ask for it or amendments to make the legislation more palatable. They get the frills, not the meat."[50] Lesniak's argument has some credibility because the top legislative priorities of special interests usually have well-financed groups on both sides and the legislator offering "access" can collect from all of them, thereby presumably preserving his or her autonomy.

Another development militating against influence-peddling is the large and rapidly increasing share of campaign funds raised by the governor and the legislative leadership. In 1987, campaign committees controlled by the Republican governor and Assembly leader raised $1.9 million, and a committee controlled by the Democratic Senate president raised $1.7 million, much of it from PACs.[51] All these committees spent their money on races targeted entirely on the basis of competitiveness, not ideology. Thus, a lobbyist "hit up" for a contribution to, say, the Senate president's committee has no idea who will eventually wind up with the money. All these developments lead a prominent student of the legislature to conclude: "Lobbyists created a Frankenstein, and now they don't know how to control it. And I think the money they give doesn't buy them very much because people are expected to contribute and nobody gets anything special by contributing."[52] An indication that lobbyists may agree with this assessment is that the NJBIA, seeing no end to the spiraling requests, recently

49. 1987 Gallup Survey, 9–10.

50. Dan Weisman, "Political Hardball: PACs Fill Void as Party Influence Wanes," Star-Ledger, March 23, 1987.

51. ELEC report, January 19, 1988.

52. Alan Rosenthal, quoted in Weissman, "Fourth Branch of Government."

convened its own workshop on campaign reform. Even legislators seem weary of the endless fund-raising events. In the Gallup survey, they favored "restricting PAC contributions" by a margin of 63 to 27 percent, with 10 percent expressing no opinion.[53] In 1990, after a lobbyist publicly accused four Democratic Assembly leaders of a shakedown, the blue ribbon Ad Hoc Commission on Legislative Ethics and Campaign Finance reviewed the matter once again. As in previous years, however, no legislation on campaign contributions resulted.

There are several important elements of continuity in New Jersey's interest-group politics, all related to the state's enduring localist orientations. The interest groups that have remained important over the past fifty years—education, labor, and small business—are those with large and relatively cohesive representation in members' districts. Almost all the issues the state government deals with remain narrow and distributive in character, or at least are defined that way. The newest groups with a presence in Trenton are the targets of greatly increased state regulation—illustratively and most notably, builders, the financial community, insurance interests (and their frequent nemeses, the lawyers), and the health-care industry (and their largest clientele, senior citizens). Very rarely, aroused public opinion may intervene in debate on these special-interests issues. The most notable of these now are quality-of-life and environmental concerns, and skyrocketing auto insurance rates. In a contracting economy, taxes also return to the forefront of the public's attention. However, the continuing absence of true mass media in the state—particularly mass audience television stations—makes it extremely difficult for public opinion, rather than special interest opinion, to form. As a journalist has put it, "The most powerful lobby in Trenton is ignorance."[54]

It is probably not true that the strong party organizations of the past actually resulted in weak interest groups, because the parties, as we have described, were themselves fragmented rather than aggregative organizations. The party caucuses in the legislature may indeed have dictated state

53. *1987 Gallup Survey*, 13. Senior legislators (serving more than five years) with more experience with the "incumbency advantage" were more likely (70 percent) to favor restrictions than were their more junior colleagues (56 percent favoring restrictions).

54. Brian O'Reilly, "Lobbying: A Survey," *New Jersey Reporter*, February 1978, 16.

policy then, but state government did little of relevance to interest groups, and what pertinent state action there was gave interest groups control over their own affairs.

It would thus be fair to say that, today, no small number of interest groups dominate the state. Rather, in the absence of strong aggregative institutions like political parties or statewide media, there are myriad small fiefdoms, and influence in Trenton indeed has passed from the hacks to the PACs.

9

New York: Powerful Groups and Powerful Parties

David L. Cingranelli

On March 2 and 3, 1987, typical days during a legislative session, members of the following state groups descended on the capital complex in Albany to demonstrate grass-roots support for their group's policy proposals: the International Ladies Garment Workers Union, the Cable Television Association, the Builders Association, the Commission on Independent Colleges and Universities, the Energy Association, the Association of Public Broadcasting Stations, the Farm Bureau, the Coalition on Smoking and Health, the Association of Realtors, the Telephone Association, the Conference for the Aging, and the Council of Family and Child Caring Agencies. It is safe to say that the presence of these groups in Albany affected the schedules of nearly every state legislator and many heads of state agencies. It is also safe to say that the messages those groups brought to the state capital were heard and that, in many cases, interest-group positions affected public policy.

According to Sarah McCally Morehouse and Harmon Zeigler, both of whom wrote in the early 1980s, New York at the time had strong political parties but weak interest groups.[1] The thesis of this chapter is that, since then, New York has become one of those rare states with both powerful parties and interest groups. Over the last decade, the political parties in the state have become less dominant and interest groups have become stronger. As a result, New York now has many interest groups competing

1. Sarah McCally Morehouse, *State Politics, Parties, and Policy* (New York: Holt, Rinehart & Winston, 1981), chap. 3. See also L. Harmon Zeigler, "Interest Groups in the States," in Virginia Gray, Herbert Jacob, and Kenneth N. Vines, eds., *Politics in the American States*, 4th ed. (Glenview, Ill.: Scott, Foresman, 1983), chap. 4.

vigorously with one another and with the political parties over the course of public policy.

To understand the relationship between the political parties and the interest groups, it is useful, first, to look at some of the things that are distinctive about New York State as an environment for interest-group activity. Then some important aspects of the New York interest-group system, including the number, variety, and types of interest groups active in the state and the nature of government regulation of groups, will be explained. This information about the nature of the interest-group system and the environment in which interest groups must function provides an essential backdrop for addressing four important questions: Are interest groups powerful in New York? Which are more powerful than others? What attributes of interest groups are most directly associated with interest-group success? And what are the future trends in interest-group activity in the state?

Because New York State politics has been the subject of much scholarly research and writing, this chapter owes a great deal to those who have asked these and similar questions in the past. In order to update those earlier studies and to get some "insider" perspective, a questionnaire was mailed to all members of the New York State legislature and to a sample of lobbyists in 1987.[2] After reviewing the responses to those questionnaires, I interviewed a sample of legislators from both houses and parties, members of legislative staffs, professional and amateur lobbyists, and executive branch officials.

THE CONTEXT

It is difficult to appreciate the economic, social, and cultural diversity of New York State. New York, the nation's second most populous state, is the home of what may be the world's leading metropolis and contains the largest state park in the continental United States. While New York is known as the place of hustle, high pressure, and high finance, dairy farming remains one of the state's major industries. New York has long been the gateway to America for European immigrant groups and is now experienc-

---

2. The response rate to the mail questionnaire was low (about 15 percent), so no statistical analyses of the responses were performed.

ing a substantial and rapid increase in its African American and Hispanic populations. Government programs are being created to assist the assimilation of these groups, because New York State and its local governments have traditionally played an active role in economic and social affairs.

Government leaders may be reluctant to admit it, but the state's reputation as a big spender and big taxer is well deserved. The capital complex in Albany, built during the Rockefeller years, was constructed mainly from Italian marble on a scale that would have pleased the pharaohs of ancient Egypt; it is a fitting place for the "Empire State" to conduct the affairs of government. On most indicators of per capita spending for health, education, welfare, libraries, police, and corrections, New York ranks near the top among the states. The total state budget in Fiscal Year 1991–92 was approximately $55 billion. In terms of per capita state and local taxes it ranks second.[3] Thus, the stakes of public-policy-making are high for everyone.

Perhaps they are highest for the governor. New York has produced more of the nation's presidents and vice presidents and major party candidates for those positions than any other state in the union. Anyone who is a popular governor in the state has a chance to achieve high national office, and that fact of political life influences what legislation is proposed and even the fate of legislation considered during the year and a half immediately preceding a presidential election. In late 1987, for example, officials of the State University of New York (SUNY), the state's public university system, proposed a major and costly initiative designed to improve undergraduate education. One of the chief SUNY lobbyists for the proposal predicted that the initiative would be adopted if Governor Mario Cuomo decided to make a run for the presidency. Otherwise, she admitted, the whole idea was probably doomed. The implication was that the proposal might not have been made, might have been different, or might have been introduced at a different time if the governor had been perceived by this state-agency lobbyist as not having presidential ambitions. Cuomo, of course, did not run in 1988, and SUNY's proposed undergraduate initiative died a quiet death.

Partly as a result of the large rewards at stake, aggressiveness, even stridency, in the way claims are staked out and defended characterizes the state's political style and culture. This heat in the political arena stems

3. David R. Morgan, *Handbook of State Policy Indicators*, 4th ed. (Norman, Okla.: University of Oklahoma Bureau of Government Research, 1982).

from the rich cultural diversity of the state and the rough-and-tumble heritage of Tammany Hall. Within New York's political culture, the ability to defend a position eloquently in free and open debate is highly prized by those who participate in the government process. Paul Smith describes the state's political style:

> The personal characteristics of assertiveness, knowledgeability, and so forth, when coupled with the intense competition among interests in the state, yield a political process marked by continual maneuverings, energetic discussions, and general activity. . . . The result is a good deal of vigorous debate, often punctuated by charge and counter-charge, that tends toward a process that is more open than closed, despite some incentives to the contrary.[4]

Because of this predominant political style, interest groups are an accepted and welcomed part of the state's political life.

Group leaders face an unusual challenge in New York because usually they must cope with an important political cleavage—New York City versus upstate. One lesson that can be drawn from a recent compilation of case studies of the politics of thirteen states is that geographic conflict is common in state politics.[5] The upstate-downstate conflict within New York is an excellent illustration of this point. Polling results have repeatedly shown that New Yorkers perceive "serious conflict" between upstate and the City. Thus, few New Yorkers were surprised by Mayor Ed Koch's famous remarks in a 1982 *Playboy* magazine interview characterizing life upstate as "wasting your life."[6] Within New York there is even serious debate over which chief executive is more powerful—the governor or New York City's mayor. One could imagine a similar debate in Illinois but in very few other states. Some interest groups draw members primarily either from upstate (e.g., farmers) or the city (e.g., tenants' organizations), but the geographic cleavage cuts through most groups. Thus, one of the most difficult challenges facing almost every interest-group leader is how to reconcile the conflicts between upstate and downstate members. Failure to do so often means that the group will lack internal cohesion and will consequently not be able to achieve its goals.

---

4. Paul A. Smith, "E Pluribus Unum," in Alan Rosenthal and Maureen Moakley, eds., *The Political Life of the American States* (New York: Praeger, 1984), 258.

5. Rosenthal and Moakley, *The Political Life of the American States.*

6. Smith, "E Pluribus Unum," 249.

Phases of the Policy-Making Process

Leaders must also adapt their strategies to two distinct phases in the policy-making process in New York State that are defined by the annual budget cycle.[7] During the "fiscal phase," lasting from January until around the end of March, the legislature acts on budget bills introduced directly into the legislature by the governor. These bills allocate or set aside pots of money for particular public purposes, such as supporting local governments, school districts, and other continuing or new state programs. In the subsequent "program and regulation" phase, members of the legislature, legislative committees, the governor, the executive departments, and other state agencies introduce bills for consideration. While during the "fiscal stage" the focus of the legislature is almost entirely on money bills, the emphasis during the program and regulation stage is on fleshing out substantive programs and on divvying up the money that had already been set aside.

In the fiscal stage there is considerable cooperation among interest groups that have a shared interest in getting a larger portion of the pie devoted to programs within a particular policy arena. For example, representatives of the interests of local school districts—associations of teachers, principals, superintendents, parents, and the like—often cooperate to increase the amount of resources that will be allocated to primary and secondary education. During the later phase, as specific programs are defined, there will be more conflict among those same groups.

Recently, conflict within the "education lobby" has occurred over such issues as child-abuse legislation, tenure rights of teachers, banning the sale of candy and soda in the schools, and schoolbus safety requirements. This distinction between phases is crude, for there is always some conflict within lobbies during any stage of the policy process, and there are some occasions when lobby groups usually at odds with one another form coalitions for or against a particular proposal. But the fact that groups commonly thought of as adversaries during the program and regulation phase often work together on money bills during the fiscal stage is noteworthy.

Within both phases, competition between the Republican party and the Democratic party is intense. The New York City area, accounting for about half the state's population, is dominated by the Democratic party. Long Island and most of upstate New York is dominated by the Republican

7. This discussion of the two stages of the budget cycle relies heavily on James R. Ruhl, *The Legislative Logjam in the States: The Case of the New York State Senate* (Ph.D. diss., State University of New York at Albany, 1986), esp. chap. 3, "The Senate Logjam Environment."

party, but the larger upstate cities of Buffalo, Syracuse, and Albany remain Democratic strongholds. Statewide elections to fill open seats are usually quite competitive, with a slight edge going to Democrats. There are about 1 million more registered Democrats than Republicans, and, according to a 1982 *New York Times* poll, people who identify psychologically with the Democratic party outnumbered Republican party identifiers by about four to three.[8] Of the last nine gubernatorial elections (starting in 1990 and working backward from there), five were won by the Democrats and four by the Republicans. The Democratic majority, 95 to 55 (in 1991) in the Assembly is long-standing and enormous. The Republican majority in the Senate is also long-standing, but more tenuous at 35 to 26 seats. Party competition within the legislature has been maintained through creative gerrymandering of Senate districts, giving some advantage to the Republican party in Senate elections.

There are some signs that the Republican party is weakening as a force in state politics. The GOP has abandoned New York City, holding only one of thirty-five city council seats in 1989. The Democrats have commanding control of the Congressional delegation. The acknowledged leader of the Republican party in the state for over a decade, Senate Majority Leader Warren Anderson, retired in January 1989. The Republican party passed a stiff test in 1990 by holding onto its narrow majority. This was a significant election, because the 1991–92 legislature reapportioned legislative districts for the 1990s. Before the 1990 election, Jonathan Bush, brother to former President Bush and state party finance chairman, said that unless the Republicans beat Governor Cuomo (which they did not do) and hung onto the state Senate in 1990 (which they did do) they would become the minority party in New York for the next 250 years.[9]

As long as the Republicans retain control of the state Senate, however, New York will continue to have one of the most competitive and partisan legislatures in the nation.[10] During the legislative process, Democrats almost automatically oppose Republican initiatives, and Republicans vote

8. The results of a survey of characteristics of the New York State electorate conducted by the *New York Times* in October 1982 are reported by John K. White and Dwight Morris, "The Electoral Riddle," in Peter W. Colby, ed., *New York State Today: Politics, Government, Public Policy* (Albany: State University of New York Press, 1985), 71–80.

9. Jeffrey Stinson, "Republicans Vanishing in New York," *Press & Sun Bulletin*, January 15, 1989, 3-E.

10. See, e.g., Alan Hevesi, "The Renewed Legislature," in Colby, *New York State Today*, 152.

against Democratic proposals, unless there is some really good reason to do otherwise. At legislative committee meetings, Republicans usually sit at one end of the table with their staff members, and Democrats sit at the other end. Lobbyists favoring Democratic proposals stand or sit behind the Democratic end, while lobbyists favoring Republican proposals provide similar support for their champions. Partisanship is maintained by regular meetings of the four party caucuses, where vote tallies that for all practical purposes bind members on floor votes are taken. When party leaders go to the floor on issues, the outcome is almost always certain.[11]

Partly because of the importance of caucus votes, many have called New York a "leadership dominant" political system.[12] A former flamboyant lobbyist for the International Brotherhood of Teamsters is reported to have said, "There are only two votes in the legislature: those of Senator Warren Anderson [then majority leader] and Speaker Steingut [then Speaker of the Assembly]."[13] The governor provides the third vote in what Gerald Benjamin has called "government by triad."[14] The occupants of the key leadership roles in the legislature have changed. Saul Weprin became Speaker of the Assembly in 1991, and Ralph Marino became majority leader of the state Senate in 1989. For years, the dominant coalition in New York State politics has been between the governor and the Speaker of the Assembly against the majority leader of the Republican-controlled Senate.

There has been great pressure from the press to reform the current system of "government by triad," and party leaders probably will not be able to resist those pressures for long. A series of democratizing reforms probably will be enacted in both chambers during the 1990s, giving rank-and-file legislators more autonomy in the legislative process. The reforms should be similar to those enacted in the U.S. House of Representatives in the mid-1970s. Such changes, if they occur, will provide even more points of access for interest groups. During my interviews, however, few legislators or staff members expressed dissatisfaction with the current distribution of legislative power. Senator Warren Anderson was not surprised. When

11. Ibid.
12. Ruhl, *Legislative Logjam*, 66; Steve Kroft, "The Magic and Myth of the Big Lobbyist," *The Empire State Report* 1 (April 1975), 125. See also John J. Pitney Jr., "Leaders and Rules in the New York State Senate," *Legislative Studies Quarterly*, November 1982, 491.
13. Steve Kroft, "The Magic and Myth of the Big Lobbyist," *Empire State Report* 1 (April 1975), 121.
14. Gerald Benjamin, "The Albany Triad," *Empire State Report* 13 (November 1987).

compared with other states that have strong legislatures, he said, the power of New York's legislative leaders is about average. Moreover, he argued, strong legislative leaders can better negotiate with the executive branch, and high-profile leaders help take the heat off rank-and-file legislators. Alan Rosenthal's comparative analysis of the roles of legislative party leaders within the fifty states lends some support to Anderson's position.[15]

The Legal Environment for Interest Groups and PACs

In 1977, New York took a major step toward public disclosure of lobbying activities when its leadership created the Temporary State Commission on Lobbying. The commission maintains a public clearinghouse of the identities, activities, and expenditures of those attempting to influence state government decision-makers. The Lobbying Act establishing the commission replaced a much weaker and almost unenforceable set of regulations and provided for the first comprehensive lobbyist disclosure reform in more than seventy years. A bipartisan, six-member commission is empowered to conduct investigations, issue subpoenas, and impose civil penalties of up to $5,000 on dilatory lobbyists, clients, and public corporations (for violations of the Lobbying Act). The act applies to lobbyists and clients or employers of lobbyists who in any calendar year either anticipate or actually expend, incur, or receive more than $2,000 of combined reportable compensation and expenses for lobbying activities. In essence, it requires lobbyists to make periodic reports of how much they earn and from whom, and of how much they spend and on what.

Some local governments meet the $2,000 criterion and therefore register; most do not. The Lobbying Act specifically excludes from the definition of "lobbyist" "any officer, director, trustee, employee, counsel or agent of the state of New York when discharging their official duties." The temporary state commission is unhappy with this provision because state agencies are major players in the legislative process. In 1990 it recommended that the Lobbying Act "should be amended to require State agency officials who lobby to register and report as legislative representatives, and the agencies themselves should be required to report as clients."[16]

Over time, the Lobbying Act will probably be toughened in a variety of ways, but even now there is widespread agreement that the law is tough, reasonable, and aggressively enforced. Legislators and staff members must

15. Alan Rosenthal, *Legislative Life* (New York: Harper & Row, 1981), 167–72.
16. New York Temporary State Commission on Lobbying, *Annual Report 1990*, 13.

report receiving any gift valued at $50 or more, and lobbyists must report giving such gifts. Once reports are filed, it is not uncommon for a lobbyist or the recipient of the gift, or both, to be the subjects of follow-up inquiries from the commission. During my interviews at the capital I asked whether most lobbyists really registered, because noncompliance was an alleged problem with the earlier regulations. One legislative staff member's response was typical: "The smart ones do," he said, "and I won't deal with those who don't."

The legislature spent much of 1988 developing and enacting new legislation on the ethics of legislators and staff members. By most accepted measures (salary, staff, length of legislative sessions, etc.), New York already has one of the most professionalized state legislatures in the nation.[17] Pursuing more independence from New York's powerful interest groups, the legislature in 1988 passed an "ethics law" limiting the amount of outside income that someone serving in the state legislature could earn. Passage of the law would stop some interest groups from using such income to achieve their goals indirectly. Former Assemblyman Peter Berle writes that a subtle use of money "involves allocation of business to financial concerns in a way which profits the legislator. For example, the legislator may be on the banking committee and may also maintain a private law practice. Without any real communication between legislator, lobbyist, or banker, certain routine legal matters are referred by the banks to the legislator's law firm."[18]

The ethics law seems to be a step in the right direction, but as several legislators pointed out, it will make state legislators more dependent on their legislative positions for their livelihoods. As a result, it will still be difficult for legislators of moderate means to say no to groups that might contribute resources to the next election campaign. Dependence on PAC support is exacerbated by the now well-known and well-documented escalation in the costs of campaigns, caused largely by the increased costs of purchasing media time.

THE GROUP UNIVERSE IN NEW YORK

In Albany, interest groups are visible, numerous, diverse in the interests they represent, vigorous, and pervasive in the policy process. In 1973 only

17. Alan Rosenthal, *Legislative Life* (New York: Harper & Row, 1981).

18. Peter A. Berle, *Does the Citizen Stand a Chance? Politics of a State Legislature: New York* (Woodbury, N.Y.: Barron's Educational Series, 1974), 52.

110 of the organizations registered with the New York secretary of state were represented by professional lobbyists.[19] In 1989, some 971 clients were represented by 1,699 lobbyists at the state capital.[20] In order to be really "in the game," groups must not only maintain a presence at the state capital but also have a large membership distributed geographically throughout the state, make campaign contributions (recorded with the Lobbying Commission), and from time to time demonstrate grass-roots support for the policies advocated by the group's leaders.

More interest groups have been establishing an Albany presence, and expenditures on lobbying activities have been higher. Table 9.1 shows the growth in numbers of lobby groups and spending between 1978 and 1989, the years for which the Temporary Commission has good, comparable information. The spending figures are probably understated. Statistics have shown that, through the years, the bulk of annual lobbying expenditures has been devoted to compensation of paid lobbyists, which made the Lobbying Commission wonder out loud whether those subject to the jurisdiction of the Lobbying Act "actually report all that is necessary and required to be disclosed."[21] The commission's concern is understandable. During the legislative session, the New York State Electric & Gas lobbyist travels to Albany about once a week, apparently to meet with legislators and staff members about policies affecting his industry, but in 1986 he reported receiving only $684 in compensation for his lobbying efforts.[22]

More than 25 percent of the $15.5 million in 1986 lobbying expenditures was accounted for by business, commerce, and industry. Table 9.2 is a breakdown of lobbying expenses by type of interest group. This compilation is possible because the Lobbying Act requires that a description of the subject or subjects on which the lobbyist has worked be provided in certain statements and reports filed with the commission.[23]

---

19. Carol Greenwald, "Post-Watergate Lobbying Laws: Tokenism v. Real Reform," *National Civic Review*, October 1974, 470. Because lobby registration laws were weak before 1977, this report probably underestimated both the number of organizations represented and the number of lobbyists.

20. New York State Temporary Commission on Lobbying, *Annual Report 1990*, 2. The increased number of registered lobbyists was due in part to the more strict regulations requiring registration of lobbyists passed in 1977.

21. New York State Temporary State Commission on Lobbying, *Annual Report 1986*, 10.

22. Ibid., 33.

23. Ibid., 16.

Table 9.1. Lobby Representation and Spending in New York State, 1978–1989

Year	No. of Lobbyists	No. of Clients	Spending in Millions
1989	1,699	971	$26.0
1988	1,632	874	22.1
1987	1,590	776	17.7
1986	1,482	735	15.5
1985	1,382	662	15.1
1984	1,320	669	12.4
1983	1,381	625	10.9
1982	1,659	596	9.6
1981	1,624	580	8.2
1980	1,732	671	6.6
1979	1,294	580	5.5
1978	n.a.	n.a.	5.7

Source: New York Temporary Commission on Lobbying, *1990 Annual Report*, 2–3.

n.a. = not available

Table 9.2. Lobbying Expenditures by Type of Interest Group, New York, FY 1986

Nature of Client's Business	Lobbying Expenses
Banking and finance	$ 940,000
Business, commerce, and industry	4,300,000
Communication	570,000
Education	1,100,000
Energy	960,000
Housing and construction	570,000
Health	1,400,000
Insurance	1,100,000
Labor	1,400,000
Law	270,000
Public and community interest	810,000
Racing and wagering	680,000
Local government	740,000
Transportation	640,000

Source: New York State Temporary Commission on Lobbying, *1986 Annual Report*.

GROUP STRATEGY AND TACTICS

James Ruhl, a former veteran staff member in the state Senate, believes that each group's influence is determined by three factors: its organization and agenda, its lobbying activities, and its election activities. Strong interest groups have focused agendas, activist, participatory members, and full-time, paid leaders. In the legislative process they are represented by a lobbyist who represents only them, who is active year-round whether the legislature is in session or not, who has access to accurate information, who drafts bills, and who is able to develop trust among legislators and legislative staff and a reputation as an expert in a particular area of legislation. They participate in electoral politics by forming PACs, making campaign workers available, and contributing to a political party and to individual candidates.

Organization and Agenda

During 1987 a legislative battle between the Teamsters union and the school nurses' organization in New York apparently did not end the way one might have expected, given Ruhl's formula. The school nurses were backing a bill banning the sale of candy and soda in schools in the mornings; several businesses were opposed to the legislation but did not lobby seriously until the bill had passed the state Senate without debate. Then the battle really began. Many businesses and associations worked hard to stop the bill in the Assembly, including the longshoremen's union, Pepsico, Nestle, and even the School Boards Association, which argued that the bill deprived local boards of their rightful decision-making authority. An equally large but seemingly less powerful array of groups backed the bill, including the Parent-Teacher Association, school nurses, and dietitians. Few of the groups favoring the bill even had lobbyists in Albany. The bill passed the Assembly and, despite a concerted attempt by the forces against it to convince the governor to veto the bill, Cuomo signed it into law.

He probably signed the "soda and candy bill" because it was a good idea and because people with expertise and commitment worked hard for it. One way an interest group without a lot of money can demonstrate the commitment of its membership is through grass-roots activities, and in Albany demonstrating grass-roots support has been refined to an art. Leaders usually make elaborate arrangements well in advance of large-scale mem-

bership visits, typically including a reception, breakfast, luncheon, or dinner (which group members and state policymakers attend) and appointments for members to speak with their own legislative representatives at
the capital about the group's concerns. Even though such grass-roots visits
take up a great deal of the time available to legislators during session days,
the visits are welcomed as an opportunity to gather important information
about the impact of existing or contemplated policies on specific constituencies and as a chance to win votes for the next election.

Jeffrey Schmalz described the Roman Catholic church grass-roots day in
1987 as follows:

> Two thousand Roman Catholics—led by all eight bishops of New
> York State, including John Cardinal O'Connor—swept through the
> halls of state government today. They lobbied for the Catholic view
> on legislation, calling for greater aid to the poor. . . . Throughout
> the day, nuns, priests and lay people, carrying a list of legislators by
> diocese, moved from office to office and detailed the more than two
> dozen items on the church agenda.[24]

In the early 1970s, when most public-interest groups were formed in New
York, they were, unlike the Catholic church, small, poorly financed, and
generally ineffective.[25] A common lobbying tactic was grass-roots demonstrations culminating in confrontations with legislators in Albany, which
got them visibility but few real results. Since those early days, strategies
and tactics of such groups have changed greatly. In the words of a competi-
tor lobbyist who represented a major corporation, "Their leaders grew up."
Now, he says, their tactics are determined less by ideology and more by
goals.

But some public-interest groups and other less powerful groups still occasionally violate the norms regulating interest-group behavior. One norm is
"apprenticeship." New groups and new leaders are expected to keep a low
profile for two to three years until they develop adequate subject-matter
expertise and an appropriate network of contacts. Another norm is "cour-
tesy" even under the most adverse circumstances. Conforming to this norm

24. Jeffrey Schmalz, "2,000 Catholics Lobby Leaders in Albany Visit," *New York
Times*, March 10, 1987, A-1.

25. See Edward L. Schapsmeier and Frederick H. Schapsmeier, *Political Parties and
Civic Action Groups* (Westport, Conn.: Greenwood Press, 1981), for a short history of
the origin and development of these groups.

requires that lobbyists be patient and persistent, never loud and obnoxious. Groups are also expected to avoid publicly opposing and embarrassing policymakers.

While most pressure-group leaders are probably aware of these norms, they are often intentionally ignored by less-powerful groups tired of playing by the rules and losing. One lobbyist, Franklin "Dutch" Volk, a true believer in his cause—allowing citizens to own and carry handguns—has a reputation for flaunting all the rules. His attitude is "I don't care what they think of me as long as they vote for my bills." By most accounts his confrontational tactics are effective. Environmental groups in Albany also have a reputation for using unorthodox tactics, such as publishing and publicizing "good" and "bad" voting records and handing out plastic ostrich eggs to members of the legislature who have "buried their heads in the sand" on important environmental issues. Usually such strategies are short-term. They are adopted by groups with less professional leadership and by newer groups that are on the outside looking in at the policy-making process. In general, as groups mature, they use unorthodox tactics less and less.

Lobbying Activities

Although legislators and their staff members often spoke admiringly about the power of grass-roots lobbying, many of the most successful lobbyists in New York in terms of fees earned from lobbying activities are less visible, low-key contract lobbyists with former ties to state government. Most of the successful contract lobbyists also are lawyers. The law firm of DeGraff, Foy & Conway was founded by the late former legislator George Foy. Joseph Carlino, another successful lobbyist, was Speaker of the Assembly in the early 1960s. Samuel Roman, a former assemblyman and former deputy commissioner of the State Harness Racing Association, now represents clients from the horse-racing industry.

All have expertise in a particular area of public policy, are knowledgeable about the policy-making process, and have personal contacts within the government. In 1975 Steve Kroft profiled Victor Condello, who in 1974 ranked fourth in the state in earnings from lobbying activities.[26] Condello's law firm then represented nine clients and earned approximately

26. See Kroft, "The Magic and Myth," 120.

$82,000 in lobbying fees that year. In 1986 the firm represented forty-one clients and reported receiving more than $1 million in lobbying fees, probably making him the top lobbyist in the state.[27]

Condello illustrates the qualities that make a lobbyist effective. His political connections and experience go back to 1947, when he became a law assistant in the New York City Corporation Counsel's office. He has been dealing with governors and legislators ever since. By 1950 Condello had become the city's legislative representative in Albany, by 1957 he had the title "Assistant to the Mayor," and before long he left City Hall to go into business for himself.[28]

Now Condello is on friendly terms with leaders of both parties. He is almost invisible, working behind the scenes, dealing almost exclusively with leaders rather than rank-and-file members of the legislature, never throwing parties, and almost never issuing press releases. He is able to work this way because of his extensive contacts and expertise. He told Kroft, "If there is a railroad bill I want, I'll take it to the Department of Transportation and try to sell them on it. If I can convince them to introduce it, the chances of it passing are greatly enhanced."[29] Working through the state bureaucracy keeps Condello's profile low and also helps ensure good results, since state agencies are allowed wide discretion in implementing the policy once enacted.

State agencies promulgate hundreds of rules, regulations, rates, and rate changes each year, so they are prime targets for lobby activities. Among the state agencies that reported being contacted by lobbyists in 1990 were the Department of Agriculture and Markets, the Ranking Department, the Commission on Cable Television, the Department of Environmental Conservation, the Board of Equalization and Assessment, the Department of Health, the Insurance Department, the Office of Mental Health, the Office of Mental Retardation and Developmental Disabilities, the Department of Motor Vehicles, the Department of Social Services, the Department of Transportation, the Education Department, the Board of Regents, the Office of Energy, the Public Service Commission, the Labor Department, the Department of Economic Development, the Office of Parks, Recreation, and Historic Preservation, the Office of Energy Research and

27. New York State Temporary Commission on Lobbying, *Annual Report 1986*, 5.
28. See Kroft, "The Magic and Myth," 119.
29. Ibid., 121.

Development, the Liquor Authority, and the Division of Housing and Community Renewal.[30]

Because a large proportion of all state laws are passed in the final weeks of each legislative session, the successful lobbyist must have a good understanding of the labyrinth of rules and customs that govern the legislative process. After nearly four decades in the state capital, Condello is a master at playing the game to achieve his goals. His advice is often sought by other lobbyists and even legislators. In the final analysis, Condello's initial success in Albany, and his success today, are based largely on his integrity and on the quality of the work he produces.[31] He has been described as one of the foremost authorities on railroad law in the United States and is certainly tops in New York State. While in many other states the wheeler-dealer old-style lobbyists are being replaced by technical experts, in New York the most successful lobbyists are both wheeler-dealers and technical experts.

Election Activities

Pressure groups can also demonstrate the active commitment of the membership to the leadership's agenda through campaign contributions. The costs of financing a state legislative campaign in New York is high and has grown at a rate of about 10 percent each election campaign since 1984. In 1988 the average Republican candidate for the state Senate spent $47,048, while the average Democratic candidate spent $37,366. That same year the average Republican candidate for the state Assembly spent $17,908, while the average Democratic candidate spent $27,263.32. Members of the majority party in both chambers spent more because they were better able to attract contributions from political action committees (PACs).[32]

A March 1986 list of PACs, committees that raise funds from their memberships to provide financial support for candidates, included just under 400 political action committees formed to support candidates for public office in New York.[33] Under New York State law a PAC is an "unauthorized committee" working without the knowledge or permission of a

30. New York State Temporary Commission on Lobbying, *Annual Report 1990*, 9.
31. Ibid., 124.
32. Diana Dwyre and Jeffrey M. Stonecash, "Where's the Party?" *American Politics Quarterly* 20 (July 1992), 326–44.
33. The list of PACs was compiled by the New York State Board of Elections and included in *The New York State Directory*, 440–88.

candidate. Unlike candidate committees, PACs are not restricted in the amount of money they can receive from any single donor. Table 9.3 shows the types of PACs that contribute the most.

It is important to note that the information in Table 9.3 reflects cash contributions but not nonmonetary assistance, such as campaign services or other in-kind labor. Thus, because (more than the other types of interest groups) unions can and do supply campaign workers at election time, the campaign contributions of unions are understated. Even without in-kind contributions, however, unions are an important source of campaign funds in state and local elections in New York. The table also understates the PAC contributions of the real-estate industry. Although only two real-estate PACs contributed more than $5,000 during the period covered by the report, both contributions were substantial—one amounting to $141,933, by the Realtors PAC, and another of $387,760, by the Real Estate Board PAC. The contribution by the Real Estate Board PAC was the largest contribution in 1986. Other PACs making contributions in excess of $75,000 in 1986 were the Bear, Stearns Political Campaign Com-

Table 9.3. New York PAC Contributions over $5,000 (Between January 10, 1985, and January 11, 1986) by Type of Interest Group

Type of Interest Group	No. of Contributions		
	Greater Than $5,000, Less Than $10,000	Greater Than $10,000, Less Than $50,000	Greater Than $50,000
Unions	8	16	4
Banking / insurance investment	4	15	6
Real estate	0	0	2
Other corporations and industrial assns	11	12	4
Occupational and professional assns	11	4	0
Law firms	1	2	2
Utilities	1	2	0
Other	3	3	1

Source: Compiled from a listing of actual PAC contributions that appeared in *The New York State Directory 1986–1987*, 440–88.

mittee ($303,195), the Voice of Teachers for Political Education COPE ($189,117), the Grumman Corporation ($183,992), Solomon Brothers Inc. ($171,400), the United Federation of Teachers COPE ($153,111), the Neighborhood Preservation Political Action Federation ($143,959), the Public Employees Federation ($102,526), the Allstate Insurance Company ($83,500), Cigna Corporation ($81,664), and Local 1814 of the International Longshoremen's Association ($78,535).

Much of the money contributed by PACs is given to majority-party incumbents who occupy safe seats, or to campaign committees run by the Republican and Democrat leaders of the Senate and Assembly. Diana Dwyre and Jeffrey Stonecash argue that the emergence of these legislative campaign committees as major actors in campaign financing reduces the hold particular PACs have on particular members of the legislature.[34] However, interest groups do target lawmakers who control key committees with jurisdiction over matters of particular interest to each of them. For example, Assembly Health Committee Chairman Richard Gottfried (D–Manhattan) collects thousands of dollars from drug manufacturers, doctors' groups, and hospital associations each year. Similarly, the insurance industry contributes a great deal to the campaign coffers of Senate Insurance Committee Chairman Joseph Bruno (R–Troy). According to Julian Palmer, director of New York State's chapter of Common Cause, there's probably no vote-selling going on. But "contributions lead to access. Access leads to influence."[35]

THE MOST POWERFUL INTEREST GROUPS IN NEW YORK

Measuring the relative power of interest groups is difficult, and any particular ranking will be controversial. But legislators, lobbyists, and legislative staff all agree that some groups in the state are much more powerful than others. In developing a ranking of New York's groups, I considered several criteria that were sometimes mentioned in the returned questionnaires and were brought up repeatedly in the in-depth, unstructured interviews. Ac-

34. Dwyre and Stonecash, "Where's the Party?"
35. Hilary Waldman, "Political Gifts Could Be Put to Better Use," *Press & Sun Bulletin* (Binghamton, N.Y.), March 5, 1989, E-3.

cording to the participants in the policy-making process, the strongest groups are those that often influence the passage, defeat, or delay of legislation; the approval, disapproval, or delay of legislation by the governor; the adoption, rejection, or delay of any rule or regulation by a state agency having the effect of law; and the outcome of any rate-making proceeding by a state agency. Groups that could exercise influence in these ways over a broad range of public policies were considered more powerful than groups that were influential in only one or a few policy areas.

On the basis of those criteria, the business and public-employee lobbies are the two strongest in the state. Within the business lobby, the State Business Council and the Chamber of Commerce and Industry are the two strongest groups representing diverse business interests, followed closely by the Bankers Association, the Association of Realtors, and the Associated Industries of New York. No interest group representing a single corporation has as much clout on as wide an array of issues as any of these groups does. Within the public-employee lobby, the New York State Federation of Teachers and the Civil Service Employees Association are probably the most powerful groups.

Although almost everyone interviewed agreed that business associations and public-employee unions were the most powerful groups in the state, there was no consensus on which of the two types was most powerful. Zeller, who studied the role of interest groups in New York State politics in the 1930s, argued that business interests stood above all others as most powerful in the battle for legislative influence in Albany.[36] In agreement with this assessment is former Assemblyman Stephen Solarz of Brooklyn, who reportedly said that the poor, the consumers, the nonunionized workers, and the young have little voice among the lobby groups in Albany, while the monied interests have an inordinate amount of influence.[37]

Business interests remain powerful, but it is difficult to make the case today that their lobby is preeminent. In 1948 Warren Moscow identified a wider array of powerful groups and concluded that, over the years, the most effective lobbyists had been the Roman Catholic church, the teachers' lobby, the Conference of Mayors, the Association of Towns, public utility companies, railroads, newspapers, the New York State Federation of Labor,

---

36. Belle Zeller, *Pressure Politics in New York: A Study of Group Representation Before the Legislature* (New York: Prentice Hall, 1937), esp. chap. 3, "Business Interests."
37. Kroft, "The Magic and Myth," 125.

and the Associated Industries of New York.[38] And Joseph Zimmerman, writing in 1981, agreed that the power of business interests was not what it used to be, mainly because of the increased clout of unions, the rise of public-interest groups, and the consumer movement.[39] Furthermore, a 1980 rating of New York's "business climate" (based on tax levels, services commonly offered to businesses, and union regulations) ranked it as the worst in the fifty states, raising serious questions about the effectiveness of the state's business lobby.[40] There is no indication that the business climate has improved since then. In response to a survey of 3,379 corporate executives in the state conducted in 1990 by the Business Council, 57 percent reported that they wanted to move their firms out of New York. An even larger portion, 70 percent, said they would prefer to expand outside of New York if they could, and 81 percent said they thought New York was tougher on business than any other state.[41]

Still, the business lobby has been successful as an agent of public-policy change, so it deserves to be ranked among the most powerful lobbies in the state. A major achievement of the business lobby was the passage of the long-sought corporate tax cut bill in 1987. Indeed, some would argue that 1987 was the one of the best years business lobbyists have ever had in the state. In addition to the corporate tax bill, the state approved a $4.5 billion cut in personal income taxes, a new Department of Economic Development, $160.7 million in economic development programs, liability protection for corporate directors, and several other probusiness bills.[42]

The business lobby seems to be especially influential during bad economic times. In the early 1990s, the state became mired in a deep economic recession, resulting in more aggressive demands from the business lobby and increased conflict between the business and public-sector labor lobbies. Daniel Walsh, former Assembly majority leader and now president and chief spokesperson for the New York State Business Council, threw down the gauntlet when he proposed in 1991 that the salaries for all

38. Warren Moscow, *Politics in the Empire State* (New York: Alfred A. Knopf, 1948), 200–204.

39. Joseph F. Zimmerman, *The Government and Politics of New York State* (New York: New York University Press, 1981), 97–98.

40. Philip L. Rones, "Moving to the Sun: Regional Job Growth, 1968–1978," *Monthly Labor Review* 101 (March 1980), 15.

41. Alan Breznick, "Enterprising Concerns," *Empire State Report*, February 1991, 17.

42. Jon Sorensen, "A Banner Year for Business," *Empire State Report* 13 (September 1987), 12–18.

240,000 state workers be frozen for at least two years. Contract negotiations between state workers and the governor's office in 1992 resulted in agreements that essentially followed this recommendation. Walsh is also pushing for another round of corporate and income tax cuts and has extracted a "no new taxes" pledge from Governor Cuomo. Public-sector unions expect to recover from these losses when the state's economy improves.

The clout of public-sector unions was increased greatly by the 1977 act that authorized unions representing state employees to collect an agency shop fee from the paychecks of nonunion members in the bargaining unit. This act made all state employee unions major actors in the lobbying process almost overnight. In fact, every legislator who responded to my mail survey ranked organized labor among the top five interest groups. The groups mentioned most often were the teachers' unions (the United Federation of Teachers and the Teachers Association), unions representing state employees (the Civil Service Employees Association, the Public Employees Federation, and the American Federation of State, County, and Municipal Employees), the AFL-CIO, and associations of police and firefighters.

Generally, legislators thought unions were the most effective interest groups as elections approached, while business groups, such as the Business Council and banking and insurance associations, were often listed among the five most effective groups during more routine legislative sessions. This may indicate that at election time candidates may value campaign workers and votes (which unions may be able to supply) even more than PAC contributions.

One reason business groups are perceived as legislatively powerful is that, having fewer members, they usually are more cohesive, consistent, and specialized in their demands. The larger a group's membership, the more heterogeneous it will be, and the longer and more varied its policy agenda will be. For example, when the Roman Catholic church lobbied state government in 1987, among the items sought were elimination of abortion, opposition to giving terminally ill people the right to refuse lifesaving measures, an increase in welfare benefits, better access to health care for those without medical insurance, tax credits for parents who send their children to private schools, more housing for the homeless, and more day-care centers for low-income families.[43] While some of the agenda was purely Catholic, much of it was part of the state's most recent Democratic party plat-

43. Schmalz, "2,000 Catholics," A-1, B-5.

form. In the wake of the recent U.S. Supreme Court decisions giving more discretion to the states on abortion policies, the Roman Catholic church is expected to focus more of its considerable resources on antiabortion efforts. As a result, it may become a more powerful force in New York politics.

In the next category of groups, ranking below business associations and public-sector unions, in descending order, are the Teamsters, the public utilities, the New York State Catholic Conference, and the local government lobby (New York City, the NYS Conference of Mayors, the NYS Association of Counties, and the School Boards Association). Groups that have less power but that are still important in the state are the NYS Medical Association, the senior citizen lobby (especially the American Association of Retired Persons), the State Board of Regents, the NYS Hospital Association, the farm lobby (especially the Farm Bureau), and consumers groups such as the New York Public Interest Research Group (NYPIRG). Unlike the other groups in this last category, senior-citizen groups and consumer groups are making their positions known on a wide range of policy proposals and are increasing in power. As the baby-boom generation ages and as advances in technology allow people to live longer, an increased voice for senior citizens in public-policy formation is virtually guaranteed.

While none of those whom I interviewed and none of the responses to my questionnaires listed local governments or associations of local government officials as among the most powerful interest groups, I consider them to be moderately powerful, just as Warren Moscow did in 1948[44] They maintain a high profile in Albany and have excellent access to legislators. Today one could even make the case that the New York City lobby alone is the biggest and most powerful lobby in the state. During 1986 the City reported paying its lobbying staff $196,318 and spending another $109,974 on lobbying expenses. The City's Board of Education also spent approximately $90,000 on lobbying activities that year.[45] Other important local government lobbies in the state are the NYS Association of Counties, the NYS Conference of Mayors and Other Municipal Officials, and the School Boards Association. New York also has several important quasi-public agencies called public authorities. Among the most active public authori-

44. Moscow, *Politics in the Empire State*, 200–204.
45. New York State Temporary State Commission on Lobbying, *Annual Report 1986*, 39.

ties on the lobbying scene at the state capital are the Port Authority, the Power Authority, and the Off-Track Betting Corporation.[46]

Although none of the legislators ranked public-interest groups as among the most powerful, there are also several "good government" lobbies that are well known, active, and apparently effective in Albany, including Common Cause, the NYPIRG, Change New York, and the Consumer Assembly. In addition, the growing consumer movement has caused many older New Yorkers to support these groups, which had previously served the young almost exclusively. As a result, group leaders are willing to cooperate with business interests and even to form alliances when it furthers their goals to do so. By all accounts, the power of these good-government groups is growing.

A BALANCE OF STRONG PRESSURE GROUPS AND PARTIES

Powerful parties in New York have not prevented the emergence of equally powerful interest groups. Instead, strong parties provide strong groups with access to the policy process. While both Morehouse and Zeigler once characterized New York's interest groups as weak, it would be difficult to do so today. A state's interest-group system would be considered "weak" if some interest groups are able to gain access and exercise influence over the policy-making process only when a particular party is in power; if parties make use of pressure groups to accomplish their legislative ends; if parties occasionally discipline unruly pressure groups; or if pressure groups must do business with party leaders who "clear" legislation.[47] On the basis of these criteria, New York has a powerful interest-group system.

Many others who have written on the subject also have argued that the state's interest-group system is strong and diverse. In 1948 Warren Moscow wrote that the public would protest if it were known that a lobbyist had helped draft a bill in Washington, but in Albany it happens all the time and no one gets excited about it.[48] In 1981 Zimmerman wrote that the role of interest groups in shaping public policy "cannot be overestimated."[49] In

46. Ibid.
47. Morehouse, *State Politics, Parties, and Policy*, 106–7.
48. Moscow, *Politics in the Empire State*, 200.
49. Zimmerman, *Government and Politics of New York State*, 97.

1984 Paul Smith argued that interest groups were "always in at least partial opposition to one another," that they operated "at every level of politics," and that they served "to structure and limit power in the state."[50]

Since two-party competition is so strong in statewide elections and within the legislature, all interest groups have good access to the policy-making process at all times. The major parties in New York are not particularly ideological, and this fact increases the access most groups have to the elected representatives of both parties. There are numerous recent examples of the Republican party in New York supporting positions we normally think of as "liberal." For example, rather than stand aside while New York City almost went bankrupt in 1975, Republicans in the state Senate worked hard on a solution to bail the city out. And instead of opposing the spread of unions, the Senate supported union shops and dues checkoffs for public employees, making public-sector unions a much more powerful force in state politics. In 1977, when it looked as if the Democrat-controlled Assembly was going to pass legislation requiring businesses to upgrade the benefits packages for employees, the former head of the State Business Council, Raymond Schuler, went to Senator Warren Anderson for help. But Schuler found out that being the state's leading Republican did not put Anderson automatically on the side of business. "Andy told me I should go and sit down with Ray Corbett (former head of the state AFL-CIO) and negotiate," recalled Schuler. "He wanted us to agree to a fair solution among ourselves."[51] In 1987 Republicans in the Senate put ideology aside to work hard on a plan to subsidize the cost of prescription drugs for low- and moderate-income senior citizens in the state.

Not to be outdone, Governor Cuomo, the leader of the Democratic party in the state, prides himself on his politically conservative positions on many issues. On the day after the 1984 presidential election Cuomo told an interviewer:

> One of the Senators . . . is supposed to have said, "We have read all of Governor Cuomo's speeches and they are New Deal." I laughed. What are you when you reduce public employees by 9,000? What are you when you say [that] need should be the criterion [for welfare benefits]? What are you when you come out for a

50. Smith, "E Pluribus Unum," 263.

51. Jay Gallagher, "Senator to Leave a Large Legacy," *Press & Sun Bulletin* (Binghamton, N.Y.), June 5, 1988, 1-B, 6-B.

tax cut? What are you when you refuse to raise the basic taxes? What are you when you spend more on your defense budget, which we call corrections, than any other governor in history?[52]

Parties need the active support of interest groups in order to maintain and enhance their legislative majorities and to capture the governor's seat. Party platforms and ideologies are handy to have, but in many situations parties cave in to group demands. These compromises occur often, usually quietly, receiving little notice. But sometimes the cave-ins occur in the glare of media attention and everyone is reminded of the power that groups wield in the state. One well-known cave-in occurred in the fall of 1986, when a popular Democratic incumbent governor, Mario Cuomo, was running for reelection, and Republican members of the state Senate feared that the coattail effect of a landslide might endanger their majority control. A bill was before the legislature to allow a public takeover of the unpopular Long Island Lighting Company (LILCO). Normally, the Republican party would have little to do with a bill that allowed the public takeover of any private company, but the pressure applied by citizens groups, and the election anxieties of Long Island Republican senators, were so strong that the bill passed with Republican party sponsorship.

In New York, interest groups must reckon with party leaders who have the power to "clear" legislation, but this does not seem to limit the influence of interest groups in the legislative process. Much has been made of the power of the Senate majority leader and the Assembly Speaker to "star" a bill, thereby preventing it from reaching the floor for a vote. It is probably this kind of well-known power on the part of legislative party leaders that led both Zeigler and Morehouse to categorize New York as a "weak interest group state."

Power within the New York state legislature is more concentrated in the leadership than is true for the U.S. Congress. Differences between bills passed in the state Senate and the Assembly are worked out by the leaders of those legislative chambers and their staffs, not by more representative conference committees. Real discussions about the merits of certain legislation are more likely to take place during party caucuses than in committee or during floor debate. When caucus votes are taken, members rarely deviate from the party line in committees or on the floors of their respective chambers. There are no conference committees to work out the differences

52. Fred Barnes, "Meet Mario the Moderate," *The New Republic* 8 (April 1985), 18.

between Assembly and Senate bills; party leaders take on this role. In short, there is tremendous party discipline within the New York legislature, and the formal organization of both chambers gives considerable power to party leaders. But the powers of legislative leaders in New York are more fragile and the access to legislative policy-making by interest groups is more free than might be apparent to the casual observer. In short, the power of legislative party leaders has not been a major obstacle to interest-group access.

Party leaders must please groups or lose control of their party, or even be replaced. Legislative party leaders realize that they are elected and have great formal power because having it serves the interests of their respective party caucuses. "How long do you think I would remain majority leader if I continued to star bills that my party wanted to consider?" Senator Anderson asked. As the majority leader of the Senate, who represented an up-state district, Anderson was not personally in favor of the bill that allowed a public takeover of LILCO, but most Long Island Republican senators were, so there was no star on that bill.

Party leaders also must please groups in order to maintain majority control within their house of the legislature, or, in the case of the minority, in order to make progress toward gaining majority control. Because New York State legislators who are in the minority party within their own chamber have very little power, the principal responsibility of the Senate majority leader and the Speaker of the Assembly is to maintain their party's control of their respective legislative chambers. This effectively means that party leaders must do everything in their power to ensure that the rank-and-file members of their own party are reelected. Thus, leaders must negotiate with all interest groups perceived as having the power to influence state legislative election outcomes. This pressure is especially intense now on the Senate majority leader, where the Republican majority is slim, and on the governor, since both major parties have a good chance of winning any statewide race in New York.

TRENDS IN THE ROLE OF INTEREST GROUPS IN STATE POLITICS

Governments are becoming increasingly important as lobbyists. Inter-governmental lobby activity within the state has surged as a response to the rapid increase in the size and complexity of domestic programs since the mid-1960s and to the increased financial dependency of general-purpose local governments and single-purpose local governments (especially school districts) on the state. Agencies of New York City are represented well in Albany, and New York State itself has what are perhaps the most elaborate lobbying organizations in the nation's capital of all the states.[53] Unless the trend toward the centralization of spending decisions stops, lobbying activity by local governments in the state capital should continue to intensify.[54] Local government lobbies also are influential, because all legislators must maintain a local base of electoral support and most return to the district when the legislature is not in session.

But local governments cannot supply resources for campaigns, and the support of PACs is becoming more necessary for a successful state election campaign. The professionalization of the New York State legislature and the increased cost of conducting state election campaigns is causing an increase in the influence of groups able to contribute resources (money or labor) to those campaigns.

And we can expect more registered lobbyists and PACs in the future. It is becoming increasingly important for interest groups to be represented by professional lobbyists. As the scope and extent of New York State government activities has increased, state policies touch more peoples' lives in more significant ways. Groups that for years had disdained taking a visible role in state politics, such as senior citizens, dentists, physicians, and college professors, have developed effective lobbying organizations. If we continue on the path of big government, the political awakening of interest groups will also continue. As long as the political parties in New York remain strong and competitive, the quality of public policy in the state is enhanced by the existence of an equally powerful interest-group system.

53. David L. Cingranelli, "State Government Lobbies in the National Political Process," *State Government 1983*, vol. 56, no. 4, 122–27.

54. Russell L. Hanson in "The Intergovernmental Setting of State Politics," Gray, Jacob, and Vines, eds., *Politics in the American States*, 47, argues that there is a national trend toward increased local governmental lobbying at the state level.

10

Pennsylvania: Individualism Writ Large

Patricia McGee Crotty

Politics in Pennsylvania is a for-profit enterprise. In fact, Pennsylvania could serve as the prototype for Daniel Elazar's individualistic political-culture model. This culture produces an interest-group structure dominated by organizations that focus on increasing their members' economic well-being rather than on achieving benefits for society as a whole or on increasing the sense of solidarity among their members. Groups in individualistic states are controlled by professionals and participate in the political process through lobbying government officials rather than fostering grass-roots activities.[1] By examining the way its institutions structure group activity, the background and opinions of its political leaders, and the outcomes of recent political decisions, we can see the degree to which Pennsylvania's interest groups approximate the individualistic model and can determine which groups are powerful in the state.

Pennsylvania has come a long way from being dominated by its railroads, major manufacturers, and big unions. A former governor of Pennsylvania commented that before the 1960s the Republican party was owned and operated by big business, and the Democratic party by the AFL-CIO, and that there was little between.[2] These segments are no longer so powerful. Unless they work sub rosa, the era of big steel, big oil, and the railroads appears to have passed. Major private unions are maintaining defensive stances, primarily on the national level; the AFL-CIO has achieved few victories in the state in recent years.

1. John J. Harrigan, *Politics and Policy in States and Communities*, 2nd ed. (Boston: Little, Brown, 1984), 31.
2. See Neal R. Peirce, *The Megastates of America: People, Politics, and Power in the Ten Great States* (New York: W. W. Norton, 1972), 231.

Pennsylvania is a diverse state that lacks a common identity.[3] Among its 12 million people are a large number of ethnic, religious, and racial minorities. Subcultures as different as the peaceful Amish farmers of central Pennsylvania and the radical protest group MOVE exist within the state. Pennsylvania's geography also contributes to its diversity. The Alleghenies divide Pennsylvania's two major cities, Philadelphia and Pittsburgh. Northwestern Pennsylvania's forests and high plateaus have oil and gas wells liberally interspersed among them. This area is populated with proud, hardworking individuals who prefer to remain aloof from Harrisburg's politics. The numerous small farms across the central part of the state provide a visual and cultural contrast to the urban areas at the extremities. The coal regions in the northeast contain second- and third-generation Americans who still have strong ties to their ethnic heritage.

The state's economic diversity produces divisions that are reflected in its politics. A rural-urban division characteristic of prereapportionment politics still exists. Pennsylvania ranks eighteenth in the nation in the value of its farm products and eighth in the value of its farmland and buildings.[4] Farming provides the third largest source of income for the state.[5] Within the manufacturing and service sectors, economic divisions exist. Heavy manufacturing is in trouble, and it is questionable whether Pennsylvania's coal, steel, and iron industries will be able to survive.[6] Traditional union strength is also declining. In the steel industry alone at least 200,000 jobs have been lost in the last ten years, more than 60 percent of the total. Those involved in heavy manufacturing believe Pennsylvania is neglecting them to devote its time to attracting high-tech industries. A division also exists between the manufacturing and service sectors. Service-sector employment increased to 2,772,000 in 1990, while manufacturing employment decreased to 1,328,000.[7] The growth in the service segment, which includes finance and insurance interests, depends to a large extent on out-

3. Paul Beers, *Pennsylvania Politics Today and Yesterday* (University Park: The Pennsylvania State University Press, 1980), 1.
4. *Statistical Abstracts of the United States 1990*, 109th ed. (Washington, D.C.: Government Printing Office, 1990), 644. (Hereafter cited as SAUS.)
5. Philip Klein and Ari Hoogenboom, *A History of Pennsylvania*, 2nd ed. (University Park: The Pennsylvania State University Press, 1980), 481–92.
6. Neal Peirce and Jerry Hagstrom, *The Book of America: Inside Fifty States Today* (New York: W. W. Norton, 1983), 96–119.
7. SAUS, 401.

of-state investments. Thus, Pennsylvania's financial institutions can flourish at the expense of its manufacturers, and this division is often reflected in conflicting demands for state programs to foster economic development.

The activities of the state's smokestack and mining industries have left visible scars on the environment. In Pennsylvania's profit-taking culture, "clean is beautiful" often loses out to "muck is money" in guiding industrial development. The ravages created by this development are evident from the coalfields of eastern Pennsylvania to the abandoned oil wells and steel mills of the state's western region.

In 1977 Pennsylvania was aptly described as a snowbelt state with old cities, an aging population, heavy capitalization in limited growth industries, and business and political rigidity.[8] Employment problems led the state to owe the federal government $1.3 billion for unemployment compensation.[9] By 1990 this debt was substantially reduced, but an estimated $1 billion is needed to repair or replace Pennsylvania's crumbling infrastructure. A look at Pennsylvania's commitment to revitalizing its economy should reveal which of its multiple economic interests achieved lobbying victories during the 1980s and whether they can retain them during the economic recession Pennsylvania faces in the early 1990s.

THE POLITICAL SETTING

In politics as well as economics, Pennsylvania suffers from a lack of common identity. This has led to an absence of strong leadership and a diffused political power structure, which at times have allowed corruption to flourish. The state's lack of popular consensus encourages citizens to become involved in local rather than state politics.[10] Pennsylvania has 5,663 local units of government—more than any other state except Illinois, and in the amount of self-governing authority that it devolves on local units, it is ranked seventh in the nation by the Advisory Commission on Intergovernmental Relations. These factors should affect the state's interest-group structure. Groups follow power. When localities hold a significant amount

8. Peirce and Hagstrom, *Book of America*, 96–119.
9. Beers, *Pennsylvania Politics Today and Yesterday*, 456.
10. Klein and Hoogenboom, *History of Pennsylvania*, 96–119.

of authority, lobbies will focus on local as well as state units of government. In addition, local units themselves should play an important role in lobbying Harrisburg.

Localism has also affected the political parties in the state. Both parties contain major factions that form around loyalties to the Pittsburgh region or the Philadelphia region. Ballots in statewide elections reveal party efforts to balance tickets with candidates from both ends of the state. There is a strong inclination in southwestern Pennsylvania to vote Democratic, and labor's endorsement remains important. The southeastern faction more closely mirrors the changing face of the national Democratic party with its need to attract minorities, white-collar workers, and suburbanites. Although the Republican party is similarly divided, differences between its two factions are not as evident.

Once a one-party Republican state, Pennsylvania is now a swing state with control over state government varying between the parties. Out of a possible score of .500, which indicates a perfectly competitive state, Pennsylvania's index of party competition between 1981 and 1988 was .47.[11] Since 1954, the parties have alternated in the governor's office for eight-year periods and frequently split control of the legislature.

The state's elections are structured to foster control by the party organization. Primaries are closed, party labels appear on a ballot with a straight-ticket lever, and direct action by the people through the use of the initiative or the recall is not allowed. Party strength is reflected in voter registration figures. Of the approximately 6.2 million registered voters, 43 percent are Republican, 52 percent are Democrats, and less than 5 percent are Independents.[12] Thus, in their efforts to sway officials and residents, groups must also contend with the political-party organization. The parties' control over selecting candidates for special elections was challenged unsuccessfully in court during 1991.

Party strength is an important factor in the Pennsylvania legislature, which has a regular promotion pattern from party whip to floor leader to Speaker.[13] Legislative roll-call votes reveal high levels of party cohesion.[14]

---

11. See John F. Bibby et al., "Parties in State Politics," in Virginia Gray, Herbert Jacob, and Robert Albritton, eds., Politics in the American States: A Comparative Analysis, 5th ed. (Glenview, Ill.: Scott Foresman / Little, Brown, 1990), 92.

12. SAUS, 263.

13. Harrigan, Politics and Policy, 212.

14. James Eisenstein and Roger Karapin, "The Relationship Between PAC Contri-

These factors limit the control that groups have over legislators. Group influence is also mitigated because the Pennsylvania legislature is professionalized.[15] It has come a long way from the days when the Sun Oil and Pennsylvania Railroad lobbyists were known as the state's 51st and 52nd senators.[16] In addition, a corrupt-practices law passed in 1978 strengthened regulations on the interactions of legislators and lobbyists.

Pennsylvania's laws and political practices encourage interest groups to focus attention on lobbying the executive branch as well as the legislature. Because of the item veto, governors can eliminate unwanted items in bills that the legislature passes. The governor's office serves as an important recourse for lobbyists who are attempting to prevent the passage of certain laws or to eliminate riders from bills.

INTEREST-GROUP LOBBIES AND STATE REGULATIONS

Registration

The access private groups have to public officials is structured by the rules the state has adopted to regulate group activity. Pennsylvania laws require that groups attempting to influence the political process both register and report their expenditures, but set no maximum limit to the amount of money that can be spent on campaigns or lobbying efforts. The lobbying registration law requires individuals who spend more than $300 a month contacting legislators and agencies to register with the clerk of the House and the secretary of the Senate.[17] Comparing Pennsylvania with states with stronger requirements highlights the loopholes in reporting. In 1989, lobbyists in Pennsylvania reported spending $362,291, some $20,000 less than in 1987. In 1987, lobbyists in New York reported spending $18 million,

---

butions and Roll Call Votes in the Pennsylvania House of Representatives: A Preliminary Analysis" (Paper presented at the Pennsylvania Political Science Association Meeting, State College, Pennsylvania, March 1981), 18.

15. Thomas R. Dye, *Politics in States and Communities*, 5th ed. (Englewood Cliffs, N.J.: Prentice Hall, 1985), 158–59.

16. Peirce, *Megastates*, 262.

17. Act 171, October 4, 1978; Act 318, November 26, 1978.

and in California it was $75.6 million. One estimate of actual spending by Pennsylvania lobbyists in 1989 was $40 million.[18]

Because groups are narrowly defined, registration lists contain only a portion of the groups that engage in lobbying. Criteria exempt many grass-roots, amateur, and professional lobbyists who spend less than the minimum, and government workers acting in their official capacity are also excluded. Thus, much of the lobbying public-interest groups engage in is not recorded as interest activity. Private nonprofit organizations who receive government contracts, and consulting firms or research groups whose

Table 10.1. Profile of Registered Organizations in Pennsylvania, 1986–1987

Categories	Subtotals	Total
I. Selective benefits focus		
A. Business		166
1. Primary industries		
Manufacturing	74	
Extracting and utilities	61	
Farming	11	
Other	20	
2. Service sector		465
Banking and insurance	181	
Retail sales and service	155	
Transportation	72	
Health	57	
B. Professional organizations		155
Government workers	57	
Medical	50	
Labor	24	
Miscellaneous	24	
II. Nonprofit and ideological organizations[a]		93
III. Not identifiable from registration data		103
Total organizations		982

Source: State lobby registration lists for 1986–87.

[a]May be underrepresented because of reporting requirements.

18. "The Role of Lobbies in Pennsylvania," *Wilkes-Barre Times Leader,* June 27, 1990, 5a.

findings affect government policy, need not register. Finally, the registration lists do not reveal the size of the groups or the skill of their leaders.

Registered Groups

Even with these exceptions, registered lobbyists outnumbered legislators by more than three to one in 1991. Approximately 17 percent of the registered lobbyists are contract lobbyists who work for two or more unrelated groups. Some 72 percent of the registered lobbyists represent business interests, a percentage associated with states where groups have a moderate amount of political power.[19] These business groups are divided among the manufacturing, financial, and service sectors of the economy, but banking and finance groups outnumber manufacturers by more than two to one.

The range of registered groups is narrow, possibly a result of the numerous exemptions in registration requirements or of the narrow range of functions the state controls. Other than business interests, occupational groups are most common. This reinforces Pennsylvania's image as a state in which groups primarily seek selective benefits for their members. (An overview of these organizations can be found in Table 10.1.) When registration lists are divided by function, transportation, health, and education groups predominate. Except for sportsmen and religious organizations, few single-issue interest groups or grass-roots lobbies are registered. The stability of the interest-group community is demonstrated by the fact that these proportions remained approximately the same between 1986 and 1991. This consistency is also evident in data on Political Action Committees (PACs).

PAC Regulations

PAC registration data supplement information obtained from the lists of registered lobbies and lobbyists. Pennsylvania's Election Financing Act, Act 171, took effect in 1979 and established similar registration requirements for candidate, lobby, and party PACs. There is no upper limit on the amount that can be contributed to campaigns, although each PAC must report campaign expenditures. In Pennsylvania, PACs are not as essential a source of money for candidates as they are in states that place limits on the amount any one individual can contribute to a campaign.

19. L. Harmon Zeigler, "Interest Groups in the States," in Virginia Gray et al., *Politics in the American States*, 4th ed. (1984), 111–19.

Of the PACs registered in 1991, at least 100 were established by political parties and 83 by individual lobbyists. Cross-referencing the PAC lists with lobby registration lists indicates that most interest-group PACs in Pennsylvania are related to business interests or are formed by contract lobbyists. It is difficult to determine the affiliation of many PACs because registrants are not required to list affiliation.

The role of PACs is growing. In the late 1980s the number of registered PACs was 1,136, and national PACs have become involved in state elections. Interviews with party leaders reveal a great deal of animosity toward PACs and the belief that they are eroding the party's control over its candidates. To date, these leaders have been unable to convince elected officials to pass legislation limiting PACs. Pennsylvania's legislators are actively seeking PAC money. PAC administrators acknowledge that reverse lobbying is occurring. Candidates are approaching PACs, requesting assistance, and explaining how they would support the PAC's cause. Legislators' responses to the survey used in this study reveal that many confuse a lobby group with its PAC.

Statistics assembled by Common Cause indicate that since 1983, in terms of contributions, the top five PACs include the Pennsylvania Trial Lawyers' Association; the Pennsylvania State Education Association (PSEA); Pennsylvanians for Effective Government; the Pennsylvania Chamber of Business and Industry's PAC; the state medical society; and the American Federation of State, County, and Municipal Employees (AFSCME). Other high-spending PACs include bankers, hospital associations, insurance, real estate, construction, and union interests. Approximately half the money raised in contributions for the 1990 governor's race came from contributions of $5,000 or more from individuals and PACs. Approximately 50 percent of campaign money came from business sources, and 20 percent came from law firms, many of which were based outside Pennsylvania. Two of the PACs that contribute the largest amounts to campaigns are comprised solely of government workers: the PSEA and AFSCME.

Bureaucratic Lobbying

Before the era of PACs, Pennsylvania politicians received large amounts of campaign funds from "macing"—that is, requiring contributions from patronage appointees. Until 1955, Pennsylvania's governor had more patronage positions to dispose of than any other governor, or even the U.S.

President. Only 20 percent of public employees were protected by merit regulations. By 1980 approximately 55 percent were merit employees.[20] In addition to an expanded civil service, the professionalization of the bureaucracy was increased by the passage of the Public Employees Relations Act (Act 195) in 1970. This act allows state employees, except for police and firefighters, to organize, to bargain collectively, and to strike. Since the act was passed, 25 percent of all school strikes within the fifty states have occurred in Pennsylvania. Each year for the last decade an average of thirty-one strikes have been called in Pennsylvania.[21]

Act 195 dramatically increased both the independence of state workers from elected officials and the impact bureaucrats have on the policy process. This, combined with the independence of local units from state control, constitute the principal reasons that government workers have become important lobbyists in their own right. Approximately 11 percent of the individuals employed in Pennsylvania work for state and local governments, and 20 percent of these employees are unionized.[22]

Two recent developments represent attempts by Pennsylvania's legislature to limit the way both public and private groups lobby the administrative branch. In the early 1980s a regulatory review process that makes the adoption of regulations more cumbersome and difficult was established. In 1981 a sunset law was passed to give the legislature more control over agencies.[23] Even with these limits, elected and appointed officials enter freely into lobbying efforts by means of public demonstrations, court cases, proxy lobbyists, advisory boards, and public-relations techniques. In 1991, daily protests by state workers during the budget impass in Harrisburg, and news reports on Philadelphia's efforts to obtain financial aid from the state, revealed clearly that public workers and local units of government are lobbyists in their own right, though infrequently recognized as such.[24] They are also capable of misusing their power. Between 1987 and 1991, three major statewide scandals involved administrators and judges—not legislators—accepting bribes for political favors.

Based on their expertise, information-processing capacities, innovative-

20. Klein and Hoogenboom, *History of Pennsylvania*, 500.
21. "Public Enemy No. 1? It's a Striking Teacher," *Wilkes-Barre Times Leader*, September 8, 1991, 10c.
22. *Pennsylvania Statistical Abstracts 1987* (Harrisburg, Pa.: Department of Commerce, 1988), 5, 158.
23. Act 142 (December 22, 1981).
24. "More Villains," *Philadelphia Inquirer*, May 9, 1991, 20a.

ness, and partisan neutrality, Pennsylvania ranks high in the quality of its administrators.[25] This professionalism enhances their commitment to their position as well as their susceptibility to the influence of similarly trained professionals in the private sector. Because national mandates limit the control state legislators have over public-policy formation, and grant discretion to state administrative agencies, bureaucrats become the focus of lobbying efforts. This trend is especially obvious in environmental policy.

Groups that cannot achieve their goals in the legislative or administrative arenas look to the courts for relief. In addition to serving as referees, Pennsylvania's judges openly participate in the political process. They are elected on partisan ballots for fixed terms. Their recent lobbying efforts include court suits to eliminate a two-tiered judicial pension system, and struggles to prevent a more stringent corrupt-practices bill from passing the legislature.

BACKGROUND STUDIES AND SURVEY ANALYSIS

Background Similarities Between Politicians and Lobbyists

Pennsylvania's institutional framework and its lobby and PAC registration lists indicate that interest activity is dominated by business interests and that bureaucrats freely enter into the lobbying process. Examining the personal background of state officials and their responses to questions on interest-group activity provides a fuller picture of which lobbies are influential. Background studies are important because they indicate who government officials consider to be their professional peers in the private sector. Such individuals can frequently obtain access to policymakers through a "good old boy" network.

Biographies of legislators serving in 1986 and 1990 reveal that the three most common positions they held before serving in the state legislature were in business (primarily insurance and real estate), the law, and education (Table 10.2). It is important to note that, in 1986, House members listed "legislator" most frequently as their profession, and this was the third

25. Richard C. Elling, "State Bureaucracies," in *Politics in the American States*, 4th ed. 275–77.

Table 10.2.   Pennsylvania Legislators' Professions, 1986 and 1990

Profession Listed	House		Senate	
	1986	1990	1986	1990
Legislator	78	149	9	31
Business	43	22	17	3
Law	38	18	15	14
Education	20	3	4	0
Government	9	3	1	0
Farming	5	4	2	2
Medicine	4	1	0	0
Labor	4	2	1	0
Clergy	0	0	1	0
Total	201	202	50	50

Sources: Senate Legislative Directory, 1985–86 and 1989–90; House Legislative Directory, 1985–86 and 1989–90.

most common listing for state senators. By 1990 almost two-thirds of the state's legislators perceived themselves as career politicians. In Pennsylvania's individualistic culture, politics is a job, not merely an avocation.

The backgrounds of cabinet members reveal that professionals outnumber politicians. Since 1986 approximately 66 percent of the eighteen department secretaries were trained in the area dealt with by their departments. A similar situation exists for registered lobbyists. Most of the individuals who lobby for just one interest group worked in a related occupation before becoming lobbyists or still work in that profession. The heads of contract lobbying firms, however, are usually lawyers, former legislators, or administrators. If political-power theorists are accurate, the predominantly legal and business background of legislators, agency officials, and lobbyists gives these interests special access routes into government. Responses to surveys conducted on interest-group activity will help reveal whether shared backgrounds result in special influence.

Survey Responses

In order to determine what groups are perceived to be powerful by political activists, legislators, cabinet heads, and a random sample of fifty lobbyists were surveyed in 1986, 1988, and 1990. Because no major differences based on party affiliation or house membership were discovered, and because responses remained remarkably consistent over this period, responses will be considered as a whole. Generally, legislators view pressure groups in a positive manner, as necessary elements in the political process, but they are closely divided on whether more stringent regulations over groups are required and whether PACs have too much influence in Pennsylvania.

Lobbying tactics perceived as effective by legislators include working with the legislature to identify, build support, or testify on bills; providing information to legislators; and offering financial aid during campaigns. Few legislators see groups as spokespersons for constituents or look to groups to provide information on how the administration is thinking. In addition, legislators do not perceive government bureaucrats as lobbyists. The influence of the administration on the legislative process was mentioned by only three legislators. This is surprising since the legislature spends most of its time responding to policies suggested by governors and argued for by their administrators.

The range of groups identified as important was quite narrow. Five groups predominate: the Pennsylvania State Education Association, the Pennsylvania Chamber of Business and Industry, the Pennsylvania Trial Lawyers Association, the AFL-CIO, and the insurance lobby. These groups are consistently mentioned as powerful by at least 25 percent of legislators responding to the surveys. Four common reasons were given for why groups achieve power: financial resources, number of members, organizational ability, and research skills. Money was most commonly mentioned as a reason for the power of business and professional organizations, and numbers were said to be the reason for unions' strength. The fact that approximately half of the respondents believed a group's expertise increased its power indicates that a new, technical lobbying style is becoming more respected in Pennsylvania.

Bureaucrats' responses to the survey echo the legislators' assessments of which groups are powerful. Bureaucrats shared the legislators' positive view of the role of groups and believed the most effective techniques groups use include testifying or tracking bills in the legislature. In addition to the five groups mentioned as powerful by legislators, bureaucrats and lobbyists included their own special constituencies. Almost all the lobbyists believed the legislature and administration were receptive to their ideas. Their responses indicate that the techniques they use most frequently involve contacting administrators rather than legislators.

Survey results reinforce the findings revealed in the examination of Pennsylvania's institutions and regulations. Lobbying the administration is important, although not as visible as lobbying the legislature. The lobbies perceived as powerful are business, legal, labor, and education groups. Pennsylvania politicians view lobbyists as professionals; few consider grassroots organizations important. Survey responses indicate that officials in Harrisburg respect groups led by paid lobbyists rather than groups led by amateurs.

The importance of past legislative or administrative experience is demonstrated by the fact that the two individuals mentioned most frequently as effective lobbyists were once high-level officials: one was a former legislator, the other was a former cabinet secretary. The importance of money is also evident in the survey responses received from the legislators. Financial resources were seen as the major reason why the trial lawyers are powerful; ranked second to personal skills as the reason for business' power; and ranked second to number of members for education's power.

DECISION-MAKING

The reputation, access, and resources of interest groups are not proofs of power. There must be a connection between these attributes and the ability to reach goals in dealing with government. The decisions the state makes indicate how accurate the perceptions of those involved in the lobbying process are. This study concentrates on the fiscal benefits groups have been able to structure into public policy, as well as on program and budget decisions made between 1986 and 1991.

Policy Changes

In 1984, in order to avoid tort reform, law and insurance lobbies acted in concert to obtain the catastrophic accident tax (CAT), a yearly fee on registered motor vehicles. In 1990 after a protracted struggle, Pennsylvania adopted tort reform legislation that allows automobile policyholders to limit their right to sue in court. This victory resulted because medical and business lobbies combined with insurance interests to pressure for liability limits and because Pennsylvania's citizens were irate about rising automobile insurance rates and a proposed increase in the catastrophic accident tax.

Pennsylvania's 1986 banking law reveals the strength of financial lobbies. It allows bank holding companies in surrounding states, except for New York, to acquire Pennsylvania banks if those states give Pennsylvania banks reciprocal rights. This reciprocity was extended to all states in 1990, a delay prompted by smaller banks' efforts to be protected from large New York institutions. This law illustrates three facts about banking lobbies in Pennsylvania: the power of the savings-and-loan lobby, which achieved an exemption from the law, the influence that national banking lobbies have within the state, and the advantage that large firms maintain over small firms within the same industry. One reason for the success of bankers in the state is their lobbying strategy. The lobby assigns an officer of a major bank within the legislative districts to each legislator. These bankers present the "local" bank's perspective on bills that relate to banking.

Divisions within Pennsylvania's business sector were evident in the passage of a 1990 antitakeover law. The state Chamber of Business and Industry led a successful fight for its passage, but it includes "opt out" clauses that firms can use to remove themselves from any of the law's three provisions. Many of the largest firms have chosen to do so in spite of organized labor's and professional managers' support of this law.

According to employment statistics, organized labor's strength is diminishing, yet the AFL-CIO was frequently mentioned as a powerful group by state legislators. This organization, however, appears to be concentrating its efforts on gaining protection through national legislation rather than state legislation. In 1986 another large union, the United States Steel Workers, was involved in a bitter struggle with USX, the former United States Steel Corporation; Pennsylvania did little to help the union achieve its goals. The last obvious victory for labor in the state was the passage of a state right-to-know law in 1984 that requires organizations to inform their employees of hazardous materials in the workplace. Court challenges by industry delayed implementation of this law until 1987.

Four policy decisions made between 1986 and 1991 reveal the power of bureaucrats as lobbyists. First, records of those who testified during the reauthorization of the state's Public Utility Commission (PUC) in 1986 made it clear how little the consumer enters into the lobbying arena when proxy lobbyists speak for them before agencies like the PUC. Pennsylvania bureaucrats structure grass-roots responses by providing staff members to represent citizens before government agencies. The state is noted for these "proxy" lobbyists.[26] At least three major offices serve this purpose: the Consumer Protection Office in the Department of Justice, the Public Utility Commission advocate, and the Bureau of Advocacy in the Department of Aging. Second, the medical society lost a major battle in the legislature, which included $2.25 million in the 1987 budget to create a twenty-one-member health-cost containment council—another set of government paid, proxy lobbyists—to gather data on medical costs for consumers. Third, the passage of an agency shop bill for unions of public officials in 1988 enhanced union power in the public, not private, sector.

Finally, employees' success in preventing the sunsetting of the state Liquor Control Board illustrates how vigorously state workers lobby for selective benefits. Pennsylvania's individualistic culture includes strong puritanical strains. Commercial interests of hotel and tavern owners benefit as profits are enhanced if the state monopolizes liquor sales. Government workers successfully united these liquor interests with labor groups and fundamentalist religious organizations to thwart Governor Richard Thornburgh's attempt to end the state's liquor monopoly. This was accomplished through a public-relations campaign that raised fears about uncontrolled access to alcohol and through initiating court suits that delayed action until a new governor, William Casey, who supported the Liquor Control Board, took office.

Pennsylvania has one of the strictest antiabortion laws in the nation. The passage of this law was accomplished by a marriage of convenience between the Pennsylvania Catholic Conference, pro-life organizations, and fundamentalist religious groups. The Catholic bishops were willing to be practical and to refrain from publicly threatening Catholic politicians. The result was a law that does not mirror Catholic dogma but is a political success.[27] Pro-choice forces challenged the law in federal courts. This issue is one of the few areas where grass-roots involvement played an important role in Pennsylvania's policy decisions.

26. William Gormley Jr., *The Politics of Public Utility Regulation* (Pittsburgh: University of Pittsburgh Press, 1983), 147.
27. Thomas O'Hare, "Pennsylvania Catholics and the Abortion Control Act of 1989" (Paper delivered at the annual meeting of the American Political Science Association, San Francisco, 1990).

Budget Victories

In Pennsylvania, lobbies seek support through the passage of referenda, bond issues, tax policies, and earmarked revenues that guarantee benefits over a period of years. Agricultural and business interests were successful in obtaining popular approval of referendum issues on borrowing funds for infrastructure repairs (1982) and subsidies for farmers (1988). Local units of government, however, failed to obtain popular support of a referendum that increased their taxing powers.

Earmarking revenues restricts legislative control over financing. In Pennsylvania, the largest earmarked benefits, gasoline tax revenue and lottery proceeds, accrue to groups rarely mentioned as influential by legislators: the highway lobby and senior citizens. This may be because both groups concentrate their efforts on lobbying the administration. Senior-citizen lobbies have successfully prevented any diversion of lottery proceeds, even during the budget crisis in 1991. Proceeds were earmarked in 1972. One legislator explained that this was done to "white shroud" a gambling law and obtain enough votes for its passage. Receipts from the lottery amounted to more than $650 million in 1989, of which 25 percent was given to the elderly for property tax or rent rebates and inflation dividends, 20 percent to transportation assistance, 30 percent to nursing homes and medical providers, 15 percent to prescription drug assistance, and the remainder to county aging programs.[28] Thus, local governments, transportation organizations, medical facilities, and drugstores benefit indirectly from the lottery.

Transportation politics in Pennsylvania are complex. Competition for resources exists among automobile, trucking, railroad, water, and air transport industries. Pennsylvania's transportation lobbies include thirty-five auto clubs, twenty-five trucking groups, eleven railroad organizations, eleven water transport associations, and three air freight companies, as well as highway construction firms and related industries. These groups rarely present a united front to Pennsylvania officials and often lobby against each other. In the past, a major conflict involved the struggle between railroad and trucking interests.[29] Presently, mass transit interests vie with the highway lobby over state support.

28. Pennsylvania Department of Revenue, "The Pennsylvania Lottery Annual Report, 1989," 198–99.

29. Andrew Hacker, "Pressure Politics in Pennsylvania: The Truckers v. the Railroads," in Alan F. Westin, ed., *The Uses of Power* (New York: Harcourt Brace & World, 1962).

Only California and Texas have more federal highway miles, and Pennsylvania has more highway employees than any other state in the union. In 1988, taxes on gasoline and turnpike tolls returned $932 million, the second highest amount in the nation.[30] Trucking and automobile interests are comfortable with the regulatory relationship they have established with the Pennsylvania Department of Transportation (PennDOT) and the Pennsylvania Turnpike Commission. In order to raise revenues to maintain the turnpike, the Turnpike Commission raised tolls by 60 percent in 1986. This was done in executive session immediately before a new sunshine law, which would have opened such meetings to the public and the press, was to take effect. During the 1991 budget struggle the highway lobby successfully defended the earmarked funds PennDOT and the Turnpike Commission receive for highway maintenance. For the first time, however, mass transit interests received their own source of earmarked revenues from new taxes on transportation related businesses.

Two groups that have also succeeded in locking in financial benefits are the Pennsylvania Federation of Sportsmen and state workers. Through combining with environmental interests, sportsmen successfully lobbied the legislature to obtain a refund option on the state tax form. Taxpayers may elect to have all or part of their tax refunds donated to the state's wildlife conservation fund. State workers obtained a generous pension plan that serves as the model for the rest of the nation.[31] To date, state workers have prevented Pennsylvania from following the lead of northeastern states that have modified investment projections and reserve requirements in order to reduce the level of support government contributes to these funds.[32]

Because of a surplus in the state treasury, both personal and corporate income taxes were reduced in 1987: a reduction of one-quarter of 1 percent for personal taxes and of 1 percent for business taxes. This large reduction in the corporate tax, from 9.5 percent to 8.5 percent, is evidence of the strength Pennsylvania's business lobbies can have when they act in concert. While the legislature was considering this issue in the closing days of the 1986 session, it was difficult to find Chamber of Business and Industry

30. *SAUS*, 60, 599, 601.

31. Richard Aronson and John Hilley, *Financing State and Local Government*, 4th ed. (Washington, D.C.: The Brookings Institution, 1986), 202.

32. "Cities and States Seek Fiscal Aid from Employee Pension Funds," *New York Times*, July 21, 1991, 1a.

lobbyists to interview. All were busy contacting legislators. The same was true during the budget stalemate in July 1991, when these victories were reversed.

Fiscal Stress

The budget crisis in 1991 revealed which lobbies were successful in maintaining advantages during times of fiscal stress. The fistfight in the state House during a budget vote was an indication of the pressure and frustration legislators faced during this time. To cover a $454 million deficit, a $13.9 billion state budget that raised taxes by $2.86 billion was adopted thirty-five days after the fiscal year began. Pennsylvania's personal income tax was raised from 2.1 percent to 2.8 percent, and corporate taxes went from 8.5 percent·to 10.5 percent.[33] The large rise in the corporate tax rate, and the subjection of numerous business services to the sales tax for the first time, indicate that business lobbies, even when united, cannot control Pennsylvania's politics during times of fiscal stress.

The influence of teachers as lobbyists is enhanced by the fact that approximately half the state's budget is allocated to education. The importance of this function is also reflected in the fact that the Pennsylvania State Education Association (PSEA) was the most frequently mentioned, powerful lobby in survey responses. As is true with business interests, the education community contains varied groups that have contradictory goals. These divisions were evident during the adoption of the 1991 budget when elementary and secondary schools, special education, and higher education interests competed for scarce revenue. The power of the PSEA is revealed in the 7.2 percent increase in funds allocated for basic education, the largest increase in the state's history.

The power of local governments as lobbyists is also revealed in the 1991–92 budget. The large increase in education funding reduced pressure on localities to raise taxes. The state's Department of Community Affairs budget was increased from $35 million to $45 million. Counties received additional levels of state support for the services they provide, and the new earmarked revenues for mass transit have been attributed to the skills of the Philadelphia lobby.

---

33. "House Vote Set," *Philadelphia Inquirer*, August 3, 1991, 1b.

OVERALL SUCCESS

Tactics

In Pennsylvania, lobbying power varies according to the issues, groups, and tactics involved. Former politicians and contract lobbyists who head large firms are perceived as powerful by legislators and other lobbyists. This reflects the state's penchant for old-style lobbying that stresses personal contact. Responses to surveys also reveal that a new style of lobbying is becoming more important in the state. The new style emphasizes information-processing for legislators and bureaucrats. The growing role PACs play in campaign financing is another indication of this. Although PAC contributions are perceived as effective lobbying techniques, there is no hard evidence that money buys legislators' votes on issues. The large tax increases levied on business interests in 1991 support this interpretation. Campaign contributions are more important for groups that must compete for annual budget appropriations than for recipients of earmarked funds or for groups that concentrate on influencing bureaucratic decisions.

Defensive tactics that involve preventing items from reaching the public agenda or that maintain the status quo are frequently as important as marshaling new laws or regulations through government. The highway and senior-citizen lobbies successfully protected their privileged status during the 1991 budget struggle. Lobbying success can also be achieved by removing issues from annual legislative battles. These tactics include obtaining separate funding sources, entitlements, or court decisions that mandate levels of support. In addition to the highway and senior-citizen lobbies, business, farming, and welfare interests have successfully insulated state sources of funding. Financial victories by Pennsylvania's "have nots" have occurred recently in national, not state, forums.

Much of the increase in welfare, Medicaid, corrections, and special-education funding in Pennsylvania's 1991–92 budget can be attributed to national mandates.[34] All segments of Pennsylvania's politics use the federal government as a lobbying forum. Pennsylvania's legislature attempted to limit the administration's power by suing in court to require that all federal funds be channeled through the legislature. Since 1988, interests as varied as pro-choice advocates, business groups, school districts, welfare recip-

34. "A Do Right Budget," *Philadelphia Inquirer*, August 6, 1991, 8a.

ients, and prisoners have brought suits in federal courts claiming that Pennsylvania's laws violate constitutional requirements.

Although they have lobbyists registered in Harrisburg, the largest firms in the manufacturing, finance, and service sectors focus their major efforts in Washington. One banking representative indicated that policies established by the national government affect his company more than those adopted by the state. A manufacturing representative echoed these estimates and added that, because the national government has preempted state authority in many fields, it is the manner in which Pennsylvania implements federal laws and guidelines that most affects his company's activities within the state. He therefore concentrates on lobbying the administrative branch.

Powerful Lobbies

Results derived from the institutional, reputational, and decision-making approaches in this study reveal the groups that are powerful in Pennsylvania. There are three structural or institutional indicators of power: having an agency devoted to the group's cause, such as the Department of the Aging for senior citizens; appearing on state lobby registration lists; and having a PAC that donates a large amount of money to campaigns. Two reputational indicators of power are sharing background similarities with legislators and being mentioned as powerful by at least 25 percent of the respondents surveyed in 1986, 1988, and 1990. Finally, three decision-making indicators include having a guaranteed revenue source, winning a major program victory between 1986 and 1991, and, during this time period, achieving a major budgetary victory that was not reversed during the budget crisis in 1991.

Results reported in Table 10.3 allot one point for each factor. Although many lobbies benefit from decisions made in national forums, this study describes patterns in Pennsylvania, so only state factors are considered. Based on this methodology, powerful lobbies from the private sector include chamber of commerce, insurance, medical, transportation, and banking interests. Public-sector labor and education interests are also powerful, as is the Pennsylvania Trial Lawyers Association, a group whose members work in both sectors. All groups except for the Trial Lawyers cooperated in responding to questions on their lobbying activities. The Pennsylvania Trial Lawyers Association apparently believes its lobbying success is enhanced by secrecy. When reputational indicators of power are eliminated

Table 10.3. Indicators of Powerful Lobbies in Pennsylvania, 1986, 1988, 1990

Function	Institutional			Reputational				Decision			Total
	Agency	List	PAC$	Background	Survey '86	'88	'90	Set Income	Budget Victory	Policy Victory	
Aging	x							x	x		3
Agriculture	x	x						x			3
Banking	x	x	x	x						x	5
Commerce	x	x	x	x	x	x	x	x		x	9
Criminal justice	x										1
Education	x	x	x	x	x	x	x		x	x	9
Environment	x							x		x	3
Government workers	x	x	x	x				x	x	x	7
Insurance	x	x	x	x	x		x			x	7
Labor	x	x	x		x	x	x				6
Lawyers	x	x	x	x	x	x	x				7
Medicine	x	x	x				x			x	5
Transportation	x	x						x	x	x	5
Welfare	x										1

Source: Compiled by author from survey data collected in 1986, 1988, and 1990.

from the analysis, group scores, except for welfare and criminal justice interests, are remarkably similar.

Pennsylvania interest-group activity is a multiplicity of business, professional, and governmental groups vying with one another for special treatment by the state. Most of these groups seek selective benefits for their
members; very few work for ideological causes. Many groups see the government itself as a source for profit-making activities as well as a regulator
of private practices. Members of Pennsylvania's most powerful lobbies receive government salaries, tax incentives, and consulting fees. For example, teachers, lawyers, and public workers are often government employees;
banks and insurance companies buy and float government bonds; and business ventures profit from location incentives and government contracts.

Political pluralism has also affected Pennsylvania. Although its groups
are concentrated in commerce, education, transportation, and medicine,
each functional area contains numerous groups. This pluralism is enhanced
by developments in the influence that groups have vis-à-vis the political
party. Pennsylvania's parties have been weakened by the proliferation of
interests, but they have not been able to obtain legislation limiting these
groups and their PACs. In addition, professionalized contacts between officials
and their colleagues in the private sector supplement the influence that is
based on personal ties among lobbyists, administrators, and legislators.

This tendency toward fragmentation is enhanced by the willingness of
Pennsylvania's groups to use national institutions to increase their power
within the state. Congress and the federal courts provide lobbying arenas
that have been used by business and welfare interests and by Pennsylvania
legislators and administrators to achieve policy goals and selective benefits
denied them by state decisions. The importance of lobbying the executive
branch is clear from the responses of administrators and lobbyists to survey
questions, yet it is not recognized by members of the legislature. In Pennsylvania, there is a noticeable lack of grass-roots lobbying activity. The
state's professionalized pluralism, combined with its individualistic culture,
could result in a hyperpluralism that prevents Pennsylvania from adopting
policies that transcend particular interests. However, the individualistic
nature of group politics in Pennsylvania also reduces the likelihood that
any one group or interest will dominate the state.

The author wishes to acknowledge the assistance of members of the Pennsylvania state
legislature and the administrators and registered lobbyists who responded to survey questions and granted me personal interviews.

11

Rhode Island: The Politics of Intimacy

Mark S. Hyde

"It's not like the old days, when the brewery used to send over ten cases of beer and a case of glasses." Thus began one veteran state senator's description of lobbying in Rhode Island. His basic point, that lobbying and politics generally have become more sophisticated in the state, is confirmed by political participants and observers alike. However, there are constants in Rhode Island that provide the framework for politics in general, including group activity. These factors are as important to an understanding of interest groups as they are to changes that have occurred over the past twenty years.

The famed Narragansett brewery, for many years the sponsor of Boston Red Sox radio and television broadcasts, is now closed and no longer provides free beer for legislators. Nevertheless, social interaction, taking place within a complex network of personal, family, group, business, and political relationships, is still the major component of interest-group activity in Rhode Island. This network is possible because of the state's most obvious characteristic—its small size.

THE SETTING FOR POLITICS

Rhode Island ranks 50th among the states in land area and 40th in population, but with a population density of more than 900 people per square mile only New Jersey is more densely populated. Imposed on Rhode Island's landscape is a set of political boundaries that divide the small, densely populated state into an intricate, overlapping political jigsaw puzzle.

There are five statewide elected offices—governor, lieutenant governor, attorney general, secretary of state, and treasurer—with each serving only a two-year term. In addition to the two U.S. senators, Rhode Island has two seats in the U.S. House of Representatives. The state Senate has fifty members and the House has an even 100, all serving two-year terms. Overlying the state electoral system boundaries are thirty-nine cities and towns. In terms of size and population, the state is about the equivalent of a metropolitan area in, for example, neighboring Massachusetts. But viewed in political terms, Rhode Island is thirty-nine municipalities and one state government (with more than 20,000 state employees) compressed into a small space—and because of the two-year election cycle, compressed in time as well.

The many political units are dotted with the usual business, fraternal, and service associations found in all states. An added factor in Rhode Island is the heavy Catholic population. More than 65 percent of the residents belong to the church, the highest proportion of any state in the nation. Of the 159 parishes in the state, many were founded by immigrants—mostly French-Canadian, Irish, and Italian—who came to the state in the late nineteenth and early twentieth centuries. These ethnic groupings still play an important role in the lives of many residents. Portuguese-Americans have settled on the east side of Narragansett Bay, while newer Hispanic and Southeast-Asian immigrants are concentrated in Providence.

The many political units, the Catholic and ethnic organizations, plus the usual array of voluntary associations crowded into the small state result in many political, business, and social elites often knowing and interacting with one another in several different contexts. A leader of one interest group said that, at times, it appears everyone in the state is president of something. One state legislator calls the whole process resulting from this personal interaction of elites in differing contexts the "Rhode Island shuffle." The state has an intimate area, and context, for the practice of state politics.

POLITICS IN RHODE ISLAND

As well as being the most Catholic state, Rhode Island has been one of the most Democratic states in the country; the Democrats have pretty much held sway in the state for fifty years. Until the middle 1930s, Yankee Republicans controlled the state and its burgeoning urban and ethnic population. In the 1930s the Democrats finally gained control of the governorship and both houses of the legislature. The state Senate majority was achieved by the controversial seating of two Democrats in disputed elections. Their seating was followed immediately by a wholesale housecleaning of all Republican appointees, including replacement of the entire state Supreme Court. Since that time, the Republicans have occasionally captured the governorship and other statewide offices, but the Democrats have always been in the majority. In the 1980s the Republicans at times controlled three of the five statewide offices, but Democratic control of both houses of the legislature has been unyielding. At present, the Republicans hold one U.S. Senate seat (John Chafee) and one of the two House seats (Ronald Machtley). All else belongs to the Democrats, including commanding majorities in the house (89–11) and the senate (45–5). Republican Machtley took the First District congressional seat away from twenty-eight-year Democratic incumbent Fernand St. Germain, chairman of the House Banking and Finance Committee, in 1988. It was Machtley's first try at any elective office, and his victory is generally attributed to St. Germain's ethical problems surrounding his association with the banking/savings-and-loan industry.

The political structures of state government remain unreformed. All five statewide officers serve only two-year terms; the governor and lieutenant governor run separately instead of being elected as a team. The legislature is part-time, with a scheduled sixty-day session. Compensation is $5 for each day of the session, or $300 per year, and individual rank-and-file legislators lack even minimal support services.

The Democrats are well organized, especially in the legislature. As any members of a party with a substantial majority, they sometimes have difficulty sorting out their line of succession in running for statewide offices. This has led twice, 1976 and 1984, to divisive primaries that helped contribute to general election losses. But after the electoral defeats, the Democrats have regrouped for the next set of statewide elections. Morehouse rates Rhode Island political parties as "strong" in general organizational strength.[1] Cornelius Cotter and his colleagues, in their work on party organizations in the states, rate the Rhode Island Democrats as "moderately strong" and the Republicans as "moderately weak."[2]

1. Sarah M. Morehouse, *State Politics, Parties, and Policy* (New York: Holt, Rinehart & Winston, 1981).

2. Cornelius P. Cotter et al., *Party Organizations in American Politics* (New York:

In the legislature the Democrats have traditionally been well organized. Through the 1988 session, House Speaker Matthew Smith and Senate Majority Leader John Revens ran tight ships. Some veteran Rhode Island politicians perceived them as reformers, at least when contrasted to 1960s House Speaker Harry Curvin. Curvin would simply tell the party's legislative caucus what was to be passed and gavel through "skeleton" bills—that is, legislation consisting of only a title or bare outline. But compared with party activity in other states, recent Rhode Island legislative leaders would likely be viewed as strong party regulars. While veteran legislators praise discussion of bills in the Democratic caucus, with ideas "percolating up" from the membership, there was no question that the Speaker and the majority leader were firmly in charge of their respective bodies, with committee chairs working closely with the party leadership. In 1989 both Smith and Revens were gone—the former Speaker to an appointed position in the court system, and the Senate majority leader to a futile primary effort for the party nomination for state treasurer. In 1990 Revens was once again elected to the state Senate, but he no longer holds a leadership position.

The transition in the House was orderly, with Majority Leader Joseph DeAngelis moving up to Speaker and taking firm control of that body. In their caucus, divided Senate Democrats selected Newport Senator David Carlin as majority leader, but he was challenged on the floor by a combination of dissident Democrats and some of the nine Republican senators. He was stripped of the power to name committee chairs, and the decision-making process in that body was clouded at best. The Democratic lieutenant governor, Roger Begin, said the factions were not based on issues— "It's a matter of alliances, personalities, friendships."[3] The differences certainly led to unstatesmanlike conduct, with Democratic senators on the losing side suffering such indignities as assignment to the least desirable parking spaces in the lot farthest from the statehouse.

The leader of the minority faction, Carlin's chief rival for majority leader, was Judiciary Chairman John Bevilacqua of Providence, son of former House Speaker and State Supreme Court Chief Justice Joseph Bevilac-

Praeger, 1984). For a fuller discussion of party alignment in Rhode Island, see Darrell M. West, "Party Realignment in Rhode Island," *Comparative State Politics Newsletter* 8 (December 1987), 12

3. M. Charles Bakst, "Senate Wrangling Gets 1989 Session Off to Raucous Start," *Providence Sunday Journal*, January 8, 1989, C-2.

qua. The elder Bevilacqua resigned from the court in the midst of an impeachment inquiry. His Republican ally was Minority Leader Robert Goldberg of South Kingstown, son of former Family Court Chief Judge William Goldberg. In the 1991 session, Bevilacqua wrested control of the Senate from Carlin and was chosen majority leader. Carlin is unlikely to challenge him again, and both houses are now once again tightly organized.

GROUPS OPERATING IN RHODE ISLAND

The group with the largest membership in Rhode Island is the Roman Catholic church, but except for matters relating to human reproduction, the church plays no obvious, overt role in state politics. Because so many elected officials and their constituents are Catholics, the church has little opportunity to view elections or issues as Catholic/non-Catholic dichotomies.

The one recent attempt at direct political activity by the church ended in failure. In the November 1986 election, Rhode Island voters were asked to ratify a number of amendments to the state constitution approved by a constitutional convention the previous summer. The Paramount Right to Life/Abortion Amendment would have, given a reversal of Roe v. Wade by the U.S. Supreme Court, banned all abortions in Rhode Island. The amendment was defeated at the polls by a large margin, despite public pronouncements from the bishop of the statewide diocese for voters to approve the measure. The bishop even appeared on radio talk shows to answer questions about his position on the proposed amendment. A solid majority of Catholics voted contrary to the urgings of their bishop.

An election-day exit poll of more than 1,400 voters indicated that 56 percent of Catholics voted against the amendment to limit abortions, with 44 percent casting favorable votes.[4] While other religious and social groupings showed even less support for the amendment, the lack of response from Catholics to the cue from their bishop indicates the church had little influence on an issue of great importance that it chose to highlight.

A good indicator of the range of group activity in Rhode Island politics is the list of groups registered to lobby. The state has a fairly restrictive registration law, so virtually any group involved in politics is registered.

4. Alpha Research Associates, General Election Exit Poll Results (Manuscript, Providence, Rhode Island, 1986).

Table 11.1 lists by category groups that were registered to lobby over four of the last five legislative sessions.[5] The analysis covers four sessions, not for comparative purposes but to guard against year-by-year idiosyncrasies.

Business has the largest number of groups, ranging as high as 33.3 per-

Table 11.1. Groups Registered to Lobby in Rhode Island, 1987–1991

	Legislative Session							
	1987		1988		1990		1991	
	N	%	N	%	N	%	N	%
Labor	15	11.1	21	10.0	24	9.2	18	7.0
Business	38	28.2	69	32.7	79	30.4	86	33.3
Banking	3	2.2	7	3.3	13	5.0	12	4.6
Utilities	7	5.2	8	3.8	6	2.3	10	3.9
Insurance	14	10.4	15	7.1	20	7.7	20	7.8
"Sin" industries (liquor and tobacco)	4	3.0	9	4.3	8	3.1	10	3.9
Professionals	12	8.9	11	5.2	18	6.9	16	6.2
Single issue	4	3.0	6	2.8	11	4.2	8	3.1
Realtors, builders, and contractors	4	3.0	8	3.8	10	3.8	13	5.0
Health industry	9	6.7	22	10.4	13	5.0	12	4.7
Governmental units	1	0.7	6	2.8	8	3.1	7	2.7
Public interest	6	4.4	8	3.8	21	8.1	17	6.6
Other (includes elderly, environment, and education)	18	13.3	21	10.0	29	11.2	29	11.2
Total	135	100%	211	100%	260	100%	258	100%

Source: Compiled from official list of registered lobbyists in the Rhode Island Office of Secretary of State.

Note: Data for 1989 not available.

5. The lists of registered lobbyists and groups were examined for the years 1984–91, excepting 1989, the list for which year was unavailable. Only the most recent four years of the available data are shown in Tables 11.1 and 11.2.

cent of all groups registered in 1991. Labor has about 10 percent of the groups in 1987, 1988, and 1990 but falls to just under 7.0 percent in 1991. Insurance (1987) and the health industry (1988) are the only other categories to reach the 10 percent level in any year. When one combines the separate categories of banking, insurance, "sin" industries, and other specialized business categories, more than half of all registered groups in Rhode Island in these four legislative sessions are business-oriented.

A recent study of the political activity of business in the state indicates the scope of political action by business firms in Rhode Island.[6] More than 75 percent of the firms included in the study had contacted a town official in the previous two-year period; almost 63 percent had done so at the state level. Just over 40 percent of the firms belonged to a business association, other than a chamber of commerce, that employed a lobbyist, but only 6 percent of the surveyed firms had a political action committee.

The Rhode Island business community is therefore a very active player in the interest-group game, and the members of the community are diverse in size and focus. Firms registered to lobby over the last few years include both General Motors Corporation and Cozy Cab Inc. The major banks in Rhode Island are Fleet National, Old Stone, and Hospital Trust (owned by Bank of Boston). Major insurance companies on the scene include Amica, Nationwide, and Allendale. In addition, numerous business associations keep track of the interests of the banks and insurance companies as well as hairdressers, physical therapists, accountants, and other business/occupational/professional groupings. Business groups such as the Rhode Island Association of Beer and Wine Wholesalers and the Rhode Island Licensed Beverage Association have become more active and visible because of much publicized "bottle bills," which would require deposits on beverage containers, being introduced each session.

Major utilities include New England Telephone, Providence Gas Company, and Narragansett Electric. Labor unions maintaining a visible presence in group activity include the Rhode Island AFL-CIO, teachers unions (the NEA and the AFT), and other public-employee unions, such as firefighters and correctional officers. The leading environmental group, with a high profile statewide, is Save the Bay. Probably the best known and most respected public-interest group is the Rhode Island Public Expenditure

6. Mark S. Hyde, John Carroll, and William E. Hudson, "Business and Politics: Interest Group Activity at the State Level" (Paper presented at the Annual Meeting of the Midwest Political Science Association, Chicago, 1987).

Council, a business-funded, nonprofit organization that does detailed analyses of public-finance issues and presents its findings to the public.

LOBBYISTS

The Rhode Island lobbying law requires lobbyists and groups hiring them to register with the Office of the Secretary of State; elected officials and government employees are exempt when acting in their official capacity. While in the statehouse, each lobbyist must wear a badge identifying him or her as such. Organizations or individuals hiring a lobbyist must file regular reports with the secretary of state indicating fees paid to the lobbyist and expenditures connected with promoting or opposing legislation.

About 220 to 320 lobbyists register for each session of the General Assembly (see Table 11.2). Many groups that rely on their members to lobby on a voluntary basis have multiple agents registered—for example, the American Association of Retired Persons (AARP) usually has at least a half-dozen member lobbyists. Some public-employee unions, such as firefighters, correctional officers, and AFSCME locals, do the same. On the other hand, some individual lobbyists represent more than one group. In all three legislative sessions there is a core group of approximately twenty to thirty lobbyists, most of them attorneys (see Table 11.2). Groups represented by these people are most often businesses, business associations, and utility companies. We shall discuss this core group of lobbyists again when describing the tactics and assessing the relative power of groups in the state.

Table 11.2. Registered Lobbyists in Rhode Island, 1987–1991

	Legislative Session			
	1987	1988	1990	1991
Total lobbyists	219	273	335	319
Lobbyists representing multiple groups	13	20	35	39
Multiple-group lobbyists that are attorneys	11	18	28	30

Source: Compiled from official list of registered lobbyists, Rhode Island Office of Secretary of State.

Note: Data for 1989 not available.

In order to get a clearer picture of who is lobbying, and why, a question-naire was mailed to all 261 lobbyists registered for the 1986 legislative session. Four envelopes were returned as undeliverable, and 98 usable questionnaires were mailed back, for a return rate of 38.1 percent. The mean age of the respondents was forty-five years, with just over 75 percent of the lobbyists being male. (In the 1985, 1986, and 1987 sessions, the actual percentage of males was just about 75 percent.) They are well educated; 84.7 percent had at least some college education. Half the lobbyists had been on the job two years or fewer, but 24.7 percent of them had been lobbying for ten years or more, indicating a mixed group in terms of experience. When asked to indicate their party identification, 45.9 percent claimed to be Democrats, only 6.1 percent said they were Republicans, and 44.9 percent identified themselves as Independents. The small Republican percentage is not surprising given the overwhelming Democratic majority among elected officials and the electorate.

In terms of compensation, 45.9 percent of the lobbyists in the sample said they were paid, but only 11.2 percent indicated that salary was the primary source of their income. The most common occupations listed among the lobbyists were executive director of a group, businessman, lawyer, and union representative. Just over 6 percent of the respondents had previously held political office. On the average, lobbyists knew approximately 35 members of the 150-seat legislature on a first-name basis.

STRATEGIES AND TACTICS

A useful concept when considering the tactics of interest groups in bringing about their desired ends is an inside-versus-outside strategy.[7] An inside, or direct, strategy consists of tactics that require direct contact between group representatives and public officials. An indirect, or outside, strategy involves working through the constituency of and/or relevant media for the public officials one wishes to influence.

In Rhode Island, groups use primarily an inside strategy involving direct lobbying of various types, largely because of the intimate nature of state politics described in the introduction. However, some groups make good use of media outlets to pursue their interests, while others donate campaign money for mostly statewide elections.

7. Ronald J. Hrebenar and Ruth K. Scott, *Interest Group Politics in America* (Englewood Cliffs, N.J.: Prentice Hall, 1982).

Direct Lobbying

In addition to the survey of lobbyists mentioned earlier, 62 out of 150 state legislators and senators (41.3 percent) responded to a mail questionnaire about group activity in the state. Legislators and lobbyists agreed on the most widely used tactics by interest groups. By an overwhelming margin, both samples cited testimony at legislative hearings and personal presentation of arguments as the most employed techniques. Both groups also agreed that personal presentation of arguments was most effective. Legislators felt testimony at hearings was the next most effective tactic, while lobbyists found testimony and having an influential member of his or her group contacting relevant decision-makers to be equally effective.

Therefore, direct lobbying through personal presentation of arguments is viewed as the most common and effective lobbying technique in Rhode Island. The technique is successfully carried out by combining long hours at the statehouse during legislative sessions with social interaction at evening functions, or by having the necessary credentials and experience to gain quick access.

At the statehouse, lobbyists representing individual groups become influential by being available for consultation at virtually any time in the session and by explaining the down side as well as the up side of proposed legislation. Because the legislature is part-time with little professional staff to help, they rely heavily on lobbyists to provide information on which way to cast a vote or a justification for a decision already made. And well-prepared lobbyists who attend every session and are willing to discuss all sides of a bill perform that function best. In the mail survey, 88.7 percent of the legislators agreed that lobbyists make the legislature work better by providing useful information to members.

At a workshop organized by the secretary of state to introduce new lobbyists to the entire process of legislating, the praise from legislators for most lobbyists was effusive. Comments from legislators included: "Lobbyists are the most valuable resource we have" and "[There is] no greater service for a legislator than having a group of well informed lobbyists." But the praise was tempered by advice to new lobbyists to provide a full and accurate assessment of the legislation, even if it hurt in the short run. The long-run gains, said the legislators, would be worth it. From the chairman of the House Labor Committee: "Tell the truth to legislators or you will lose your credibility." A majority-party senator: "You must be credible. If you know the down side of a bill, tell it. If not, tell [the legislator] you do not." And from a Republican legislator, "As long as we know where you're coming from, we are glad to hear from you."

Lobbyists agree that effectiveness comes from telling everything one knows about a bill; in fact, one veteran lobbyist defined integrity in his profession as "telling the truth [to a legislator] when it hurts." In a private interview, former Speaker of the House Matthew Smith used the phrase "cumulative repetition of positives" to describe how one became a respected and effective lobbyist in the legislative arena.

These standards of behavior have been set by a group of full-time (at least during legislative session) lobbyists who interact with legislators on a regular basis. They are part of the whole social and interpersonal activity that surrounds sessions, not merely a political part of the legislative session. Two of the better-known members of this group are George Nee, of the AFL-CIO, and Paul Hicks, representing the Rhode Island Petroleum Association.

The group of twenty or so lobbyists, most of them attorneys, who represent more than one group (see Table 11.2) are for the most part contract lobbyists who work for the groups on a fee basis, with additional funds provided for entertainment expenses.

Some of these lobbyists are influential because of previous political experience. Dennis Roberts is the patriarch of a family long active in Democratic politics and is himself a former mayor of Providence and governor of the state. His brother, Thomas, was a State Supreme Court Chief Justice, and his nephew, Dennis II, another lawyer/lobbyist, is a former two-term attorney general of Rhode Island. One of the elder Roberts law associates, Kelley Sheridan, is also among the group. Joseph Walsh, another attorney in the group, was a state senator, mayor of the state's second largest city (Warwick), and a Democratic candidate for governor. Others of these contract lobbyists seem to specialize by substantive area and build more general avenues of influence as a result. For example, in 1985 attorney John G. Coffey represented twelve groups, half of which were utility companies. Yet still others seem to have attained the position solely by working the long hours and staying at the job long enough to become well known and respected by state decision-makers.

Social functions also provide the opportunity for face-to-face interaction and personal presentation of arguments. These generally take the form of receptions or dinners held at hotels or country clubs for all members of the Assembly. On occasion, a small dinner is provided for a specific committee, although recent publicity about such small affairs seems to have made them less popular as a technique for gaining access. But the general idea of social lobbying is well established in Rhode Island. A freshman legislator estimated that between his election in November and the opening of the legislative session in early January he had received from interest groups twelve dinner, five luncheon, and five breakfast invitations. In addition, he had received twelve to fourteen invitations to meet with groups in the House or Senate lounge.[8]

In 1986, among other activities, the president of the Rhode Island Share & Deposit Indemnity Corporation (the private insurer for a number of the state's credit unions and banks) attempted to influence a banking bill before the legislature by holding a dinner party for the House Finance Committee before the public hearing on the bill. Commenting on the activities surrounding that bill, John Tabella, then lobbyist for the Rhode Island Public Interest Research Group, said, "The banks have professional lobbyists. . . . These lobbyists attend all the political cocktail parties and many throw receptions for General Assembly members. It puts us at a disadvantage."[9] In somewhat of a reversal, the recent (1984–90) Republican governor, Edward DiPrete, formed a type of club that had breakfast with the governor several times a year. The minimum dues were $1,000, and although membership rolls swelled with lobbyists and others, negative publicity put an end to the organization.

Public officials, not required to register as lobbyists, generally gain access to other decision-makers within the context of political party. For example, Democratic mayors of cities meet with their city's legislative contingent to present their agendas. Republican executives, however, have considerably less access to the Democratic legislature.

When Democrat Joseph Garrahy was governor (1976–84), heads of departments, such as Corrections, would lobby among legislative chairs and party leaders for their respective programs. Republican Diprete frowned on his department heads promoting their programs independently in the Democratic legislature, but even if he had encouraged such behavior, differences in party would make access difficult. With the recent downturn in the state's economy resulting in sharply reduced state revenues, and another Democrat, Bruce Sundlun, in the governor's office, department heads now lobby to avoid budget cuts rather than promote programs.

8. Katherine Gregg, "The Press Rarely Gets on Lobbyists' Guest Lists," *Providence Sunday Journal*, January 25, 1987, C-8.
9. Jan Brogan, "Banking Lobby," *Providence Journal*, July 6, 1986, F-2.

Indirect Lobbying

Indirect lobbying is not widely used in Rhode Island. The lobbyists who responded to the survey were asked to indicate the most widely used and, from their perspective, the most effective lobbying techniques. Letter-writing and campaign contributions were listed as the most common indirect techniques, but they lagged far behind the more direct techniques discussed earlier. And they were not seen as effective; contributing money to campaigns was thought to be the most effective indirect technique, but only 7.1 percent of the lobbyists listed it as most effective. The legislators were in agreement about the most-used techniques but gave a slight nod to letter-writing (8.1 percent) over campaign contributions (6.5 percent) as the most effective.

Because the legislative districts are small in size and population, elaborate campaigns are not conducted below the statewide level in Rhode Island. An effective campaign for the state legislature can be waged for a few thousand dollars, although more is often spent.[10] Legislators can "walk their district" to contact voters, and of course radio or television advertisements would be wasted on audiences living outside the district. Even as a whole, the state does not constitute a single media market.[11] At any rate, electoral strategies to influence decision-makers below the statewide level are not generally employed and are not seen as potentially effective. Political influence in Rhode Island is certainly not gained by threatening to withhold electoral support from members of the legislature or senate.

Campaign contributions for statewide offices are more common by groups. There is a long tradition that firms doing business with the state are expected to make contributions to gubernatorial campaigns. These groups range from large construction firms to small suppliers. As of July 1, 1988, contributions to candidates from any source were limited to $2,000 per calendar year.[12] Groups or businesses, however, can maneuver around

10. A notable exception to the moderate expenditures for legislative seats was the 1988 primary race of Patrick J. Kennedy, son of the U.S. Senator from Massachusetts, Edward M. Kennedy. A junior at Providence College, the younger Kennedy reported spending $87,694 to unseat incumbent John M. Skeffington Jr. in the Democratic primary. He was unopposed in the general election.

11. Malcolm Jewell, *Representation in State Legislatures* (Lexington: University of Kentucky Press, 1982).

12. In 1990, candidates for governor had the option of using public funds for their campaigns. The state matched the first $1,000 of each private contribution, up to a

the limit by splitting contributions among several individuals. For example, during the 1988 gubernatorial campaign the Donatelli family of North Providence gave to the incumbent governor, Edward DiPrete, $22,905 between July 1 and election day, despite the new law. This was achieved by having several family members and different businesses owned by the family donate up to $2,000 individually. The Donatelli Building Company is one of the state's major construction firms, and two members of the family had been business partners with the governor's son, Dennis, in an apartment development project.[13]

In Rhode Island, PAC contributions, rather than direct group or individual contributions, are largely confined to out-of-state organizations donating to congressional and U.S. Senate races.

The organization with the widest scope of lobbying activity is Save the Bay, an environmental group that takes its name from concern about pollution of Narragansett Bay. With about 10,000 members, eighteen full-time employees, and an annual budget of more than $800,000, it is the largest environmental group in New England.[14] It has a part-time, paid lobbyist (shared with one other group), and several of its staff are registered to lobby.

Save the Bay makes good use of the mass media, especially television, by providing many on-the-scene photo opportunities for local reporters when an environmental issue is raised. One reason for the high profile is the group's attempt to win approval of numerous bond issues that provide money for state environmental projects.

According to the group's former executive director, Trudy Coxe, members serve on "dozens" of committees set up by the state Department of Environmental Management and has a solid working relationship with the department. Save the Bay has used the courts, as well, to push its agenda. In conjunction with the Conservation Law Foundation, the organization filed a lawsuit under provisions of the federal Clean Water Act against two Providence jewelry firms for illegal dumping of toxic waste. The suit was the first in the nation of this type that allows citizens to seek recourse in the courts against polluters.

---

total of $750,000. Candidates who accept public funds had to limit total expenditures to $1,500,000. No candidates accepted public money in 1990.

13. Russell Garland, "A Tangled Tale of Campaign Finances," *Providence Sunday Journal*, February 5, 1989, B-1.

14. Peter Lord, "Save the Bay Efforts Expand to Mass. Communities," *Providence Sunday Journal*, November 13, 1988, C-1.

Court action has also been used by the American Civil Liberties Union to address constitutional issues, such as separation of church and state. The U.S. Supreme Court heard a successful challenge from Rhode Island on the question of prayers at public-school graduations. A citizen group organized by a radio talk-show host challenged the self-voted pensions of the General Assembly in the state courts but lost.

THE RELATIVE POWER OF GROUPS AND LOBBIES

In general, the two most powerful lobbies in Rhode Island are the business and labor communities, and while the power of business is on the rise, that

Table 11.3. Groups Nominated as Among Most Powerful in Rhode Island, 1987

	Legislator Nominations		Lobbyist Nominations	
	N (221)	%	N (237)	%
Labor[a]	51	23.1	58	24.5
Business	27	12.2	41	17.3
Banking	28	12.7	26	11.0
Utilities	23	10.4	16	6.7
Insurance[b]	17	7.7	21	8.9
"Sin" industries (liquor and tobacco)	14	6.3	6	2.5
Elderly	12	5.4	4	1.7
Professionals	11	5.0	12	5.0

No other groups, including single-issue, environmental, realtors, builders, contractors, health industry, handicapped, and government units, received at least 5 percent of the nominations from either legislators or lobbyists.

Source: Compiled by author from 1987 survey.

Note: Respondents were asked to name the three most powerful groups.

[a]Includes the Rhode Island chapters of the NEA and the AFT.
[b]Includes Blue Cross / Blue Shield.

of labor is waning. In the two mail surveys, respondents were asked to name the three most powerful groups in Rhode Island. Because many answered by category (e.g., business) instead of by specific organizations as requested, all the responses were put into categories (see Table 11.3). Labor and specific unions were named most often by both legislators and lobbyists as being the most powerful groups in Rhode Island. Of 221 total nominations by legislators, 23.1 percent were references to labor. For lobbyists, 24.5 percent of 237 nominations were unions or labor. The second and third rankings were also the same for both groups—business and banking. The legislators ranked utilities as fourth most powerful and the insurance industry as fifth; the lobbyists had the latter two categories reversed in their rankings.

When one combines the more specific business categories with the general category, 49.3 percent of the nominations by the legislators and 46.4 percent of those by lobbyists mention business as having the most power among groups in the state. Other than business and labor, only the elderly and professional groups received even 5 percent of the nominations.

The legislators mentioned twenty-five different specific groups as among the three most powerful, while lobbyists mentioned twenty-nine. Consistent with the more general categories, the two groups mentioned most often by both samples were the Rhode Island Chamber of Commerce Federation and the Rhode Island AFL-CIO. After the Chamber and the AFL-CIO, the groups most often mentioned were Blue Cross / Blue Shield and Save the Bay. When asked why some groups were more powerful than others, the respondents in both samples gave wide-ranging answers that are difficult to categorize and summarize. However, the common theme seemed to be the importance of money. The crux of the argument was money for a full-time lobbyist (rather than for campaign donations), and preferably one who had a personal relationship with legislators, who was well informed, and who had a great deal of integrity. The money would also be needed to support staffing and other resources necessary to draft or to keep up with all relevant legislation. The focus on what made groups powerful was clearly on the process of legislating rather than electioneering.

A majority of legislators and lobbyists also agreed that the power of labor had been diminished while that of business had been enhanced. This is likely attributable to the changing nature of the economy in Rhode Island as well as in neighboring states, such as Massachusetts—manufacturing is being replaced by service. With the decline of blue-collar workers and difficulty in organizing the service sector, the power of labor decreases relative to that of business. Other groups seen as increasing in power were banks and environmental groups—the latter reference clearly to Save the Bay.

Thus, the powerful groups in Rhode Island among the business community are banks (Fleet National is the largest), insurance companies, and associations that represent them or business in general (such as the Chamber of Commerce). Powerful labor unions other than the AFL-CIO are the public-employee unions, such as the American Federation of State, County, and Municipal Employees (AFSCME), and teachers unions—that is, state chapters of the NEA and the AFT. Public utilities are powerful, and any group with one of the top ten or fifteen contract lobbyists must be considered as powerful. Because of its successful organization that supports a full complement of activities, Save the Bay is a group whose power is increasing.

It must be remembered that interest-group conflict often takes place within the context of the state's party system. The Democrats are the well-organized majority party, and while groups must sometimes deal with Republican governors or other statewide officers, the Democrats are the dominant force. For example, 78.6 percent of the lobbyists surveyed for this study agreed with the statement that once the party leadership of either house agreed with the lobbyist's position, committee chairs and the rank and file would usually follow. And 73.4 percent of the lobbyists agreed that it was more effective to lobby committee chairs and party leadership than the rank and file. Among the legislators, 87.1 percent believed committee chairs would follow the cues of party leaders on issue positions, and 82.3 percent believed lobbying party leaders and chairs would be more effective than dealing with the rank and file.

Perhaps given the right issue and commitment of time, an individual can make an impact on the legislative process in Rhode Island. During the 1985 legislative session, a Rhode Island small businessman, upset about his wife breathing secondary cigarette smoke at her job, set about getting legislation concerning smoking in the workplace passed. Gerald Maldivir took leave from his company, registered as a lobbyist, and spent every day of the session working for his cause. He drafted a bill based on legislation from other states, buttonholed every member of both houses that he could find, and kept track of the whole process on his personal computer. He allied himself with the state chapters of the lung and heart associations and had them urge members to write letters; he spent his nonsession time on radio talk shows all over the state. Maldivir emphasized the ease in traveling to all sections of the state for appearances; the trip across Rhode Island is only about forty-five minutes by car.

The bill was passed, in slightly different form, by both houses. But near the end of the session, before a compromise version could be passed, the bill ended up in what one lobbyist referred to as the "black hole." This is the bargaining process near the end of every legislative session among party leaders and other political actors that determines the fate of most legislation. Maldivir says he "completely lost track" of the bill during the last two weeks of the session, but it did become law. While a direct connection between Maldivir's efforts and consideration of the bill is likely, the ultimate success was determined by legislative leaders at the end of the session—and Maldivir's views were probably not a major consideration.

A more typical example of the intimate nature of Rhode Island politics is revealed in the state's ongoing banking crisis. On January 1, 1991, his inauguration day, Governor Bruce Sundlun closed forty-five banks and credit unions in the state because on the previous day their private insurer, Rhode Island Share & Deposit Indemnity Corporation (RISDIC), had collapsed and declared itself insolvent. This was the first public revelation that RISDIC was in serious trouble, and Sundlun's move froze the accounts of about 300,000 people, approximately one-third of the state's population. While many of the smaller institutions opened within a few months, the largest credit unions and banks that held the bulk of the deposits were not opened and still had accounts frozen nine months later.

Two of the issues raised after the governor's January 1 action were how RISDIC could have failed and why some banks and credit unions in the state had federal insurance while those that had been closed did not. The answer to the first question was that RISDIC was a creature of the very institutions it insured; member institutions provided the capital, and their officers constituted RISDIC's board of directors. As Rhode Island's economy declined in the late 1980s—especially the real estate component—some larger RISDIC-insured credit unions and banks became financially shaky. Although two RISDIC institutions had failed in 1990, few people knew that other, larger institutions were in trouble because RISDIC, much to the surprise of the public, had been given the right to audit its own institutions instead of having the State Department of Business Regulation do so. The RISDIC audits were evidently infrequent, sloppy, and overly optimistic. Thus, the forty-five credit unions and banks insured by RISDIC were insulated from any effective outside regulation, and any problems were certainly hidden from depositors and the public in general.

The reason for the lack of federal insurance emerged after the collapse. In 1986, legislation was introduced requiring that all banks and credit unions in the state be federally insured, which meant the end of RISDIC. On the House side, the bill was referred to the Finance Committee. The committee chair was Representative Robert Tucker, whose wife would serve as director of one of the closed RISDIC credit unions from 1987 to 1990. Tucker later failed to indicate his wife's position on any financial disclosure statements that elected officials must file with the state Ethics Commission. The vice chair was Representative Robert Bianchini, also head of the Rhode Island Credit Union League, a trade association. As an elected official, he was not registered as a lobbyist.

At the hearings, Peter Nevola, president of the RISDIC, argued forcefully against the requirement of federal insurance, having made his case earlier as well at a RISDIC-funded dinner for the entire House Finance Committee at a private Providence club. One supporter of the legislation at the hearings was Republican Attorney General Arlene Violet, a former nun whose first electoral race was for the office she then held.

Violet had recruited Robert Stitt, a New York investment banker who had retired to Rhode Island, to prepare a report on the financial status of the institutions insured by RISDIC. The report indicated potentially severe financial problems that indeed surfaced four years later. Not wanting to alarm the public and perhaps cause a run by depositors, Violet asked the committee to go into closed session to receive some confidential information.

At that point in the hearings, Tucker and Bianchini apparently met with the Democratic leadership of the House, and the decision was made not to accept the report in either open or closed session, effectively killing the bill. The existence and content of the Stitt report were unknown to the public until after the collapse of RISDIC.

The extent of the old-boy network surrounding RISDIC and the closed institutions became clearer when the General Assembly appointed a nine-member commission, headed by Washington attorneys, to find out what happened. The early sessions of the public hearings revealed that some insiders, including Democratic officeholders, had withdrawn large sums of money from RISDIC institutions days before the insurer collapsed.[15]

Salvatore Mancini—mayor of North Providence, State Democratic

15. Mike Stanton, "RISDIC Commission Urges Lawsuits Against 14 Insiders," *Providence Journal*, September 6, 1991, 1.

Committee chair, director of a closed credit union—withdrew $150,000 from RISDIC institutions in the last week of December 1990. He disputes the commission's claim that he withdrew another $65,000 on December 27. Mancini's nephew was also accused of taking out money based on insider information. John Correia—Democratic state senator—withdrew $210,000 from the East Providence Credit Union where he was a vice president, including $150,000 three days before the credit union was closed. At the public hearings, Correia argued that because he had quickly deposited the money in another (federally insured) institution he had not really withdrawn the money but only completed "a transaction."

Peter Nevola, president of RISDIC, withdrew $63,000 from one of his organization's insured credit unions on December 31, *after* the emergency meeting at which RISDIC declared itself insolvent. His wife and mother-in-law withdrew more than $100,000 from RISDIC institutions in the last ten days of December. In all, the commission has demanded that fourteen people return money to the closed institutions that had been withdrawn because of insider information, but whether that will ever happen is questionable.

Although the general public and all but a very few of the depositors were unaware of the impending crisis, the state's network of overlapping elites evidently spread the word among themselves.

Politics in Rhode Island is, to a great degree, traditional politics and party politics. The art of compromise is still clearly understood and practiced well in the state. Because of the state's small size and its structure of overlapping elites, political bargaining is done mostly on a face-to-face basis by people who know one another well. And while political conflict can become intense, those with experience know that success means that acrimony cannot be carried from one battle to another. Besides, in Rhode Island you may be related to or scheduled to eat dinner with your opponent that evening.

It is, indeed, the politics of intimacy; many top-level political discussions are held (or at least started or continued) at weddings, banquets, sporting events, and other social occasions. Except when extraordinary events such as the banking crisis occur, this part of the political process remains unobserved. But the logical extension of that informal process is the pattern of direct, face-to-face group activity described earlier.

In Rhode Island a group achieves its goals primarily by becoming inti-

mate with the political process through hiring a lobbyist with an established reputation, developing such a person in-house, or, as in the case of
Bianchini, merging an elective and advocacy position. More indirect
methods, such as campaign contributions and use of the mass media, are
not seen as effective unless dealing with statewide elections or bond referenda.

But there may be changes in the traditional politics of the state. The
banking crisis has exposed more fully to the public the workings of an
insulated system. Other recent scandals involving the arrest of a state senator, the removal of two judges, and the indictment of a Democratic mayor
have left voters angry. The Republican party is heavily recruiting candidates for the legislature and seems to be having considerably greater success
than in the past. If Republicans do make major gains in the House and the
Senate, and/or Democratic legislative leaders lose their seats in the 1992
elections, the tightly controlled legislative process may open up.

All recent political activity in the state has been played out against the
backdrop of a serious economic decline made worse by the banking crisis.
This has undermined even further the power of labor, including public-
employee unions. With state revenues falling well behind projections, public unions have been content to avoid layoffs and "givebacks" rather than
ask for increased wages and benefits. But a rebounding economy will eventually restore the influence of the public unions, although other unions
that have lost membership and influence as the state's economy moved
from manufacturing to service are unlikely to rebound.

The major banks in the state, influential before the banking crisis, are
more so afterward. Some of the closed institutions will probably be taken
over by the bigger, federally insured banks in the state, even though the
larger banks are also feeling the effects of the general recession. Being in a
position to help with at least some of the closed institutions, and more
generally being available for advice to elected officials, has given these
banks an even more advantaged position. Increased Republican strength in
elected offices, if it comes, will likely add to this advantage.

Thanks are due to the Political Science Data Center assistants at Providence College;
to all the lobbyists, elected officials, heads of groups, and others who provided written
or oral interviews; and to former House Speaker Matthew J. Smith. The term "politics
of intimacy" was coined by Professor Elmer Cornwell of Brown University.

12

Vermont: Interest Groups in a Rural Technopolity

Frank Bryan and Ann Hallowell

"Vermont," says Neal Peirce, "is perhaps the only place in America a stranger can feel homesick for before he has even left it."[1] This is because Americans think of the Green Mountain State as kind of a national pastureland of yesteryear.

With its citizen legislature, town meetings, and low-keyed and personalized politics, Vermont has remained the quintessential "M," or moralistic, culture state.[2] Geography isolated Vermont from the "I," or individualistic, culture brought by the urban industrial revolution to most of America. Yet what is not generally understood is that the state has also always been a full partner in America's technological advancement.[3] Rapid growth and the coming of high-tech economic infrastructure since World War II reinforced this fact and has placed Vermont in a unique position. What happens when a state carries an "M" culture environment into the postmodern world where a new decentralist culture supported by information technology is the ascendant pattern? What happens when "M" culture collides not with "I" culture but with something far different and far newer?

1. Neal R. Peirce, *The New England States* (New York: W. W. Norton, 1976), 233.

2. The typology of political cultures (or, more correctly, subcultures) used here is the one used by Daniel J. Elazar in his *American Federalism: A View from the States*, 3rd ed. (New York: Harper & Row, 1984), chap. 5, "The States and the Political Setting."

3. While southern New England gets most of the ink for "high-tech" advancements, when the New England Telephone Company needed a city to try out a new technology recently, they chose Burlington, Vermont, because of the larger number of households there with personal computers. Throughout the 1980s Vermont was a national leader in the percentage of its labor force employed in high-tech industries. This statistic does not include agriculture, which in the modern period is perhaps the most high-tech industry of all.

Ironically, this collision features an elite set on rapidly centralizing state government at the very time that high technology is reenergizing the communal, decentralized society preserved by Vermont's noninvolvement in the urban industrial revolution. Interest groups are a metaphor of this irony. Vermont is creating a marketplace *arena* for interest-group activity apropos of "I" culture even though there never has been (and now never will be) and "I" culture to support it.

When Theresa G. Feeley served in Montpelier in 1979 and 1980, she did so as a citizen legislator representing about 3,500 people. In 1986 she was still in Montpelier, but at that time Theresa Feeley, lobbyist, represented twenty-two different interest *groups*. She and other prominent lobbyists, such as Bill Gilbert (former secretary of administration and former commissioner of the Public Service Department), Bob Sherman (former press secretary to Governor Madeleine Kunin), David Wilson (former commissioner of the Department of Social Welfare and secretary of the Agency of Administration), and even former Governor Thomas Salmon, are or have recently been part of a cadre of Vermont lobbyists with strong connections to government and especially to the Montpelier establishment.

In short, over the years Vermont towns have steadily lost political power in Montpelier. Between 1957 and 1969, according to G. Ross Stephens's centralization index, Vermont led every state but Alaska on increasing centralization of state government.[4] Pushed by a progressive environmental ethic and a centrist mentality on education policy, this movement continued throughout the 1970s and 1980s. The result is that influence is peddled more and more at the center, where an "I" culture expression of marketplace wheeling and dealing is fast developing.

INTEREST GROUPS IN RURAL TRANSITION, 1930–1965

Although the thesis of Vermont politics between 1930 and 1965 was thoroughly rural and Republican, several elements were coalescing as an emergent antithesis. (1) After World War II, the communications revolution hit Vermont like a whirlwind, bursting through the geographic barrier that had isolated the state for a century. (2) Agricultural technology began to

4. G. Ross Stephens, "State Centralization and the Erosion of Local Autonomy," *Journal of Politics* 36 (February 1974), 44–76.

wipe out the hill farms, opening up new and picturesque lands for settlement. This, coupled with new technological comforts that made life in Vermont more pleasant year-round, transformed the state into a "beckoning country," and population began growing rapidly. (3) The Democratic party made a substantial breakthrough in 1952 (in terms of percentage gains in the vote for governor) and in 1958 elected its first Democrat to the U.S. House of Representatives in a century (Vermont has only one U.S. congressperson). Four years later, for the first time in a century, a Democrat—and a liberal at that—Philip Hoff, won the governorship.

During this time, Vermont was considered a state where interest groups were "moderately strong" (as opposed to either strong or weak).[5] Yet the evidence for this ranking is skimpy. Indeed, Vermont's placement in the middle category instead of the "weak" category may have been driven by deduction, for the state ranked high on variables associated with interest-group activity: a simple economy, a weak party system, a less professionalized legislature, and a weak governor. Harmon Zeigler points out, for instance, that strong parties leave "no room for interest groups" and that states with strong interest groups "typically do not have complex economies." He goes on to assert that "legislators with professional staffs do not rely upon lobbyists for information, hence lobbyists are not influential" and that "strong lobby states have weaker governors than weak lobby states."[6]

In the national eye, Vermont has historically fit all these predictors of strong interest-group activity. First, it was the most one-party state north of the Mason-Dixon Line. The Republicans were nagged by a progressive-conservative split among party leaders and elected officials. While this split weakened party leadership, it did not penetrate to the grass roots to provide a bifactional order analogous to some southern one-party states. The dominant pattern—friends-and-neighbors politics—was highly unstructured. For their part, the Democrats (at least until the mid-1950s) maintained a loyal opposition that dutifully contested statewide elections. But they had no hope (and, some say, no intention) of winning.

More important, the cohesion of the parties in Montpelier and the de-

5. Sarah McCally Morehouse, *State Politics, Parties, and Policy* (New York: Holt, Rinehart & Winston, 1981), 111.

6. See L. Harmon Zeigler, "Interest Groups in the States," in Virginia Gray, Herbert Jacob, and Kenneth N. Vines, eds., *Politics in the American States*, 4th ed. (Boston: Little, Brown, 1983), 97–131. Zeigler also points out that strong lobby states have small bureaucracies. This also fits Vermont because Vermont has a small bureaucracy in the aggregate, even though its per capita bureaucrats figure is substantially higher than the national average.

gree to which they opposed each other on roll-call votes has always been quite low, with the exception of several legislative sessions during the Hoff administration and several later sessions. There has been substantial opportunity in the legislative process in Vermont for interest groups to exert substantial influence (see Table 12.1).

Second, agriculture dominated the state's economy for years. There was also a limited but reasonably active small-business/light-industry sector that featured influential ancillary sectors in banking, insurance, and utilities, and the tourist trade has been a growing factor throughout the century. But in general the Vermont economy was not complex. Almost everybody outside the major population areas farmed. Even many who lived in population centers were supporters of or supported by agriculture. Other rural enterprises, such as extractive industries (marble and granite) and forestry and wood products, were also important. Clearly Vermont was a state where a few dominant economic sectors, free from the cross-pressures of overlapping interests, had the potential to exert strong influence. Small business (represented by Associated Industries of Vermont) and agriculture (represented by the Farm Bureau) might well find Vermont legislators sitting ducks.

Third, the nature of the Vermont legislature itself made it seem like prime hunting ground for organized interests. It was huge (246 members in the House, 30 in the Senate) and relatively unorganized and unstructured. It had minuscule staff services, and legislators had no offices or personal phones in the statehouse complex. Huge percentages of legislators—more than half until the 1950s—were typically serving their first term. Even

Table 12.1. Average Party Activity Scores in the Vermont House of Representatives, 1951–1978 (Roll Calls = 987)

Legislative Sessions	Democratic Cohesion	Republican Cohesion	Index of Party Likeness
1951–63	35	25	82
1964–67[a]	68	33	58
1968–78	53	41	73

Source: Compiled by the authors.

Note: The Index of Cohesion for any given roll call ranges from 0 (the party is evenly split on the vote) to 100 (the party is totally unified). The Index of Party Likeness ranges from 0 (one party's vote is exactly opposite the other's) to 100 (both parties vote precisely the same).

[a]Sessions when Democrat Philip Hoff actively promoted a legislative agenda.

into the 1980s one-third of the legislators serving in any given legislative year had never served before. Lobbyists ought to be strong in a place that relied almost totally on nonlegislative sources of information and policy analysis—things lobbyists have always been adept at providing.[7]

Finally, Vermont's weak governorship and small bureaucracy would also be likely to lead to stronger interest groups. Using Joseph Schlesinger's Index of Gubernatorial Power, Vermont scored 13 out of a possible 20 (the highest score) in the 1960s; the average American state scored fifteen.[8] Moreover, Vermont's governorship was weaker than even its relatively homogenous socioeconomic environment would predict it ought to be.[9]

Based on these facts, one would expect interest groups in Vermont to be strong. Accordingly, most studies concluded that there was in Vermont a continuing battle between two dominant groups—Associated Industries of Vermont (AIV) and the more powerful Farm Bureau—which meant that the interest-group system in Vermont should be scored "moderately strong." It is our contention, however, that these interest groups were quite weak, as was the group system itself.

The Morehouse ranking for Vermont, which was used by Zeigler in his important study of state interest groups, was based on a 1954 report by Belle Zeller.[10] This in turn was based on the case study by Oliver Garceau and Corinne Silverman, which treated the Associated Industries of Vermont as it sought to wield its influence in the 1951 session of the legislature.[11] In the late 1970s Morehouse changed Zeller's rankings in eleven cases, but not Vermont's.

7. The standard comparative measure of legislative capacity to act independently of interest groups was published in 1971; it ranks Vermont 42nd in its capacity to avoid outside influences (such as interest groups) and 34th in its capacity to gather information. See Citizen Conference on State Legislatures, *State Legislatures: An Evolution of Their Effectiveness* (New York: Praeger, 1971).

8. Joseph A. Schlesinger, "The Politics of the Executive," in Herbert Jacob and Kenneth Vines, eds., *Politics in the American States*, 2nd ed. (Boston: Little, Brown, 1971).

9. John L. Sullivan, "Political Correlates of Social, Economic, and Religious Diversity in the American States," *Journal of Politics* 35 (February 1973), 70–84. See also Frank M. Bryan, "The New England Governorship: People, Position, and Power," in Josephine F. Milburn and Victoria Schuck, eds., *New England Politics* (Cambridge, Mass.: Schenkman, 1981), 75–106.

10. Belle Zeller, *American State Legislatures*, 2nd ed. (New York: Thomas Y. Crowell, 1954).

11. Oliver Garceau and Corinne Silverman, "A Pressure Group and the Pressured: A Case Report," *American Political Science Review* 48 (September 1954), 672–91.

Well into the 1980s, therefore, Vermont's interest-group structure was still being explained in the context of the politics of the early 1950s, but even the validity of this 1950s assessment is questionable. A close reading of the Garceau and Silverman study indicates that Associated Industries of Vermont was not a highly active lobbying force in Montpelier. In a year when political circumstances could have maximized the influences of AIV, Garceau and Silverman identify only one legislative success. This occurred early in the session when, through quiet negotiations with labor groups outside the legislature ("lobbying" was not employed), AIV compromised its way to an acceptable version of an occupational disease bill. After this initial success, AIV was quite ineffective. In fact, according to Garceau and Silverman, *both* labor and industry were weak. In terms of AIV they conclude: "Business endorsement of a policy was considered, in the AIV office, a surety of defeat. . . . This, be it noted, is not because labor was strong, but because business interests remained essentially weak."[12]

If business was weak, does that mean the Farm Bureau was strong? Not necessarily, for this kind of vacuum mentality, often penned from the city by urban political scientists ("Someone must control these people"), is a function of applying "I" culture thinking to an "M" culture environment. In the political marketplace, where influence rises and falls in a zero-sum game, one would expect that agriculture must be strong if labor and industry were weak.

More significant is that agriculture as an interest group did not *need* to be strong. The Vermont legislature during the period was dominated by farmer-legislators or legislators with relatives who farmed. When Garceau and Silverman studied interest groups in the Vermont House in 1951, four of ten lawmakers were farmers. Indeed, the authors themselves agree that farming interests were dominant, but in a very informal way. One legislator is quoted as saying:

> You can't talk about "Farm Bureau" activity on this bill. Farm sup-
> port or opposition is not always organized. It's the same with any
> group. For example, when this bill came up, or when any bill comes
> up, the members of the Agricultural Committee sit around for
> awhile in their committee room and discuss the effects of the bill on
> them as farmers. Sure, they're all farmers and probably all Farm
> Bureau members. But is this an organized group? Not really. At

12. Ibid., 677.

least not organized in such a way that you can point to direct Farm Bureau influence.[13]

In other words, it is different to say "Farming interests were strong in the Vermont legislature" (which they were) than to say "Farming *interest groups* using their lobbyists were capable of exerting important influence." Thus, we reach the general conclusion that placing Vermont among the eighteen states in the Morehouse ranking that had "moderately strong" interest groups (with AIV and the Farm Bureau dominating) is substantially exaggerated.[14]

A more subtle yet perhaps equally important reason why the Vermont legislature was cast as being controlled by lobbyists to a greater degree than it really was is the temptation to conclude that the legislators were being duped. Farmers could be "had" because, with lower levels of education and a clear amateur status in the state capital, they did not have the sophistication to understand that lobbying was going on. How, this theory asks, could a highly unorganized crowd of nonprofessionals representing districts that, on average, contained less than 2,000 people *not* be influenced by lobbyists? This theory is suggested by Garceau and Silverman and then adopted by Duane Lockard in his important work on Vermont.[15]

There are two reasons to question this interpretation, however. First, Garceau and Silverman's data are incomplete and inadequate. They are based on only fifty-six interviews selected *nonrandomly*. Yet, they extend their analysis of this small group to conclude that less than one-third of all 276 legislators had ever heard of Associated Industries of Vermont and that "one-third had never heard of Arthur Packard, for a generation the presi-

---

13. Ibid., 686–89.

14. In a short section on interest groups in his text on Vermont State Administration, Andrew Nuquist (*Vermont State Government and Administration* [Burlington: Government Research Center, University of Vermont, 1966]) does not single out the Farm Bureau or the AIV but includes them in a short list of the most active groups. The list also includes public utilities groups, the railway brotherhood, the dairymen's association, labor organizations, the Vermont Patrolmen's Association, the Vermont Highway Union Conference, the Vermont Teachers' Association, and the Wholesale Beverage Association. In the best treatment of Vermont politics of the period, Duane Lockard, himself relying heavily on Garceau and Silverman (see note 11), entitles his section on interest groups and the Vermont legislature "Low Pressure Politics." See Duane Lockard, "Vermont: Political Paradox," *New England State Politics* (Princeton: Princeton University Press, 1959), 35–45.

15. Duane Lockard, "Vermont."

dent and lobbyist for the Farm Bureau."[16] Their findings, broken down in percentage tables, represent Ns that are too small to be taken seriously.

More significant is the fact that the closest observer of Vermont politics at the time, Andrew Nuquist, believes that the researchers themselves had been snookered. Nuquist said that the parochial and "Yankee" ethic that pervaded the legislature in those days often meant that, with a wink and a knowing look, Vermont legislators dearly loved to "put on" eager social scientists who often came to the legislature to "study these backward old farmers." Nuquist believes (as do we) that a judgment asking us to believe that one-third of the legislators had never heard of Arthur Packard is absurd.[17]

What happened, it seems to us, is that a rural "M" culture was being measured in urban "I" culture categories. It would have been quite difficult to "pressure" Vermont legislators precisely *because* they represented such tiny constituencies and precisely because they believed that pressure groups were outside the acceptable way of things (the great majority of them, remember, had been raised in the town-meeting tradition). Pressure was exerted from time to time, to be sure, yet relative to what is generally considered to be standard in American interest-group politics, there is no evidence that Vermont's system should have been labeled "moderately strong" during the early period. However, such a classification, although wrong for the time it was intended to reflect, is right for the present. Vermont has caught up with its ranking.

TRANSITION: BEGINNINGS OF A NEW INTEREST-GROUP POLITICS, 1965–1977

Between 1965 and 1977 the sociopolitical dynamics that had been under way throughout the earlier period began to intensify. What had been an agrarian, Republican state was now something different. Antithesis was becoming thesis. Vermont became a two-party state. Farming ceased to be the dominant activity in rural Vermont, where most of the population is located. Furthermore, in the 1960s and 1970s Vermont experienced its first major population increase since before the Civil War. The people who came to Vermont moved into the countryside, not into the larger towns. But they did not come to farm.

16. Garceau and Silverman, "A Pressure Group and the Pressured," 685.
17. Interview with Andrew Nuquist, November 17, 1968.

Vermont's economy became more diversified. Leading this diversification was the IBM plant in Essex Junction, which now employs more people than live in any one of more than two-thirds of Vermont's towns. The ski industry and tourist trade flourished. Second-home development provided economic transfusions in many rural towns. Cottage industries, such as the now nationally recognized "Ben and Jerry's Ice Cream," began to catch on. The tertiary component of the work force grew much faster in Vermont than in other parts of America. In short, Vermont experienced a third-wave breakthrough, which, given its small size and isolation throughout the previous century, had a massive impact on the state. We have said elsewhere that this condition is best described as a rural "technopolity."[18]

In terms of political structure, three important transitions were established by 1977. First, government became profoundly more centralized. To reiterate, G. Ross Stephens's landmark 1974 article on state centralization revealed that during the previous decade none of the forty-eight adjacent states outdistanced Vermont on the degree of state centralization of services.[19] The second event was the growth and, more important, the *rationalization* of the state bureaucracy. Between 1968 and 1972, under the direction of Governor Deane Davis, Vermont shifted from a department form of state administration to an agency form. The governor's "span of control" was both narrowed and strengthened. A wide array of independent and quasi-independent departments were placed "in line" under the agency apparatus. Although Vermont's system was still (by Weberian logic) quite fragmented, it was strengthened immensely by Davis's innovations. At the same time, the Vermont legislature began turning more and more power over to the agencies (as did legislatures all over the nation). Symbolic of this movement was the shift of control of one of the legislature's most prized possessions, Vermont's white-tailed deer herd, to wildlife managers in the Department of Fish and Game.

Finally, the legislature reapportioned. Whereas before legislators representing as few as 13 percent of Vermont's population could elect a majority in the state's House of Representatives, now no majority could be formed that did not represent a majority of the people of the state. The House also reduced its membership from 246 to 150.

For interest groups this means, first, that a more competitive party system would seem to predict a weaker interest-group system. Under Demo-

18. Frank M. Bryan, *Yankee Politics in Rural Vermont* (Hanover, N.H.: University Press of New England, 1974).
19. Stephens, "State Centralization."

crat Philip Hoff, Democratic cohesion in the House jumped dramatically. Certainly, there was less room for interest groups to score points in the legislatures of 1966, 1967, and 1968, when they had to contend with Hoff's legislative coalition. Also, the increasing variety of Vermont's economy also suggests a defoliation of the habitat for interest groups. The growing strength of the bureaucracy would predict a weakening of traditional interest-group politics as bureaucrats themselves competed for the attention of lawmakers. The smaller, reapportioned legislature would, it is presumed, provide a more complex district structure for individual legislators, thus weakening the influence of single dominant groups. Yet between 1966 and 1977 the number of organizations registering lobbyists at the capital in Montpelier doubled.

There are a number of explanations for this paradox. For instance, the *nature* of the new two-party competition does not foretell weaker interest groups. Vermont's party system became competitive, it is true, but this did not translate into stronger party organizations. Vermont has leveled off its partisan playing field. But whether it has viable party organizations that can compete with interest groups in the legislative arena is problematical indeed. Another explanation is that, in contrast to the situation in the past, when farmers were so powerful in numbers that they lacked an incentive to become strong organizationally, increasing economic diversity and complexity has placed the economic sector in a zone where there is enough diversity to increase the number and activity of interest groups. However, this increased economic diversity was not of a scale to create the multiplicity of groups that would work to the disadvantage of major interests.

It is difficult to rationalize the parallel increase in strength of state agencies in policy-making and the increase in interest-group activity. The most plausible explanation is that legislators, confronted by the unregistered lobbying tactics of bureaucrats with their technical knowledge and monopoly over information, turn more and more to interest groups as the only *countervailing* source of information and technical advice. It is interesting too that the vitality of lobbying organizations is enhanced by the need to lobby the *agencies* themselves after the legislature adjourns every year. For instance, leading Vermont lobbyist Bob Sherman says he lobbies the executive all year and that in many cases executive agencies get more attention than the legislature. Thus, the agencies are becoming life-support systems for lobbying firms between legislative sessions. The more lobbyists turn their attention to bureaucracies, the more the hypothesis that legislatures are losing control of the lawmaking function is confirmed.

The political system in the transition period was ripe for an increase in interest-group activity for three other reasons. First, there was the tremendous growth of political power in Montpelier. When policy was more diffused in the towns and cities around the state, lobbying in Montpelier was far less important. Now that major decisions on many more fronts are being made in the capital, organizations are focusing their activities there.

Second, there has been a great buildup in the number of lobbyists that have registered to represent groups now served by government that were not served before. The increase in public-sector activity on all fronts is its own stimulant for a more developed interest-group system. Finally, there is a growing mentality on the part of political elites in Vermont that interest-group politics is a necessary evil that must accompany political progress. Interest groups became more and more accepted in Vermont because the "I" culture politics they represented was viewed as an indicator that Vermont's politics was "growing up." We shall return to this final consideration in the discussion section, but first we need to describe the characteristics of interest-group activity in Vermont since 1978, the time when, as experienced and respected Vermont newsperson Debra Sline has said, lobbying "came of age in Montpelier."[20]

DIMENSIONS OF INTEREST-GROUP ACTIVITY SINCE 1978

The socioeconomic characteristics of the transition phase have become institutionalized in the contemporary period. Vermont agriculture continues to decline, the variables associated with life in the rural technopolity are more pronounced, and the Democratic party is even more successful. The balance of power is now slightly in the Democrats' favor.

As far as interest groups are concerned, the period began with the significant strengthening of legislation governing interest-group activity. The major statute governing interest groups, passed in 1939, underwent major revisions in 1976. Registration procedures and fees, disclosure requirements for expenditures, and enforcement penalties were all addressed. But this in no way reduced interest-group activity. Since then, several developments have taken place:

1. Executive lobbying from the governor's office has become an important factor. Said Sline in early 1988: "There is perhaps no greater sign of

20. *Barre/Montpelier Times Argus*, January 31, 1988.

the heightened impact of lobbying than the fact that the Governor herself has hired lobbyists to push key initiatives in the past two years."[21]

2. The number of advocacy groups relying on the state for funding increased as Reagan administration spending-cuts shifted the arena of interest from Washington to Montpelier.

3. The number of organizations hiring contract lobbyists and the total number of lobbyist registrations (plus the number of nonregistered lobbyists) have continued to grow dramatically (see Table 12.2). Although it is difficult to ascertain exactly why, the empirical record is clear: As the 1990s began, the Vermont legislature became prime hunting ground for special interests. Symptomatic of this change is that, for the first time, Vermont has been faced with a serious revolving-door problem. Key government figures have resigned and hung up their shingles as lobbyists. This caused a minor uproar in Vermont politics in 1987 and 1988, and again in 1991, when a former high-level state administrator, who had since returned to a law practice and lobbying, again took up a key role in government (administration secretary) in the new administration of Governor Howard Dean.

4. The number of PACs has increased dramatically in Vermont. Between 1978 and 1987 the number of PACs filing campaign contributions for the elections of all statewide offices (excluding congressional seats) more than doubled, increasing 154 percent from 24 to 61. Growth of PAC contributions for candidates running for a seat in the Vermont legislature has also increased dramatically. Of all the contributions made in the elections of 1980, 1982, 1984, and 1986, some 41 percent were made in 1986. The three leading contributors were the Vermont Realtors Association, the Vermont Labor Council (VCOPE), and the business group BIZPAC.

The principal political development was the rise of a more disciplined Democratic party in the state House of Representatives in the 1985–86 and 1987–88 sessions of the legislature. That this has occurred at precisely the same time interest groups have become a more important force in the legislature continues to challenge the hypothesis that the two tend to be mutually exclusive. There is nothing to do at this point but leave the problem alone, much as a Vermont farmer treats a huge boulder in the middle of a field: work around it. What we can do is be more specific about the details of the pressure-group activity that takes place in Montpelier.

21. Ibid.

Table 12.2. Basic Data on Registered Vermont Interest Groups: Selected
Years, 1939–1989

Year	No. of Organizations Registered	No. of Lobbyists Registered	No. of Lobbyist Registrations[a]	Lobbyists per Legislator
1939	67	51	—	0.18
1949	52	61	—	0.22
1959	73	67	—	0.24
1969	84	63	—	0.35[b]
1973	119	135	—	0.75
1975	112	145	189	0.81
1977	149	187	245	1.02
1978	146	183	255	1.02
1979	134	173	215	0.96
1980	129	177	221	0.98
1981	150	192	—	1.07
1982	120	152	229	0.84
1983	144	212	285	1.18
1984	168	217	296	1.21
1985	175	230	319	1.28
1986	162	227	357	1.26
1987	231	280	484	1.56
1988	221	315	470	1.75
1989	246	352	597[c]	1.96

Source: Compiled from raw data in the archives of the Vermont Secretary of State.

[a]Many lobbyists work for more than one interest group, and many interest groups hire more than one lobbyist. This figure represents the number of times a single lobbyist registered under a single organization.

[b]This figure jumped because the number of legislators dropped from 276 to 180 after reapportionment in 1969.

[c]The jump was caused in part by lobbying firms of two or more lobbyists listing each lobbyist in the firm with each interest group lobbied by the firm.

Who Lobbies?

In the 1987 session of the Vermont legislature, 280 lobbyists registered. They represented 231 organizations for a total of 484 registrations. There were three lobbyists for every two lawmakers in Montpelier. In the last year for which accurate data are available, 1989,[22] some 352 names appeared on the list of registered lobbyists, representing 246 organizations, for a total of 597 lobbyist registrations, two lobbyists for every lawmaker.

In the 1980s the largest category of organizations registered was business and particularly insurance and banking. Business accounted for about one-quarter of all groups registered in the 1989 session, and insurance companies dominated lobbying by business groups. Beyond this, it is difficult to place groups and organizations in categories. The category "medicine, health, and social services" is much more visible in current sessions, reflecting expansion of the agenda of public concerns and a centralization of functions in Montpelier. It accounted for 13 percent of groups registered during the 1989 session. Finally, "professional groups" began appearing in the top categories in the 1977 session (see Table 12.3) and have remained there ever since. This matches the growing tertiary flavor of Vermont's socioeconomic makeup. In short, the kinds of interest groups that seem to dominate (at least in numbers) in Montpelier reflect the changing character of the state itself.

How Much Is Spent?

The 1976 amendments to Vermont's lobby disclosure law did not include strong financial disclosure provisions. Groups were required only to estimate total expenditures by categories, which are few in number and necessarily wide. The last category is set low, at $10,000 per year, and is open-ended.

In the 1989 legislative session, only 198 of the 250 organizations registered filed financial disclosure statements. The gap between those registering and those disclosing expenditures is substantial, probably as a result of the tendency of groups to register every session even though they anticipate no legislation of particular interest to them. As one observer recently stated, they are "covering themselves." This fact somewhat distorts the tremendous increase in the number of groups registered in recent years, for although the number registered increased by 68 percent since 1977, the number of groups that filed financial disclosures increased by only 51 percent (Table 12.4).

22. With the passage of a new lobbyist registration bill in 1990, confusion about requirements created a "black hole" for registrations at a key point in the 1990 session. Data for the 1991 session are incomplete as this chapter is being completed.

Table 12.3. Who Lobbies Vermont? Categories of Registered Organizations: Selected Years, 1939–1989

1939		1959		1973		1977	
B.I.B.[a]	31%	B.I.B.	34%	B.I.B.	35%	B.I.B.	28%
Transport.	16	Transport.	9	M.H.S.S.	11	Prof. groups	9
Utilities	16	Utilities	9	Utilities	8	Utilities	9
S.L.G.[b]	16˙	Agriculture	9	C.G.R.[d]	8	C.G.R.	6
Others	21	M.H.S.S.[c]	9	Others	38	Others	48
		Others	30				
Out-of-state		Out-of-state		Out-of-state		Out-of-state	
organizations	31%	organizations	23%	organizations	25%	organizations	20%

1981		1983		1987		1989	
B.I.B.	19%	B.I.B.	19%	B.I.B.	23%	B.I.B.	33%
M.H.S.S.	9	M.H.S.S.	8	M.H.S.S.	9	M.H.S.S.	13
Prof. groups	9	Prof. groups	7	Prof. groups	9	C.G.R.	12
Utilities	6	C.G.R.	7	Utilities	6	Prof. groups	8
Others	57	Others	59	Others	53	Others	46
Out-of-state		Out-of-state		Out-of-state		Out-of-state	
organizations	23%	organizations	32%	organizations	25%	organizations	21%

Source: Compiled from raw data in the archives of the Vermont Secretary of State.

[a]Business, insurance, and banking.
[b]State and local government.
[c]Medicine, health, and social services.
[d]Citizens groups and religion.

Actual spending increased by an estimated 244 percent over the last decade. Spending estimates are conservative, arrived at by establishing arbitrary amounts to each category of expenditures. In other words, we estimated that each organization spent the midpoint amount in the category in which it placed itself, and those that indicated they spent more than $10,000 spent $12,500 (Table 12.4). In real dollars the $1,101,500 we estimate lobbyists spent in the 1989 session comes closer to the $320,000 they spent a decade earlier.

Who Spends?

A detailed analysis of the spending of each group that filed disclosures for the five sessions reviewed here between 1977 and 1989 reveals that only

Table 12.4. How Much Is Spent? Expenditures of Interest Groups Lobbying the Vermont Legislature, 1977–1989

Year	No. of Organizations Registered with Legislature	No. of Organizations Disclosing Lobbying Expenditures	Organizations Disclosing Expenditures Reported Spending (in Dollars)				Estimated Total Expenditures by Those Disclosing[a]
			0–1,000	1,001–5,000	5,001–10,000	10,000+	
1977	149	131	72	43	9	7	$ 320,000
1981	150	119	51	33	23	13	458,000
1983	144	112	38	40	23	11	449,000
1987	231	166	70	49	19	28	657,500
1988	221	165	44	50	23	48	944,500
1989	250	198	55	61	27	55	1,101,500

Source: Compiled from raw data in the archives of the Vermont Secretary of State.

[a]These figures are calculated on the following assumptions: those that estimated spending between $0 and $1,000 spent $500; the $1,001–$5,000 category equals $3,000; the $5,001–$10,000 category equals $7,500; and the $10,000+ category equals $12,500.

two, the Central Vermont Public Service Corporation, Vermont's largest utility, and the Vermont League of Cities and Towns, reported spending more than $10,000 in all five sessions. Four other groups, the American Petroleum Institute, Planned Parenthood, the Vermont Chamber of Commerce, and the Vermont Ski Association, reported spending over $10,000 in the last four sessions we looked at in detail: 1981, 1983, 1987, and 1989. It is noteworthy that no agricultural groups, with the possible exception of the Tobacco Institute, were big spenders in any of the four sessions. Associated Industries of Vermont reported spending more than $10,000 in 1983, 1987, and 1989.

Clearly the amount and range of interest groups spending over $10,000 in 1989 (see Table 12.5) demonstrates the varied character of Vermont's interest-group system. "High tech" (IBM), utilities (Central Vermont Public Service Corporation and Green Mountain Power), communications (AT&T), transportation (Central Vermont Railroad), professional groups (the Vermont State Medical Society), business (Associated Industries of Vermont, the Vermont Chamber of Commerce), good government (Common Cause, the Vermont League of Cities and Towns), and other nonprofit public-interest groups (Planned Parenthood, Vermont Low Income Advocacy)—all registered in the cohort that spent more than $10,000 in 1987 and 1989. Even a narrowly defined single-interest group such as the Tobacco Institute appeared in this category. Vermont Seat, which lobbied for a statewide seat-belt law, spent over $10,000 in 1987. There truly has been a proliferation of interests playing the game in Montpelier.[23]

What Do the Legislators Think of Interest Groups and Lobbyists?

We surveyed the 1987–88 session of the legislature to determine the impressions the lawmakers themselves have of interest-group activity in Montpelier Table 12.6).[24]

23. Although there has been a sharp increase in the number of public relations firms lobbying in Vermont, contract lobbying, although increasing in significance, is still not a dominant element. John Downs, a highly experienced observer of Vermont politics and a lawyer who began lobbying in Montpelier in 1949, says lobbying in Vermont is conducted primarily on a "cost per time" basis and that "the days of six-figure incomes for contract lobbyists have yet to be realized."

24. A questionnaire was hand delivered to the legislature with a stamped, self-addressed envelope. Although there was no follow-up, 121 (two-thirds) of the total membership in both houses responded. This excellent return rate not only validates the

Table 12.5.   Who Spends the Most? Interest Groups Reporting Spending of over $10,000: Selected Years, 1977–1989

	1977	1981	1983	1987	1989
Central Vermont Public Service Corp.	x	x	x	x	x
Vermont League of Cities & Towns	x	x	x	x	x
American Petroleum Institute		x	x	x	x
Planned Parenthood		x	x	x	x
Vermont Chamber of Commerce		x	x	x	x
Vermont Ski Areas Assn		x	x	x	x
Associated Industries of Vermont			x	x	x
Green Mountain Power		x		x	x
AT&T and affiliates				x	x
Central Vermont Railway				x	x
Common Cause				x	x
Eckerd Family Youth Alternatives Inc.				x	x
IBM				x	x
National Federation of Independent Businesses				x	x
Tobacco Institute				x	x
Traffic Safety Now Inc.				x	x
Vermont Low Income Advocacy				x	x
Vermont State Medical Society				x	x
Vermont Natural Resources Council			x		x
Motion Picture Assn		x			x
American Insurance Assn					x
Bank of New England					x
Blue Cross and Blue Shield of Vermont					x
Bombardier Credit Inc.					x
Central Vermont Landfill Inc.					x
Champlain Pipeline Inc.					x

Source: Compiled from raw data in the archives of the Vermont Secretary of State.

When legislators were asked to rate the influence of interest groups in the recent past, the Vermont Natural Resources Council, the Vermont League of Cities and Towns, and the Vermont Chamber of Commerce

study (checks were made to ensure that the returns were representative of major cohorts in the legislature) but also indicates the concern with the question of interest groups in this (the 1988) half of the 1987–88 session. Also important was a new and much stronger lobbyist control bill that had been introduced in the session studied.

Table 12.6. How Vermont Legislators Ranked the Interest Groups (N = 121)

The Top Dozen Interest Groups Ranked on Question I	Question I Influence This Term				Question II Influence in General			
	Mentioned			Influence Index[a]	Mentioned			Influence Index
	1st	2nd	3rd		1st	2nd	3rd	
Vermont League of Cities & Towns	24	11	6	100	19	9	8	83
Vermont Natural Resources Council	17	18	11	98	25	12	8	107
Vermont Chamber of Commerce	5	12	7	44	13	16	8	79
Vermont Education Assn	7	3	8	35	6	7	6	38
Associated Industries of Vermont	4	9	4	34	6	10	8	46
Farm Bureau	5	3	9	30	2	6	0	18
The "Administration"	5	6	3	30	3	1	1	12
The Alliance for the Mentally Ill	4	3	1	19	Not mentioned			—
"Utilities"	4	2	1	17	4	4	2	22
Vermont Public Interest Research Group	4	0	2	14	5	3	2	23
COVE, The Coalition of Vermont Elders	3	1	2	13	2	1	1	9
The "Governor"	4	0	1	13	Not mentioned			—

Source: Authors' 1988 survey of legislators.

Note: Legislators were asked: "Please identify the three interest groups you feel are presently most influential in this legislative session" (Question I) or "the state in general" (Question II). Some 121 of the 180 Vermont legislators are included in the study.

[a]Figured by multiplying the number of first mentions by 3, the number of second mentions by 2, and the number of third mentions by 1.

stood out. When asked to rate the most influential of interest groups in the 1987–88 legislature, two of these, the Vermont League of Cities and Towns and the Vermont Natural Resources Council, outdistanced all the rest—probably because some important bills in the second half of the session were of interest to these groups, including a "growth bill" that included statewide land-use controls.

Several groups named by legislators as most influential were not included in the big-spender category. Associated Industries of Vermont and the Farm Bureau were mentioned in both sets of responses. It is interesting that they appear adjacent to each other in the rankings on influence, well down the list. Their scores regarding influence in the 1988 session were very close, but the AIV's index of influence scores is more than double that of the Farm Bureau (46–18) when it comes to assessing their general influence over time.

These data do not indicate that Democrats and Republicans disagree significantly on who peddles the most influence in the legislature—with one exception. The exception is that party members tend to list the sources of pressure that they are most likely to oppose as being most powerful. Thus, in the 1988 session, Democrats listed the Vermont League of Cities and Towns, which opposed the growth bill that was the key feature of the Democratic legislative agenda, as more influential than the Vermont Natural Resources Council, which led the support for the growth bill. The Republicans, who strongly attacked the growth bill, did the opposite. Associated Industries of Vermont was ranked sixth by the Republicans and third by the Democrats. The "administration" and the "governor" were ranked fifth and sixth by the Republicans (the governor was a Democrat) and thirteenth and twelfth by the Democrats. The Vermont Education Association was ranked fourth by the Republicans and sixth by the Democrats. The Farm Bureau was ranked eighth by the Republicans and fourth by the Democrats. In every case, party members chose the group one would expect them to disagree with most as more influential.

Still, certain interest groups are not so closely affiliated with a single party that their affiliation seriously distorts perceptions of influence, although legislators are less apt to list as influential pressure groups organizations that do not "need" to lobby them (because there is a natural policy linkage between them).

RECENT DEVELOPMENTS

In 1990 a new lobbyist disclosure law was passed, making data-collecting for that year impossible because the law went into effect while the legislature was in session. Moreover, there are serious concerns about the consistency of the reporting. Vermont's Secretary of State, James Douglas, is worried about loopholes, and controversy has emerged over how to close them. The principal change in the new law is that actual dollar-figure spending amounts must be reported, instead of estimates by category.

Data for the 1991 session of the legislature, compiled by Vermont's highly respected Associated Press reporter Christopher Graff, indicate spending by 266 companies and 290 registered lobbyists at $1.6 million (see Table 12.7 for the top spenders).[25] This figure is not out of line in any important way with projections we might have made based on our figures from previous years.

Over the last two decades, there has been a sharp rise in interest-group activity in Montpelier. At the same time, Democratic strength in the legislature has increased as well. As far as Vermont is concerned, however, the hypothesis that strong interest groups are less at home in systems featuring strong parties needs qualification. At the beginning of this chapter we suggested that we would place new interest-group activity in Vermont in an overall framework of political development. Such a framework may suggest how to resolve this dilemma.

First, the rise of competitive parties at the ballot box in the *postmodern* period cannot be equated with the old-style political competition featured in the *industrial* period. Second, the rise of a disciplined party system in the Vermont legislature between 1985 and 1988 is a historical anomaly. The Speaker of the House, Ralph Wright, and his majority leader, Paul Poirier, developed an effective working relationship. Most observers of Vermont politics see the rise of Democratic cohesion as a product of this personalistic power center. It is not a systemic outgrowth of Vermont's political culture—in fact, it is contrary to it. Most of the recent Republican cohesion is related to a reaction to Wright's leadership.

25. Christopher Graff, "1.6 Million Goes to Lobbying," *Burlington Free Press*, July 26, 1991, 1B.

Table 12.7. Big Spenders Among Vermont Interest Groups, by Amount Spent, 1991

Interest Group	Amount Spent	Percent of Total
Business / industry	$675,498	39
Insurance	216,035	12
Gambling / liquor / tobacco	183,543	11
Utilities	146,886	9
Transportation	115,222	7
Social services	114,343	7
Misc. (including recreation, education)	62,671	3
Real estate	53,011	3
Municipalities	47,663	3
Environment	33,875	2
Agriculture	31,503	2
Unions	28,679	2

Source: Vermont Secretary of State.

Wright himself was raised in the Boston, Massachusetts, area and is a Marine Corps veteran who exults in (and often brags about) his capacity to organize and "produce results." He came to Vermont with values fashioned on big city streets. In short, he articulates perfectly the litany of the old, urban-style political boss. This ideological framework of urban industrialism (the "I" culture) is supported in Vermont by political elites who believe that a trip through the urban-industrial era with its attendant political culture is preordained and natural. They see both a disciplined party system and the rise of interest-group politics as part of the same scenario, as a necessary (if not pleasant) wave of the future.

We, on the contrary, argue that this state of affairs is not generic and in fact countervails the dominant thesis of Vermont's politics as it is currently unfolding. Our thinking is based on the number of kinds of interest groups in the new system. Interests as such have become dramatically diffused, not concentrated. Indeed, interests come and go in the Vermont legislature today as never before, reflecting the conditions of high-tech society whereby all groups (political, economic, and social) nimbly adjust their activities to match current conditions. The growing centralism of state policy-making over the last thirty years (which is itself antithetical) has simply provided a centralized arena to draw these groups into battle. But the high-tech and democratic character of Vermont politics means that so many new groups are forming every year in so many different sectors of the public weal that it seems likely the interest-group system *as a system* will fall of its own weight.

In short, Vermont's leaders are forever trying to drive the square peg of urban-industrial ("I" culture) politics into the round hole of postmodern techno-democratic politics. Most of them were *educated* in the second-wave, interest-group pluralistic tradition. Most of them, and also a majority of the "attentive public" and opinion-making elite in Vermont, were born and *raised* elsewhere, many in America's largest cities. Their fundamentally conservative outlook accepts and defines interest groups as a necessary evil (i.e., contrary to Vermont's "M" culture traditions) that (lamentably) must be accepted by "realists" as Vermont works it way back through the urban-industrial mind-set on our way to the future.

But if the rise of interest-group politics is seen, rather, as a product of the deconcentration of society and the enabling power of postmodern information technology, it can be defined in "M" culture terms and promoted as a positive good. Our prediction is that Vermont will, for the near term, be plagued by this tension. Its leaders want to go one way—backward—but its society is determined to move forward. If our view is correct, the concentration of power in Montpelier will be reversed. The number of interest groups will continue to increase, and their capacity to organize and bring influence to bear will also improve, but be directed at a wider variety of substate arenas. This will mean that as the twenty-first century proceeds, the pressure-group *paradigm* itself (a product of the old centrist, urban-industrial condition), which has dominated political science over the last half-century, will melt away as information technology decentralizes and then democratizes the policy-making process.

13

West Virginia: Coal and the New West Virginia Politics

James R. Oxendale and Allan S. Hammock

Throughout much of West Virginia's history, extractive industries have been at the center of the state's economic, social, and political systems. Only three counties in West Virginia have neither coal nor natural gas (yet even those three have significant timbering). The most significant of the extractive industries is coal. West Virginia and coal are inextricably intertwined, a fact that prompted Sarah McCally Morehouse to assert that West Virginia was a state "run by a single industry—coal."[1] The present political system cannot be understood without some familiarity with the evolution of the coal industry in the state.

With the discovery of large tracts of coal and gas in West Virginia in the latter half of the nineteenth century, representatives from numerous eastern firms came to the state and purchased either complete titles to millions of acres in the mineral-rich areas of the state or at least the mineral rights to such lands.[2] Extracting the coal from West Virginia was not easy. The state lacked a sufficient transportation network because the terrain in the coal areas was nearly impassable, and, perhaps most important, West Virginia did not have sufficient population to mine all the coal the industry needed. This population shortage prompted the state to allow Consolidation Coal Company and the New River Coal Company to pay for a state commissioner of immigration to represent West Virginia in Europe and in

1. Sarah McCally Morehouse, *State Politics, Parties, and Policy* (New York: Holt, Rinehart & Winston, 1981), 113.

2. John A. Williams, *West Virginia: A Bicentennial History* (New York: W. W. Norton, 1976), 105–7. See also John A. Williams, *West Virginia and the Captains of Industry* (Morgantown: West Virginia University Foundation Press, 1976).

the South to attract coal miners.[3] Thousands of non-English-speaking Europeans and southern blacks were imported into West Virginia to work the mines.

In importing workers, most coal operators constructed entire communities in which the company owned everything: churches, homes, stores, medical services, law enforcement, and so on. According to the federal government Coal Commission of 1925, in 1920 some 80 percent of West Virginia's coal miners lived in company-owned houses.[4] Such a situation had an enormous impact on political developments in West Virginia because it allowed the companies to control the political systems of these areas. Coal-company power was not seriously challenged until the New Deal permitted unions to organize the state's coal miners, thereby creating conditions that allowed miners to compete with the industry for political influence at the state and local level.

No one disputes that the coal industry dominated West Virginia's political institutions for most of its history. In many states this is not unheard of. But a remarkable fact about extractive industries, such as coal and timbering and to a lesser degree gas-drilling, is their provocative nature. They generate conflict because they are destructive to the environment and because, realistically, their destructiveness can be diminished only by government action. Government regulation increases the cost of doing business, and therefore the industries attempt to inhibit or reduce government interference with their operations.

The most destructive of the state's industries is coal. Coal mining, be it strip or deep, is land-scarring. Coal mining also produces the omnipresent slag pile or slate dump that, aside from being aesthetically obnoxious, slowly releases poisonous fumes into the atmosphere. In some instances these slag piles pose even more immediate danger. In 1972 at Buffalo Creek, an 80,000-ton slag pile released 21 million cubic feet of water that killed 125 people, destroyed 1,000 homes, and caused $50 million in property damage.[5] The Pittston Company slag pile was unregulated. Indeed, the State Department of Energy is not noted for its vigorous enforcement of even the lenient West Virginia laws. At the time of the Buffalo Creek

3. Evelyn L. Harris and Frank J. Krebs, *From Humble Beginnings* (Charleston: West Virginia Labor History Publishing Fund Committee, 1960), 19–20.

4. Homer L. Morris, *The Plight of the Bituminous Coal Miner* (Philadelphia: University of Pennsylvania Press, 1934), 86.

5. Neil R. Peirce, *The Border South States* (New York: W. W. Norton, 1975), 151; Gerald M. Stern, *The Buffalo Creek Disaster* (New York: Random House, 1976), ix.

disaster there were hundreds of such piles in the coalfields, and most continue to exist.[6]

Coal mining has been, and to some extent remains, a labor-intensive industry. It is also a dangerous industry. More than 20,000 miners have been killed in West Virginia mines in the twentieth century, and that figure does not include the additional thousands who have died of various lung diseases directly attributable to coal mining or the tens of thousands who have been crippled or maimed by this work.[7] Such an industry clearly invites political conflict, because many of the dangers of coal mining can be lessened by government action.

A good example of how difficult it can be to improve mine safety is found in the case of rock-dusting in the mines. William Graebner's *Coal-Mining Safety in the Progressive Period* notes that, by the second decade of the twentieth century, mining experts in the United States and Europe agreed that the best and cheapest method to prevent coal-dust explosions in the mines was rock-dusting.[8] One might assume that such a consensus would result in legislation to mandate this inexpensive and lifesaving procedure, but it did not. Even though legislation was introduced annually in the state legislature, it got nowhere until 1953. When the legislature finally ordered rock-dusting, however, it was purely cosmetic because the federal government had already required such a practice beginning in 1952.[9]

Another key political issue regarding mining has been taxation. Most states or nations that have extractive industries impose severance taxes based on the fact that extraction reduces the value of land rather than increasing it. When the natural resource is depleted the industry moves on. In extracting coal there are additional costs. Water systems, highways, topsoil, scenic beauty, and the health of the society are to varying degrees damaged by coal mining.

There was no serious move to impose a severance tax in West Virginia until 1953. Governor William Marland, in his first address to the legislature, proposed a 10-cent-a-ton tax on coal. The proponents of the tax looked formidable: the United Mine Workers (John L. Lewis, leader of the

6. According to Brian Long of the West Virginia Department of Natural Resources, in 1990 there were approximately 150 coal refuse impoundments in the coalfields.

7. West Virginia Department of Mines, *Annual Report and Directory of Mines* (Charleston, W.Va., 1982), 41–42.

8. William Graebner, *Coal-Mining Safety in the Progressive Period* (Lexington: University of Kentucky Press, 1976), 43–47.

9. Howard B. Lee, *My Appalachia* (Parsons, W.Va.: McClean, 1971).

mine workers, testified before the legislature), the AFL, and the CIO, the West Virginia Education Association, and the seven-member state congressional delegation lobbied for the tax.[10] The declared opponents consisted of the coal operators, the Chamber of Commerce, the Republican minority in the legislature, and several newspapers, including the influential *Charleston Gazette*. By a 14–4 vote, the tax proposal was defeated in the Senate Finance Committee, demonstrating the power of the coal industry in the legislature and the relative weakness of labor as a political force in the state. Not until 1970 was a modest severance tax imposed.

The severance-tax battle of 1953 showed the extent of coal-industry power in both parties in West Virginia. Until 1940, the Democratic party was quite conservative, so naturally the two traditionally oriented Democratic governors from 1933 to 1940 implemented New Deal policies only grudgingly and openly resented the growth of unions in the state. They were the last Democratic governors to openly voice such opinions. The spread of unions through the coalfields totally changed the nature of the Democratic party in the state, and by the early 1940s a new political coalition, which eventually became known as the Statehouse Group, was established.[11]

The Statehouse Group had no particular policy agenda. Its primary purpose was to gain and remain in power, which it did through an extended patronage system and by placating both of the main players in state politics—labor and management. This was relatively easy to do (except during such incidents as the severance-tax battle) because the unions in the state promoted no social program. The United Mine Workers (UMW), a conservative union, became increasingly friendly with management, and for the most part its only political concerns were unemployment compensation and worker compensation laws.[12] The UMW took little action to reform the environmental aspects of mining, such as water purity; the extremely low tax rates on the industry; the state's regressive tax system; or the lack of basic public services and educational facilities in the coalfields. Such issues were occasionally raised in the *UMW Journal*, but they were never top political priorities either in lobbying the legislature or in securing commitments from candidates.

10. Paul F. Lutz, "Governor Marland's Political Suicide: The Severance Tax," *West Virginia History* 19 (October 1957), 16.

11. John H. Fenton, *Politics in the Border States* (New Orleans, La.: House Press, 1957), 87–99.

12. Peirce, *Border South States*, 169.

The insensitivity to the safety aspects of mining on the part of the UMW leadership reached its peak in the aftermath of the Farmington disaster. On November 20, 1968, an explosion at the Consolidation Mine No. 9 at Farmington, West Virginia, killed seventy-eight miners. Tony Boyle, then UMW president, showed up at the site and praised Consol as a safety-conscious company, ignoring the fact that the Farmington mine had been cited numerous times for violating a simple antiexplosion requirement—essentially insufficient rock-dusting.[13] Boyle's cavalier treatment of the safety issue was probably the event that galvanized the political forces in West Virginia seeking change.

EVOLUTION OF INTEREST-GROUP POLITICS IN WEST VIRGINIA

Historians, politicians, and lobbyists generally agree that the traditional interest-group elite in West Virginia comprises coal, oil and gas, railroad, and manufacturing interests. These sectors were predominant in all branches of the state government. John Hurd, president of the West Virginia Chamber of Commerce, noted in an interview with the authors that before 1960 the number of permanent lobbyists in the legislature was rarely more than eight or ten and that the undisputed leaders were the representatives from the West Virginia Coal Association, the West Virginia Railroad Association, the West Virginia Oil and Gas Association, and the West Virginia Manufacturers Association. These people had close relationships with the legislative leadership—the Speaker of the House of Delegates and the president of the Senate—through whom policies satisfactory to these interests were worked out. The relationship among these six has been described as "clublike."[14] In addition to these association representatives, particular industries, such as coal, railroads, manufacturing, oil, and gas, as well as banks and utilities, had representatives at the legislature, but these were not generally full-time lobbyists.

Labor unions also had permanent representation in the chambers, and according to most observers their impact was not insignificant. Over the years, the AFL-CIO and the UMW were the dominant labor groups in the

13. Bret Hume, *Death and the Mines* (New York: Grossman, 1971), 15–16.
14. Interview with John Hurd, president of the West Virginia Chamber of Commerce, December 7, 1987.

state. More recently, the West Virginia Education Association has emerged as another important labor organization. Between the mid-1960s and the mid-1970s, West Virginia underwent major changes in interest-group activity. Like much of the nation, West Virginia was in the midst of significant social and political change in an era punctuated by consumerism, environmentalism, and populism. The political establishment was totally unprepared for the movements that hit the state in the late 1960s and early 1970s. The two major reform groups were the Miners for Democracy, which sought to oust the traditional leaders of the United Mine Workers, and the Black Lung Association, which sought to provide compensation to the victims of pneumoconiosis, a chronic lung disease among coal miners.

Reforms started ordinarily enough. In 1967 the legislature passed a relatively strong strip-mine bill, and throughout 1967 and 1968 there was agitation for other environmental legislation, stronger coal-mine safety standards, and compensation for lung disease. The critical point was reached with the Farmington disaster of November 1968. The entombment of seventy-eight miners in the Consol mine, and the Boyle statement, were the catalysts for a major reformulation of coal policy.

The following year, 1969, was turbulent. The Black Lung Association closed virtually every mine in the state and filled the state capitol building with miners while the legislature debated a black-lung-disease bill. Essentially out of fear, the legislature passed it. Late in the year, the president of the UMW ordered the assassination of Jock Yablonski, his reformist rival in the union, an act of barbarism that ended Boyle's leadership and the close working relationship of the union with the state business and political establishment. The traditional interest groups were caught off guard by these events. For decades, political activities had been channeled through a tightly controlled union hierarchy or through local political organizations with their ties to economic elites. The political structure of West Virginia was not ready for middle-class reformers, not to mention a popular-based mass movement. The assault on the capital, and the democratization of the UMW, were novel and ominous. Over a three-year period, coal and other business interests suffered two costly defeats in the legislature: a moratorium on surface mining in counties that had no strip mines, and stringent and punitive standards for surface mining; and the imposition of a severance tax on coal. These were unambiguous losses in an institution that had for decades largely shared the same political views as the coal industry. The business community in general, but most decidedly the coal industry, learned from these defeats. They responded to the new political realities by employing the tools that helped them function efficiently and profitably in their business environment—they mobilized their organizational skills and money to counter future onslaughts by the state's populist groups.

CONTEMPORARY INTEREST-GROUP ACTIVITY

Interest-group activity has grown considerably in recent years. Since the coal industry losses of the late 1960s and early 1970s, there has been growth in the number and types of groups operating in the state. The number of organizations lobbying the legislature nearly doubled in fifteen years (see Table 13.1). Growth has been the greatest among businesses, with general business lobbies nearly doubling (from 32 to 55).

The coal industry had more than a fourfold increase—from six groups to eighteen. Health and medicine tripled in number. (This was undoubtedly due to issues of cost containment in hospitals and to funding the public-employee insurance and the Medicaid program.) The public-interest category had significant growth, but it includes an array of groups ranging from the Humane Society to Citizens Action and is not comparable to the growth of the coal lobby, for example. Three categories had fewer representatives: oil and gas, women's issues, and religious groups. The decline in religious and womens' groups probably reflects a lull in the abortion debate, while the decline in oil and gas has no particular meaning because the increase in utilities probably more than compensates for any loss in that category—the two groups are quite related. Just as the number of groups has increased, so have the costs of lobbying the legislature. Table 13.2 sets out the expenditures declared by registered lobbyists during the 1977 and 1987 sessions of the state legislature.

The cost of lobbying has far outpaced the increase of lobbying organizations. The number of lobbying groups has doubled over the fifteen years, but the amounts spent have increased fourfold. Business expenses kept pace with the increase, but their expenditures would skyrocket if the disclosure requirements included salaries or living expenses for the lobbyists. No other groups come close to spending the amounts spent by businesses.

Although groups are not monolithic in their approach to the legislature, harmony rather than conflict is the general pattern among the state's businesses. The economy of West Virginia is relatively homogeneous. Nearly

Table 13.1. Registered Lobbying Groups, West Virginia, 1976 and 1991

Type of Group	No. of Organizations Represented	
	1976	1991
General business	32	55
Utilities	13	27
Industry	11	30
Health and medicine	10	30
Oil and gas	9	8
Labor	9	11
Education	9	9
Insurance	8	20
Banking and finance	8	8
Public employees	7	8
Religious	5	4
Women	5	3
Government	3	9
Public interest	2	10
Railroads	2	3
Professional associations	1	13
Gambling	1	1
Timber / land	1	5
Agriculture	1	1
Press	1	1
Elderly	1	2
Environment	0	2
Political party	0	1
Total	140	279

Source: Data on file with the Clerk of the West Virginia Senate and the West Virginia Secretary of State.

all of southern and central West Virginia is dominated by extractive industries, coal or oil and gas. Other sections, except for the eastern counties, are oriented toward chemicals, heavy industry, metals, glass, or manufacturing. In many counties, two or three basic industries are the lifeblood of the area, so retailers, banks, insurance agencies, lawyers, accountants, and so on, find their economic fates linked to coal, chemicals, timbering, oil

Table 13.2. Lobbying Expenditures, West Virginia, 1976 and 1991

Type of group	1976	1991
Business	$25,391	$106,424
Labor	2,152	3,495
Education	1,289	4,646
Government employees	1,146	1,411
Agriculture	—	3,968
Government	—	13,713
Others	500	900
Total	30,478	133,557

Source: Data on file with the Clerk of the West Virginia Senate and the West Virginia Ethics Commission.

and gas, steel, or a dominant manufacturing plant. Thus, while business lobbies have proliferated, as a result of the homogeneity of the state, open conflict among them is the exception rather than the norm.

This is not to imply that divisions do not occur among business groups. Certainly, there is potential for significant conflict between the extractive industries and the tourist industry, since tourism in West Virginia is based on outdoor activities, but this has yet to occur, because the tourist sector is so poorly organized. In the 1991 session of the legislature, coal had thirty-three lobbyists registered. The state's ski and whitewater-rafting industries were not represented at the legislature.

An example of modest intrabusiness conflict can be found in the banking community. As in many states, on the issue of branch banking, larger banks differ with smaller banks, and these differences are reflected in distinct points of view being presented to the legislature. With the recent triumph of the larger banks, and the introduction of branch banking, all banking groups have united and are now a powerful presence in West Virginia politics.

One of the more fascinating intraindustry divisions occurred in 1985 between two groups that are ordinarily allies: the coal and railroad industries. Coal companies, which face stiff competition in both their domestic and foreign sales, charged that the railroads were abusing the rail bed monopoly they enjoyed in delivering coal to the eastern seaboard. They did this, it was argued, by charging rates far beyond the cost of haulage. To remedy this, the coal companies proposed that competition be permitted on tracks that passed through the coalfields. The railroads clearly did not want to share an extremely lucrative market. Such a profound split between these two giants is rare—and some would say unprecedented. The battle was joined, but in the end there was no contest. The railroads faced united opposition from all groups interested in the health of the mining industry. In the final vote, the railroads lost in the Senate 34 to 0 and in the House 71 to 27.

The coal industry clearly won this battle. The popular and scholarly literature leads one to believe that the coal industry won this battle because it is practically hegemonic in its legislative power. To ascertain whether this perception was shared by legislators, a survey of members of the West Virginia legislature was conducted in December 1987. Each legislator was asked to rate the degree of influence interest groups had on politics and policy in the state House of Delegates and Senate. Presumably, if coal were as dominant in the 1980s as it has been throughout most of the state's history, organizations associated with the coal industry should be rated by legislators as among the top influential groups in the legislature.

At first glance the data (Table 13.3) are surprising. Coal does not turn out to be the most influential interest operating in the legislature. Of the forty-five different groups evaluated by legislators, only three are directly involved in the mining sector: the United Mine Workers, the Appalachian Power Company (which controls numerous coal mines), and the West Virginia Coal Association. The UMW (ranked seventh), Appalachian Power (ninth), and the Coal Association (tenth) are superseded by such organizations as the National Rifle Association, the West Virginia School Service Personnel Association, and the West Virginia Federation of Labor (ranked 1, 2, and 3, respectively).

Three other groups in the top ten are labor organizations: the West Virginia Education Association (WVEA, fourth), the West Virginia Trades Council (fifth), and the Building and Construction Trades Council (eighth). The WVEA obviously has an agenda beyond labor questions, but most of its energies are devoted to bread-and-butter issues for teachers. Rounding out the top ten is the West Virginia Bankers Association (sixth). Thus, six of the top ten groups are labor organizations.

If one expands the analysis in the table to the top fifteen groups, the list includes the West Virginia Chamber of Commerce (eleventh), the West Virginia Manufacturers Association (twelfth), the West Virginia Hospital Association (fourteenth), and the West Virginia Auto and Truck Dealers Association (fifteenth). Of the top fifteen organizations, seven represent business interests, six represent organized labor, and two were single-issue

Table 13.3.   West Virginia Legislators' Perceptions of Interest-Group Influence in the West Virginia Legislature, 1987

Interest Group	Mean Score[a]	Rank Order
National Rifle Assn	4.016	1
W.Va. School Service Personnel Assn	3.842	2
W.Va. Labor Federation	3.649	3
W.Va. Education Assn	3.550	4
W.Va. Trades Council	3.508	5
W.Va. Bankers Assn	3.491	6
United Mine Workers	3.466	7
Building & Construction Trades Council	3.406	8
Appalachian Power Co.	3.344	9
W.Va. Coal Assn	3.333	10
W.Va. Chamber of Commerce	3.288	11
W.Va. Manufacturers Assn	3.203	12
W.Va. Surface Mining & Reclamation Assn	3.189	13
W.Va. Hospital Assn	3.122	14
W.Va. Auto & Truck Dealers Assn	3.052	15
W.Va. Farm Bureau Inc.	2.982	16
American Federation of State, County & Municipal Employees	2.967	17
W.Va. Retailers Assn	2.910	18
W.Va. Federation of Teachers	2.807	19
Fraternal Order of Police	2.894	20
W.Va. Medical Assn	2.850	21
W.Va. Oil & Gas Assn	2.796	22
Consolidation Coal Co.	2.722	23
W.Va. Wholesalers Assn	2.706	24
W.Va. Assn of Counties	2.666	25
W.Va. Municipal League	2.661	26
W.Va. Assn of Elementary School Principals	2.603	27
W.Va. for Life	2.602	28
League of Women Voters (W.Va.)	2.601	29
W.Va. Motor Truck Assn Inc.	2.518	30
W.Va. Beverage Distributors	2.482	31
W.Va. Citizen Action Group	2.362	32
Blue Cross and Blue Shield of W.Va.	2.333	33
W.Va. Safety Council	2.285	34
National Organization for Women	2.250	35
W.Va. Dental Assn	2.222	36

Table 13.3. *Continued*

Interest Group	Mean Score[a]	Rank Order
W.Va. Railroad Assn	2.222	37
W.Va. Consumer Finance Assn	2.160	38
United Transportation Union	2.150	39
W.Va. Highlands Conservancy Inc.	2.037	40
Common Cause of W.Va.	2.035	41
W.Va. Funeral Directors Assn	2.017	42
W.Va. Cable Television Assn	1.946	43
The Tobacco Institute	1.865	44
W.Va. Tobacco Council	1.678	45

Source: Authors' survey of legislators, December 1987.

Note: The survey was developed in cooperation with the select panel of members of the West Virginia House of Delegates and Senate drawn from both the northern and the southern regions of the state. Each panel member was asked to review a complete list of registered lobbyists and to indicate which names on the list ought to be included on a short list of important or influential lobbyists in West Virginia. The procedure enabled us to pare the original list from 190 to 45. The list of 45 was then sent to every member of the legislature (N = 134). Sixty legislators (44.7%) responded.

[a]The mean score is the average of scores of legislators, rating the degree of influence of each interest group from 1 to 5, with 1 = "very little influence" and 5 = "a great deal of influence."

groups, the NRA and the Hospital Association. (The Hospital Association is interested in more than a single issue, but its focus rarely extends beyond that which directly affects hospital operations.)

The data indicate that the top groups are associated with either business or labor, with an indeterminate advantage given to labor with six of the top ten groups. But do the results reflect reality? One of the most debated issues in the study of state and local politics is whether reputed power corresponds with the actual exercise of power. Do these labor groups exercise the power the survey would attribute to them? There is no unambiguous yes or no, but it is doubtful that the West Virginia Farm Bureau, ranked sixteenth in influence, is more influential than the West Virginia Medical Association, ranked twenty-first; the West Virginia Oil and Gas Association, ranked twenty-second; the Consolidation Coal Company, ranked twenty-third (the largest coal producer in the state); or the West

Virginia Beverage Distributors, ranked thirty-second, which has rarely, if ever, lost a battle in the legislature.

The survey results lead one to conclude that labor unions are powerful, independent players in legislative politics, but the facts do not necessarily support this conclusion. Throughout the late 1970s and early 1980s labor's top legislative priority was collective-bargaining rights for public employees. The WVEA and the State Federation of Labor (AFL-CIO) expended all of their political resources in these attempts, yet the legislature never came close to passing such a bill, even absent a right-to-strike clause. Eventually labor accepted defeat on this issue, and collective bargaining is no longer even debated in the legislature. If the six labor groups were among the most influential in the legislature, they should be able to put a limited collective-bargaining bill on the governor's desk.

On the other hand, labor has had some legislative successes. One of its major victories, especially for the WVEA, was getting the legislature to authorize a referendum on statewide property-tax reappraisal, in which the voters overwhelmingly gave their approval. Reappraisal would greatly benefit education and by all accounts force the major landowners in the state— coal companies, railroads, oil and gas drillers, and timbering enterprises— to pay taxes that reflected market values. However, success in the legislature did not result in implementation of the reappraisal. The traditional power groups, through their influence in the county courthouses and in the executive branch, by propaganda efforts through the media, and in grassroots organizing, have prevented enforcement of this important reform.

The influence configuration among contemporary interest groups in West Virginia appears confusing. The legislative survey indicates that labor is a significant force in legislative policy-making, and that is undoubtedly true. The results, however, significantly understate the influence of business interests in the legislature.

LOBBYISTS AND LOBBYING TACTICS

One relatively recent lobbying tactic in West Virginia has been the institutionalization of coalition activity. Beginning with the agitational activities of the late 1960s, organized labor formed a loose coalition of labor groups known as the United Labor Committee (UNLC). The UNLC became a formal organization in the 1970s, meeting every Monday morning when the legislature is in session to formulate their legislative agenda, map out their lobbying strategies, and share perspectives on legislators and legislation. Throughout the remainder of the year, they meet quarterly.

The United Labor Committee has its business counterpart in the Business and Industry Council (BIC). In 1981, under the leadership of the West Virginia Coal Association and the West Virginia Chamber of Commerce, BIC was formed. The purpose of BIC was to "[provide] a means for the business and industry community to consolidate and coordinate efforts regarding legislative, governmental and regulatory matters in this state."[15] BIC was originally composed of state trade associations, but in recent years corporations have been permitted membership. Its members include:

Appalachian Power Co.
Builders Assn of W. Va.
C&P Telephone Co.
Cecil I. Walker Machinery Co.
Charleston Chamber of
   Commerce & Devel.
Contractors Assn of W.Va.
Flexible Pavement Council of
   W.Va.
Merit Enterprises
W.Va. Cable Television Assn
W.Va. Coal Assn
W.Va. Forestry Assn
W.Va. Manufacturers Assn
W.Va. Motor Truck Assn
W.Va. Petroleum Council
W.Va. Retailers Assn
W.Va. Soft Drink Assn

Associated Builders & Contractors
Builders Supply Assn of W.Va.
Cannelton Holding Co.
Charles Ryan Assoc.
Consolidation Coal Co.
CNG Transmission Co.
Indep. Oil & Gas Assn of W.Va.
Tri-State Coal Operators
W.Va. Chamber of Commerce
W.Va. Consumer Finance Assn
W.Va. Hospital Assn
W.Va. Mining & Reclamation
   Assn
W.Va. Oil & Nat. Gas Assn
W.Va. Petroleum Marketers &
   Convenience Store Assn
W.Va. Self-Insurers Assn
W.Va. State Medical Assn

According to John Hurd, executive director of the West Virginia Chamber of Commerce, BIC's founders had two immediate goals: (1) to provide a united business front to the legislature and governor and (2) "to give recognition to those who supported the business philosophy."[16] BIC fulfills these goals in two ways. While BIC is not a registered lobbying organiza-

15. West Virginia Business and Industry Council, *1987 Ratings and Analysis of the West Virginia Legislature* (Charleston, W.Va.: W.Va. BIC, n.d.), 1.
16. Interview with Hurd.

tion, it is actively involved in the legislative process. During the session, BIC members, who are lobbyists for their individual trade associations, meet weekly to plan strategy and decide which issues to cooperate on. Occasionally they assign individual lobbyists to selected legislators in order to make use of friendships, campaign supporters, or constituency relationships. Clearly such a strategy gives the business community, at least those in BIC, another important contact with regard to issues and personalities in every legislative session.

Its second major function is to rate legislators on legislative issues that are important to business. This rating system is important because the business community uses it to determine PAC and individual contributions to political campaigns. According to a former BIC chairman, when the ratings first came out in 1981, several legislators called wanting to know why they had scored so low. Since then, members sometimes call to ask whether a given vote will be included in the ratings.

One possible indication of BIC's influence, or at least the influence of business, is a comparison of the average support score for BIC in its first rating with later support scores. In 1981 the average support score for BIC was 47 percent in the House and Senate. In 1991 the Senate average was 56 percent and the House average was 73 percent.[17] While the Senate change was moderate, the House increase was dramatic. It is likely that BIC has been a major contributor in this change through its influence in the legislative and electoral activities of the business community.

Other lobbying tactics employed in West Virginia are typical of legislatures everywhere: wining and dining (legislative banquets are held almost nightly throughout the session) and the more respected though not necessarily more effective information-providing functions of lobbying. Most larger groups employ both tactics. For years the West Virginia Coal Association had three or four lobbyists working the legislature. The senior lobbyist was Ned "Big Daddy" Watson, a descendant of the founders of Consolidation Coal and former chairman of the House Judiciary Committee. Watson occupied the "Coal Suite" in one of the major hotels in Charleston. The suite apparently never closed during the legislative session. It was fitted with a well-stocked bar, food, and card tables and was a safe haven from the eyes of the press and the public.

In recent years, however, the Coal Association lobbyists are generally permanent employees of the association who specialize in health, tax, and operational aspects of mining. In interviews with lobbyists representing

17. W.Va. Business and Industry Council, *1987 Ratings*.

both management and labor, the coal lobby was mentioned by all as being especially effective. Clearly, the financial resources of the Coal Association are a major factor in its ability to provide a complete panoply of activities in its lobbying efforts. Probably no other groups come close to the expertise marshaled by this organization. Presently, interest groups are eschewing the traditional wheeler-dealer lobbyist and are contracting with public-relations or law firms to represent them before the legislature, or using in-house personnel who are experts at dealing with legislators. This is perhaps principally due to the conviction between 1988 and 1990 of two Senate presidents, a Senate majority leader, and West Virginia's only three-time elected governor for essentially shaking down lobbyists and campaign contributors.

A more ambiguous area of interest-group activity in the legislative process is in the hiring of staff and the use of outside counsel to draft legislation. Unlike the wealthier and more populous states, West Virginia's legislature has relatively few full-time employees, and its committees have no permanent legal staff. Therefore, the legislature routinely hires dozens of lawyers during the legislative session to serve as committee counsel or to work for the leadership. Frequently these attorneys represent major interests in the state and are thus in strategic positions to influence the wording of legislation that might affect their clients. For example, one of the most important law firms involved in influencing the legislature is Jackson & Kelly, whose attorneys have served as clerks of both chambers' judiciary committees.[18] Jackson & Kelly is the largest, most prestigious and most powerful law firm in the state. Among its clients are West Virginia Water Company, GTE, Cabot Corporation, B. F. Goodrich, Johns-Manville, Ernst & Whitney, Union Carbide, the West Virginia Coal Association, Beth Energy, Arch Mines, Ashland Oil, Consolidation Coal, Island Creek Coal, Westmoreland Coal, Cannelton Industries, Carbon Industries, General Motors, and Ford Motors.[19]

Occasionally such outside firms write major legislation. A significant example of this is a 1986 bill that radically restructured coal-mine safety and environmental enforcement in West Virginia. The bill created a new Department of Energy (essentially the old Department of Mines) and transferred most environmental enforcement to it from the Department of Natural Resources. The new law also removed a conflict-of-interest provision from the code, thereby permitting the Energy Department director to have

18. Hume, *Death and the Mines*, 125.
19. *Martindale & Hubbel Law Directory* (Summit, N.J.: Martindale & Hubbel, 1988), 7:1005B.

holdings in the mine or reclamation businesses. (The U.S. Department of Energy disallowed this provision, and a recent director had to divest his mining-related businesses.) Environmental and union groups opposed much of this legislation; the coal industry strongly supported it. According to a coal executive interviewed for this chapter, the bill made the department "more of a coal advocate than an industry antagonist." This bill was drafted by the Charleston law firm of Bowles, McDavid, Graff & Love. Among the Bowles clients are Ashland Oil, Bright of America, Cecil Walker Machinery Corporation, Exxon Corporation, Devon Energy, FMC, McJunkin Corporation, Monsanto Corporation, Midwest Corporation, NRM Petroleum, Peabody Coal, Sonat Exploration Company, Taywood Mining, Terry Eagle Mining, Southeastern Gas Company, and the West Virginia Mining & Reclamation Association.[20]

Another increasingly common tactic is the fostering of cooperation between previously antagonistic groups. Perhaps the most surprising example of this is the cooperation between the coal industry and the UMW. Although the UMW and the coal industry had a sweetheart relationship, from the late 1960s to early 1980s, relations between the UMW and the coal operators were extremely hostile. The UMW reformers who took over the union in 1972 represented the more militant attitudes of the rank and file in their enmity toward the coal operators. Thus, throughout the 1970s, it seemed as if strikes, legal and wildcat, had become a permanent feature of life in the Mountain State. However, given the recent sharp downturn in the West Virginia economy, and some changes in lobbying personnel by the operators, this mutual antipathy appears to be diminishing. For example, John Hatcher, then chairman of the House Judiciary Committee, reported that during the waning days of the 1987 session Mark White of the Coal Association and Mike Burdess of the UMW met in his office and went through a bill line-by-line until they agreed on a final product. According to Hatcher, this simply would not have occurred two or three years earlier.[21]

INTEREST GROUPS AND THE EXECUTIVE

Interest groups also have significant influence on policy-making in the executive branch. The executive agencies in West Virginia are imbued with amateurism. This occurs for two reasons: First, West Virginia's public em-

20. Ibid., 996B.
21. Interview with John Hatcher, December 16, 1987.

ployees are among the poorest paid in the nation. This results in high turnover in state government employment, which is frequently perceived as training for employment in the private sector. For example, there has been a flow of employees from the Department of Natural Resources and the Bureau of Mines (now the Division of Energy) into the mining industry. Since its founding in 1966, the West Virginia Mine & Reclamation Association has had three chief executives, the last two of which have been former executives in the Department of Natural Resources. The current Surface Mine Association president, Benjamin C. Greene, and his vice president, William B. Raney, were at one time chief and vice chief of the DNR's reclamation division.

The second reason for the amateurism in state government is the large number of citizen boards and commissions appointed throughout the state bureaucracy that have significant regulatory power. In many cases the legislature requires that the groups being regulated be represented on the boards. Even if that is not required, the governor invariably follows that practice anyway, thereby creating a kind of state corporatism. For example, two of the five appointed members of the Air Pollution Control Commission must be representatives of industries engaged in business in the state; four of the six members of the Board of Banking and Financial Institutions must be executives of banking and financial institutions; the Mine Board of Appeals has three members, one representing industry, one representing labor, and the third selected by the other two; the Reclamation Board of Review, the Water Resources Board, and the Coal Mine Health and Safety Board do not have statutory requirements for industry/labor representation, but the boards are invariably dominated by industry and union representatives.

An example of how the system operates in the state can be seen in the creation of the Health Care Cost Review Authority. When the Authority was created in 1983, Governor Rockefeller appointed former State Senator William Gilligan (a bitter foe of the Authority) as one of the agency's three directors. According to the *Charleston Daily Mail*, "hospital officials . . . admitted they were pleasantly surprised" at the appointment of Gilligan, himself a hospital board chairman. A second Rockefeller appointee's spouse, shortly after her appointment, began a chain of outpatient health centers. When the three appointments were named, the spokesperson for the West Virginia Hospital Association, which strongly opposed the creation of the Review Authority, stated: "It sounds like a group dedicated to doing a good job."[22]

22. *Charleston Daily Mail*, May 6, 1983, 1C.

If the Morehouse statement that West Virginia is a state run by a single industry were true once, it is true no longer. Undoubtedly the coal industry is influential—probably the most important single interest in the state—but as the state's economy has become more diverse and the labor movement more coordinated and democratic, no single industry is able to dominate as it once could. Business is clearly the most powerful and well-organized interest. Labor is competitive, but it is in no position to formulate a legislative agenda and have its acceptance guaranteed by more than a handful of legislators. It can, however, prevent legislation that could seriously weaken the labor movement or reduce the benefits it has won in the past.

Certain groups have built a niche for themselves in the interest-group configuration, and within a narrow range of issues they appear to be quite powerful. The top two in the survey are prime examples. The National Rifle Association (NRA), while generally having no lobbyists at the legislature, is extremely powerful because of its philosophy. West Virginia is a hunter's state; some school systems close the first week of deer season, and coal companies cease operations during this period. Therefore, on the gun issue, the NRA is powerful. The School Service Personnel Association, representing staff workers, is also quite successful—primarily because of the skill of its lobbyist. Although it is a low-profile association, it has done quite well on the one issue with which it is concerned, the pay and benefits of its members. Indeed, while West Virginia teachers invariably are underpaid in national or regional surveys, the school service personnel always fare well.

There have been some major changes in interest-group influence since the writings of Peirce and Morehouse, and it is likely that the 1990s will bring other changes in this regard. Coal production has increased over the last several years, but employment has dropped. The number of miners is at a twentieth-century low. It took 102,000 miners to produce 143 million tons in 1946; in 1990 some 171 million tons were mined by 28,876 miners.[23]

As the industrial labor force has declined, union membership has also declined across the board—in chemicals, metallurgy, glass, and manufacturing—all of which will probably produce comparable losses in political influence. Education groups also face problematic futures. The U.S. Census Bureau projects population losses in the state to continue through the year 2010, which means fewer students and therefore fewer teachers. These

23. West Virginia Coal Association, *Coal Facts, 87* (Charleston, W.Va.: W.Va. Coal Association, n.d.), 17.

population changes increase the power of the elderly, who put increased budgetary demands on state government while not contributing to education revenue at the local level because of property-tax exemptions.

At present there are on the horizon no new groups that could seriously challenge West Virginia's traditionally powerful business community. The most obvious candidates are environmentalists and representatives of the tourist sectors, but no such coalition has yet emerged.

West Virginia is one of the most rural states in the nation. Hunting and fishing are ways of life for tens of thousands of state residents. Tourism is growing, and much of this is predicated on outdoor activities. With the exception of the surface-mine battles of the late 1960s early 1970s, environmental groups alone, or in concert with representatives of the tourist sector, have not been able to convert potential into actual power when confronting major groups. During the 1989 session of the legislature, despite evidence of groundwater contamination caused by mining, they were unable to get an effective bill out of the legislature.

Perhaps more telling is that most environmental groups endorsed Gaston Caperton for governor in 1988. He won, but throughout his first term the Division of Mines was under attack not just by environmentalists but also by the U.S. Office of Surface Mines, which in 1991 finally gave notice that unless the state hired more inspectors and enforced the law the federal government would assume complete control of mine inspections in the state. Environmental groups are frequently marginalized in West Virginia by the business community. Environmental issues are put in a context of job loss, and in a state that perennially leads the nation in unemployment and in which everyone living in the coalfields knows someone who has been unemployed, environmental damage is generally seen as preferable to more poverty. Absent a major catastrophe, it seems unlikely that environmental groups will compete seriously as major forces in the West Virginia interest configuration.

Politically, the business community has not reduced its activism; on the contrary, in the late 1980s it created two new groups whose primary thrusts are political. A Business Roundtable was created to deal with developmental efforts—it will work with government agencies in these matters. At the same time, a Business Foundation was created to promote the interests of business politically. The foundation solicits business men and women to run for public office, and to lobby state government. Whether these efforts will be successful is unknown, but clearly there is vitality in the business community. It is active, innovative, and optimistic. These characteristics are not evident in any other major interest groups.

14

The Changing Nature
of Interest-Group Activity
in the Northeast

Clive S. Thomas

The Northeast is the oldest and most complex region of the nation, and consequently it has developed a very diverse pattern of interests and interest groups among the various economies and peoples of the twelve northeastern states. Significant changes have occurred in the interest-group scene in all northeastern states, yet there has been considerable continuity in the state political cultures, which set the parameters of individual state politics. This pattern of change in terms of technology and technique within a context of the continuity of long-term individual state political traditions and styles is a central theme in our analysis of northeastern interest groups.

This chapter uses the analytical framework developed in Chapter 1 to synthesize the information from the individual state chapters in order to identify regional characteristics such as the types of groups that are active, lobbyists, group power, and group tactics.[1] This data is then used to determine ways in which interest groups in the Northeast differ from their counterparts in other regions.

---

1. This chapter's data are based on the synthesized data contained in the individual chapters for the twelve northeastern states and the other thirty-eight states contained in the Hrebenar-Thomas study. The most complete results for the fifty states published from this study to date can be found in Clive S. Thomas and Ronald J. Hrebenar, "Interest Groups in the States," chap. 4 in Virginia Gray, Herbert Jacob, and Robert B. Albritton, eds., *Politics in the American States: A Comparative Analysis*, 5th ed. (Glenview, Ill.: Scott, Foresman / Little, Brown, 1990).

THE CHANGING LOBBYING GAME IN THE NORTHEAST

The greatest change in northeastern interest groups since the 1960s has been a significant expansion in three dimensions of interest-group activity. The number of groups active in state lobbying has increased; the range or type of groups has broadened; and the frequency and intensity of lobbying activities has increased significantly.

These changes in interest-group activities have not taken place in a political vacuum. Broader political changes that swept the Northeast have had an impact on the interest-group system to varying degrees. For example, the continued relative decline of agriculture in all the northeastern states has resulted in the reduction of agricultural interest-group activity and power in the state capitals. The causes for the decline of agriculture range from the overall American decline of agriculture as a political force in state legislatures following reapportionment in the 1960s, to the reduced economic and numerical clout of farmers as the nation's economy continues its restructuring from primary and industrial activities to a postindustrial service economy.

A second major change has been the emergence of a more balanced two-party system in most of the Northeast. Political scientists have long contended that a relationship exists between political parties and interest groups: changes in the former are quite likely to have an impact on the latter, and vice versa. It has also been suggested that interest-group systems would become stronger as parties became weaker. The reapportionment revolution throughout the nation during the late 1960s and early 1970s also contributed to a broadening of the number of interests being represented in northeastern state capitals. More urban representatives were elected, and more urban interests sought access to more politically hospitable legislatures and hastened the decline of agricultural interests. In addition, as rural northeastern states such as New Hampshire continued to urbanize and industrialize, their interest-group universes have also diversified.

Urbanization and industrialization in turn resulted in growing demands on state and local governments for additional services, greater tax revenue, and larger budgets. Government and its clients became more important in many northeastern states that had long-standing traditions of relatively insignificant public sectors—particularly in the higher-education sector.

Power has shifted in most of the northeastern states, and now widely diversified urban and public-sector interests tend to dominate legislative debates.

The rise of public-sector groups representing state and local employees and public school teachers has changed the balance of power in state legislatures across the region. In some states, public-employee associations and education groups have become the most powerful lobbies. All this increased government activity has also brought an array of often nonregistered government agencies onto the lobbying scene at both the state and local level.

In every state of the region, the loopholes of existing lobby registration laws result in the serious underreporting of government lobbyists. All the northeastern states have provisions for registering lobbyists and require reporting of some types of lobby expenditures. Most have some provisions for regulating campaign financing and conflict of interest. In the post-Watergate era of political reform, states such as Massachusetts have been in the forefront of this movement. However complex, though, these laws usually have as their primary objective the disclosure of interest-group activities rather than the restriction or prohibition of most activities. The relative comprehensiveness of lobbying laws in the Northeast, compared with those found in the South, is largely a function of the greater media focus on lobbying in the Northeast and the passage of laws to attempt to deal with the more serious problems.

Lobbying also means more than just interest-group activities in the state legislatures. The various state chapters make it clear that interest groups are increasingly lobbying the governor and the various offices of the executive branch and using the courts in terms of filing litigation or *amicus* briefs to achieve their policy goals, Clearly, interest-group lobbying in the northeastern states is moving in the direction of the patterns found on the national level, where seemingly any agency of government is a potential site for lobbying activities.

Overall, the above-mentioned changes have tended to promote a more competitive group style of politics in the Northeast. Enhanced competition has required an increased sophistication in lobbying strategies and tactics that have manifested themselves in all northeastern state capitals. This professionalization has occurred in terms of interest-group organizations, the skills of the lobbyists, and the range of lobbying techniques used to influence public policy.

MAJOR INTERESTS ACTIVE IN THE NORTHEAST

Since the 1960s, there have been significant changes in group activity in the Northeast as a result of the developments mentioned earlier. The Northeast, prior to the 1960s, was already the most diverse region. As noted above, there has been a considerable expansion in the number and range of groups seeking to influence state government. Many new interests, including social-issue, public-interest, and single-issue groups, have entered the political arena, and other, more traditional, interests have proliferated. Business and local government lobbies have become more specialized and numerous in the region because several groups do not see their specific interests as being fully served by their umbrella group, such as a chamber of commerce or league of cities. The third dimension of this expansion is that groups are lobbying more intensively than twenty or even ten years ago. They have more regular contact with public officials and use more sophisticated techniques.

Northeastern interests are presented in Table 14.1 on the basis of their degree of effectiveness in influencing public policy in each state. The top nine interests are active and influential in at least eight of the twelve northeastern states. However, only general business organizations (with nine "most effective" rankings and three at the second level of effectiveness) are powerful in all twelve northeastern states. In contrast, organized labor (seven "most effective" and two "second-level") is influential only in nine states. The interests in the table represent the power elite of interest groups in the states. Perhaps 75 percent of the lobbying effort in terms of time and money is attributable to the top fifteen interests.

One interesting tendency in the northeastern states (as well as in the rest of the nation) is the increasing prominence of lobbies representing individual cities, special local government districts, and state agencies. In all states the most prominent state agencies are the Departments of Education or Public Instruction, Transportation, and Welfare, in addition to state universities and colleges. Associated with this rise of government lobbying has been the increased prominence of public-sector unions, particularly state and local employees and teachers unions. Ideological groups, which are also often single-issue groups, such as those who are against abortion, have also become quite active in recent years. Public-interest organizations, particularly good government, senior citizen, and, increas-

Table 14.1. Ranking of the Most Influential Interests in the Twelve Northeastern States

Rank	Interest	Most Effective	Second-Level Effectiveness	Total Rank Points
1	General business organizations	9	3	21
2	Schoolteacher organizations	9	1	19
3	Insurance companies / organization	7	4	18
4	Traditional labor organization (AFL-CIO)	7	2	16
5	Manufacturers (companies / assns)	6	3	15
5	General local government organizations	6	3	15
7	Individual banks and financial institutions	6	2	14
8	State / local government employees	5	3	13
9	Utility companies and assns	3	6	12
10	Bankers' Assns	5	1	11
11	Realtors' Assns	4	2	10
12	Lawyers (bar and trial assns)	3	3	9
13	Individual traditional labor unions (Teamster, UAW, and others)	4	0	8
14	Environmentalists	1	6	8
15	Health-care organizations	1	5	7
16	Contractors / builders / developers	2	2	6
17	Public-interest groups	0	6	6
17	Senior citizens	0	6	6
17	Doctors	0	6	6
20	Cities and towns	2	1	5
21	Retailers (companies / assns)	2	0	4
22	Sportsmen / hunting / fishing / gun groups	1	3	4

Table 14.1. *Continued*

Rank	Interest	Most Effective	Second-Level Effectiveness	Total Rank Points
23	K-12 education interests	1	1	3
23	Religious interests	1	1	3
23	Universities / colleges	1	1	3
26	General farm organizations	0	3	3
27	Trucking and private trans- portation organizations	1	0	2
27	Forest product companies	1	0	2
27	Tourist industry groups	1	0	2
27	Oil and gas (companies / assns)	0	2	2
30	Liquor / wine / beer interests	0	2	2
30	Gaming interests	0	2	2
30	Tobacco interests	0	2	2
34	State agencies	0	1	1
34	Women / minority groups	0	1	1
34	Newspapers / media	0	1	1
34	Taxpayer groups	0	1	1

Source: Compiled from the Hrebenar-Thomas listing in Table 14.2 and the twelve chapters on interest groups in the northeastern states.

Note: Rankings were calculated by allocating 2 points for each "most effective" ranking and 1 point for each "second level of effectiveness" placement in the Hrebenar-Thomas listing in Table 14.2 and adding the totals. Where a tie in total points occurs, interests are ranked according to the number of "most effective" placements.

ingly, environmentalist groups, are other forces that now have a significant presence in nearly all northeastern state capitals.

The range of interests represented is extremely broad. It is important to note that each state has its own unique collection of interest groups. We now turn to an evaluation of the individual states and the groups that form unique interest-group systems in each state.

INTEREST GROUPS AND PUBLIC POLICY IN THE NORTHEAST

The term "group power" in this study is used in two distinct but interrelated ways. It may refer to the power of specific or individual groups, interests, or lobbies, or to the power or impact of interest groups as a whole on the political system of a particular state. With regard to the dimension of specific interest-group influence, we focused on the ability of a group to achieve its self-defined goals. It is difficult to definitively measure individual group power, because numerous variables or influences are involved, several of which are extremely volatile or dynamic in nature, such as the political climate and public opinion, and power relationships between public officials.

Individual Interest-Group Power Assessment

In order to assess the power of northeastern interest groups, we used a combination of quantitative and qualitative techniques. The results are summarized in Table 14.2, which compares the most influential interest groups in the twelve northeastern states, as listed by Sarah McCally Morehouse a decade ago, with the findings from our study.[2] The Hrebenar-Thomas listing includes two paragraphs for each state. The first paragraph lists the interest groups assessed as the most consistently influential during the 1980s; the second contains the interests that are declining in power; those rising in power, but not yet in the first rank; and those that are more ephemeral or only occasionally active.

By comparing the Morehouse and the Hrebenar-Thomas rankings, we can discern the changing influence of individual groups and interests in the Northeast. States previously dominated by one or several powerful interests, such as Maine, where timber, the shoe industry, and utilities once

2. Morehouse's assessment was based on thirteen books and one journal article on state politics. She relied heavily on the series of books on the subregions of the nation by Neal R. Peirce and her own *State Politics, Parties, and Policy* (New York: Holt, Rinehart & Winston, 1981), 108–12. An updated version of the Morehouse table was produced by Michael Engel, *State and Local Politics: Fundamentals and Perspectives* (New York: St. Martin's Press, 1985), 241–42. Most of the updating, however, appears to be based on Neal R. Peirce and Jerry Hagstrom, *The Book of America* (New York: W. W. Norton, 1983).

Table 14.2.   Most Effective Interest Groups in the Twelve Northeastern
States: An Alternative Assessment to Morehouse

Morehouse Assessment	Hrebenar and Thomas Assessment

Connecticut

Connecticut Manufacturers' Assn; Insurance lobby; Farm Bureau Federation; Grange; AFL-CIO	Connecticut Business & Industry Assn; AFL-CIO; Insurance Assn of Connecticut; Connecticut Conference of Municipalities; Northeast Utilities; Connecticut Education Assn; American Assn of University Professors
	Connecticut Bankers Assn; Northeast Bankcorp; Connecticut National Bank; Connecticut Hospital Assn; Connecticut Assn of Health Care Facilities; Tobacco Institute; Connecticut Beer Wholesalers; Connecticut Retail Merchants Assn

Delaware

Dupont Chemical Co.; insurance lobby	Delaware State Chamber of Commerce; Delaware State Education Assn; Delaware Trial Lawyers Assn; Delaware State Bar Assn; Delaware Bankers Assn and Banks (esp. Wilmington Trust); corporate interests and corporate law firms; chemical manufacturers (esp. I.C.I. Americas, Hercules, DuPont, Occidental); AFL-CIO and traditional labor unions (mainly during elections)
	Utilities (esp. Diamond State Telephone Co., Delmarva Power & Light); Farm interests (esp. Delaware Farm Bureau); insurance; environmentalists; volunteer firemen; Delaware Assn of Realtors; senior

Table 14.2. *Continued*

Morehouse Assessment	Hrebenar and Thomas Assessment
	citizens; Home Builders Assn of Delaware; Delaware Contractors Assn; National Rifle Assn; Common Cause; League of Women Voters; local civic and community groups; Pilots Assn for the Delaware Bay & River

Maine

Morehouse Assessment	Hrebenar and Thomas Assessment
Big three: electric power, timber, textile and shoe manufacturing; Farm Bureau; Grange; liquor and beer lobby; horse-racing lobby; conservation groups	Environmentalists (esp. Audubon Society and Natural Resource Council); Maine Teachers Assn; AFL-CIO, paper industry; utilities (esp. the Central Maine Power Co.); Maine Municipal Assn; banking; insurance; Sportsmen's Alliance of Maine; Maine State Employees Assn
	Maine Nuclear Referendum Committee (antinuclear); Maine Assn of Realtors; Chamber of Commerce and Industry; Maine Christian Civic League; women's groups; medical groups

Maryland

Morehouse Assessment	Hrebenar and Thomas Assessment
Bankers; industrialists; AFL-CIO; liquor lobby	Banking and financial institutions; insurance; business assns; AFL-CIO and traditional unions; AFSCME; local gov'ts (assns and individual units)
	Environmentalists (esp. The Chesapeake Bay Foundation); health care professionals and organizations (esp. doctors); public utilities (esp. Baltimore Gas & Electric, Chesapeake & Potomac Telephone); horse-racing

Table 14.2. *Continued*

Morehouse Assessment	Hrebenar and Thomas Assessment
	industry; professional / occupational groups (esp. Trial Lawyers)

Massachusetts

Labor; Catholic church; public-utility interests; Real Estate Lobby; Associated Industries of Mass.; Chamber of Commerce; Insurance Companies; Mass. Federation of Taxpayers Assns; racetrack interests; state employees; liquor interests	Associated Industries of Mass.; Life Insurance Assn of Mass. and individual insurance companies; Mass. Teachers Assn; AFL-CIO; Mass. Municipal Assn; Mass. Hospital Assn; Professional Firefighters of Mass.; Mass. Assn of Realtors/Greater Boston Real Estate Board
	Citizens for Limited Taxation; utilities; Mass. Bar Assn; Mass. High Tech Council; Mass. Public Interest Research Group; Gun Owners Action League; League of Women Voters; Chamber of Commerce; Mass. Medical Society (3)

New Hampshire

Public utilities; paper manufacturing; lumber; racetrack lobby	Pro-development groups (esp. realtors, construction, Business & Industry Assn); bankers (esp. New Hampshire Bankers Assn); insurance industry; tourism / hospitality industry (esp. New Hampshire Hospitality Assn)
	Medical groups; conservation groups (esp. the Trust for New Hampshire Lands, Society for the Protection of New Hampshire Forests); State Employees Assn; NEA-New Hampshire; New Hampshire Municipal Assn and individual

Table 14.2. *Continued*

Morehouse Assessment	Hrebenar and Thomas Assessment
	municipalities; fish and game interests; the *Manchester Union Leader*; criminal justice lobby (police, sheriffs, etc.); citizens groups (e.g., Common Cause, Citizens Alliance [formerly Clamshell Alliance]); utilities (esp. Public Service Co. of New Hampshire)

New Jersey

Morehouse Assessment	Hrebenar and Thomas Assessment
Johnson & Johnson; Warner-Lambert Pharmaceuticals; Prudential Insurance; Campbell's Soup; Becton Dickinson; First National State Bank in Newark; N.J. Manufacturers' Assn; Hess Oil; Garden State Race Track; N.J. Farm Bureau; N.J. Education Assn; Chamber of Commerce; AFL-CIO	N.J. Education Assn; N.J. Business & Industry Assn; builders and developers (esp. realtors, N.J. Builders Assn); Trial Lawyers; Johnson & Johnson; Prudential Insurance
	AFL-CIO; banks (esp. First Fidelity, Midlantic, First Jersey, United Jersey); Chamber of Commerce; environmentalists; N.J. Farm Bureau; N.J. School Boards Assn; pharmaceutical companies (other than Johnson & Johnson); Alliance for Action (business-labor road construction coalition); casino industry; insurance companies; Petroleum Council; senior citizens (esp. N.J. Federation of Senior Citizens); N.J. Municipal Assn

New York

Morehouse Assessment	Hrebenar and Thomas Assessment
Education lobby: Board of Regents, New York State Teachers Assn, New York Federation of Teachers; Associated Industries of New York; Empire State Chamber of Commerce; Bankers Assn; AFL-CIO; Teamsters;	Public employees (Civil Service Employees Assn, Public Employees Assn, AFSCME, New York Federation of Teachers); AFL-CIO; Teamsters; Business Council; Chamber of Commerce & Industry;

Table 14.2.   *Continued*

Morehouse Assessment	Hrebenar and Thomas Assessment
state medical assn; Roman Catholic church; New York City lobby	New York Bankers Assn; Assn of Realtors; Associated Industries of New York; local gov't lobby (esp. New York State Assn of Counties, New York State Conference of Mayors, New York City); New York School Boards Assn; New York State Catholic Conference
	New York State Medical Assn; State Board of Regents; New York State Hospital Assn; senior citizens (esp. American Assn of Retired Persons); New York Public Interest Research Group

Pennsylvania

Steel companies (U.S. Steel, Republic Jones & Laughlin, Bethlehem); oil firms (Standard, Gulf, Sun, Atlantic); public utilities; service industries; Pennsylvania State Teachers Assn; Welfare Rights Organization; AFL-CIO	Pennsylvania Chamber of Commerce and Industry; Pennsylvania Trial Lawyers Assn; Pennsylvania State Education Assn; insurance industry; Pennsylvania Motor Truck Assn; Pennsylvania branch of the American Automobile Assn; auto dealers
	Utilities; AFL-CIO; Pennsylvania Bankers Assn; state and local employees (esp. AFSCME); oil and gas; steel companies; senior citizens (esp. American Association of Retired Persons)

Rhode Island

AFL-CIO, Associated Industries of Rhode Island; insurance companies; public utilities; banks; racetrack assns	Business (esp. Rhode Island Chamber of Commerce Federation); banks (esp. Fleet National); AFL-CIO and traditional labor unions; school

Table 14.2. *Continued*

Morehouse Assessment	Hrebenar and Thomas Assessment
	teachers (NEA and American Federation of Teachers); insurance companies (esp. Blue Cross / Blue Shield); utilities; public employees (esp. AFSCME)
	Save the Bay (environmentalist group); liquor lobby (esp. Rhode Island Licensed Beverage Assn, Rhode Island Liquor Store Assn, Rhode Island Assn of Beer and Wine Wholesalers); Tobacco Institute; Rhode Island Medical Assn; Rhode Island Bar Assn; Certified Accountants; senior citizens

Vermont

Morehouse Assessment	Hrebenar and Thomas Assessment
Farm Bureau; Associated Industries of Vermont	Vermont Natural Resource Council (environmentalists); Vermont League of Cities & Towns; Vermont Chamber of Commerce; Vermont Education Assn; Associated Industries of Vermont
	Utilities (esp. Central Vermont Public Service, Green Mountain Power); Vermont Farm Bureau; Vermont Public Interest Research Group; senior citizens (Coalition of Vermont Elders); the Governor's Office; administrative agencies; Alliance for the Mentally Ill

West Virginia

Morehouse Assessment	Hrebenar and Thomas Assessment
Union Carbide; Bethlehem Steel; Occidental Petroleum; Georgia Pacific; Baltimore & Ohio Railroad; Norfolk and Western Railway Co.;	West Virginia Coal Assn; United Mine Workers; West Virginia Bankers Assn; Jackson & Kelly (state's largest law firm); West

Table 14.2. *Continued*

Morehouse Assessment	Hrebenar and Thomas Assessment
Chesapeake & Ohio Railway Co.; United Mine Workers	Virginia Education Assn; West Virginia Federation of Labor (AFL-CIO); West Virginia Chamber of Commerce
	Railroads; National Rifle Assn; School Services Personnel Assn; West Virginia Surface Mine and Reclamation Assn (strip-mine owners); oil and gas (esp. West Virginia Oil & Gas Assn, Independent Oil & Gas Assn); chemical companies (esp. Union Carbide and DuPont); Georgia Pacific

Sources: The Morehouse assessment is reprinted with permission from Sarah McCally Morehouse, *State Politics, Parties, and Policy* (New York: Holt, Rinehart & Winston, 1981), table 3.2., "Listing of the Significant Pressure Groups by State," 108–12. The Hrebenar and Thomas assessment was compiled from survey research conducted by the authors of the individual state chapters in this volume.

Note: The designation "Education Assn" in the formal name of a group indicates a schoolteachers' organization; the designation "Medical Assn" (or "Medical Society") in the formal name of a group indicates a general practitioners' organization.

AFSCME = American Federation of State, County, and Municipal Employees.
AFL-CIO = American Federation of Labor–Congress of Industrial Organizations.
NEA = National Education Association.

controlled the state, have developed into pluralist interest-group systems. The interests that do exert considerable influence must share power with other groups. Because of increasing political pluralism, the days when one interest or a handful of interests could dictate policy on a wide range of issues also appear to be gone.

As for the power status of the so-called traditional interests in the Northeast—business, agriculture, labor, education, and local government—three of these have maintained or enhanced their power, while two appear to have lost ground. Education interests, especially schoolteachers, are ranked second only in the Northeast, but they are top-ranked in each of the other regions. Business is top-ranked in the Northeast but can manage only a third or fourth rank elsewhere. Labor remains very influential in the Northeast, where it is the fourth-ranked effective interest.

Other interesting differences in the Northeast's ranking of effective interests includes the third most effective position, held by insurance interests, which rank much lower in other regions. Agricultural interests, still powerful in the other regions (ranked between sixth and eleventh), are only the sixteenth-ranked interest in the Northeast—as one would expect, given the relatively small economic role of agriculture. Perhaps, most unexpected is the high ranking given to environmentalist groups (fourteenth) in the Northeast, as compared with their twenty-fifty or twenty-sixth ranking in the other three regions.

Contrary to some predictions, increased political pluralism and interest-group fragmentation within the business community does not appear to have significantly affected business influence overall. Certainly some more traditional businesses (such as banking) may have declined, but these have been replaced by service and other businesses among the ranks of the most powerful groups. On the other hand, agriculture appears to have suffered an irreversible decline in its political influence.

Organized labor has managed to gain or hold on to its political influence better in the Northeast than in the South and the West. Teachers, and to a lesser extent public employees, are the new face of labor in the Northeast as also throughout the nation. The rise of state-employee associations is a noteworthy phenomenon in the changing configuration of group power in the region. It seems to be linked to the increased role of government since the 1960s, which also has enhanced the power of many state agencies, particularly departments of education and transportation and state university systems.

Less-significant gains have been made by health-care groups, environmentalists, and senior citizens, and single-issue groups, such as the anti-nuclear-power groups in Maine, have also experienced a series of successes, although many of these groups tend to be ad hoc in nature and to appear and disappear as their issues ebb and flow.

The successes of these nonestablishment interests, including social-issue and minority groups, do not appear to have been significant enough across the northeastern states to have upset the relative influence of the traditionally powerful groups. Indeed, the changes in the hierarchy of group power across the Northeast, as in the other regions, has been far less dramatic over the last twenty-five years than the major expansion in group activity might lead us to assume. This is not surprising when we consider the factors that constitute individual group power. The players in the game may have been changed by the addition of new groups, but the rules of success, particularly command of resources and building-up long-term relationships with public officials, remain virtually unchanged.

Overall Group Power Evaluations

Turning to overall group power, we define this as the extent to which interest groups as a whole influence public policy when compared with other components of the political system, such as political parties, the legislature, and the governor. As with individual group power, researchers have encountered problems in assessing this factor. However, drawing on the research from the Hrebenar-Thomas study, we have classified the fifty states according to the impact interest groups have had on their respective state policy-making systems.

It is not an easy task to evaluate overall group power within a given state. Other scholars have attempted to assess this aspect of group power, with varying methodologies, mixed results, and many questions left unanswered. The first such study, by Belle Zeller, was based only on the assessments of political scientists. The Zeller study argued that group strength was primarily a function of political-party strength and inversely proportionate to it.[3] Subsequent research explored this idea and attempted to develop it further. Work by Morehouse, for example, used measures of party strength to define the relationship more accurately.[4] Zeigler and van Dalen, and Zeigler, added the variable of economic and social development.[5] As noted in Chapter 1, these theories predicted the gradual transformation of "strong" group systems into "moderate" and eventually "weak" systems as economic and social pluralism advanced.[6] The results from the

3. Belle Zeller, *American State Legislatures*, 2nd ed. (New York: Thomas Y. Crowell, 1954), 190–93 and chap. 13, "Pressure Group Influence and Their Control"; L. Harmon Zeigler, "Interest Groups in the States," chap. 4 in Virginia Gray et al., *Politics in the American States: A Comparative Analysis*, 4th ed. (1983).

4. Morehouse, *State Politics, Parties, and Policy*, 107–17.

5. L. Harmon Zeigler and Hendrik van Dalen, "Interest Groups in State Politics," chap. 4 in Herbert Jacob and Kenneth N. Vines, *Politics in the American States: A Comparative Analysis*, 3rd ed. (Boston: Little, Brown, 1976), 94–110; Zeigler, "Interest Groups in the States," 111–15.

6. Two other studies have attempted to assess aspects of overall group power in the fifty states, but these based their assessments on studies of only one aspect of the pro-

Hrebenar-Thomas study enable us to suggest an alternate way of approaching an understanding of overall group power.

We find little to support the categorization of states into strong, moderate, and weak group systems. First of all, this categorization gives the incorrect impression that groups in some states are literally weak or powerless and thus of little consequence in state politics. Even in those states where groups are not all-powerful, certain interest groups, such as the United Automobile Workers and the automobile makers, are undeniably powerful in Michigan politics.

A more accurate and informative way to designate the overall impact of groups is to use terminology that avoids the inaccurate impression that groups are not important but that communicates the degree of their significance in state policy-making vis-à-vis other political institutions. We describe the impact of a particular group system as having a *dominant*, a *complementary*, or a *subordinate* impact in relation to other aspects of the system. We also provide two intermediate categories that are a combination of two of these pure types of interest-group power systems.

The inverse relationship between party strength and group impact does not always hold, and socioeconomic development and increased professionalization does not always lessen the impact of groups on a state's political system (see Chapter 1), but this is not to argue that these variables are insignificant. Instead, their effect on overall group power appears to be different from that originally predicted. For instance, party strength generally has considerable influence on the overall impact of groups, but although weak party systems are invariably accompanied by dominant group systems, strong parties do not always mean weak group systems, as the case of New York illustrates. Furthermore, developments in California in the early 1990s demonstrate that increasing party strength may not result in a decrease in overall group influence. We also suggest that there is no automatic progression from dominant to subordinate status resulting from socioeconomic development and increased professionalization of government. In fact, groups often increase their influence as such developments occur. All this leads us to conclude that party strength and socioeconomic develop-

cess: Wayne L. Francis, *Legislative Issues in the Fifty States: A Comparative Analysis* (Chicago: Rand McNally, 1967); Glen Abney and Thomas P. Lauth, "Interest Group Influence in the States: A View of Subsystem Politics" (Paper delivered at the 1986 annual meeting of the American Political Science Association, Washington, D.C.). Francis concentrated on the legislature, while Abney and Lauth based their listing on a survey of administrators.

ment and professionalization are not the only factors that influence overall group power. In fact, in some circumstances they may not even be the most important variables. What is clearly needed is a more sophisticated analysis of these relationships. While we do not claim to have developed a definitive theory, a combination of quantitative and qualitative analysis of the data from the Hrebenar-Thomas study suggests that a more comprehensive understanding can be provided by reference to the components of our analytical framework described in Chapter 1.

Each of the seven factors in our analytical framework has some influence on overall group power. The problem is, however, that the impact of each appears to vary from state to state and from time to time within a state, and thus the combined influence of all seven factors will vary accordingly. For example, the moralistic political culture has controlled corruption in Vermont despite its one-party system and fragmented policy-making system. In contrast, New Hampshire's Moralistic-Individualistic political culture does not have a similar restraining influence on corruption.

Table 14.3 provides a listing of the states according to overall group power. States listed in the "dominant" column are those in which groups as a whole are the overwhelming and consistent influence on policy-making. The "complementary" column contains those states where groups tend to have to work in conjunction with or are constrained by other aspects of the political system. More often than not, this is the party system, but it could also be a strong executive branch, competition between groups, the political culture, or a combination of all these. The "subordinate" column represents a situation where the group system is consistently subordinated to other aspects of the policy-making process. The absence of any states in this column indicates that research reveals that groups are not consistently subordinate in any state. The "dominant/complementary" column includes the states whose group systems alternate between the two situations or are in the process of moving from one to the other. Likewise, the states in the "complementary/subordinate" column are those whose group systems alternate between being complementary and subordinate.

The overall northeastern interest-group system is closest to the "complementary/subordinate" end of the continuum. Four of the five complementary/subordinate states in the nation are in the Northeast: Connecticut, Delaware, Rhode Island, and Vermont; the only other such state is Minnesota, in the upper Midwest. Only West Virginia, with its long history of domination by the coal industry, which has somewhat lessened in recent years, appears to fit better the dominant category filled by many of its neighboring southern states.

Northeastern and midwestern interest-group systems continue to be weaker than those found in the South and West. If the fifty states were grouped by regions in Table 14.3, we would see some interesting patterns. The South has a strong pattern of dominant interest-group systems; the West is largely a dominant/complementary type of interest-group politics, the Midwest is overwhelmingly complementary, and the Northeast is complementary with a strong complementary/subordinate subcategory. Clearly, the Northeast, with its weaker interest-group system, represents the extreme end on the continuum of interest-group power vis-à-vis other institutions, such as political parties.

LOBBYISTS AND LOBBYING IN THE NORTHEAST

Americans tend to be suspicious and distrustful of interest groups and lobbyists. The misuse of political power by railroad, banking, and other powerful interests during the late nineteenth century contributed to a legacy of distrust and suspicion among the public with regard to interest groups and particularly the lobbyists who represent them. Because huge amounts of money are often at stake in many legislative battles, interest groups have used almost any means at their disposal, sometimes illegal ones, to secure access to public officials and influence government decisions in their favor. Despite these perceptions, lobbying on the state level has significantly changed with the passage of public-disclosure laws and increased media-monitoring of the interest-group scene in most state capitals.

A lobbyist is a person an interest group designates to represent it to government for the purpose of influencing public policy in that group's favor. Many, including the popular press and some academics, tend to group all lobbyists together in the same category, but there are five major categories of lobbyists: contract, in-house, government lobbyists and legislative liaisons, volunteer or citizen, and hobbyist or self-styled (see Chapter 1). It is important to distinguish among the five types of lobbyists because different types have different strengths and weaknesses. With different backgrounds and experiences, the various categories are perceived differently by public officials, and these perceptions determine the nature and extent of a lobbyist's power base.

Increased numbers, more women, and professionalism all characterize the lobbyist corps in the Northeast during the past two decades. We esti-

Table 14.3. Classification of the Fifty States According to the Overall Impact of Interest Groups

	States Where the Overall Impact of Interest Groups Is—			
Dominant (9)	Dominant / Complementary (18)	Complementary (18)	Complementary / Subordinate (5)	Subordinate (0)
Alabama	Arizona	Colorado	Connecticut	
Alaska	Arkansas	Illinois	Delaware	
Florida	California	Indiana	Minnesota	
Louisiana	Hawaii	Iowa	Rhode Island	
Mississippi	Georgia	Kansas	Vermont	
New Mexico	Idaho	Maine		
South Carolina	Kentucky	Maryland		
Tennessee	Montana	Massachusetts		
West Virginia	Nebraska	Michigan		
	Nevada	Missouri		
	Ohio	New Jersey		
	Oklahoma	New Hampshire		
	Oregon	New York		
	Texas	North Carolina		
	Utah	North Dakota		
	Virginia	Pennsylvania		
	Washington	South Dakota		
	Wyoming	Wisconsin		

Source: Compiled from the fifty state chapters of the Hrebenar-Thomas study.

mate that women make up 20 to 25 percent of lobbyists in the Northeast and the West, as compared with 12 to 15 percent in the South. In terms of direct lobbying, the most common and still most effective tactic is the use of lobbyists. In fact, until recently it was the only tactical device used by the vast majority of groups, and it remains the sole approach used by many today.

Perhaps the greatest change has been the proliferation of professional contract lobbyists and lobbying firms in many northeastern capitals. These full-service lobbying firms often provide a wide variety of services and represent up to as many as twenty-five clients. Another trend is for more and more lobbyists to become "specialists" in a particular field of lobbying, reflecting the increased specialization of government. Typical of these specialists are the various "public-relations" lobbying firms in West Virginia that specialize in. representing only business interests, and Connecticut's Joseph Coatsworth, whose clients are health and hospital groups. In addition, in all northeastern states, lawyers and law firms are increasingly moonlighting as lobbyists.

Clearly, the days of "booze and bribes" in most northeastern capitals are over, but the wheeler-dealers still exist in a more subtle manifestation. Like their predecessors, the new breed of lobbyist realizes the need for a multifaceted approach to establishing and maintaining good relations with public officials. This includes everything from participating in election campaigns to helping officials with their personal needs. Even more important, the modern lobbyist is quite aware of the increased importance of technical information, the increased professionalism and changing needs of public officials, and the increased public visibility of lobbying. The result is a low-key, highly skilled, and effective professional who is a far cry from the old public image stereotype lobbyist.

New tactics have supplemented the traditional work of the lobbyist. Grass-roots lobbying, public relations, media campaigns, and to a lesser extent demonstrations and sit-ins form the major indirect tactics, the ultimate purpose of which is to enhance direct access and influence. Other successful tactics include the building of coalitions with other groups, and contributing workers and especially money to election campaigns, particularly by establishing a political action committee (PAC). PACs are used more frequently in the Northeast than in the rest of the nation. These tactics are viewed not as a substitute for a lobbyist but as a means of enhancing the ability of the group's lobbyist to gain access to and influence public officials. Interest-group leadership generally chooses the most cost-efficient and politically effective method to achieve their goals; because of the high costs, they employ the newer techniques only if absolutely necessary. Despite the limitations, these new techniques are being widely and increasingly used on the state level. One reason the range of tactics and strategies is broadest in the Northeast is that the high degree of intense competition among the groups and between the political parties has led to escalations in interest-group conflicts.

Combined state- and national-level campaigns are often planned and implemented by interest groups. Many state groups have national affiliates. For example, the National Education Association has an extensive and sophisticated national organization that provides all sorts of aid and advice to its local state affiliates. When needed, state affiliates are sometimes activated to participate in lobbying in Washington, D.C. Large corporations set general policies on political involvement that are followed by the state offices of these organizations.

HOW DIFFERENT ARE INTEREST-GROUP SYSTEMS IN THE NORTHEAST?

Interest-group politics in the Northeast share both similarities and differences with the other three regions studied. There are no significant uniquely northeastern patterns. While there are certainly variations among the four regional systems and from state to state, these do not appear to be uniquely regional. Increasingly, state and regional interest-group systems share more patterns with one another and with the national pattern found in the nation's capital.

There are, however, several patterns that appear to differentiate northeastern interest groups from those in other regions. These differences derive primarily from the diversity of the Northeast's society and economy and its mixtures of different political cultures and traditions. Despite a historical dislike for "big government" in many parts of the Northeast, government has become a significant lobbying force, as have teachers and other public employees. The group systems as a whole are relatively powerful but are often in competition with equal or superior powerful institutions, such as political parties in Connecticut, Massachusetts, and New York. The professionalization of lobbying in many northeastern capitals approaches that found in the most professionalized lobbying corps of Sacramento, California.

The established interests—business, labor, education, and professional groups—as well as state and local government agencies, still dominate the political processes in most northeastern states. It is primarily their command of extensive resources that has enabled them to maintain, and in some cases enhance, their influence.

All in all, there are many subtle differences among the various states in the Northeast, the fifty individual states, and the four regions. But in the final analysis (at least in this regional study), what is remarkable is the growing number of similarities among what are often quite different states and regions, as well as the increasing congruence between interest-group politics on the state level and on the national level in Washington, D.C. Perhaps it is predictable that the Northeast, the region that contains the cities that dominate the nation's financial, intellectual, communications, and national political institutions, would be a leader in institutionalizing these changes on the state level.

About the Contributors

JOHN C. BERG is a professor of government at Suffolk University in Boston. He received his Ph.D. in political science from Harvard in 1975. Professor Berg has been active in city, state, and national government.

FRANK BRYAN is an associate professor of political science at the University of Vermont. He is a well-known expert on politics in rural areas and is the author of *Rural Politics*.

DAVID L. CINGRANELLI is an associate professor of political science at the State University of New York at Binghamton. He teaches courses on American national government, intergovernmental relations, and public policy. He is the author of *Human Rights: Theory and Measurement*.

PATRICIA McGEE CROTTY is a professor at East Stroudsburg University in East Stroudsburg, Pennsylvania. Her research interests are public policy, intergovernmental relations, and lobbying. She has been a policy adviser to Pennsylvania state government and has been a lobbyist for environmental and social organizations.

ROBERT EGBERT is an associate professor of political science at Plymouth State College in Plymouth, New Hampshire. He teaches American government courses, including state and local, interest groups, and political parties classes. He is the chair of the board of directors of the New Hampshire Civil Liberties Union.

MICHELLE ANNE FISTEK is an associate professor of political science at Plymouth State College in Plymouth, New Hampshire. She teaches courses on the Congress and the presidency, American national government, public policy, and public administration. Professor Fistek has a long history of activism in state and local politics.

ANN HALLOWELL is a graduate student at the University of Vermont and has worked with Frank Bryan on various state government projects. She is currently an elected member of a Vermont city council.

ALLAN S. HAMMOCK received his Ph.D. from the University of Virginia. He is an associate professor and chair of the Department of Political Science at West Virginia University in Morgantown, West Virginia.

DOUGLAS I. HODGKIN is professor and former chair of the Political Science Department at Bates College in Lewiston, Maine. He received his Ph.D. from Duke University and he teaches courses on political parties, interest groups, and the legislative process. Dr. Hodgkin has served as president of the Northeastern Political Science Association. He has also served for ten years on the Maine Commission on Governmental Ethics and Election Practices and briefly on the staff of the Maine state legislature.

RONALD J. HREBENAR is professor of political science at the University of Utah. He is co-author or co-editor of *Parties in Crisis, Interest Group Politics in America, The Japanese Party System,* and *Interest Group Politics in the American West.*

MARK S. HYDE is professor of political science at Providence College in Rhode Island. He teaches courses on state politics, interest groups, and political parties. Professor Hyde is a frequent contributor to such journals as *Polity, Journal of Politics,* and *Social Science Journal.*

JANET B. JOHNSON is associate professor of political science at the University of Delaware. She received her Ph.D. from Cornell University and she is the co-author of *Political Science Research Methods.* She has been very involved in environmentalist activities in her state.

RONALD C. LIPPINCOTT is an assistant professor in the Department of Government and Public Administration at the University of Baltimore. He received his Ph.D. from the University of North Carolina at Chapel Hill. Dr. Lippincott has had extensive experience in government and policy analysis.

SARAH McCALLY MOREHOUSE is professor of political science at the University of Connecticut at Stamford. She received her Ph.D. from Yale University. She is the author of *State Politics, Parties, and Policy* as well as articles and chapters on state governors, legislatures, and political parties.

JAMES R. OXENDALE is professor of political science in the Division of Social Sciences at West Virginia Institute of Technology in Montgomery, West Virginia.

JOSEPH A. PIKA is an associate professor of political science at the University of Delaware. He received his Ph.D. from the University of Wisconsin at Madison and has written extensively on the presidency.

BARBARA G. SALMORE is professor of political science at Drew University in Madison, New Jersey. She is co-author of *Candidates, Parties, and Campaigns: Electoral Politics in America*.

STEPHEN A. SALMORE is professor of political science in the Eagleton Institute at Rutgers University in New Brunswick, New Jersey. Among his many articles and book chapters are several on public opinion and on campaigning on the state level. He is co-author of *Candidates, Parties, and Campaigns: Electoral Politics in America*.

CLIVE S. THOMAS is professor of political science at the University of Alaska Southeast in Juneau. He received his Ph.D. at the London School of Economics and has taught previously at Iowa State University. He is the author, co-author, or editor of several books, chapters, and articles on interest groups and public policy.

LARRY W. THOMAS is chair of the Department of Government and Public Administration and associate professor at the University of Baltimore. He is also the acting director of the Schaefer Center for Public Policy. Among his many articles are ones on state legislatures, the courts, policy implementation, and intergovernmental relations.

Index